Dark Matter

Marxism and Culture

Series Editors:
Esther Leslie (Professor in Political Aesthetics at Birkbeck, University of London) and Mike Wayne (Reader in Film and Television Studies at Brunel University)

Other titles available:

Red Planets
Marxism and Science Fiction
Edited by Mark Bould and China Miéville

Marxism and the History of Art
From William Morris to the New Left
Edited by Andrew Hemingway

Magical Marxism
Subversive Politics and the Imagination
Andy Merrifield

Philosophizing the Everyday
The Philosophy of Praxis and the Fate of Cultural Studies
John Roberts

Marxism and Media Studies
Key Concepts and Contemporary Trends
Mike Wayne

Dark Matter

Art and Politics in the Age of Enterprise Culture

GREGORY SHOLETTE

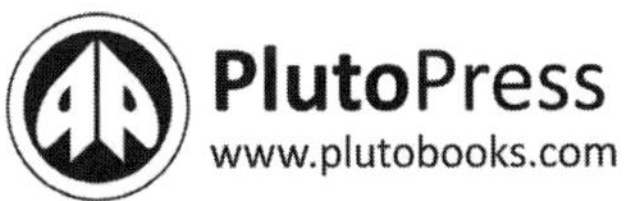

First published 2011 by Pluto Press
345 Archway Road, London N6 5AA

www.plutobooks.com

Distributed in the United States of America exclusively by
Palgrave Macmillan, a division of St. Martin's Press LLC,
175 Fifth Avenue, New York, NY 10010

British Library Cataloguing in Publication Data
A catalogue record for this book is available from the British Library

ISBN 978 0 7453 2753 2 Hardback
ISBN 978 0 7453 2752 5 Paperback

Library of Congress Cataloging in Publication Data applied for

This book is printed on paper suitable for recycling and made from fully managed and sustained forest sources. Logging, pulping and manufacturing processes are expected to conform to the environmental standards of the country of origin.

10 9 8 7 6 5 4 3 2

Designed and produced for Pluto Press by
Chase Publishing Services Ltd, 33 Livonia Road, Sidmouth, EX10 9JB, England
Typeset from disk by Stanford DTP Services, Northampton, England
Simultaneously printed digitally by CPI Antony Rowe, Chippenham, UK and
Edwards Bros in the United States of America

This book is dedicated to Lucy R. Lippard, whose tireless energy remains an inspiration to me as an artist and writer; to the memory of Sophie Saroff (1917–88), comrade and mentor; and to Patrick Sholette (1958–2010), brother, worker, and friend.

CONTENTS

SERIES PREFACE

Marxists frequently point out the crisis of the present and proclaim "We've never had it so bad—now is the time for revolution." And here we go again. But, by any account, the events of the past couple of years have been turbulent and critical. Bank bailouts, meltdowns in major financial institutions, long-established businesses going to the wall, the collapse of economies and economic zones, rising world unemployment, humanly-induced ecological disasters, and that perennial feature of the post-war world, ongoing war and occupation. There is a widespread perception of systemic instability and many fear worse to come. In the realm of culture, there are concrete threats ahead—the arts, which in such times of crisis are perceived as a luxury, face a period of cutbacks. Universities are slashing courses in the Arts and Humanities, now defined, under current funding regimes, as "of no financial value"—the only legitimate measure today. Our series, Marxism and Culture, continues in this bleak context, in which there is less and less to lose.

Eighty years ago, Walter Benjamin and Bertolt Brecht planned a journal, in order, as they saw it, to seriously wage the intellectual civil war against their many reactionary or incompetent fellow critics. It was to be called *Krisis und Kritik* [*Crisis and Criticism*] and drew in figures such as Lukács, Adorno, and Marcuse. Its character was political, "standing on the ground of class struggle," and "its critical activity anchored in clear consciousness of the basic critical situation of contemporary society." At that moment, the many forms of crisis—social, economic, political—appeared to be ever more manifest and they pressed themselves in to become part of the context of criticism. The critical moment is, precisely, the moment of the splinter, the shattering. Critical is derived, of course, from crisis. It is defined as a turning point, an interruption, a change in quality. This sense is most explicit when it is used in chemistry or physics: where it relates to the value of a measurement, such as temperature, at which an abrupt change in a quality, property, or state occurs. The critical moment proposes a before and after or a wavering on the cusp of those two moments.

Our book series would hope to address such a critical moment. It is a decidedly "post-post" one. The delusions of the 1980s, which took on concrete "critical" form in Post-modernism, seem otherworldy now. Post-marxism, post-feminism, "the third way"—these appear as the concerns of another epoch. It is not uncommon to hear talk again of that oldest of Marxist bugbears, Imperialism. And today Capitalism—and its anti-, are even part of the media's vocabulary.

This current volume investigates a terrain of critical art practice, or, better put, tactical media work that exceeds the white walls of the gallery and takes the battle of and in representation—in all its senses—to the streets. It builds on previous work in our book series, melding the work on Marxism and Art History (edited by Andrew Hemingway) with the analysis of the Everyday (John Roberts). It brings to light the "dark matter" of the art world, the unrepresented "missing mass," wresting creativity from professionals and commodifiers, in order, not least, to rewrite art history and re-invigorate the everyday.

Esther Leslie (Professor in Political Aesthetics at Birkbeck, University of London) and Mike Wayne (Reader in Film and Television Studies at Brunel University)

ACKNOWLEDGMENTS

A substantial roster of groups and individuals made this decade-long study possible. Foremost among them are Carol Duncan and Andrew Hemingway, whose support and insights over many years cannot be overestimated. I am also indebted to Janet Koenig, and Ariana Sholette, as well as a remarkable group of teachers including Hans Haacke, Jean-Pierre Gorin, Steve Fagin, Benjamin Buchloh, Charlotte Schatz, and Jeanne Burford. My gratitude extends to my friends David Stern, Sue Giffard, and Rachel Stern who provided me with a place to work in a time of need; Olga Kopenkina for her guidance and encouragement; Jeffrey Skoller for his enduring intellectual engagement and friendship; Lucia Sommer who expertly helped with the project survey as well as designers Noel Douglas, Emily and Scott Santoro; Lize Kirwin who generously provided access to The Archives of American Art, and the staff of the Museum of Modern Art Archive for their able assistance with research in the PAD/D Archive. This book would also not have been possible without the adept editing of Esther Leslie, David Castle, and Tim Clark from Pluto Press, as well as a host of artists, friends, and scholars who have contributed in countless ways to my knowledge of this subject for several decades, including: Dennis Adams, Alexander Alberro, Melody Aleen, Jerri Allyn, Aryeen Anastas, Rasheed Araeen, Doug Ashford, Todd Ayoung, Scott Berzofsky, Brett Bloom, Mary Ann Calo, Jessica Cannon, Ron Clark, Keith Christensen, Salem Colo-Julin, Maureen Connor, Jim Costanzo, Ivet Curlin, Edward DeCarbo, Ana Devic, John Duda, Dan Eisenberg, Andrea De Felice, Ed Eisenberg, Marcelo Expósito, Nina Felshin, Marc Fischer, Kirsten Forkert, Emily Foreman, Rene Gabri, Aaron Gatch, Benj Gerdes, Philip Glahn, Leon Golub, Dara Greenwald, Libertad Guerra, Brian Hand, Marc Herbst, Robbert Herbst, Brian Holmes, Nataša Ilić, Paul Jaskot, Fred Lonidier, Tom Klem, Lisa Maya Knauer, Carin Kuoni, Steve Kurtz, Dejan Kršić, Nicolas Lampert, Ernie Larson, Pedro Lasch, Marc Leger, Martin Lucas, Rikke Luther, Jerry Kearns, Mary Kelly, Martin Krens, Moukhtar Kocache, Ed Marszewski, Lydia Matthews, Micki McGee, Josh McPhee, Karen van Meenen, André Mesquita, Sherry Milner, Nicholas Mirzoeff, Naeem Mohaiemen, Alan Moore, Barbara Moore, Beverly Naidus, Catherine Queloz, Trevor Paglen, Herb Perr, Jenny Polak, Tatjana von Prittwitz, Yasmin Ramirez, Gene Ray, Gerald Raunig, Oliber Ressler, Scott Rigby, Tim Rollins, Martha Rosler, Ellen Rothenberg, Julia Rothenberg, Orla Ryan, Sabina Sabolovic, Rasha Salti, Dread Scott, Jacque Servin, Stephanie Smith, Åsa Sonjasdotter, Christoph Spehr, Nancy Spero, Blake Stimson, Eva Sturm, Bill Talen,

Nato Thompson, Daniel Tucker, Igor Vamos, Vanni Brusadin, Wolfgang Zinggl, Vera Zolberg, Dan Wang, O. K. Werckmeister, Nicholas Wisniewski, Chin-tao Wu. I am also grateful to the publications *Afterimage*, *Artforum*, *Circa*, *The Journal of Aesthetics and Protest*, *Proximity*, and *Third Text* for their support (and who in a different form first published some of this book's ideas and material), and to Professional Staff Congress union ADT Local #2334 and Queens College City, University of New York for making possible the release time from teaching to complete the manuscript.

EXORDIUM: AN ACCIDENTAL REMAINDER

Many years ago, when I began my initial research for this book, I purchased a volume of essays by the late art critic Craig Owens, a New York-based art historian and theorist closely identified with 1980s post-modernism. *Beyond Recognition: Representation, Power, and Culture* was published in 1992, two years after Owens died of complications from AIDS.[1] Though I never met Owens, his ideas about the politics of contemporary art left their mark on my intellectual development. *Beyond Recognition* was of particular interest to me for several reasons. One of these centered on a short essay the critic wrote in 1984 entitled, "The Problem With Puerilism."[2]Drawing on the social art history and cultural theory of Stuart Hall and Thomas Crow, the two-page essay roundly denounced the gentrifying effects of the East Village Art Scene, then in full bloom on New York's Lower East Side. Originally published in *Art in America* magazine, Owens' commentary is one of the first texts that links contemporary art with what we now call neoliberalism: the radical deregulation and privatization of the post-war Keynesian economy initiated by Thatcher and Reagan.[3] The cultural changes brought on by the rise of neoliberalism runs like *a leitmotiv* throughout this book. However, there was another reason I wanted to look over the text republished in *Beyond Recognition*: in its original form in the magazine his essay was accompanied by several anti-gentrification street graphics created by PAD/D, the group I had worked with in the early 1980s (and in fact, to my knowledge "The Problem With Puerilism" is about the only occasion when PAD/D was referred to in any major art magazine).

Owens' brief editorial in *Art in America* was in fact a barbed rejoinder to a far lengthier article that unabashedly eulogized the gritty, self-proclaimed Bohemianism of this new, East Village art market. Both texts appeared in the same 1984 Summer issue. At the center of the debate stood dozens of commercial art galleries that had sprung up in what was then one of the most ethnically diverse and working-class sections of Manhattan. The presence of these new Bohemian artists, dealers, and their posh clientele had begun pushing up rents and accelerating the exodus of low-income residents out of the neighborhood. Owens took to task the mannered affect of East Village art, a mostly painterly and expressionistic style largely churned out for novice collectors riding the mid 1980s stock-market boom, but he also deftly focused on the symbiosis between art and real estate. In a sense, "The Problem With Puerilism" offered an early description of what was to become a new urban lifestyle woven from equal parts entrepreneurship and avant-garde dissent. A decade later such simulated Bohemia

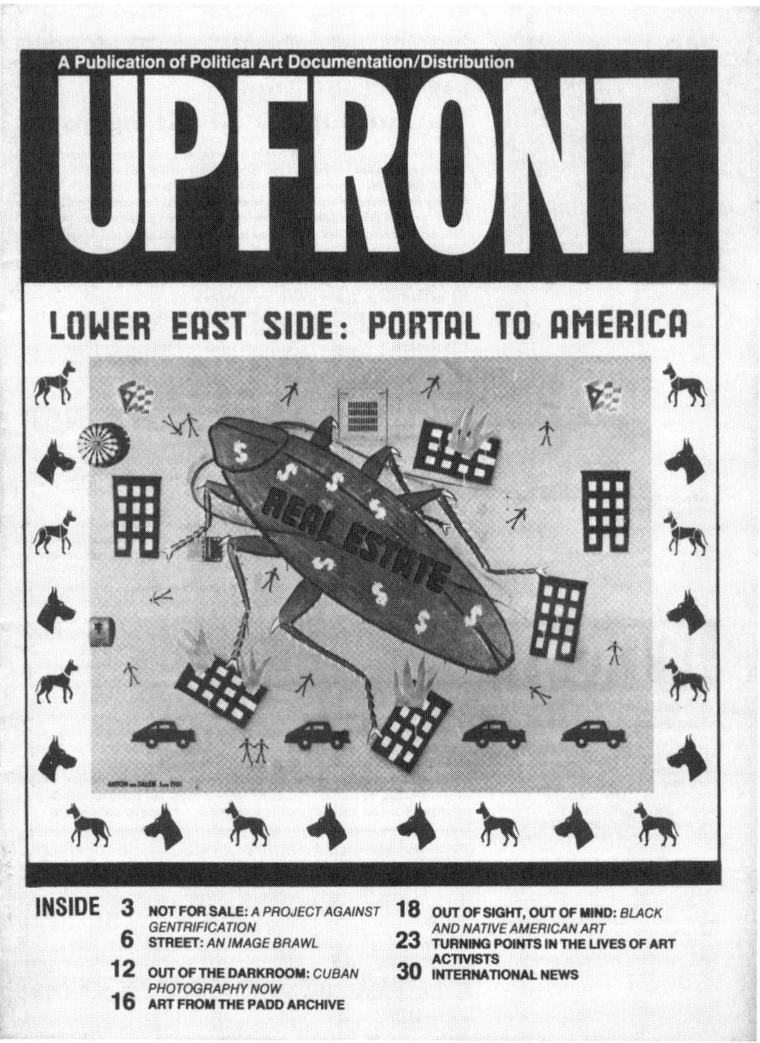

Upfront newsletter was produced on a semi-annual basis by the artists' collective PAD/D (Political Art Documentation/Distribution) and featured illustrations, reports, reviews, and full-length articles about engaged art practices in the New York City region and beyond. On the cover of this issue on gentrification, from Summer 1983, is a large stencil mural by artist Anton van Dalen ("Lower East Side: Portal to America"; medium: latex and spray paint stencils on wall; size: 148x180ins; exhibition date: May 31–June 28, 1981). It was located inside CHARAS/El Bohio (at 605 E. 9th Street, New York, NY), a former public school building occupied in the 1970s and 1980s by Nuyorican community activists. In 1998 a private developer purchased the building from the City with the intention of transforming the former school into luxury apartments and the mural was painted over. Image courtesy Gregory Sholette Archive.

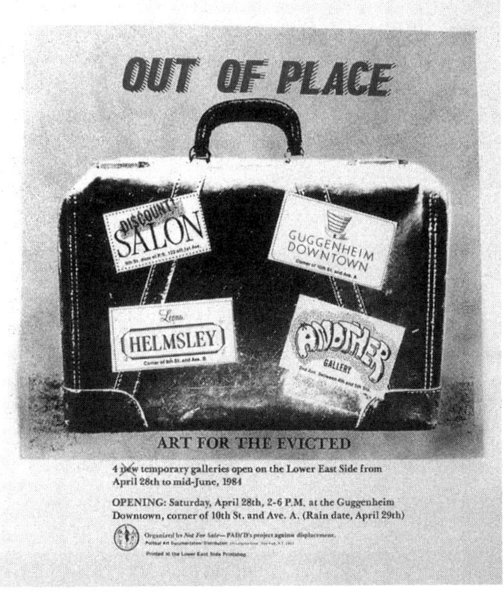

PAD/D's Not For Sale committee launched its anti-gentrification guerrilla project OUT OF PLACE on the streets of Manhattan's East Village in the mid 1980s by designating the façades of four boarded-up buildings as mock art galleries. Pictured here is the poster for the project and the then derelict Christa Dora building transformed into the mock art venue "Leona Helmsley Gallery" (named for one of the city's real estate moguls). A series of graphic works were wheat-pasted onto each of these illegal venues explicitly protesting the role of artists in displacing local residents and small businesses. The opening of the project took place at the "Guggenheim Downtown" on the corner of Avenue A and 10th Street on April 28, 1984 during the height of the East Village Art Scene. Images courtesy Gregory Sholette Archive.

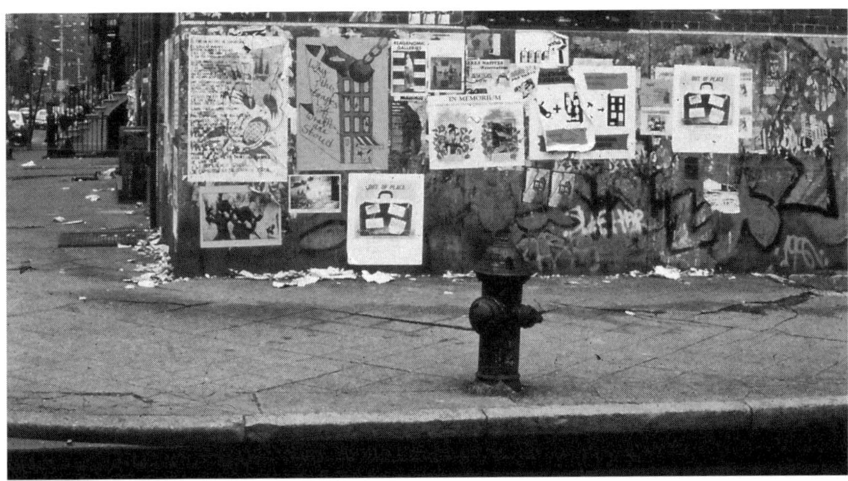

would spread from New York City to Chicago, London, Berlin, Copenhagen, Mexico City, Budapest, and beyond. The critic's essay did not end on a pessimistic note however, and instead, in a gesture invoking Benjamin's "The Author as Producer," Owens called upon artists to reject their own class interests in order to work "within the community to call attention to, and mobilize the political and economic interests East Village art serves (as the artists affiliated with PAD/D, who are responsible for the illustrations accompanying this text, have done)."[4] Owens parenthetical comment referred to several graphics that had been part of a guerrilla-style poster campaign PAD/D directed (ineffectively) against the gentrification of the Lower East Side. The street exhibition was entitled *Not For Sale*, and it overtly parodied the informal character of East Village art galleries in a bid to stimulate some form of social involvement by an otherwise politically passive art scene. By linking his text with these agitational graphics, Owens likewise shifted the tenor of his commentary from that of a purely analytical tract, to something approaching political pedagogy, and therefore closer to the tendentious style of Benjamin's anti-fascist essay.

However, when I opened the posthumous collection of his writings the *Art in America* essay appeared quite different. There were no reproductions of PAD/D's images, and no parenthetical statement praising the group's anti-gentrification stance. I turned to the index. There I found an entry entitled PAD/D 266. But this index entry was all that remained of PAD/D, a small residuum certain to be overlooked by even the most observant reader. The most interesting angle to this minor art-historical mystery is not why or how PAD/D's presence was excised from the text—such editorial oversights happen all the time and no doubt my book is no exception—but rather it is the way this textual ellipsis relates to my own project, which seeks to unearth this and other accidental remainders, or, more accurately, to point to their present absence. Granted, it is a warning that almost certainly comes too late. With increasing, often cybernetic energy, a shadowy social productivity now haunts the very notion of a proper artistic canon with its exemplary practices and necessary acts of exclusion. These ghosts pour out from the crypts and basements of culture's dwelling places, including its poorly kept records and shadowy archives of over-productivity. They multiply faster than any newly devised tomb (or text-tomb) could even hope to retain them. Along with the explosive activity of non-artists, the increasing visualization of countless failed professionals, and the diminutive trace of activist groups such as PAD/D, the uncomfortable but growing presence/absence of culture's missing excess mass announces its arrival. Think of this book therefore, as a tentative "lumpenography" of artistic dark matter.[5]

INTRODUCTION: THE MISSING MASS

The dreaming collective knows no history.

Walter Benjamin[1]

Dark Matter

Astrophysicists describe *dark matter* (and *dark energy*) as forming an invisible mass predicted by the *big bang* theory, yet so far only perceived indirectly by observing the motions of visible, astronomical objects such as stars and galaxies. Despite its invisibility and unknown constitution, most of the universe, perhaps as much as 96 percent of it consists of dark matter, a phenomenon sometimes called the "missing mass problem." The gravitational presence of this unseen force presumably keeps the universe from flying apart. This book borrows the metaphor of an unknown but ubiquitous stellar mass and applies it to the world of art and culture. Like its astronomical cousin, *creative dark matter* also makes up the bulk of the artistic activity produced in our post-industrial society. However, this type of dark matter is invisible primarily to those who lay claim to the management and interpretation of culture—the critics, art historians, collectors, dealers, museums, curators, and arts administrators. It includes makeshift, amateur, informal, unofficial, autonomous, activist, non-institutional, self-organized practices—all work made and circulated in the shadows of the formal art world, some of which might be said to emulate cultural dark matter by rejecting art world demands of visibility, and much of which has no choice but to be invisible. While astrophysicists are eager to know what dark matter is, the denizens of the art world largely ignore the unseen accretion of creativity they nevertheless remain dependent upon.

Consider the destabilizing impact on high art were some of these hidden producers to cease or pause their activity. What would happen for example if the hobbyists and amateurs who purportedly make up a billion-dollar national industry in the US simply stopped purchasing art supplies or no longer took classes with "professional" artists, or ceased going to museums to see what bona fide artists do?[2] And why consider only the tactical withdrawal of amateur participation, which is by definition marginal? What about the dark matter at the heart of the art world itself? Consider the structural invisibility of most professionally trained artists whose very underdevelopment is essential to normal art

1st ISSUE POLITICAL ART DOCUMENTATION /DISTRIBUTION

February 1981

PAD: Waking Up In NYC

PAD (Political Art Documentation/Distribution) is an artists' resource and networking organization coming out of and into New York City. *Our main goal is to provide artists with an organized relationship to society;* one way we are doing this is by building a collection of documentation of international socially-concerned art. **PAD** defines "social concern" in the broadest sense, as any work that deals with issues—ranging from sexism and racism to ecological damage or other forms of human oppression. We document all kinds of work from movement posters to the most personal of individual statements. Art comes from art as well as from life. Knowing this makes us want to learn more about the production, distribution and impact of socially-concerned art works in the context of our culture and society. Historically, politicized or social-change artists have been denied mainstream coverage and our interaction has been limited. We have to know what we are doing. In New York. In the US. In Canada and Latin America. In Europe. In Asia and Africa. **The development of an effective oppositional culture depends on communication.**

UN CERTAIN ART ANGLAIS!

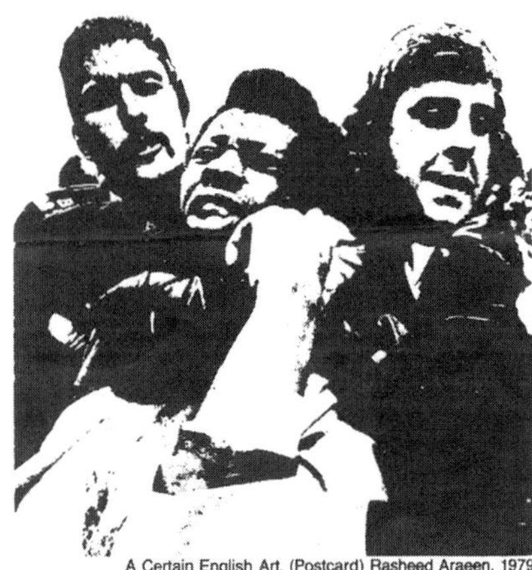

A Certain English Art, (Postcard) Rasheed Araeen, 1979

PAD celebrated its first birthday with a Valentine's evening of entertainment and discussion around a slide show of political art (followed by dancing, but not in the streets—yet). We began in February 1980 as an amorphous group of artworkers dimly aware of a mutual need to organize around issues, but without much notion of how to do it. We met at Printed Matter once a month and agreed to start collecting documentation so we would have a physical core from which to reach out. For a while we looked at each other's work, discussed it, and thought about a social club and various possibilities for cultural activism. Then in late Spring we were offered a room in a former high school on the Lower East Side under the aegis of Seven Loaves—an umbrella group for community arts organizations. Suddenly we existed physically. We *had* to be in the world, and that led to the present structuring, still in process.

We have three kinds of meetings now: 1) The relatively flexible core or work group of 15-20 people gets together on three Sunday afternoons a month at the Seven Loaves space (when not too cold). Here we deal with: soliciting and handling of the archive materials; how to connect with other cultural organizations in NYC with similar purposes so there's no overlapping and duplication of work. (For instance, we are working with Cityarts Workshop, which has an impressive resource center on the community mural movement, and with Karin di Gia of Gallery 345, who has a collection of original political art.) We are also beginning to connect with and inform each other about the political events and struggles taking place in the city, understanding the ways these relate to national and international situations. Finally, we are thinking about collectively created issue-oriented exhibitions in public spaces, such as windows, subways, libraries, etc.

2) The open meetings with which we began. They take place on the second Sunday of every month at 8 PM at Printed Matter (7 Lispenard St., NYC 10013; 925-0325). Here reports are made from the work group and a brief visual or verbal presentation is given by a **PAD** member or guest as a sort of laboratory to stimulate discussion, education, consciousness raising and activism.

3) We are just beginning a series of public events centered around specific social issues seen in their historical perspectives, focusing on how they were opposed or supported by the socially concerned art of the time; for instance in May, a day on militarism in the "cold war" era, the Vietnam era and today, discussed by people from WRL (the War Resisters League), CARD (Committee Against Registration for the Draft) and artists who have done work with anti-militaristic content. We want to understand how the dialectic between oppositional art and society changes and takes different forms at different moments. These public afternoons will be publicized, and will lead up to an Autumn conference, at which we hope to bring together a wide coalition of cultural groups and artists. (For more information on events, see the "Calendar" section of **PAD**.)

PAD's theory is going to develop out of real experience instead of from the idealized and romanticized notion of a

The first newsletter of PAD/D (Political Art Documentation/Distribution), a single folded offset page published in February 1981, approximately one year after the group's founding. Shown is the group's mission statement "Waking Up in New York City," as well as the artwork "Un Certain Art Anglais!" by artist and founder of the journal *Third Text*, Rasheed Araeen. Image courtesy Gregory Sholette Archive.

world functions. Without this obscure mass of "failed" artists the small cadre of successful artists would find it difficult, if not impossible, to sustain the global art world as it appears today. Without this invisible mass, the ranks of middle and lower level arts administrators would be depleted, there would be no one left to fabricate the work of art stars or to manage their studios and careers. And who would educate the next generation of artists, disciplining their growing numbers into a system that mechanically reproduces prolific failure? Furthermore, by purchasing journals and books, visiting museums and belonging to professional organizations, these underdeveloped "invisibles" represent an essential pillar of the elite art world whose pyramidal structure looms over them eternally out of reach. And yet there is no material difference between an earnest amateur on the one hand, and a professional artist made invisible by her "failure" within the art market on the other; except perhaps that against all the odds she still hopes to be discovered? How would the art world manage its system of aesthetic valorization if the seemingly superfluous majority—those excluded as non-professionals as much as those destined to "fail"—simply gave up on its system of legitimation? Or if they found an alternative to it by creating a Peer-to-Peer (P2P) network of support and direct sales bypassing art dealers, critics, galleries, and curators? Indeed, to some degree this has already begun to take shape via media applications of Web 2.0. What has not happened is any move towards re-distributing the cultural capital bottled up within the holding company known as high art.

All of these forms of dark matter play an essential role in the symbolic economy of art. Collectively, the amateur and the failed artist represent a vast flat field upon which a privileged few stand out in relief. The aim of this book is to raise an inevitable question: what if we turned this figure and ground relation inside out by imagining an art world unable to exclude the practices and practitioners it secretly depends upon? What then would become of its value structure and distribution of power? The answer is not to imagine the emergence of a more comprehensive social art history in which the usual art subjects are better contextualized. Nor is it to take part in some rarified tour of this dark-matter world in which the mysterious missing cultural mass is acknowledged, ruminated over, and then re-shelved or archived as a collection of oddities. Instead, when the excluded are made visible, when they demand visibility, it is always ultimately a matter of politics and a rethinking of history. This is often the case with artists' collectives, groups, and collaborations whose communal self-embrace inevitably spotlights the general superfluity of artistic production and producers. But something has also happened in recent years to that far larger mass of inert dark matter. It is a change that dramatically alters the relationship between visible art and its shadowy other, between professional and amateur, the institution and the archive. Dark matter is getting brighter. And simultaneous with that change in status, this once missing mass has also been forced to undergo its own adaptations and mutations. The essays that make up this volume do not seek to link the growing illumination of imaginative dark-matter productivity with a market-generated notion of outsider art or some other facile locus of cultural colonization. Rather, their allegiance is with those artists who self-consciously choose to work on the outer margins of the mainstream art world for reasons of social, economic, and political critique. In a sense, these artists have learned to embrace their own structural redundancy, they have chosen to be "dark matter." By grasping the politics of their own invisibility and marginalization they inevitably challenge the formation of normative artistic values. Here "politics" must be understood as the imaginative exploration of ideas, the pleasure of communication, the exchange of education, and the construction of fantasy, all within a radically defined social-artist practice. Such informal, often highly politicized micro-institutions are proliferating today, and have been growing in number for the past 15 years at least. This kind of self-organized dark matter infiltrates high schools, flea markets, public squares, corporate websites, city streets, housing projects, and local political machines in ways that do not set out to recover a specific meaning or use-value for art world discourse or private interests. Which is why the responses to this growing illumination made so far—including the various narratives and theoretical attempts to manage dark matter, from the academicization of public art to relational aesthetics—are no doubt transitory, and merely part of a greater shift taking place within the broader cultural paradigm.

Look again at the art world and the dark matter it occludes. Few would deny that the lines separating "dark" and "light" creativity, amateur and professional, high from low have become arbitrary today, even from the standpoint of qualities such as talent, vision, and other similarly mystifying attributes typically assigned to high culture. What can be said of creative dark matter in general, therefore, is that either by choice or circumstance it displays a degree of autonomy from the critical and economic structures of the art world by moving instead in-between its meshes. It is an antagonistic force simultaneously inside and outside, like a void within an archive that is itself a kind of void. But, as I hope to show, the archive has split open, its ragged contents no longer hidden from view. Still, this growing materiality is not necessarily a politically progressive event. Increased visibility not only poses certain risks for any institution that seeks to enclose it but also—by privileging spontaneity and discontinuity, repetitions and instability—dark matter can seldom be sustained as a political force. What proves effective in the short term or locally remains untested on a larger scale. And that is the point we appear to be rapidly approaching: an encounter with matters of scale and the need for a new sustainable political culture of the Left. Dark matter's missing cultural mass is both a metaphor for something vast, unnamable and essentially inert, as well as a phantasmagoric proposition concerning what might be possible at this moment of epistemological crisis in the arts and structural crisis in global capital.

Commitment

This then is a book about the politics of invisibility that could only have been written at a moment when invisibility itself has emerged as a force to be contended with, or, conversely, a provocation to be selectively controlled. It is as much dedicated to those who refuse the capture of their invisibility, as it is to those whose very visibility has been and continues to be refused. But this is also a study of something else. We might call it the ubiquitous gaze of the "social factory" that now looks back at us tirelessly, unblinkingly, and with an unprecedented historical hunger. The collision of these visibilities and shadows, appetites and circumventions defines the spaces of my text, as well as the very conditions that artists, myself among them, must operate under within a post-Fordist enterprise culture. And yet, as odd as a book about invisible artists and artwork may seem, my methods are less orthodox still. In his essay "The Author As Producer," Benjamin called upon cultural workers to become producers transforming the very means of their artistic production.[3] What follows is my attempt to respond to that call. Throughout these pages I have sought to write *tendentiously*, in the critically engaged manner proposed by Benjamin, producing, I hope, a committed work that never disengages from its political core. By turns it invokes historical research, critical theory, empirical observation, and journalistic reportage approached from the bottom up, from the viewpoint of a cultural worker who necessarily labored at numerous ignoble jobs from janitor, to dishwasher, to industrial fabricator before becoming a college instructor, all to maintain his existence as an "artist." And while these sundry work experiences were admittedly privileged by gender, ethnicity, and education, they nonetheless remain deeply instructive for my work and mark this volume in ways that have sometimes taken its author by surprise. This fundamental identification as a cultural worker leads me to push my critique of enterprise culture beyond an analysis of representation in order to examine artists' working conditions and the power of the market. It also draws directly from my own history as an artist, specifically with two artists' collectives—Political Art Documentation/Distribution, or PAD/D (1980–88), and REPOhistory (1989–2000)—both informally structured groups whose relationship to the art world was, and remains, marginal at best. Finally, whenever possible, attempts to define art and aesthetics have been avoided. For obvious reasons an artist is not able to step outside of such discourse into some detached critical space. Instead, I allow those who claim to make "art" to define it on their own terms, even if their identification with the practice is provisional, ironic, or tactical, as for example when artist Steve Kurtz insists "I'll call it whatever I have to in order to communicate with someone." And perhaps this playful relationship to the word "art" has its downside, given that Critical Art Ensemble, the Tactical Media group Kurtz co-founded, has received very little direct financial support from cultural foundations.[4] My aim in other words is not to separate art from non-art, the rubbish from the dross, but to examine how these self-defined cultural practices operate within a changing economy involving material and symbolic rewards and penalties, visibilities and shadows. I leave it to the reader to decide if this idiosyncratic approach permits the airing of ideas and histories that would otherwise remain in the dark. What follows therefore is one admittedly partial attempt to articulate the politics of this missing mass. To paraphrase the cosmologists: there is perhaps no current problem of greater importance to cultural radicals than that of "dark matter."

Redundancy

"We can measure the waste of artistic talent," the art historian Carol Duncan perceptively observed as early as 1983, "not only in the thousands of 'failed' artists—artists whose market failure is necessary to the success of the few—but also in the millions whose creative potential is never touched." Duncan adds that this glut of "art and artists is the normal condition of the art market."[5] As an artist trying to make my way through the complexity of New York's cultural scene in the 1980s her comments struck me as both accurate and suggestive of an unglimpsed reality just below the surface. It seemed as though some vaguely visible structural condition peculiar to contemporary art had briefly flashed up before me. After several decades of working at being an artist, political activist, writer, teacher, curator, and founding member of two political artists' collectives, Duncan's comments returned to me with a vividness that only lived experience can furnish: The oversupply of artistic labor is an inherent and commonplace feature of artistic production. Why? In preparing this study I reinterpreted the art historian's remarks as a series of questions. What do the many, necessarily "failed" artists, as Duncan calls them, actually provide to a system that handsomely rewards some of its participants? Artists are educated by the art world to see such failure as a kind of chaff that must be removed to release a small nucleus of value. Yet, even this agricultural metaphor reminds us that a "wasted" husk once protected a valuable seed. Perhaps most importantly, this creative chaff maintains and reproduces the system's *symbolic* hierarchies by exchanging information about the luminaries of the art world at openings, parties, on blogsites, doing so reflexively, like a vast field of heliotropic flowers always oriented towards a brightly lit center. Even if the soil at the margins of this field is sewn with bitterness, such gossip reinforces the apparent naturalness of the overall art economy and its hierarchies. To restate this point with a shift of metaphors, the artist Martha Rosler was once brazenly informed by an art dealer that either you're on the art world "table" or your not. The question today is, who supports the table?[6]

As peculiar as the cultural economy of fine art may be, there is no getting around the fact that an increasing number of individuals are choosing to become artists.[7]

This is all the more striking given the past 30 years in which a form of deregulated capitalism has dominated the global economy transforming increasing segments of the population into an under- or simply un-employed surplus population that exceeds even the necessary "reserve army of labor" essential to the functioning of capital. So why has art, an inherently precarious activity in the best of times, actually flourished during this process of competitive global austerity? Needless to say, the answer appears to lie not strictly within the art establishment, but is instead part of a broader change in the status of culture within the neoliberal economy of the past 30 years. For one thing, enterprise culture requires a kind of enforced creativity that is imposed on all forms of labor. Workers, whose livelihoods have been made increasingly precarious by the collapse of the traditional social welfare state, are expected to be forever ready to retrain themselves at their own expense (or their own debt), to labor continuously even when at home or on vacation, and finally, they are expected to be constantly creative, to think like an artist: "outside the box." Such universal demand for imagination and innovation inevitably places added value on forms of "creativity" previously dismissed as informal or non-professional. In a very tangible sense dark matter is simply not as dark as it recently appeared. The spread of information technologies including the World Wide Web directly enhance this process of illumination while expanding forms of creative economic discipline into the affective and domestic spheres of human life. As never before, producing, copying, re-mixing, printing, uploading, and distributing images and information has become (almost) everyone's privilege, even their social responsibility. Digital technology also functions like a prosthetic memory permitting the excluded to document and narrate ephemeral, everyday activities and overlooked forms of expression or resistance. As Boris Groys insists, no one sits in the audience any longer, everyone is on stage.[8] Which brings me to the third and most important phenomenon and the one this book is most keen to address—the way this twin expansion of neoliberal demand and creative "mining" technology has inevitably led to a kind of rupture within a vast surplus archive "from below," a vault of pent-up ideas and desires, hopes and frustrations, littered with odds and ends, and structured (if that word applies here at all) by narrative gaps and lacunas. In an age of enterprise culture, when concepts of labor and class and resistance are being taken apart and put back together again, it is to this shadow or surplus archive that artistic dissidents and rebels now look for inspiration on "how to fight." For what post-Fordist enterprise culture and its precarious dependency on social networks have unleashed may not be fully compatible with the kind of giddy, self-regulating free market idealism digital libertarians have cheerfully promoted. The new electronic commons might instead be thought of as the return of an old commons, or, as Blake Stimson and I proposed: "the newness of the new e-collectivism, like the newness of the new Arab street, is only a rebirth of intensity, the welling up of spirits from the past, a recall to the opportunities and battle lines of old."[9] This materializing missing mass is no doubt permeated with its own historical baggage, half-submerged resentments, but also a sense of anticipation. Under these circumstances, even once formidable modes of artistic dissent such as institutional critique have become deeply ambivalent about the role of self-criticism.[10] In a sense, the once-hidden surplus archive is now eating its host. Or, more precisely, like some extraterrestrial vegetal pod it is *becoming* its host. But I am getting ahead of things.

The book begins by selectively examining politically committed forms of mostly collaborative art that arose on the cusp of the post-Fordist structural adjustment of the late 1970s and early 1980s. Following an initial chapter that serves as a broad, introductory overview of the entire project, the second chapter focuses on the archival work of the New York City based collective PAD/D. Founded in 1980 this group's collective mindset was still deeply indebted to the mass opposition movements and liberation struggles of the 1950s, '60s and '70s in which students, soldiers, women, minorities, and many workers rejected not only the culture of capitalism, but also its work disciplines within the factory as well as the office. Though it was already in decline by the early 1980s, PAD/D sought to maintain this antagonistic spirit by establishing its own separately networked art world apart from both the commercial market and that of mainstream museums and not-for-profit spaces. This quite literal counter-culture would ideally evolve its own exhibition venues, material support, and critical discourse and look forward to the post-capitalist society yet to come. Indeed, it was still possible even then to think this way about history and its inevitable forward movement towards greater social and economic democracy. In many ways, PAD/D actually harkened back as much to the organized Left of the 1920s and '30s as it did to the less formal New Left of May 1968 and after. Notably, the group's demise took place exactly as the socialist "East" finally fell apart. In retrospect, this was also the end of a phase of political and cultural experimentation by many post-colonial nations in search of an alternative to capitalism. It was also the moment when a wave of deregulation and privatization began to rapidly displace inner-city residents in places like Manhattan's Lower East Side where PAD/D's offices were located. What PAD/D left behind to a gentrified New York was its archive of social and political art, now housed within the Museum of Modern Art (MoMA).[11]

Chapter 2 addresses the obvious irony of this outcome, as well as the structural changes going on in the 1980s art community. However, it also goes inside the PAD/D Archive to examine some of its many documents about unknown or little known politically engaged artists and artists' groups. The primary question this chapter raises concerns how this entombment of a "radical" art functions, or potentially functions, within the MoMA. To look at this from the other way around, what does a key pillar of the art world establishment gain from this internalized bit of dissent, which, setting content aside, also represents a virtual core-sample of the massive overproduction artists generate at any given moment? One answer is to think of this *other* archive of critical, surplus cultural activity as a mark or bruise within the body of high art. The system must wear this mark of difference in order to legitimate its very dominance. Absolute exclusion is out of the question. Thus the image of the archive becomes an internally exiled exclusion, like a crypt or tomb that harbors meaning through a kind of negation (deathly remains) for the jurisdiction of the household above it. The surplus archive—as well as artistic dark matter—is therefore both a presence and absence within the material and symbolic economy of art. Except that an archive can never remain purely abstract, at some point it crosses the threshold into actual, content, even if, as in the case of the PAD/D Archive, this content is chaotic and messy and very much at odds with the codes and laws that order the institution within which it is housed. The chapters that follow this exploration of MoMA's encrypted *other* play upon this double nature of the surplus archive: its ambivalent structural relation as internally outlawed content which is at best a catalog of multiple aesthetic and political attractions (and perhaps also repulsions). One way to explain the structure of this book, therefore, is as an attempt to infect the "lawfully" embodied systems of exclusion and visibility beginning with the art world's inner foundation and spreading outwards: a procedure potentially brought within reach by the very demands of enterprise culture for ubiquitous creativity and amplified by its own prosthesis of electronic memory and networked intelligence. Still, there are complications.

In Chapter 3 the archive returns, but now being written directly on the skin of a gentrified city that very much wants to forget its past. This essay focuses on the momentary bubbling up and fading away of this *other* urban narrative as an openly revanchist neoliberal urbanism typified by the administration of Mayor Rudolph Giuliani swept over New York City in the 1990s. During this period the group REPOhistory carried out several site-specific, "Do It Yourself" (DIY) public art projects, using street signs to focus public attention on little known, forgotten, or politically inconvenient histories. Eventually REPOhistory ran afoul of municipal and cultural authorities, and the subaltern archive was slammed shut once more. The chapter also sets REPOhistory's work within a broader context of public art practices that emerged towards the end of the Cold War and focused on historical memory and forgetting, as if a certain archivalization was only (temporarily) possible once the danger it represented had passed. Like REPOhistory a number of these public art and history projects in Buenos Aires, Berlin, Pittsburgh, and Oakland California also mimicked the official street signs and other systems of spatial administration. As global neoliberalism turns urban spaces into zones of managed consumption and ubiquitous surveillance, it seems

Phone items to (212) 251-6800 • Fax (212) 696-0487 MANHATTAN NEIGHBORHOODS 23 NY-M

Art Signs Challenge 'History'

By Melissa Tarkington
STAFF WRITER

At the corner of William and Fulton Streets next week, passersby will be greeted by a sign welcoming them to "Gotham City." Washington Irving, the sign reads, once gave New York City this nickname after an English village whose residents practiced tax evasion by running around acting demented.

Is this history?

You decide, say artists who designed this sign and 35 others denoting infamous or little-known facts about city history as part of the Lower Manhattan Sign Project, which will be officially opened in Battery Park tomorrow. The 18-by-24-inch metal signs are being placed on lampposts primarily in the financial district along South Street Seaport, the World Trade Center, Battery Park and near the Liberty Island ferry landing in lower Manhattan.

This collection of artwork, which offers an alternative, multi-ethnic view of history, is the result of three years of research, permit-gathering and historical verification by about 60 artists, performers, writers and teachers.

"We wanted to examine and question the way history was written in a public art project," said Lisa Maya Knauer, a participating artist. "We wanted to see what kind of relationship Lower Manhattan had with history — its ties to the past and then offer our findings in an objective, scientific way."

Through words and pictures, the signs will broach such subjects as epidemics, racial and sexual equality, the slave trade, subway fires, international health care, the "inequality of the U.S. Senate," New York's Chinese community and exploitation in boxing, among others.

"Each sign has a series of questions that addresses the viewer and directly engages that person," said Alan Michelson, who researched John Jacob Astor and fur trade. "We want people to think of the place they are in — we hope everyone is going to see a different thing."

The Lower Manhattan Sign Project

The themes and locations of all the signs.

1. Potter's Field/Ellis Island
2. Indian Giver or When Will America Be Discovered?
3. Great Negro Plot of 1741
4. Leisler's Rebellion
5. Bullet made from Statue of King George
6. Homelessness: Forgotten Histories
7. Whitehall Street Induction Center
8. Origin of Pearl Street
9. Nelson Mandela's visit to NYC
10. Origin of the Word Indian
11. Indian Settlement Sites
12. India House
13. The Other J.P. Morgan
14. Stock Market Crash
15. False Democracy: Inequality of the U.S. Senate
16. Subway Fire
17. Insurance and National Health Care
18. Meal Market/Slave Trade
19. Rose Schneiderman: Union Activist
20. Chinese Community in NYC
21. Jacob Astor and Native Americans
22. The Story of the Waterfront
23. Madame Restell and Anthony Comstock
24. Office Workers Eat Their Lunch
25. What's in a Name?
26. Gotham City
27. Epidemics
28. Frances Wright: Racial and Sexual Equality
29. Vito Marcantonio: Radical Congressman
30. Civil Defense Drill Arrests 1950s
31. Boxing and Exploitation
32. Forlorn Hope/Debtor's Jail
33. The First Alms House
34. Negroes' Burial Ground/The City Limits
35. Smith Act Trials
36. United Tailoresses Society

MANHATTAN

Newsday / Richard Cornett

Tom Klem, who designated homelessness as forgotten history on his sign, said he hopes the project prompts analytical thinking. "Perhaps someone will just read the questions, stop and think. Everyone could see completely different things. We've given a lot of thought to how the public will interpret this project."

Greg Sholette, who created a sign titled "The Other J.P. Morgan," said they expected mixed reactions for challenging conventional "correct" history. "Any questioning of history is seen as threatening to so many people that we are expecting to get some backlash," he said, "and if this is seen as a liberal attack, it won't be effective at all."

Knauer said the project was initially planned as guerrilla art because they expected strong oppostion and censorship.

"We thought we would be going out in the dead of night to do it," she said. "We thought we would be prevented from doing it directly."

The project, however, has received approval from The New York Historical Society and funding from the Lower Manhattan Cultural Council and the Andy Warhol Foundation, among others. None of the organizations attempted to censor their work, Knauer said. "We believe in a full range of voices being heard — so much about history has not been shared," said Erika Sanger, coordinator of public programs at the New York Historical Society. However, Sanger said the historical society at first was skeptical about the project's authenticity.

"There were actually some historical questions," Sanger said. "I had my doubts, but I went through and researched questions with one of the artists and the artist proved me wrong."

The artists view themselves as creators of an original project.

"What makes our project different," Michelson said, "is that we have gone out and done a marker project and also that we are focusing on social history. There is almost nothing marking social history in this city."

CLOSEUP

The project is a combination walking tour and public art viewing and will run through December 27, 1992. The opening begins at 2 p.m. at Castle Clinton in Battery Park tomorrow. The artists are scheduled to lead the first walking tour from 3:30 p.m. until 5 p.m.

Maps of the walking tour are free and may be picked up at the visitors information booth at the World Trade Center.

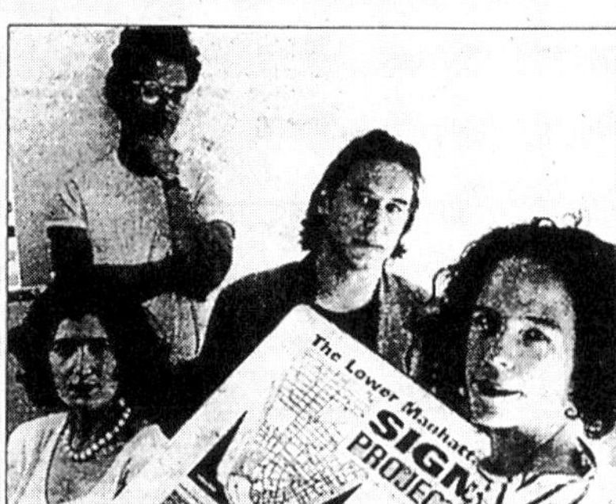

Newsday / Jon Naso

Artists Lisa Maya Knauer, Todd Ayoung, Alan Michelson and Tess Timoney with a sign by Michelson entitled "John Jacob Astor and Native Americans."

NEW YORK NEWSDAY, FRIDAY, JUNE 26

New York Newsday, June 28, 1992, reporting on REPOhistory's Lower Manhattan Sign Project including a clip-and-carry do it yourself walking tour map of the installation. Shown in the photograph from left to right are "REPOhistorians" Lisa Maya Knauer, Todd Ayoung (standing), Alan Michelson, and Tess Timoney. The newspaper is no longer in print. Image courtesy Gregory Sholette Archive.

that the battle for public memory must be played out from within the city's own repertoire of semiotic management.

Chapter 4 continues to examine the tactics of urban intervention with a study of the Illinois-based artists' collective Temporary Services. As if thumbing their collective nose at the fate of being merely another "creative glut," the group has spent the past decade developing a series of archival projects, public interventions, publications, its own publishing house, and an exhibition and program space located on Chicago's North Side. Like an independent cultural municipality, Temporary Services substitutes a gift-based economy for the managed scarcity of the market. How does it manage this host of "services," especially given that its three members no longer reside in the same city? The digital communications capacity unleashed by neoliberal capitalism has brought some of what PAD/D once imagined within reach via the Internet. However, this chapter also looks at these new forms of self-organization and networked generosity from a decidedly darker angle, one that even enterprise culture is loathe to acknowledge (although it is entwined within it). For just as powerful networking technology amplifies the power of a few artists in Illinois, it also opens the public floodgates to what Nietzsche described as *Ressentiment*, or what Eve Kosofsky Sedgwick understood as the structural complexity of ignorance.[12] Inevitably, the perforation of a once suppressed archive exposes the wounds of political exclusions, redundancies, and other repeated acts of blockage that wholly or partially shape this emerging sphere of dark-matter social production.

With Chapter 5 we return to the questions raised by Duncan in more detail by sketching the political economy of contemporary art from the bottom up. This chapter tries to describe its system of promises, self-made identities, exclusions, and hierarchies from the inside, the way an art worker sees it. Its primary case study compares the efforts to gain greater social security for artists by the Art Workers' Coalition (AWC) in the late 1960s with those of the Artists Pension Trust (APT), a private, global investment fund established this past decade, at the apex of the art market's inflationary bubble. The main point of this comparison is to understand how the ever-present "glut" of artists either define and manage their own precarious redundancy, or have it defined for them within a continuously changing capitalist economy. To put this differently, how and when does the allegedly blissful new affair between "creative" labor and neoliberal capitalism become more than an arrangement of overlapping interests? When is it more than just a shared "script," as sociologist Olav Velthuis has argued, and when does it emerge as a fully blown antagonism with potential political consequences?[13]

The sixth and seventh chapters extend and refocus these various lines of inquiry through an examination of Tactical Media (TM), a form of interventionist cultural activism that typically borrows new media technology made accessible by global capitalism in order to turn it against state and corporate authority. Its practice includes media pranks, culture jamming, digital swarming, hacking corporate websites and other hit-and-run electronic guerrilla tactics aimed at what Guy Debord described as the society of the spectacle. TM marks a moment of change within resistant cultural practices, one that divides the politically engaged art associated with 1968 from that of 1989. Unlike PAD/D, REPOhistory, AWC or many of the groups discussed in the earlier chapters, TM was not only born out of the cold cinders of the Cold War, it was immediately at home within the digital Zeitgeist of post-Fordism: a form of imaginative resistance that could only fully emerge within the precarious networked world of neoliberalism. By its own carefully invented epithets TM's principal practitioners—Critical Art Ensemble, RTMark, The Yes Men, Institute for Applied Autonomy, Bureau of Inverse Technology, 0100101110101101.org—typically mirror or mimic the appearance of entrepreneurial culture itself, including bootstrapping start-up ventures and creative micro-institutions. However this mirroring process is not as simple as appears. TM's logic claims to be above ideology, yet it remains romantically anti-capitalist, perhaps even to the point of collectively mourning an unspecified aesthetic wholeness, glimpsed here and there as mere remnants and tatters within the spectacle of enterprise culture. Curiously, this very abhorrence of ideology seems to link it with neoliberal processes of social collapse and extreme reification that may provide the raw material for new social organs to grow and cohere. After World War II, as ideological combat continued by other means, Western state and corporate interests sought to legitimate their power, publicly aligning themselves with secular democratic society and even modern experimental forms of art. Theodor W. Adorno described the art thus generated as a sham. Beneath its cheerful façade was concealed the cold brutality of capitalist instrumental logic. For Adorno, true art had no choice but to draw (regrettably) upon the dark negativity of this administered welfare culture itself. Dissonance and blackness were his ideal aesthetic response to the world of administered culture.[14] In the 1980s the culture of the welfare state and Left politics were not so much superseded with a new order as they were shattered into fragments, becoming the rubble of what Margaret Thatcher once sneeringly labeled "society." This post-modern landscape is strewn with bits and pieces of dissolved social organizations, ghosts of mass movements past, ruined states, and crippled notions of the public sphere. Yet as much as remnants of nineteenth-century culture became for Walter Benjamin a kind of allegory brimming with a potential for redemption, so too have the fragments of a lost social commons, however imperfect in reality, become today a kind of allegorical detritus.

No less than opportunistic capitalists, TM and other interventionist activists have learned to tinker with this wreckage, taking it apart, reassembling it again, parodying or clowning about with its elements, mimicking its functions. And yet by default, some of these tactical practices appear to be developing what may be the closest thing to a sustainable twenty-first century dissident culture. The penultimate chapter suggests that a new form of progressive institution building is already under way, not through traditional organizing methods, but more like an accidental side-effect of defensively generated mimicry and imitation. As if superimposing two different states of being in the world—one deeply suspicious of institutional authority of any sort and therefore informally organized, and one mimicking, sometimes with impressive precision, the actual function of institutions, these mock-institutions appear to be filling a gap left by a missing social reality. Perhaps the clearest example of this is visible in the wave of new pedagogical structures being assembled around the world by art students from the United States, Great Britain, and Europe to Asia, Africa, and the Middle East. Using materials and means they salvage from the very edifice of a crumbling social system, students and artists are reinventing sustainable democratic forms. Nevertheless, the nature of this new mock-institutionalism is quite unlike the "alternative art movements" of the 1960s and 1970s. Though it borrows from these past tendencies (after all this too is part of the rubble), the new social architecture is discontinuous and contradictory, sometimes borrowing aspects of traditional not-for-profit organizations, at other times looking more like temporary commercial structures, and still other times appearing as a semi-nomadic band or tribe stumbling across a battered social landscape made all the more dire by the economic collapse of 2007–8. The brief, concluding chapter enters this ontological "gap" from below, comparing its chiaroscuro of visibility and invisibility to Marx's historic concept of the *proletariat*, which, as philosopher Stathis Kouvelakis reinterprets it, is not the figure of some hoped-for totality to come, but the very "embodiment of the impossibility of full totality" that is nevertheless no less animated or capable of mutiny or even revolution. For in light of the massive structural adjustment foisted on us by global capital, such terminology no longer seems embarrassing, as one young scholar of Tactical Media insisted as recently as 2009. Perhaps it is now time for the contemporary *ragpicker* to search again amongst the wreckage of past rebellions and uprisings for some kind of meaning, some promissory note to the present or the future?

"It's Worse Than We Thought"[15]

I began my research for this book long before the start of the so-called Great Recession and the growing resistance to it in Greece and elsewhere.[16] Indeed, the current economic contraction has brought with it a renewal of political and cultural debate that vanished three decades ago, more or less as neoliberal enterprise culture began its ascension onto the world stage. At some point in the mid 1980s, when Western finance capital was about to triumph over a deteriorating socialist East, the flexible, entrepreneurial spirit of post-Fordism seemed to offer every cultural and ethnic interest a commodified niche-market all its own. And at this moment the very concept of class as a category of economic exploitation appeared problematic. Some Marxists argued that the situation was simply an empirical problem that would be resolved once the actual working class (as it was configured under "late capitalism") could be definitively located. Others insisted that the very narrative of class was in need of deconstruction together with the notion that history was propelled by antagonisms between the many who produce, and the few who own the means of production. At the forefront of this latter critique were Ernesto Laclau and Chantal Mouffe, a duo of anti-Marxist Leftists whose influential book *Hegemony and Socialist Strategy: Towards a Radical Democratic Politics* attempted to prove that any universal economic explanation of society is merely a fetish or myth dreamed up by Marx and elaborated on by his followers. According to Laclau and Mouffe, if economic relations really do determine human subjectivity then the economy would have to be "defined independently of any specific type of society; and the conditions of existence of the economy must also be defined separately from any concrete social relation."[17] Their alternative thesis is a greatly modified version of Antonio Gramsci's concept of hegemony, except this post-structuralist version of hegemony maintains that "social agents lack any essence."[18] If there is such a thing as political agency, therefore, it must take place within a social "text" that consists of different, differing, multiple, and sometimes conflicting social positions. No one privileged signifier—such as the economy or class status—could possibly affect all of these positions because capitalism is not a totality, it is instead a text with a multiplicity of interpretive possibilities that generate merely local conflicts of power and temporal moments of subjectivity. In a more recent essay, ostensibly about artistic activism, Mouffe reiterates her mid-1980s stance insisting that

> Every order is the temporary and precarious articulation of contingent practices. Society is not to be seen as the unfolding of a logic exterior to itself, whatever the source of this logic could be: forces of production, development of the Spirit, laws of history, etc. The frontier between the social and the political is essentially unstable and requires constant displacements and renegotiations between social agents.[19]

Thus the field of agonistic struggle inevitably includes the short-order cook in the local McDonald's food factory as well as the corporate CEO who owns the company. It comprises the museum director, as well as dissident artists demanding more rights of representation. And it encompasses the artist laboring as a graphic designer or data-entry specialist 80 hours per week along with her boss who also employs dozens of similar outsourced "creative" workers. The fact that each subject's position could just as effectively be defined by a greater or lesser degree of freedom over his or her material conditions of life is far less significant, so Laclau and Mouffe argue, than their particular hegemonic articulation within society, which always remain provisional and indeterminate. Admittedly, in 1985 this utopian desire to distance radical politics from the reductive economism of much orthodox Marxism appeared as a necessary corrective to the brittle and seriously deflated Left that a sweeping neoconservatism had all but politically decimated. The collapse of the Eastern Bloc and the Soviet Union seemed to confirm the market's final triumph on an unprecedented global scale. And yet what was traded away along with the abandonment of class conflict was a primary *raison d'être* of the Left itself, including above all its historic demand for autonomy from the economic determinism of capital (a determinism that was apparently but an illusion all along). Ironically, this theoretical trade-off made in the name of deconstructing grand historical and political narratives came at the very moment when capitalism emerged as the totalizing world system. Workers' incomes rapidly dropped in the United States and other industrial nations, jobs shifted to the global Southern hemisphere and slavery reemerged as a hidden component of the global economy. And when the system did dramatically implode in 2008 its effects were predictably universal. Capitalism's crisis was everyone's crisis—or opportunity. All at once the "unfixed character of every signifier" [20] suddenly had one common referent. Which is to say that while some socialists and intellectuals may have had difficulty locating the modern proletariat, alternatively deflating or mythologizing its composition along the way, global capitalism never doubted the existence of the working class or its whereabouts (even if capital would never describe class relations in anything like those terms).[21] That said, within some influential academic and artistic circles Laclau and Mouffe popularized a useful, if limited critique of a classical Marxism, one that dovetailed with an assortment of militant liberation struggles by women, minorities, gay people, environmentalists, anarchists and other libertarian Leftists. However, even as this position was circulating in mid-1980s intellectual circles, a less well-known, but increasingly radical critique of standard Marxism had already been initiated in the 1960s and '70s in which the extraction of surplus time and value from labor remained the locus of cultural and political struggle. That analysis has proved far more applicable to the current crisis.

Despite many strong differences, this other tendency includes a range of libertarian Marxist thinkers, including those emerging out of the Italian Autonomist movement, or Potere Operaio (Workers' Power), such as Mario Tronti, Paulo Virno, and Antonio Negri; those coming from the very different tradition associated with the Frankfurt School, such as Oscar Negt and Alexander Kluge; as well as a range of less well-known feminist, environmental, and Left-libertarian Marxists that includes C. L. R James, Raya Dunayevskaya, Mariarosa Dalla Costa, Selma James, Vandana Shiva, and theorists associated with the Midnight Notes Collective such as Silvia Federici, George Caffentzis, Harry

Cleaver, Mariarosa Dalla Costa, and younger scholars inspired by their work like Leopoldina Fortunati and the members of edu-factory collective in Europe.

As diverse as these writers are they nevertheless reassert Marx's view that labor generates its own political and resistant forces from *within* the process of capital accumulation (it's the politics of the economy, stupid).[22] Furthermore, it is capital's attempt to overcome this resistance that fuels its continual geographic and technological expansion. Impossibly, this restless process seeks to eliminate capital's own dependency on living labor.[23] In the past few decades of deregulated post-Fordism, those workers who retain a function under neoliberalism hold on precariously, while a significant portion of the world's people has become a vast and redundant surplus population. But something has happened to make this apparent surplus army increasingly visible, not only to capital, but to itself. Almost as if a long forgotten crypt had split open, the dead, the redundant laborers, the excess population, is now speaking, visualizing itself, asserting a new form of collectivism that is also an old form of collectivism. Its visibility is dependent not only on the rise of global communication technology necessary to the deregulated enterprise economy, but also on its own sheer abundance and precariousness in relation to that economy.

Now, after a hiatus in which many influential Left and cultural theorists sought to treat class and economic exploitation as just one more discursive subject position within a field of shifting social antagonisms, a new generation of intellectuals, media activists, and interventionist artists, no doubt spurred on in part by the 2008–9 financial adjustment, are beginning to re-examine the role of labor in the so-called creative economy. As necessary as it once seemed to "rethink" the critical importance of class struggle and Marxist analysis during the heady, expansionist years of neoliberalism, it now appears just as necessary to rethink capitalism and its relationship to work, history, and culture. Young artists, often working collectively, have begun to address their relationship to work. Among many recent experiments is Working Artists and the Greater Economy, or W.A.G.E., an informal group that dates from the very start of the 2008 financial meltdown (although at a time when it was still being described simply as a serious mortgage crisis). The group has demanded a "working wage" for artists because artists make "the world more interesting."[24] Other fledgling efforts at self-organization include the Teaching Artist Union, a group of NYC art instructors whose membership is open to faculty at the university and college level, as well as in high schools and the lower grades.[25] In an age of enforced creativity and enterprise culture the very concept of a unionized cultural workforce may be nearly impossible to conceptualize. Not surprisingly the group's founding manifesto begins with a somewhat strained statement of self-identification as a generation of "freelance idealists" before continuing heedfully, "we are not angry laborers." (Admittedly this mission statement was penned before the depth of the "Great Recession" was fully apparent and layoffs began to hit New York's art and teaching community.)

Chicago-based Temporary Services recently compiled a number of these group manifestos and projects into a 40-page newspaper entitled *ART WORK: A National Conversation About Art, Labor, and Economics*. In November 2009, the group used its intensively developed social networks to distribute some 15,000 copies of the publication in cities from Chicago, San Francisco, Los Angeles, and New York City, to Newark, New Jersey, Anchorage, Alaska, Washington DC, Albuquerque, New Mexico, Louisville Kentucky, and Gordo Alabama (as well as in Copenhagen, Leeds, London, Aberdeen, and Athens).[26] Meanwhile, the question of how artists choose to organize their labor under varying historical and economic circumstances has become a subject of interest to a growing number of art historians willing to risk upsetting dominant cultural paradigms by rubbing the art world—to paraphrase Benjamin—against its grain. A new wave of art scholarship is examining the role of cultural labor both within well-ensconced subject matter and historical periods, as well as amongst lesser known artists and art movements. Andrew Hemingway's important study of artists and the Communist Party USA in the 1920s, '30s, and '40s was recently complemented by Julia Bryan-Wilson's *Art Workers: Radical Practice in the Vietnam War Era*, in which the theoretical impact of the New Left on the concept of artwork in the 1960s and '70s is examined through a series of case studies that reconsider the oft-visited work of Carl Andre, Robert Morris, Hans Haacke, and Lucy R. Lippard.[27] Even an industry mainstay like *Artforum* ventured into these waters following the Great Recession by printing an excerpt of anti-capitalist musings by the Marxist theorists Michael Hardt and Antonio Negri.[28]

Meanwhile, debates, conferences, and exhibitions on the topic of art, finance, cultural markets, and creative labor have been organized by among others Carin Kuoni, director of the Vera List Center for the Arts, and Maria Lind, former director of the Center For Curatorial Studies at Bard College. Lind provocatively entitled her program, co-sponsored by the Goethe Institute, "What is the Good of Work?" In Turkey, four female curators from Zagreb who go by the collective moniker WHW (What, How & for Whom?) organized the most recent Istanbul Art Biennial around the decidedly militant theme "What Keeps Mankind Alive?" The line borrowed from the title of Bertolt Brecht and Kurt Weil's song from *The Threepenny Opera* received a blunt answer in 1928: Mankind is kept alive by bestial acts of starvation, torture, and silence. No doubt the same answer is on everyone's lips today. Most of the artists in the WHW program were not previously seen at biennials and art fair circuits, the curators making an effort to disturb business as usual in the global art world. One installation entitled *Unemployed Employees*, by Turkish artists Aydan Murtezaoğlu and Bülent Şangar even provided "creative jobs" for recent university graduates in Istanbul. The

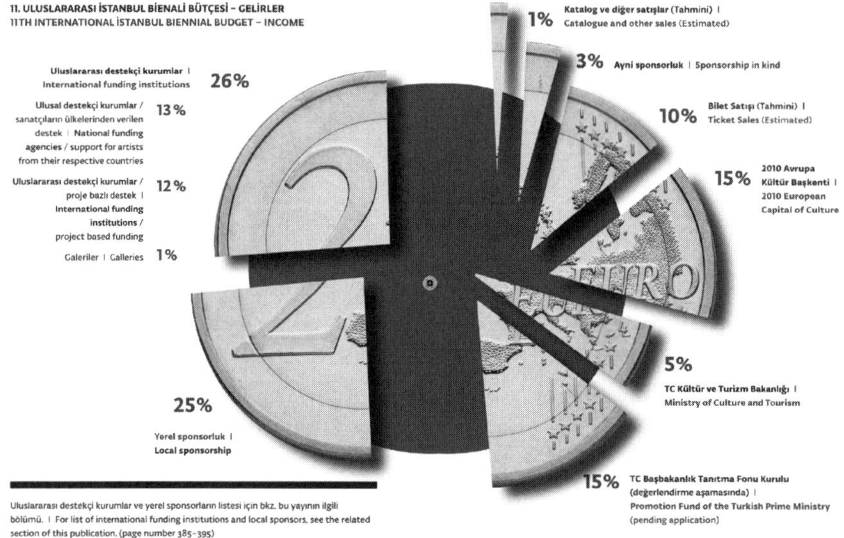

Graphic designer and collaborator Dejan Kršić worked with the collective WHW (What, How & for Whom: Ivet Ćurlin, Ana Dević, Nataša Ilić, and Sabina Sabolović) to create a series of pedagogical illustrations exploring the financial and administrative mechanisms of the Eleventh Istanbul Biennial (2009), whose title—What Keeps Mankind Alive?—the group took from Bertolt Brecht and Kurt Weil's 1928 production *The Threepenny Opera* (*Die Dreigroschenoper*). Image courtesy WHW and Dejan Kršić.

employees first had to apply for their temporary positions, which then consisted of folding and refolding piles of t-shirts, and pointlessly offering perfume samples to Biennial visitors. But perhaps it was an innovative mini-conference held recently at The New School University organized by artist Trebor Scholz that most clearly addressed the gap between theory and practice, virtual and material labor, doing so at least in part by accident. The question posed by the three-day program was whether or not the Internet is a creative "play ground," or an electronic "factory," or perhaps both at the same time.[29] Attended by a predominantly youthful, white male audience, the program included sessions described as "the Gift of Immaterial Labor," "Digital Labor and the Body," and "The Emancipatory Potential of Play." The very phrasing of the program's title—"The Internet as Playground and Factory"—is perhaps an unintentional reference to Mario Tronti's four decade's old expression "The Social Factory," in which the regulatory power of the capitalist market encloses social relations once found exclusively outside the workplace. But signs of how the new, networked economy actually extracts value from material, living labor unexpectedly bubbled up at the event when conference participants were confronted by a group of self-defined Cyber Sweat

Shop Workers distributing leaflets that bitterly, and ironically, denounced the anti-union policies of The New School, principal host of Playground or Factory.[30]

It would seem to be a given that capitalism has always secretly depended upon certain forms of production other than the obvious, male-identified physical labor of the factory or farm. This *other* productivity includes women's non-waged chores or "housework," as well as their sexual procreation that literally reproduces the workforce. But it also includes the semi-waged labor of students and children and the hidden dependency capital has with forms of slave labor, once an essential stage of what Marx described as primitive wealth accumulation, and which has now made a return in an era of deregulated labor, individual risk, and weakened states.[31] Perhaps it is time to rephrase a question first posed by Brecht some 75 years ago by asking: who builds the *digital* networks?[32] Who lays down its glass fiber cables, who cooks the meals for the system's designers and programmers as they sit in their cubicles, hour after hour, banging-out lines of html, drawing up spreadsheets, sizing images, designing templates, tagging data, and formatting websites? More basic still: who operates the injection-molding machines and lathes and grinders that stamp-out the computer chassis, mobile phones, and Blackberry's essential to the day-to-day function of the "cognitariat"? Who packs and ships the electronic components of the new, networked economy? Who hauls away its e-waste? And after piles of this electronic debris are shipped to towns and villages in Africa and South Asia, who is it that picks through this detritus for recyclable toxic metals that nonetheless pollute bodies, water, and soil? What appears to be immaterial play on one side of the digital terminal is something quite different at its other end. For somewhere on this planet a different workforce toils on a Fordist assembly line in order to make immaterial post-Fordist labor possible in the US, EU, and other developed nations.[33] It is this "other end," this invisible surplus not entitled to the Neo-Bohemian good life, that concerns us here, whether or not its ethereal "elsewhere" is located in Logos, Jakarta, or Mexico, or in some overlooked, non-union factory in London, Toronto, or New York City.

Revenge of the Surplus

The scope of these issues is well beyond this, or perhaps any single study, which is why my focus remains largely on the changing conditions of production within and around the margins of the contemporary art world, and the resistance to those changes. But the underlying issue remains that of cultural labor, and what that means today, in a "creative" economy that, as Brian Holmes pithily points out, has made art the "linchpin of the workfare system, in the financialized era of image sign production."[34] How have the conditions of artistic production changed in this context? More importantly, how do those artists who remain critical of capital's disciplinary economic apparatus manage in the art-friendly world of enterprise culture? Perhaps the Berlin-based art and media collective kleines postfordistisches Drama (KPD) has pinpointed the difficulty, with their fictional "sociological" documentary about creative industry workers just like themselves. In a series of video interviews they reenacted the mental life of art workers mulling over a set of questions including, "What do you consider a 'good life'? Should cultural producers, as role models for society, join with other social movements to work towards new forms of globalization?" Based on actual responses, the project reveals Berlin's creative workers trapped in their own feeble expectations about a "good life." We watch as they attempt to multitask hour after hour, with little or no transition between work and non-work, socializing and networking, or in some cases wakefulness and sleep. It seems the social factory has completely triumphed, and no doubt the observations from Germany are generalizable to the "cognitariat" in other global cities. The Berlin media collective's enigmatic name sums up the situation. Roughly translated into English it reads, *Small Post-Fordist Drama*. The group's operating thesis is amusingly summed up on their webpage that shows a single, acid-colored photograph of six hip-looking creative workers in a minimal office space posed precisely around an uncluttered worktable. The image appears to allude to one of Caravaggio's late, understated domestic dramas, such as his *Supper At Emmaus* (second version, 1606) in which a very ordinary-looking Christ quietly announces to several followers he has returned from the grave. As if to diminish any remaining theatricality still further, the image on the website has been reduced to the size of a postage stamp.[35]

Still, there are constant stirrings of resistance. Some of which are surprisingly familiar, though rendered in novel ways, and much that takes place not within the white cubicles of the art industry, but at the intersection of cognitive labor, precarious employment, and everyday, informal creativity.

In 2007 a very different sort of play within a play from that of KPD took place when a group of disgruntled Italian IBM workers, supported by UNI Global Union and the national IBM works councils (FIOM, FIM, COBAS national unions) carried out the first known job action in Second Life, a 3D virtual reality platform where players move about as computer generated characters or avatars in an immersive and interactive virtual world. The striking knowledge workers took explicit advantage of their dual status as both embodied and immaterial labor when they decided to collaborate "creatively" with Internet activists and graphic designers involved in Second Life Left Unity (SLLU), an anti-capitalist organization that exists only inside the online digital environment. Unionists Christine Revkin and Davide Barillari coordinated the organization of the virtual protest, generating colorful striking avatars with pixilated picket signs programmed to stage a 24-hour virtual protest against Big Blue in cyberspace. As anticipated, global media coverage was strong, and within a few months IBM capitulated to the demands of its employees' local works council, *Rappresentanze Sindacali Unitarie*

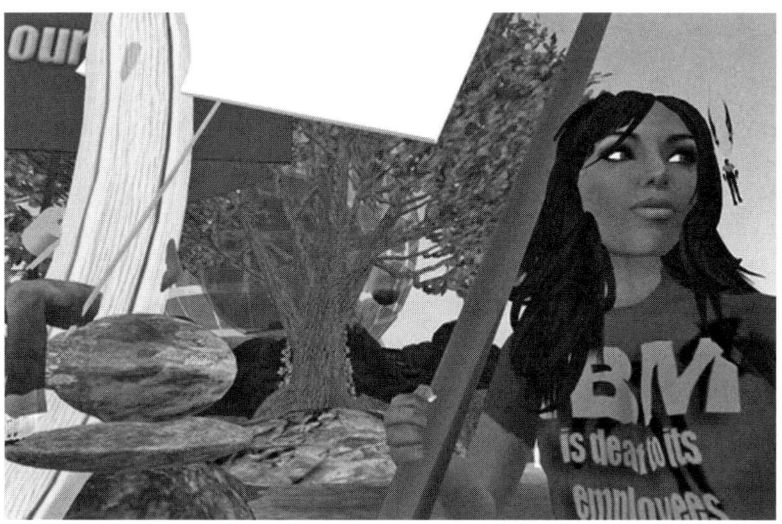

September 2007, avatars of striking Italian IBM workers stage the first virtual job walkout in the cyber-world known as Second Life. According to staff representative Davide Barillari: "Thanks to the massive use of new-generation communication tools, we moved a local problem to a global problem, so the image of the company was, for the first time, attacked ... the Virtual protest led to concrete results." Helping create the event was artist Christine Revkin, webmaster for UNI Global Union, which represents some 900 trade unions and 20 million workers employed by the global knowledge and services industries: www.uniglobalunion.org/Apps/iportal.nsf/pages/homeEn. Images courtesy Christine Revkin and Davide Barillari.

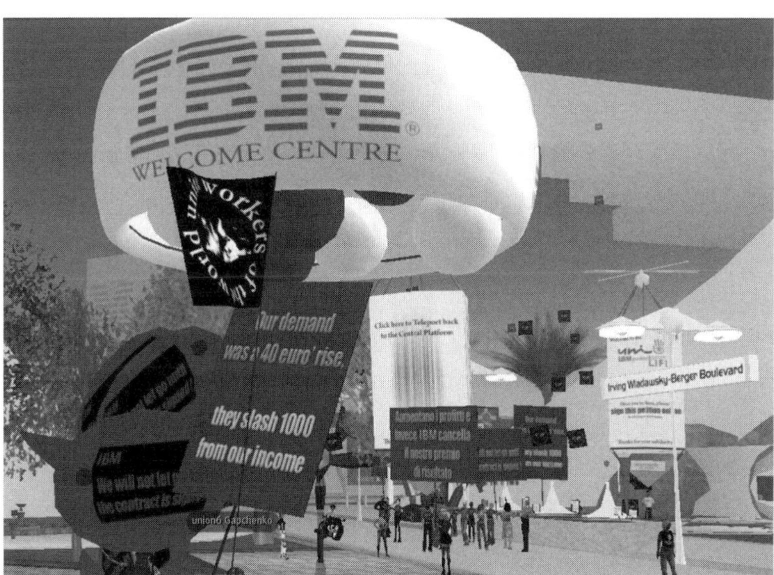

of Vimercate, agreeing to reinstate performance bonuses and contribute to the Italian national health insurance fund. The first mass union demonstration in a virtual world has serious implications in our real world: 20 days after the virtual strike in Second Life—in which some 2,000 avatars joined from 30 countries—the general manager of IBM Italy resigned. The immaterial job action was the start of a bigger international unionization project, called "unions 2.0." This small, post-Fordist drama directly improved the actual working conditions of creative laborers and reminds us, as autonomous labor theorist Bruno Gulli writes, that "communism is the liberation of time—not its framing in the factory system."[36]

Still, how does one go about mapping un-framed time and ethereal resistance? And why do so? Who is served by research into dark matter with its shadowy repertoire of tactical tricks, resentments, hidden locations, and implied link to some far broader counter-history *from below*? As Stephen Wright asserts, cultural activities that refuse to be seen at all, that are invisible-yet-undeniable, raise fundamental questions about the nature of art, labor, and creativity.[37] For example, the guerrilla projects of *Untergunther* who illegally repair public clockworks in Paris, or the anonymous sign projects of political activists such as Grupo de Arte Callejero in Buenos Aires demarcating the homes of unpunished generals from Argentina's "dirty war," as well as the sometimes obscene street provocations of the Voina (WAR) collective in Russia, or the low-tech urban interventions in São Paulo, Brazil, that theorist André Mesquita describes as zones of poetic activity at work, the online anti-corporate campaigns of the hacktivist group Anonymous, but also those everyday acts of imaginative interruption and temporal displacement carried out by temp slaves, warehouse workers, and cubicle serfs. Furthermore, the very trace of this curious mix of seen and unseen, active and inert, banal and confrontational dark matter is only possible thanks to networked global capital and the soulless specter of an absent society that haunts it. A strange inter-dependency is made possible, in other words, by the prosthetics of inexpensive communication, audio and video technologies. That this missing mass, this dark matter is materializing and getting brighter is not in doubt. Instead, what remains to be seen is just what kind of world it is giving birth to, and exactly how this "revenge of the surplus" will ultimately re-narrate politics in an age of enterprise culture.

1

ART, POLITICS, DARK MATTER: NINE PROLOGUES

Throughout history, living labor has, along with the surplus value extracted from it, carried on its own production—within fantasy.

Oskar Negt and Alexander Kluge[1]

Swampwall

For more than 30 years a close relation of mine has worked in the shipping and receiving department of a non-unionized factory in Northeast Pennsylvania. Early on in his employment he and several of his co-workers spent their work breaks attaching newspaper clippings, snapshots, spent soda cans, industrial debris, trashed food containers and similar bits and pieces of day-to-day detritus to one wall of the plant. After a few years this accumulated clutter covered most of the wall. The workers christened their impromptu collage the Swampwall. The owner of the factory, an aging sole-proprietor in a world of mergers and multinationals, long tolerated this workplace diversion until a global corporation bought out his company. A structural adjustment followed. Dozens of "redundant" employees lost their jobs. The manufacturing division of the factory was downsized, services emphasized, and post-Fordist systems of inventory and just-in-time outsourcing implemented. Needless to say, Swampwall was expunged. And though its makers remained employed they were tasked with higher productivity as their pensions, sick pay, health care, and other benefits were reduced through privatization. What was Swampwall? Notwithstanding the recent popularity of de-skilled slack art and "clutterfuck"—slap-dash cartoons pinned randomly to gallery walls; clumps of ephemera or manufactured goods spread haphazardly over museum floors; recycled cardboard and cheap packing-tape sculpture, or paintings made to appear the work of an amateur or Sunday painter—Swampwall was not art. Just compare my description of Swampwall to the way the contemporary American artist Tony Feher reputedly transforms "humble, 'forgettable' materials that he finds—bottles, jars, plastic soda crates ... into work that is rich with human emotion and fragile beauty."[2] None of the factory workers ever attended college; none had likely ever visited an art museum. Their collaborative frieze was only visible to those

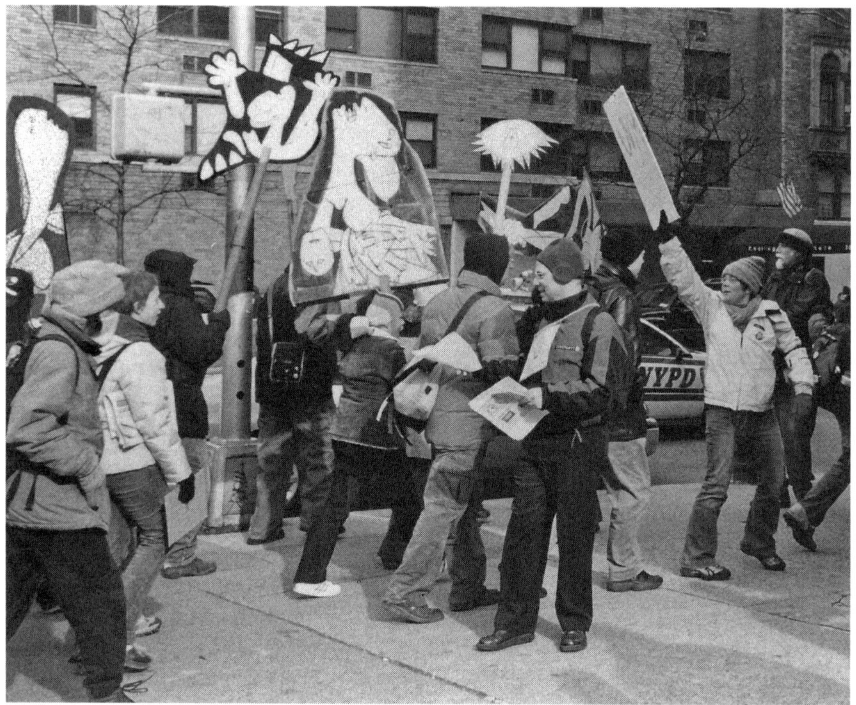

Picasso's monumental *Guernica* momentarily shifts from aesthetic object to activist intervention as the painting's anti-war imagery is re-imagined as a jigsaw puzzle of picket signs carried aloft by a flock of art students protesting the concealment of a tapestry of the iconic artwork behind blue drapes during Colin Powell's infamous UN speech leading up to the war in Iraq. This image was taken during the unprecedented global protest against US military action in February of 2003. Image courtesy Gregory Sholette.

with business in that particular wing of the plant; an uninviting, sweat-soaked warehouse filled with forklifts, loading pallets, and packing crates far from the tidy cubicles and product showrooms of upper management. As a haphazard archive of the everyday, Swampwall most closely resembled a spontaneous memorial to dead time. However, insofar as these workers made manifest a desire to direct some portion of their energy elsewhere, just as they pleased, Swampwall also represented a fantasy of autonomy. Not just any fantasy, not fantasy as illusion or self-delusion, but instead as Kluge and Negt point out, fantasy in the form of production, or, as Miriam Hansen succinctly puts it, "imaginative strategies grounded in the experience of production—protest energies, psychic balancing acts, a penchant for personalization, individual and collective fantasy, and creative re-appropriations."[3]

PAD/D

On February 24, 1980, several dozen artists, activists, and future DIY (Do It Yourself) archivists gathered at a bookstore in downtown Manhattan. They came in response to a call for volunteers circulated by art critic Lucy R. Lippard who sought assistance in organizing an archive of documentation about the many good, socially active artists that no one had heard of.[4] In the room were members of the recently formed art collective Group Material, as well as members of existing organizations such as Heresies, but also defunct groups including Art Workers' Coalition (AWC), and Artists Meeting for Cultural Change. At least one participant had been active in the 1940s with the "old" American Left.[5] There were also constituents of collectives yet to come, including the feminist-oriented cultural groups Carnival Knowledge and the Guerrilla Girls. An entire new organization was established that evening, whose ambitions, contrary to Lippard's initial intentions, went far beyond the humble task of archiving. Within a year Political Art Documentation/Distribution (PAD/D) was publishing a newsletter, programming public events, networking with other politically active cultural organizations, and producing art for street demonstrations and street projects like Death and Taxes where artists created decentralized interventions in public spaces around New York City to protest government military spending just before April 14, "income tax day." The new group opposed both the commercial *and* the not-for-profit art world, asserting contrarily that PAD/D "cannot serve as a means of advancement within the art world structure of museums and galleries. Rather, we have to develop new forms of distribution economy as well as art."[6] In order to realize this goal PAD/D sought to link a variety of exhibition spaces with activist, labor, and local community organizations, thus producing an entirely separate, left-wing sphere of culture. Populating this networked alternative art world would be those many unknown artists whose work was too political or socially involved for mainstream museums and galleries in the 1980s. For despite a substantial wave of politicized cultural experimentation that took place throughout the post-war period from the 1950s on up to the 1980s the mainstream art world remained strongly committed to abstract and formalist art, often defined by critics like Clement Greenberg and Michael Fried, or by a minimalist art that was indistinguishable from such formalism.[7] PAD/D's imagined parallel art world was not unlike the cultural organizations of the 1920s and 1930s organized by labor unions, socialists, and the Communist Party USA, except in the 1980s there was little counter-institutional power to provide support. Its stated aim was to build "an international, grass roots network of artist/activists who will support with their talents and their political energies the liberation and self-determination of all disenfranchised peoples."[8] This romantic, anti-imperialist rhetoric energized the group for a while, but neither the historical circumstances nor the technology of the early 1980s permitted PAD/D to realize its somewhat grandiose counter-institutional mission. Furthermore, the actual day-to-day tasks of organizing meetings, networking, publishing and mailing newsletters, and collecting, dating and storing archival materials took its toll on the group. Eight years after its founding PAD/D ceased meeting. Though the Archive Committee continued, the programs and activist street art ended. In a solemn editorial farewell in PAD/D's newsletter *Upfront*, the group recognized that its demise coincided with a prudent form of "political art" becoming briefly fashionable in the art world.[9] Nor was it entirely a coincidence that the organization's demise coincided with this appropriation of counter-culture by the mainstream art world and the consolidation of a decade-old rightward political shift in the US, UK, Canada, and elsewhere. PAD/D's attempt to establish autonomy from mainstream art culture ended, paradoxically, with the incorporation of its Archive into the Library of the Museum of Modern Art (MoMA), New York City, where its 50-plus linear feet of flyers, memos, news-clippings, posters, slides, and other forms of documentation now reside: something of an anti-formalist trove encrypted within what is perhaps the foundational institution of high modernist formalism. Nevertheless, the frequently ragged and fading contents of this other, surplus archive remain, still, almost entirely unheard of, as if forming a hole or zone of dark matter in the very heart of the formal art world's circulatory system.[10]

Paper Rad

MoMA and the gatekeeper galleries of the art world are far from Pittsburgh Pennsylvania where three artists collectively known as Paper Rad share studio space. Founded twelve years after PAD/D's demise, Paper Rad's DIY aesthetic incorporates electronic music (both recorded and performed live), knitted sculptures, and comic-book-like publications filled with day-glo doodles and cartoon characters.[11] But the group is probably best known for its heavily pixilated video animations that look like "claymations" or "puppetoons" made under the influence of psilocybin. Brash, youthful, and disarmingly flippant, Paper Rad is one of many insouciant and often-short-lived artists' collectives that have appeared over the past decade. *Groupettes* such as Gelitin, Bathus International, Reena Spaulings, Derraindrop, hobbypopMUSEUM, Beige Programming Ensemble, Forcefield, and Paper Rad mix visual art, fashion, and music in an ambient form of collectivism that has the same relation to previous forms of cultural mobilization (i.e. PAD/D, AWC, Group Material), as social networks such as Facebook or Twitter have to organized politics. In contrast to PAD/D's relative invisibility during the 1980s, the contemporary art world of the early twenty-first century has come to embrace this "whatever" mode of collectivism. Tate Britain, Deitch Projects, the Whitney and Liverpool Biennials are among the high-profile

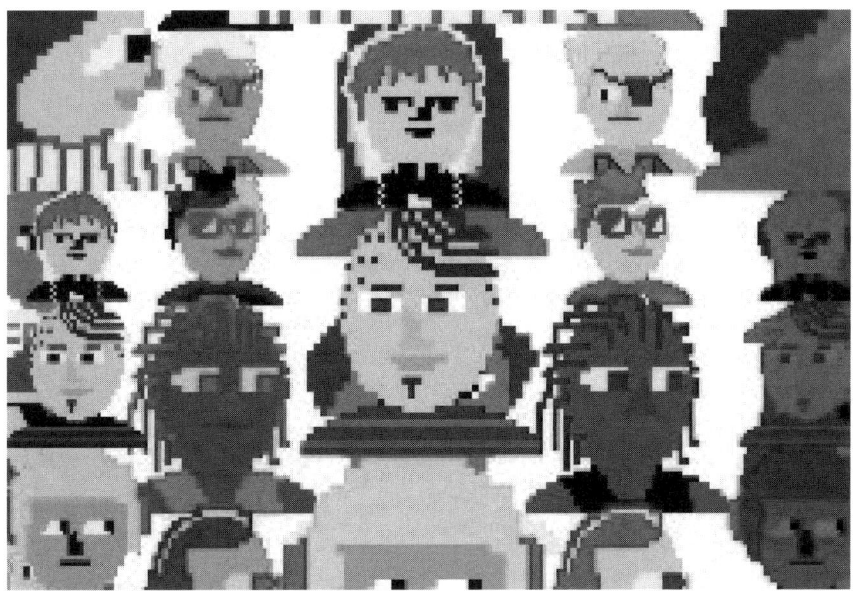

Paper Rad, "P-Unit Mixtape," 2005. An image grab from one of the delirious video projects created by the Pittsburg-based collective Paper Rad that synthesizes found materials from television, video games, and advertising sources in combination with digitally produced, zine-like imagery. The 21:08 minute music video is filled with day-glo cartoon characters, talking animals, and oblique references to the war in Iraq. It is viewable on YouTube at: http://vodpod.com/watch/971081-paper-rads-p-unit-mixtape-2005. Image courtesy Electronic Arts Intermix (EAI), New York.

institutions that have featured Paper Rad's neo-Pop art installations, performances, and video screenings, and yet the group itself claims to be most "at home" in the vertiginous arena of cyberspace. "The Internet represents a new form of chaos in which you experience all these different source materials jumbled together," insists one Paper Rad member, her sentiments echoed by the group's full-service website: a pulsating, polychromatic light-show crammed with free downloadable cartoons, memorabilia, noise music, poetry, documentation of artworks, and a series of e-mailable "get-well" postcards that, when downloaded, purportedly contain a virus capable of infecting your computer with "love."[12] Cyborg-like and spectacularly digitized, this technologically enhanced collectivism appears to have no proprietary boundaries; its communal commingling being identical with the networks that give rise to it. Nonetheless, some of these new, politically indeterminate artist's groups have commercial dealers who face particular difficulties trying to sell their multi-authored work. It seems collectors seek secure, long-term investments, whereas group identity is inherently unstable. One New York City art dealer devised his own solution to this problem: organize solo exhibitions for each member of Paper Rad, reassuring anxious collectors that behind the group's communal persona lie three distinct talents.[13]

Battles have even erupted over the organizational property of disbanded collectives and former members have disputed who has rights to the group's moniker. The Danish artists' group N55 now has only one original member, and the Guerrilla Girls split into several groups in 2000 with one iteration involved in performing as the Guerrilla Girls. Needless to say, such asset management seems antithetical to the free-wheeling, communal identity Paper Rad represents on their website:

> If you are trying to write an article, a school paper, or telling your mom or dad, or boss, basically you are screwed, you can say words like 3 member art collective, but remember that you are lying and are just trying to translate what we are trying to do into america-speak again ... if you are a art collector, policeman, or ad agency, we are no company, its individuals making things, you like the name Paper Rad? great, you don't like it, even better, run with it, ask me who i am, maybe i'll tell you [*sic*].[14]

The group's taunting identity games and refusal to be translated into "america-speak" come off as magic incantations for warding off commercial branding. And yet, this is precisely the fate that has already overtaken them. Perhaps the clearest evidence of this fall from grace is the group's response to the publication "BJ & the Dogs 2," a zine-like booklet that appeared on several websites in 2006 with all the earmarks of Paper Rad's comic-book aesthetic. Once freely downloadable, as well as available for purchase as a hard copy, the ersatz booklet was nonetheless a counterfeit pseudonymously authored by the "Paper Rad Liberation Front." Soon after it appeared online, Paper Rad's attorney responded with a Cease and Desist letter posted on the group's blog. It called the imposters identity thieves who had stolen the authentic trio's "copyrighted images, likeness, and names." Paper Rad's website subsequently assured fans "we are and always have been and always will be 'real' Paper Rad ('real'-- weird)."[15] But the beguiling ambivalence about collective forms of identity once so playfully expressed are now brought up short by the return of the real "real," the concrete demands of the contemporary marketplace.[16]

Surpluses

Workers "expressively" killing time in a factory; an archive about unknown artists gathered and organized by other, unknown artists; giddy hallucinations of a distributed collectivism colliding with everyday economic realities—no matter how often such impulses towards autonomy meet with defeat one thing is clear: capitalism and its disciplinary routines continue to be haunted by what it has promised and has repeatedly failed to deliver, namely, a life free from the bridle of scarcity and the monotony of mundane labor, while rich in human solidarity and sensual, aesthetic expressivity. Sometimes the desire flashes up for an instant, bursting forth with symbolic ferocity amongst disgruntled workers, radicalized students, women and minorities structurally marginalized or totally cut off from the system's daydream. On rare occasions it materializes as direct action, swiftly deforming existing aesthetic, political, and institutional regimes. When not suppressed by legal mechanisms that regulate so-called intellectual property or state security (and increasingly these two have merged into one), it is confronted with phalanxes of riot police who meet this overflow of anticipation with tear gas, rubber bullets, crowd nets, and improvised holding cells. Which is why this spectral expectancy is more often like a low-grade fever, smoldering wherever individual lives are no longer mediated by collective or governmental protections, wherever local conditions of life and work, time and space have been dismantled by the spread of ultra "free market" ideologies (although clearly the new capitalist world crisis is testing the limits of this narrative, which suddenly seems to be fighting for its ideological life). The most recent global financial collapse has only served to underscore this ruined landscape between promises and everyday life. All at once 30 years of consumer-driven, unregulated "growth" suddenly contracts to reveal what even many on the Left had tried to forget. As Slavoj Žižek recently opined, borrowing his words in part from Clinton's 1992 US presidential election: it's the *political* economy stupid! But his aim is not to return us to an outmoded theory of Marxist base and superstructure in which the maintenance of ideology is strictly determined by the relative health of capitalist markets. It is instead a way of reading history. "When the normal run of things is traumatically interrupted, the field is open for a 'discursive' ideological competition."[17] Žižek points out that it was Hitler, rather than social democrats or communists who won in the competition for a narrative that would explain the German economic collapse and military defeat after World War I. The question now is what narrative will come out on top today?

This long drawn out historical dreaming might well have remained just what it has always been—a patchy counter-history, marked by muted anticipations, repetitions, and defeats—and yet something has happened to alter this narrative that sometimes resembles a low-budget movie which appeals to us despite faulty dialogue, non-linear editing, and awkward *dues ex machina*. The desire for collective, cultural autonomy has become tantalizingly conspicuous of late, as has the sheer overabundance of activity, ideas, imaginative practices, and everyday creativity generated by what increasingly appears to be a massive surplus population that capital is not sure what to do with, especially when that collective body is too frightened even to over-consume. It is as if a previously overlooked mass of excess social productivity has suddenly been forced into view, as if a once-shadowed archive has spilt open. This other productivity (inventive also though intentional non-productivity) is materializing in places both familiar and unexpected, from the shantytowns of the imagination, to the depths of corporate, governmental, and institutional structures. It is fundamentally altering the formal artistic culture, or what is often simply called "art." It is also transforming the nature of the popular spectacle that dominates global society and all that remains of the public sphere. One can hardly escape an encounter with this vast and heterogeneous bounty of imaginative activity today as it radiates from homes, offices, schools, streets, community centers, artistic venues, and in cyberspace, especially in cyberspace, which uniquely marks the point of contact between the dark, surplus archive and the everyday. And it harbors its own forms of community and collectivism that are simultaneously new and archaic. So far this decentralized fraternization can only be represented by the jumbled profusion of symptoms it displays—community as dispersed networks, a love of mimicry, bathos, vulgarity, distraction, and resentment, a lack of interest in abstraction coupled with a fondness for everything that was once considered inferior, low, and discardable. Qualities that were anathema to modernist notions of serious art are essential to this informal cultural production as it ranges from the whimsical to the inspired, from the banal to the reactionary, and from the obscene to the seditious. This vast, irregular congregation includes pattern-swapping knitting circles, Flickr photo clubs, garage-kit sculptors, fantasy role-play gamers, devotees of Goth culture, open-source programmers, mash-up music samplers, right-wing groups and militias, and eBay pages filled with the work of both serious and Sunday painters. An example of this odd mix of old and new artistry is the Nike Blanket Petition, essentially a crazy-quilt made from dozens of hand-knitted fabric panels that called on the multinational apparel maker to adopt fair labor practices. The panels were submitted by anti-sweatshop crafters across the US and beyond to microRevolt, a "craftivist" group founded in Rhode Island by Cat Mazza, and just one example of an expanding network of artists weaving together early or pre-industrial technologies and digital media.[18]

There are also clusters of amateur archeologists digging up abandoned Star Wars props in the Tunisian desert, and individuals who share information about the government's alleged remote-control over their thoughts, as well as a host of sometimes ambiguous art collectives, public art interventionists, politically informed media activists, and an increasing number of professionally trained artists simply in search of "community" beyond what they can (not) find in the mainstream art world (Paper Rad being a case in point). Like a vast archive of everything previously omitted from cultural visibility suddenly spilling into view this shadowy productivity spreads across, rather than sinks deeply, into the broader social firmament. Meanwhile, cultural critics, curators, policy wonks, politicians, even "cutting-edge" management theorists and CEOs sprint to keep pace.

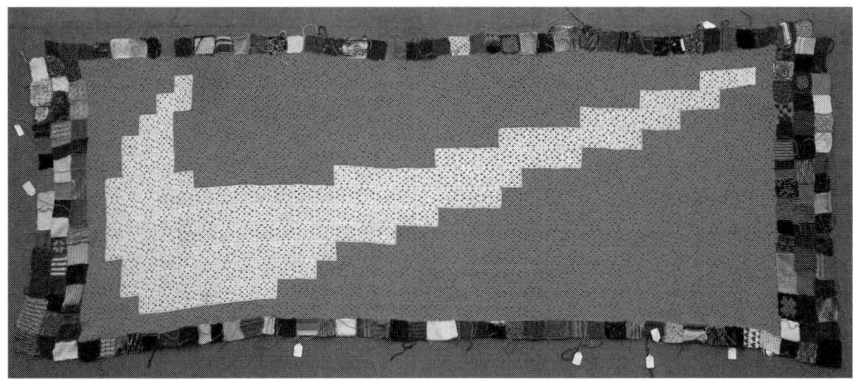

Founded Troy, New York, in 2003, microRevolt is a series of workshops, performances, and web-based projects that explore the overlaps between textiles, technology, and labor. Between 2003 and 2008 a decentralized group of international craft hobbyists from over 30 countries participated in the Nike Blanket Petition—a 15-foot-wide blanket of the Nike swoosh. Knit and crochet squares were collected on tour and by mail over the five-year period, representing a hand-stitched signature demanding fair labor conditions for Nike garment workers. In 2010 the blanket was exhibited at the Museum of Contemporary Craft in Portland, Oregon, to which executives from the Beaverton Nike headquarters were invited. Other microRevolt projects include distributing knitPro (2004), a free web application that generates textile grid patterns, as well as Stitch for Senate (2007–9), a pro-peace initiative of knitters making military helmet liners for every United States senator. Image courtesy Cat Mazza.

This then constitutes the first of several paradoxes: how is it that the same global processes that melt everything solid into air also provide a means of representing opposition to the market and to disciplinary regimes? And not merely for the privileged few, but potentially for the majority of those whose seeming superfluousness actually maintains the system? A partial answer is found in the ever more accessible technology for manufacturing, documenting, distributing, and pilfering content that has dramatically ended the isolation of so much informal social production. Capitalist innovation excels at breaking down barriers to allow for the unfettered exchange of goods and information, even when that exchange sometimes challenges a given state, party, or religion, and even when it threatens capitalist ideology itself. In different ways, recent mass demonstrations in Egypt, Tunisia, Syria, Libya, Greece, Spain, and before that in Iran, and Moldova, and Greece are a case in point. Protestors packed streets and plazas demanding fair elections, increased democracy, and an end to abusive police tactics, but it was widely reported that social networking platforms—Facebook, Twitter, YouTube, Flickr—were essential tools for organizing the demonstrations and distributing images and information. However, the "twitter revolution" did not produce the desire for social change. At best, cellular and digital technologies stitch together an ambiguous instantaneous fraternity from existing scattered needs and affects.

For no matter what form this irregularly distributed collectivity takes—electronic, virtual, embodied, veracious—it cannot be understood apart from its existence within, but more importantly resistance to, what sociologist Ulrich Beck calls the risk society: a state of "no longer trust/security, not yet destruction/disaster."[19] Precariousness, risk, indeterminacy are the inseparable counterparts of plasticity, performance, and the brightening of social productivity.[20] Which is to say that without the churning processes of capital, without its constant de-materialization and re-materialization of the familiar world in a quest to realize profits—but also, significantly, in response to acts of intermittent confrontation—all of these once-hidden cultural phantoms, redundant artists, digital zinesters, Swampwalls, and so on, would remain just what they have always been: so many specters incapable of garnering our sustained attention apart from an occasional act of haunting or brief moment of upheaval, so many shadows, so much surplus.

Crisis

By most accounts, the protracted fiscal crisis of the 1970s led to the lowering of state and local barriers that had protected workers against the fluid circulation and accumulation of capital before and just after the post-war era. Many of these regulations had been set in place after the depression of the 1930s.[21] At the same time conventional "Fordist" assembly lines and "brick and mortar" factories also underwent dismantling and reorganization. They were replaced with de-spatialized networks of "just-in-time" manufacturing that seemingly were better able to respond quickly to an ever-shifting world market for goods and services. Heavy manufacturing was also shifted from northern cities to lower-cost regions of the still-developing global south. The ostensible goal of this structural adjustment was to avoid the over-accumulation of capital that had led to falling rates of profit beginning in the mid to late 1960s. But in reality, this radical reorganization was aimed at bringing into line that most significant form of capital: productive labor, which is to say labor as a commodity in the service of capital, as opposed to free, unbridled labor in which the choice of when and how to work, or whether even to be productive or not, forms an inherent antagonism to market discipline. Such resistance was becoming widespread in the 1960s and 1970s, and not just amongst university students. In the US, unauthorized wildcat strikes reached a post-war high between 1962 and 1973, and work stoppages amongst public service employees jumped nine times. According to the American Social History Project, such confrontations were linked with a growing democratic sensibility that not only inspired a highly visible counter-culture but also "surged through the nation's factories."[22] As Silvia Federici puts it, working men and women were taking part in a "cycle of struggle that challenged the capitalist command over labor, in a sense realizing the workers' refusal of the capitalist work discipline, the refusal of a life organized by the needs of capitalist production, a life spent in a factory or office."[23]

For most workers, the "post-Fordist" economic restructuring that followed these clashes brought with it a simultaneous double leap: partly forwards, and partly backwards. New technologies, flexible work schedules, and an emphasis on mental as opposed to manual labor permitted a select few to be productive through innovation and collaboration, much in the way cultural workers had been doing for centuries. The price of this alleged liberty however, was that labor conditions in general returned to those of the early twentieth, or even the nineteenth, century: increased productivity, lower adjusted pay, cuts in benefits, weaker unions and safety protections, and far longer, if more elastic, work hours. Writing in 1996, already two decades after the start of the neoliberal "revolution," economist Doug Henwood observed that "overwork is at least as characteristic of the labor market now as is underwork. Nearly twice as many people hold down multiple jobs as are involuntarily limited to part-time work (7.8 million vs. 4.3 million)—and well over half the multiply employed hold at least one full-time job."[24] Furthermore, Henwood claimed, "we see plenty of wage polarization, a disappearance of middle-income jobs, the loss of fringe benefits, longer hours, speedup, and rising stress."[25] More than a decade later, Henwood's sobering insights have become the new reality. "Finding a market for one's labor power means entering the domain of productive labor; failing to find a market for it means falling into the category of unproductive labor," writes philosopher Bruno Gulli.[26] In other words, the radical deregulation of the economy, the "liberation" of the finance sector, and the privatization or elimination of public welfare were actually more than just an attempt to deal with falling rates of profit. According to David Harvey this neoliberal adjustment was, and remains, a political project with the ultimate aim of reasserting the power of the capitalist class project over labor. The result is that in the society of risk one either succeeds remarkably, or fails miserably. There is little gray area in-between. And most of us fall into the latter category. Either way there is no longer a sanctuary awaiting those that drop, a fact that the sweeping 2008–9 financial crisis has now laid bare. Meanwhile, excess labor capacity that might have found modest employment or public support in the post-war Keynesian welfare state is today revealed for what it has always been—if not a standing source of cheap labor (a condition that technological conversion has greatly reduced the need for anyway), then workers who have become entirely superfluous, a non-asset, a kind of dead capital. The status of this surplus population is most dramatically illustrated by the upsurge in human trafficking over the past 30 years. Slavery is a billion dollar industry today. Its "merchandise," primarily sexual slaves, but also illegal sweatshop workers, has become so overabundant that it is more economical to use and replace such labor rather than invest in the long-term value of this human capital.[27] Even those not in great or immediate peril, those who for the moment find themselves in a less precarious life situation, understand that there is an unavoidable lesson in such horrors: raw and merciless is the fate awaiting those who fail, there is no one, no institution, no net to stop your fall. It is a decidedly powerful disciplinary warning that the global media constantly reiterates, from Katrina to the Middle East, to the next global catastrophe. Nevertheless, within this precarious new world, a delicate latticework of barely specifiable social being stirs, thriving it seems on its own insecurity.

Zombie Culture

Lacking any distinct, political identity these bits and pieces of generalized dissent resist easy visualization, forming instead a murky submarine world of affects, ideas, histories, and technologies that shift in and out of visibility like a half-submerged reef. Post-'68 theorist Michel De Certeau compares the survival tactics of this everyday dissident with the primordial "simulations, tricks, and disguises certain fishes or plants execute."[28] He insists this cryptic mimicry is an "art of the weak."[29] As opposed to the committed radical of early decades who rejected capitalism *tout court*, De Certeau's rebel consumer uses the power of the market against itself. With the defeat of radical movements in the 1960s and 1970s behind him, and the neoliberal dismantling of the social welfare state just about to fully commence, De Certeau's Situationist-inspired emphasis on flexible tactics probably comes closest to grasping the outermost limits of political dissent at the start of the 1980s, at least as this potential existed within Western, developed nations. Nevertheless, this raises another seeming paradox: how is it that, in spite of the ruined social landscape neoliberal globalization leaves behind, informal non-parliamentary organizations seem today to be more, not less abundant? This book applies that question to the area of the visual arts, but holds out the hope that any serious investigation will also have implications for other areas of cultural research. For instance, one answer to how politics works in a privatized, precarious society dates from the early 1990s when a group of media activists grafted De Certeau's tenuous sedition onto the electronic flow of emerging communication technologies. According to media activist Geert Lovink, De Certeau's archaic trickster has been reanimated as Tactical Media (TM): "a short-term concept, aware of its temporality, born out of a disgust for ideology ... [TM] surfing on the waves of events, enjoying the opening up of scenes and borders, on the look out for new alliances."[30] De Certeau's "everyday" rebel had apparently gained access to a sophisticated, digital expressivity thanks to the growing accessibility of cellular and digital technologies. Patently anti-ideological and decentralized to the point of sheer dispersal, the apparently indefinite politics of this "tactical resistance" leads some theorists to conclude that an entirely new form of activism has emerged directly opposite to that of earlier generations. Media theorist Rita Raley makes this assertion in the opening paragraphs of her book *Tactical Media*, in which she immediately distances herself from the "embarrassing" and "nostalgic" desire for revolutionary transformation associated with May 1968. Raley insists that TM activists, by contrast, "cede control over outcomes," willingly surrendering political aspirations to a "postmodern roll of the dice."[31] Unwittingly, this call to randomness points to a central argument Stimson and I put forward in *Collectivism After Modernism*: new social forces ignore ideology only to place its absence at the very center of their own narrativization. This is why it is a mistake to attribute changes in social activism and collectivism solely to technological innovation, an assumption that leads to claims that politics are outmoded. Such assumptions substitute a generalized activism for political thinking; Raley's otherwise well-researched book offers a case in point. Thus, if there is a seemingly "unloaded" game of dice under way, it plays itself out at the level of plot, or more accurately a stop-gap plot device: the "extra-idealist" programmer standing in for the hot-blooded political ideologist; the cooled-down, randomized program substituting for "the old glorious communitarian ideals of Christianity, Islam, Nationalism, Communism."[32]

The near-total privatization, objectification, and marketing of life seeks to incorporate even those forms of production that historically claimed to stand outside of, or against the reach of, capitalism, on both the Left and the Right. How then to align oneself with the progressive, activist, and radical forms of art that form a rough lineage from European Dada in the aftermath of World War I, through the anti-Fascist era of the 1920s and 1930s, on up to through the Cold War, the counter-culture, the New Left, and post-colonial movments? At a moment such as this, old-fashioned appeals to the deep, transcendental meaning of high culture are no more constructive than demands for a return to the principles of the revolutionary avant-garde. If the former sought to salvage an already doubtful artistic autonomy, then the latter is incapable of breaking away from the deft grip of an all-pervasive capitalist market that seems to provide the only hope for cultural visibility today. A spirit of entrepreneurship now dominates "every phase of contemporary art," writes Chin-tao Wu, including its "production, its dissemination and its reception."[33] Art historian Julian Stallabrass recommends re-branding this enterprise culture "Art Incorporated," a satirical proposition that reflects the ascendancy of corporate marketing and finance industries today, much as Horkheimer's and Adorno's famed culture industry metaphor conveyed the administrative function of a "Taylorism of the mind" some 60 years earlier.[34] Not that managing cultural profits is new to the art world, as historian Robert Jensen points out in his book *Marketing Modernism in Fin-de-siècle Europe*. The "protean" relationship between finance and art is so central to the narrative of modernism, Jensen insists that unending attempts to separate these entwined narratives form "one of the central tropes on which modernist criticism has been based."[35] Marketing modernism at the turn of the twentieth century therefore required control over the image of the artist producer, who was to become a social outcast, and also over the archive. Somewhere between the Vienna Secession show of 1905 and the New York Armory show of 1913 this double narrative of alienation and continuity fully embedded itself within the market. Contemporary alienated artists were linked with "neglected" pre-modernist masters such as El Greco, and Impressionism and other modernist movements were provided with a linear art history unlike that of the French Academy. The result, writes Jensen, was that "classic alienated artists, like an Egon Schiele, would have learned by 1910, if not long before, that alienation sells, that to be alienated was as much a role, a way of establishing a professional identity, as occupying a position in the academy."[36] By instituting a seemingly transparent set of "laws" involving artistic alienation and successive avant-garde "isms," modern art appeared to evolve autonomously from the market, as if Hegel's historical spirit was steadily blowing on its sails. But what Jensen makes clear is that this seemingly natural historical narrative also established an unobtrusive "body of institutions, a matrix of practices that, unlike the art, was absorbed almost without resistance by the European and American public."[37] Thus, modernist art might have annoyed or vexed the public, but its antagonism was fully inscribed within the logic of the institutional art world. What appears changed today is the way this underlying institutional matrix has become automated, like a zombie, with "*x*" number of presets and so many clickable filters that go on, piling up images, exhibitions, events, randomly, monotonously, as if afraid to admit that it is comatose. This quantitative difference qualitatively shifts the art world, leading Stallabrass to mourn in exasperation that Art Incorporated churns up "all material, bodies, cultures, and associations in the mechanical search for profit making."[38] Still, profit making is proving to be an elusive goal as the neoliberal project crashes across the globe, and when even real-world economists seem to have given up explaining how, where, and why value comes into being. By contrast, zombie culture just chugs on, leading an increasing number of neoliberal theorists to speculate that creative work, including artists and art institutions, embody a previously overlooked source of value. Is it possible that the protagonist of twenty-first-century capitalism is the previous century's fantasy of the alienated artist? And if so, why a producer who has always been in oversupply?

Mining Social Productivity

"Art is money-sexy! Art is money-sexy-social-climbing-fantastic!" thunders Thomas Hoving, the former director of New York's Metropolitan Museum of Art; "Never hire anyone without an aberration in their background," blurts

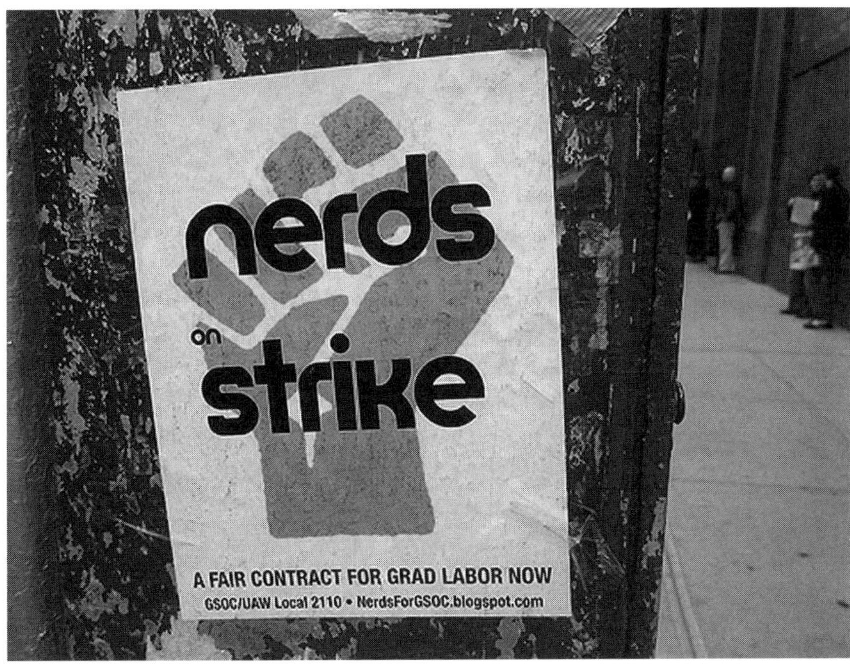

In 2006, New York University Graduate Teaching Assistants walked off their jobs seeking union recognition but failed when the university refused to acknowledge their claims thanks to changes President George Bush Jr. made in government labor legislation. As professional educational workers become increasingly precarious, such low-wage student labor is likely to become more important to universities, forcing future confrontations over wages and security. Image courtesy Gregory Sholette.

out neoliberal business guru Tom Peters; "Managing creative people will be fundamental to business success in the next century," proclaims British entrepreneur John Howkins.[39] When it comes to the movers and shakers of *capitalism 2.0*, the insubordinate image of the contemporary artist is their sexy *doppelgänger*. Forget about the avant-garde's renowned defiance, the deregulated economy celebrates deviant practices and eccentric frames of mind. French sociologists Luc Boltanski and Eve Chiapello label this post-'68 creative imaginary "The New Spirit of Capitalism" arguing that neoliberal investments in flexible organization and anti-authoritarian work environments stem from a cultural critique of capitalism taken up by artistic circles in the 1960s, rather than a response to the more materialist challenge posed by mainstream labor unions in search of expanded social benefits, shorter hours, and better wages.[40] Boltanski and Chiapello write that this aesthetic resistance to capitalism "vindicates an ideal of liberation and/or of individual autonomy, singularity and authenticity."[41] Whether or not this is truly the legacy of what Herbert Marcuse called the great refusal of the 1960s and early 1970s, when so many young people rejected a future of pointless jobs and the 2.1 family with house in the suburbs, any more than it is the legacy of critical cultural practices more generally, it is difficult to ignore the fact that unorthodox cultural labor practices are a central metaphor within the orthodoxy of the new economy, and the artist has become a virtual fetish of this creative production.[42] The overall tendency of capitalism in the post-war era involves an extremely nimble process of transforming everyday life experience and human fantasy into new forms of extractable production and value. The American academic-come-entrepreneur Richard Florida has inserted himself directly into this debate, even proposing a series of indices that allegedly measure the level of exploitable creativity in any given city, municipality, or nation. One of these indicators is the Bohemian Index. Allegedly it works by calculating among other factors the number of resident artists relative to the overall population of a given region. Presumably a high score on the Bohemian Index equals more power to attract a "creative" workforce skilled in such post-industrial sectors as finance, service, and information technologies.[43] Whether or not Florida's artist index is statistically valid or Boltanski and Chiapello's thesis outlives a careful examination of the historical facts is not the point. It is enough to note that government policy makers, urban planners, pedagogical administrators, corporate executives, and city branding experts believe the link between artists, knowledge workers, and regional economic viability is serious enough to invest in its viability. For example, Florida's consultancy website claims clients in the US, UK, Canada, Australia, and New Zealand and includes educational and media customers such as the University of California, the Chronicle of Higher Education, the University of the Arts, and the BBC.[44] Similar success stories about those peddling creative labor and knowledge-work as the engine of twenty-first-century capitalism abound.

Neither has this fascination with creative types been lost on contemporary artists, critics, and curators. While business embraces the shock and destruction of the avant-garde, artists adopt concepts such as niche marketing and networking from business. As Angela McRobbie affirms, artists today are even capable now of reinventing themselves "for the increasingly global market. They can be successful, sell their work; they no longer have any reason to be angry social critics."[45] This is the New Labour classless dream, a high-energy band of young people driving the cultural economy ahead, but in a totally privatized and non-subsidy-oriented direction.[46] One is reminded here of Socrates' pledge to Glaucon, in Book Ten of Plato's *Republic*, regarding those imitative poets and artists whose very labor deceives and seduces citizens through ruse and clever mimicry. If these cunning artists can persuade Socrates that their artistic work is in some way useful to the State then they will be permitted citizenship in his Republic. Failing that test, these arts must be kept at a distance, "lest we fall into the childish love of her which captivates the many."[47] The contemporary republic of hip culture, by contrast, needs no entreaties regarding the importance of creative workers or their fabrications. Global businesses celebrate seditious artists with prestigious cash awards and corporate "cool hunters" infiltrate gallery openings, nightclubs, and other Bohemian environs hoping to catch wind of the latest fashionable trend. Globe-trotting curators, dealers, and other gatekeepers of the elite art world emulate this search and capture method, scouring group shows and artists' studios in search of fresh, marketable talent, including the studios of incubating art students yet to graduate. Which is where Florida's creative worker and McRobbie's born-again converge—inside the school, the university, the factories of knowledge where biological, social, artistic, and communicative assets are concentrated in the form of human capital, that is the minds and bodies of students and faculty. It was only a matter of time it seems. Once life outside the factory—leisure, reproduction, sex—was organized to serve the needs of capital, enclosing and privatizing learning was inevitable, especially given neoliberalism's thirst for new intellectual property. But the knowledge factory, or edu-factory, is also a site for integrating future workers into risk society, and its primary training tool is debt. This was not always the case. According to Silvia Federici and George Caffentzis the post-war Keynesian state virtually paid workers to learn. Faced with a well-organized workforce, capital was forced to subsidize education, coming to see this expenditure as a long-term investment that would not only enhance future productivity, but also help sway labor towards the interests of the corporate business sector.

With the launching of *Sputnik 1* into near-earth orbit in 1957, educational funding was greatly accelerated. Competition with socialist nations increased tolerance of dissent in the West, especially in universities and culture. Liberal open-mindedness as well as anti-Stalinism lay behind President Kennedy's entreaty that artists are "not engineers of the soul." In a democratic society, Kennedy insisted, "the highest duty of the writer, the composer, the artist is to remain true to himself and to let the chips fall where they may."[48] The chips did fall, but far from the concert halls, studios, and salons of high culture. An increasingly militant student rebellion openly challenged US political and military ambitions, especially in Southeast Asia. As fiscal crisis and campus militarism spread, the United States disinvested in education, so that by the end of the 1970s massive faculty firings, tuition-fee hikes, and an end to open admissions in the state university system of New York (SUNY) led to a de-radicalization of campus activism. The privatization of the university followed. Federici and Caffentzis describe this retrenchment as a virtual counter-revolution in which learning as a collective, social investment was replaced by learning as a process of self-investment, preferably with cash in hand. From the 1980s onward, debt emerged as a pivotal, pedagogical tool, teaching students their obligatory place within the free market. By 2007 average student debt had grown to over $20,000, while two years earlier President Bush had approved legislation making it almost impossible to discharge such liabilities through bankruptcy.[49] In Europe, the Bologna Process has also led to rising tuition fees, centralization, and increased privatization of education. The lesson is simple: either pass through the eye of the needle and become a highly rewarded "creative" worker, or join the ranks of the vast redundant population competing for part-time jobs at or near the bottom of the economy.

Even artists—that peculiar category of labor traditionally claiming near-total freedom from economic routines—toe the free market line. And yet, even as enterprise culture hastens to assimilate even the most dissident, anti-social, ephemeral activity as a potential source of profit, something else becomes visible that involves a necessary excess of productivity, and an equally necessary act of expulsion. For if modernism, as Jensen suggests, was established through the management of a counter-institution whereby the Impressionists and their prodigy leapt over the moribund French Academy, then enterprise culture is by contrast emphatically non-dialectical. It operates horizontally, automatically, with no apparent preference regarding form or content. We come to a final enigma concerning culture under neoliberalism: it appears wholly dependent upon the presence/absence of that which it excludes, an ever-present oversupply of cultural production that is mechanically encircled and expelled, encircled and expelled, each time leaving a minor trace of *ejecta* lodged within the institution that rejects it. But something has altered this mechanized play. The once negligible traces left behind are leaking out and coagulating. For a time this inversion appeared manageable, even playful, remaining within the institution's folds as internal critique. Lately it has become less amusing. The archive is consuming its host, brandishing all the malicious resentment of the profaned, the philistine, the exile.

The third question we must explore involves the materializing of this vast, seemingly redundant productivity, this dark matter. As argued above, this missing mass has always covertly, though informally, anchored the fiscal and symbolic economy of art. And yet this productive redundancy is also an unmentionable reality stringently regulated by those who manage the art world's environs, the art critics, historians, collectors, dealers, administrators. This internal policing may explain why it is often outsiders—sociologists, anthropologists, radicals, or sometimes even uneducated non-professionals—who are willing to point out that the art world is unclothed. Take for instance a remarkable 2002 study by Columbia College in Chicago, which concluded that professional and amateur artists operated on "a two-way continuum, upon which information, personnel, financial benefits and other resources flow back and forth."[50] Rather than forming a sharp divide, formal and informal creative practitioners form a continuous spectrum of positions with semi-fixed and often shifting patterns of paid and unpaid artistic labor. The study may have been ignored, but the dynamic it explores is undergoing a fundamental change. John Roberts characterizes this as a convergence where the amateur on the "way up" the professional ladder, and the professional artist on the "way down" meet under the auspices of "deskilling."[51] The term deskilling is associated with post-1960s conceptual art in which formal painterly or sculptural craft was replaced by the use of documents, snapshots, ephemera, videos, and performances that focused on philosophical hypothesis and information exchange. And for anyone familiar with the past few decades of art-school instruction Roberts' observation comes as no surprise. But ironically, it has been left to the hobbyist and amateur to produce artworks that display a mastery of technical facility such as the time-consuming repetitive procedures of knitting and similar needle crafts, or the finely rendered fantasy figures modeled by garage-kit builders. To expand Roberts' argument then, as the amateur moves up thanks primarily to new forms of digital imaging technologies she encounters the professional traveling down, whereupon both converge somewhere in the center, often to the exasperation of all concerned. All, that is to say, except enterprising advocates of the networked creative economy.

Creative dark matter is neither fully contiguous with, nor symmetrical to the products, institutions, or discourse of high art. However, it is possible to imagine a thought experiment that would measure its aggregate impact on the art world—if, say, one were to organize an art fabricators strike, or a boycott of international art magazines demanding these journals cover creative work made by the glut of artists who go unobserved in the art world, or if art students and faculty walked out of classes and refused to attend exhibitions at The Tate, the Reina Sophia, or the MoMA, or, worse yet, collectively stopped purchasing art supplies until everyone associated with cultural production was in some way recognized by the system, including regional watercolor and sketch clubs. Needless to say, the obvious economic disruption would be inseparable from the simultaneous symbolic disruption of aesthetic valorization.[52] Nor have demands for a more inclusive cultural framework been completely absent amongst professionally trained artists. As if sensing the rising visibility of the excluded, in the late 1960s members of the New York-based collective Art Workers' Coalition (AWC) called on the art establishment not only to improve their social and economic security, but to also provide greater access to exhibition venues for other "cultural workers," including those of color, women, and even artists without commercial representation.[53] More than a decade later this same cultural democratizing urge found expression in an exhibition organized by the artists' collective Group Material. Inspired by AWC among other maverick art associations Group Material organized "The People's Choice (Arroz con Mango)," an exhibition of china dolls, family photographs, movie posters, and even a "Pez" candy dispenser collection, all chosen by the mostly Dominican neighborhood residents surrounding the collective's Lower East Side alternative art space. The objects and images Group Material exhibited in "The People's Choice" were solicited from residents of East 13th Street where their gallery space was located. The group sent a letter in Spanish to its neighbors requesting they submit for display "the things that you personally find beautiful, the objects that you keep for your own pleasure ... something that you feel will communicate to others."[54] While historical accounts of AWC and Group Material's activities often describe what they did as "institutional critique"—the practice of reflecting the art world's ideological framework back on itself—a somewhat contrary reading is also possible, and just as cogent. Much like the Situationists in France, *Tucumán Arde* in Agentina, the Artists Union in the UK, and other politically informed artists' collectives of the 1960s and 1970s, both AWC and Group Material actively acknowledged the existence of cultural values being produced and shared outside the borders of the formal art world establishment. This other reading is born out by the infamous censoring of Hans Haacke's Guggenheim Museum exhibition in 1971. Haacke, a co-founder of AWC, wanted to include in his major solo museum show two conceptually based artworks that traced the real estate investments of several family-run corporations in New York City. Drawn from public records, the informational pieces used diagrams, texts, and snapshots to present a "real time" mapping of actual social systems. But many of the properties to be displayed were of substandard, poorly repaired buildings in low-income neighborhoods of the city. Therefore, along with questioning the limits of art and what could be counted as legitimate aesthetic experiences, Haacke's projects also rendered an unflattering picture of greed and urban neglect. After some efforts at negotiation Guggenheim director Thomas Messer canceled the exhibition, explaining to the press that Haacke had deliberately pursued aims that lie beyond art when he tried to introduce an "alien substance" into the "museum organism." The alien substance of course was Haacke's focus on social reality and by extension social justice, two concerns that surpass the self-interested and frequently internecine conflicts of the art world. Nevertheless, this notorious incident has often been historicized strictly in terms of institutional critique, forgoing the very reason why Haacke's exhibition was censored in the first place. And although a promising wave of younger scholars, critics, and curators are beginning to re-narrate much of this history, most continue to seek immunity from dealing with non-art issues of social content and political justice. Something altogether different has occurred within the once gray world of business management. Unlike the allegedly "cutting-edge" art world, corporations have hastened to get out in front of this radically shifting cultural paradigm of social productivity.

Enterprise Culture

For neoliberal pundits like Charlie Leadbeater and Paul Miller the growing visibility of social production amounts to a *pro-am* (professional plus amateur) *revolution*: "the crude, all or nothing, categories we use to carve up society—

leisure versus work, professional versus amateur—will need to be rethought."[55] To Leadbeater, the materialization of a broadly distributed, creative force is the creative engine driving the neoliberal networked economy. He has urged British schools and universities to become "open-cast mines of the knowledge economy."[56] Neoliberal legal scholar Yochai Benkler actually refers to the rising visibility of intangible social production as "the dark matter of our economic production universe."[57] Curiously, this interest in culture by devotees of deregulation is typically coupled with the observation that art is inherently collaborative in nature. A bevy of popular business books makes the connection clear: *Group Genius: The Creative Power of Collaboration*; *Creativity: Competitive Advantage through Collaborative Innovation Networks*; *The Culture of Collaboration*; *Group Creativity: Innovation through Collaboration*; *Arts-based Learning for Business*; *Orchestrating Collaboration at Work*. There is even one book that attempts to teach newly precarious "flexible" workers the special survival skills of artists, and another entitled *Artful Making: What Managers Need to Know About How Artists Work*, in which CEOs and managers are presented with the powerful problem-solving skills generated by artists who work collectively.[58] All of this is curious given that communal production is a typically devalued form of social labor within the culture of art since the greatest artistic value allegedly accrues to an individual author, painter, performer, actor, and so forth. Not surprisingly, *Artful Making* opens with a foreword by Dr. Eric Schmidt, CEO of the knowledge economy's advance guard, Google. Indeed, perhaps business theorists perceive something undetectable to most artists, critics, curators, and so forth: that so-called creative work is inherently communal? As historian Alan Moore explains, "artists rely heavily on gifts—of time, space, materials, opportunities, ideas—to make their work" even as "the process of production is continuously or intermittently collective as artists come together in workshops and teaching situations, sharing ideas, techniques and processes." Nevertheless, Moore continues, the "marketable artistic product must be branded, and in this the individual producer alone is valued."[59]

One is immediately struck that this communalist, gift-giving model of production is quite at odds with the image of the contemporary artist as a scrappy, subversive knowledge worker. Where does that leave the neoliberal adoration of the artist and culture? What if it is not the alleged radicalism of art, but its demonstrated capacity to mobilize excess, even redundant productivity, that makes it an attractive model to the priests and priestesses of the new networked economy? In other words, it's not the artist's seemingly transgressive, risk-taking non-conformity, but exactly a mode of distributed risk and social cooperation denied by neoliberalism that leads certain CEOs and business thinkers to see artistic methods as near-miraculous models of "just-in-time creativity." The irony is not lost on most artists who know that the art world, as opposed to their actual conditions of production, is strictly hierarchical. They also understand, whether or not they admit it, that their assigned role in artistic valorization is literally as a form of dark matter.

The Promise

Swampwall, PAD/D, Paper Rad—imaginative expressions of autonomous production have always extended well beyond the realm of the formal art world. Nevertheless, when mainstream cultural institutions try to incorporate transient forms of art, or devise terms to package them, such as "relational aesthetics," the result typically comes off as so many frozen assets, so much art world real estate plopped down on the multi-billion dollar monopoly board. Which is to say that a certain dark, social productivity has always revealed itself to some degree, an unavoidable fact that some official art histories and museum collections reflect. This should not come as a surprise. Artists and especially artistic movements have consistently intersected with the non-artistic realm, just as within the art world one can discern an entire parallel history of art in which artists have sought to express varying degrees of opposition and autonomy towards the marketplace. Nor would most mainstream art historians deny this in principle. What is not recognized, what cannot be admitted by the maintenance crews of the high culture industry, is the degree to which not only the art world's imaginary but also its economy is stabilized by the invisible labor of this far larger shadow economy. While efforts to normalize marginalized or partially marginalized practices are inevitable, the aim of a radical art history and criticism is to place normality itself under duress by enunciating a space of critical autonomy, a dark matter space, which is never fully recoverable by the culture industry, and by virtue of that asymmetry serves to destabilize the cultural speculators of the elite art world.

However, nothing assures us that this increasingly visible social productivity, this materializing missing mass, will be a force of liberty, as some neoliberal proponents of the new economy insist. What is described in these pages as "dark matter" therefore, is not intrinsically progressive, not in the typical liberal or radical senses of that term. Instead, it possesses at best a *potential* for progressive resistance, as well as for reactionary anger. As cultural historian Michael Denning proposes, a radical reading of the historical narrative involves not only appraising the letters sent in, "but also the letters which were never sent, because the revolutions that don't take place are as disturbing as those that *do*." It is time, he insists, to "make connections between the occasional eruptions—machine breakings, store lootings, window smashings" and that *longue durée* of resistance that may not even be aware it is a *history from below*.[60] Recognizing the ambiguous militant potential of dark-matter productivity is one step towards that recognition. For if there is a resistant nucleus somewhere within this informal collectivization it is no more or less than a longstanding demand for certain promises to be met. That is why these organized and semi-organized cultural groups that make up the heart of this study—"whatever" collectivism, Tactical Media, "mockstitutions"—are not endowed here with a haughty sense of ethical superiority or moral outrage, but instead possess a complex knot of desires involving increased autonomy, envy towards elite privilege, and a demand that the centuries-old contract made between capitalism and the working class for a life free of necessity be fulfilled, not in the future, but immediately, in what Benjamin described as "now-time," a moment laden with unexpected historical possibilities.[61] Such ambiguities are an inevitable component of resistance today. Dark matter, hidden social production, missing mass, shadow archive—all these metaphors are at best a means of visualizing that which cannot be seen: the presence/absence of a vast zone of cultural activity that can no longer be ignored. Nevertheless, no amount of uncertainty relieves us of the responsibility to engage with them *politically*, as an essential element in a longstanding promise of liberation yet to be fulfilled.

2

THE GRIN OF THE ARCHIVE

Haunting implies places, a habitation, and always a haunted house.

Jacques Derrida[1]

The Ruins

The exhibition *Committed to Print* opened at the Museum of Modern Art (MoMA) in early 1988, three months after the Black Monday stock market crash ended an unprecedented capitalist expansion, and just over two years before the dismantling of the Berlin Wall signaled the termination of the Cold War.[2] Curated by Deborah Wye, *Committed to Print* featured more than 130 political posters, graphics, and artists' books made both by well-known artists—including a geometric print by Frank Stella used to raise money for the Attica Legal Defense Benefit Fund and a grim silk-screen piece by Andy Warhol from his *Death and Disaster* series—as well as printed works by artists and artists' groups unknown to most museum-goers. Examples from the latter included a stenciled octopus street-graphic by Becky Howland announcing the illegally squatted *Real Estate Show* in 1980, or "The United States of Africa," an historical map of American racism designed by Faith Ringgold to raise funds for herself, Jeane Toche, and Jon Hendricks who had been charged with desecrating the US flag during *The People's Flag Show* in 1971. *Committed to Print* garnered support from the American Section of the International Association of Critics who voted it the second most significant exhibition of 1987–88, second only to Anselm Kiefer's traveling retrospective. Not surprisingly arch-conservative Hilton Kramer denounced Wye's project, entitling his *New York Observer* review, "Show of Political Prints at MoMA Echoes the Bad Taste of the 1920s."[3] It was also heavily criticized from the Left for having lamentably left out AIDS activist graphics.[4] All in all, the ideological stakes could not have been more transparent: who would come to narrate the cultural legacy of the 1960s and 1970s? Would it be those who sympathized or perhaps even participated in its radical critique of capitalism, imperialism, homophobia, and racism? Or would it be an increasingly strident conservative movement that had been historically sidelined by the New Left and the counter-culture? The appropriation of radical Left tactics, including those of ACT UP, by the Right-leaning libertarian Tea Party suggests the latter has ultimately taken control of this historical narrative.

Included in Wye's exhibition was a searing anti-war graphic originally designed by members of the Art Workers' Coalition (AWC) in 1970. The offset poster reveals a gruesome mound of dead Vietnamese women and children slain by US soldiers. Originally photographed by Ronald Haeberle, AWC members superimposed the text *Q. And Babes? A. Yes, And Babies* over the image. Provocatively, AWC called upon MoMA to co-sponsor and distribute the work in support of a wave of national demonstrations decrying the US invasion of Cambodia and the shooting deaths of student protesters at Kent and Jackson State Universities that spring. Despite strong support from museum staff, the MoMA's board of directors officially refused the invitation, arguing that the poster's explicit political content was too far removed from the mission of an art museum.[5] With help from the Lithographers Union, AWC finally printed *Q. And Babes? A. Yes, And Babies*, after which they staged an intervention at the museum by holding the grisly graphic aloft in front of Picasso's *Guernica*.[6] Almost two decades later Wye officially displayed the contentious AWC graphic inside the institution that had rejected it, most likely for the first time. At least momentarily *Committed to Print* broke with the museum's staunch ideological separation of art from politics. Wye boldly exhibited a veritable core-sample of post-'68 dissident graphic artworks, organized the prints and posters into six contentious subject categories: Government/Leaders; Race/Culture; Gender; Nuclear Power/Ecology; War/Revolution; and Economics/Class Struggle/The American Dream. The most relevant of these categories for the thesis of this book is the show's final section on economics and gentrification. It included several printed artworks condemning real estate speculators and the relentless transformation of poor and working-class neighborhoods into neo-Bohemian zones of knowledge production. With the exception of AIDS activism, the signal feature of New York urban politics in the 1980s centered on opposition to new forms of privatized urban renewal being undertaken by municipal government in league with finance, real estate, and insurance capital. Ironically, the processes of displacement and gentrification that unfolded not only plagued the always precarious lives of artists, but artists themselves in turn fueled this very process. As Zukin, Deutsche and Ryan, and Smith have all shown, the presence of entrepreneurial cultural workers often unwittingly ramps up real estate values in economically ravaged urban neighborhoods, unleashing a series of rent hikes that eventually makes it impossible for artists to remain.[7] As they move on to still more marginal locations and repeat this process, higher-income professionals move in to the newly "regenerated" neighborhood as the new "gentry." The Midnight Notes Collective has aptly described this phenomenon in terms of *new enclosures* that recapitulate Marx's concept of original or "primitive" accumulation: the forceful theft of peasant lands and commons in eighteenth-century Europe (and earlier) that simultaneously concentrated reserves of capital and created a new, property-less class, the proletariat.[8] But what makes Wye's inclusion of anti-gentrification graphics especially notable is that by the late 1980s this process of new enclosures was not only inescapable, it was signaling the rise of what Neil Smith calls the revanchist city to come.[9] Any doubts about this process or where the city was heading were soon erased by the ruthless eviction by police of homeless squatters and anarchists from Tompkins Square Park only weeks after the MoMA exhibition closed. Thus, while AWC's anti-war poster definitively marked politically engaged artists' domestic struggles against militarism and cultural elites in the 1960s and 1970s, *Committed to Print*'s anti-gentrification graphics of the 1980s pointed to the systematic impoverishment, girdling, and revamping of domestic space that would eventually become emblematic of neoliberal urban policies at a global level. But this concept of new enclosures can and must be extended to include the instrumental harnessing of a whole range of life processes, including intellectual and artistic ideas, but also bodily organs, women's reproductive systems, genetic codes, even social affects, and, at least superficially, politically resistant histories. It is this last enclosure that leads directly to the enigma of the archive whose contradictions, gaps, and lacunae form a promissory note that if we want to know "what this will have meant," as Derrida explains, "we will only know tomorrow. Perhaps."[10]

Amongst the anti-gentrification graphics Wye included in *Committed to Print* were several works by members of PAD/D, who—myself amongst them—had spent the previous eight years fervently programming monthly discussions on art and politics, networking with activist and community organizations, publishing a newsletter, a monthly listing of Left cultural events known as Red Letter Days, and producing temporary public artworks denouncing US involvement in Central America, Reagan era anti-terrorist policies, as well as the gentrification of the Lower East Side, where the group's offices were initially located.[11] Between 1980 and 1988, PAD/D sought to establish an autonomous Left cultural sphere that would operate apart from both the commercial market and mainstream museums and not-for-profit spaces by networking non-art political activists and socially engaged artists and artists' collectives in the US, and eventually abroad. "We were disaffected with the direction of mainstream culture and fine art, and wanted to join our art directly with change-oriented politics," group member Jerry Kearns recently commented.[12] As its name implies, the group actively collected documents—posters, prints, photographic slides, announcements, news clippings, correspondence, mail art, drawings, and ephemera—related to the production of social and political art. The collection was initially housed in a small office rented from a Lower East Side community group called Seven Loaves that was part of the Nuyorican cultural center known as CHARAS/El Bohio, a former high school with links to the Puerto Rican activists known as the Young Lords as well as the vigorous NYC squatters movement of the 1960s and 1970s.[13]

The aim of this archive was also political insofar as it was meant to serve as a pedagogical "tool-kit" showing artists how to combine cultural production with radical resistance. This sort of "archival activism" was what Lucy R. Lippard had in mind when she put out a call for artists in 1979 to send her documentation about their own political and social art.[14] The request led to a flood of materials that, less than a year later, led to the formation of the PAD/D Archive and the group itself. It is ironic that the first "use" of this "activist" archive was by a mainstream cultural institution. Wye did research for her exhibition in the archive, borrowed posters and graphics for *Committed to Print* from the collection, and appears to have drawn inspiration for the show's thematic schema from dozens of hand-written index cards that made up the archive's pre-digital index system.[15] Invented out of necessity by members of the PAD/D Archive Committee—primarily Barbara Moore and artist Mimi Smith, neither of whom had formal training in library science—this DIY cataloging system amounted to a continuously generated chain of subject categories that somehow aimed to link the diverse materials that regularly arrived at the PAD/D office for inclusion in the archive. Although Moore and Smith occasionally collected some ephemera themselves, even cutting posters off a city wall in one case, it was their policy that everything mailed or delivered to the group was to be labeled, indexed, and included within the PAD/D Archive (that is, everything with one exception, addressed later in the chapter). "An archive is not a qualitative thing," explained Moore in a 2007 interview with the Chicago-based collective Temporary Services.[16] Her comment underscores both the unfiltered nature and the sheer physicality of the collection's 51.2 linear feet of documents. It was PAD/D's own mission statement that set the only tone for the collection insofar as the group sought to amass a collection of "international socially-concerned art" defined in the broadest sense as "any work that deals with issues ranging from sexism and racism to ecological damage or other forms of human oppression."[17] At the same time, the extreme open-endedness and heterogeneity of the PAD/D Archive raises questions about the interplay of light and shadow that necessarily operates within the familiar spaces of the art world.

One year after *Committed to Print* the PAD/D Archive was officially donated to the MoMA Library, a gift that coincided with the founding of the Museum's own extensive archives consisting of institutional records and other donated collections.[18] But PAD/D's entry into the Museum was made on condition that the collection was now closed to new additions, thus terminating its function as an ongoing pedagogical focal point for future art activists. One cannot help but speculate on what the Museum's first director, Alfred Barr, would have made of this hodgepodge of self-defined radical artists lovingly entombed within the heart of his institution. Barr used the institutional weight of the MoMA and its Rockefeller

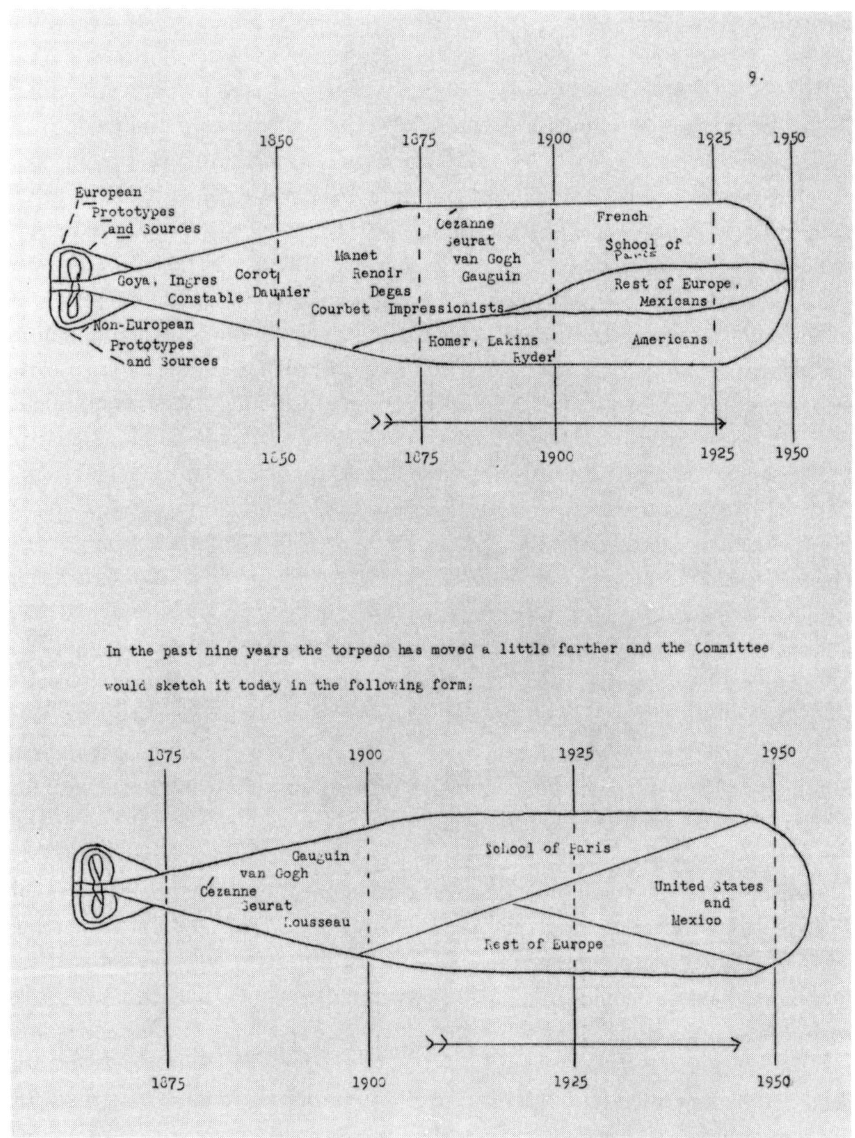

Two of the sketches made by Museum of Modern Art director Alfred Barr to illustrate the art historical thrust of his collecting strategy. "Torpedo" Diagram of Ideal Permanent Collection. Alfred H. Barr, Jr. (1902–1981), Papers, 9a.7A. The Museum of Modern Art Archives, New York. 1933. Location: The Museum of Modern Art, New York, NY, USA. Photo Credit: Digital Image © The Museum of Modern Art/Licensed by SCALA/ Art Resource, NY.

capital to singularly establish the dominant *telos* of post-war art following his visits to the 1920s Soviet Union and German Bauhaus. He even illustrated his vision of modernism, in a sketch, as a propeller-driven torpedo packed with artistic incendiaries from the School of Paris to the US and Mexican avant-gardes. Not surprisingly his sketch, now an archival document itself, shows the Americas at the very tip of the missile, providing Barr's concept of modern art with its forward momentum as well as tilting the art establishment away from Europe. But his hawkish diagram can also be read homologically in relation to the MoMA's own expansive future, a jet-propelled aesthetic economy with multiplying subdivisions for painting and sculpture, graphics, industrial design, photography, cinema, and of course the library plus its archive. For Barr, these various departmental provinces were supposed to coalesce inside one unified artistic household, and yet this imaginary sanctity never actually existed, not within the Museum, any more than in the artistic reality it sought to represent. Instead, internal divisions and dissent characterize institutional power in a museum, just as they do the most transitory of artists' groups and collectives, or the boldest of artistic movements. Notably, a familial relationship existed between PAD/D and its future host from the very get-go. During PAD/D's founding meeting in 1980, Clive Phillpot, who was then director of the MoMA's Library, proposed the name "PAD" or Political Art Documentation. It was immediately accepted. Following this christening the group added "/D" for /Distribution to reflect its expanding activist mission. What happens then, when something that is supposed to be a supplement like a glorified filing cabinet tucked out of sight into the back of a closet or in an outer borough of a city, gradually begins to seep back out into the house? Or when the "prosthesis" of memory is no longer limited to stacks of half-forgotten posters, fading photographs, or yellowing papers but includes an ocean of digital material overturning customary metaphors such as the wax-covered "mystic writing pad" that Freud once used to illustrate the simultaneous presence and partial absence of memory? How does one explain the becoming political of the archive? While we are not yet ready to address this homely haunting (or its ethereal electronic emissions), clearly something new had already begun to take shape in the 1980s, something that emerged either in spite of, or perhaps thanks to, the rise of a society of unmediated personal risk and the corporate enclosure of the commons that would soon move from the local to the global.

In the months that followed *Committed to Print*, a wave of high profile "political art" exhibitions appeared in mainstream New York museums, galleries, and cultural spaces. Displaying political commitment at an institutional level was suddenly hip in the New York art world. The Guggenheim Museum organized its first major presentation of Soviet avant-garde art entitled *The Great Utopia*, followed by the widely denounced 1993 Whitney Museum Biennial whose curators were charged with surrendering themselves to a tide of fashionable "cultural radicalism."[19]

However, it was the short-lived series of programs by The Dia Foundation that preceded the Whitney "fiasco" that were especially innovative and influential. In 1989 Dia board member Yvonne Rainier convinced the organization to turn over its SoHo exhibition space first to the artists' collective Group Material (who produced the exhibition program *Democracy*), and then to artist Martha Rosler and a group of housing activists who created three exhibitions collectively entitled *If You Lived Here*. Both projects also led to substantial scholarly publications rather than art catalogs. Dia has never again ventured into the terrain of art and politics.[20] Paradoxically however, even as these "radical" art exhibitions were being organized, the intellectual legacy of New Left culture with its promises of autonomy, democratic transparency, and collective experimentation had splintered into abject ruin. PAD/D also collapsed in 1988, the same year *Committed to Print* opened at the MoMA. Henceforth the group was destined to be interned within its own archival crypt right alongside the many other forgotten artists, authors, events, and groups PAD/D actively documented. As co-founder, Lippard later mused, "when PAD/D folded its tents in early 1988, the editorial in our magazine *Upfront* noted ruefully that we seemed to have 'reached the end of yet another cycle of organizational energy'"; Lippard adds ironically that, "we were writing that farewell at the moment when so-called 'political art' was poised on the brink of the mainstream success."[21] But the group can also be said to have fallen victim to an overly ambitious collective mission as well as a steadily "draining resistance to a reactionary decade."[22] For as important as it is to recall Immanuel Wallerstein's argument that the radical uprising of the late 1960s and 1970s transformed a range of Marxist assumptions about the role of ecologists, feminists, and other minorities who were no longer willing to wait for "the revolution" to seek justice, it is just as imperative to note Paulo Virno's painful assessment of the same period as a defeated revolution against capitalism and wage labor.[23] Significantly, the majority of the documents in the PAD/D Archive date from the years following this "defeat."

Into the Archive

"A Message To The Class of :00," reads the caption above a photo-collaged factory worker sharpening an enormous set of industrial gears. "If You Liked School ... You'll Love Work." The man's head has been replaced with the face of a timepiece. "Work:" the black and white flyer's bold Helvetica type concludes "A Prison Of Measured Time." Creased and dog-eared, the 30-year-old leaflet was produced by an experimental Left-libertarian "free-space" called the Anarchist Bookstore that was briefly located on Manhattan's Lower East Side in the mid 1980s. No doubt the cheaply produced handbill was initially intended to be wheat-pasted on a boarded-up East Village tenement or distributed at a club or art gallery. And then forgotten. Today it is entrusted to a pinkish-beige binder, one of hundreds that make up the PAD/D Archive: some 130 political prints and posters stored in flat files, and thousands of yet-to-be cataloged flyers, letters, periodicals, and other ephemera, packed inside 27 acid-free file cartons that sit on only a few shelves within the commodious MoMA Archive: a glacial-blue warehouse in Queens accessible only by appointment.[24] To the researcher, these "miscellaneous uncataloged" dossiers initially appear as a sea of tabs jutting up from corrugated boxes, each pencil-marked with the name of an artist, event, venue, or group primarily from the late 1960s to the mid 1980s. Some of these are familiar today, including groups such as ABC No Rio, Art Workers' Coalition (AWC), Artists Placement Group (APG), Collaborative Projects (COLAB), Fashion Moda, Group Material, Gran Fury, Guerilla Girls, Social and Public Arts Resource Center (SPARC), or individual artists like Conrad Atkinson, Joseph Beuys, Daniel Buren, Leon Golub, Hans Haacke, Suzanne Lacy, Martha Rosler, Adrien Piper, Nancy Spero, or Marcia Tucker. There is even a folder on the left-wing Punk band The Clash. Still, most of the names are now obscure. Their titles range from the fairly descriptive and the matter of fact—Artists for Survival, Artists and Social Change in Ireland, Bay Area Artists for Nuclear Sanity, Artists Against Apartheid, Artists Call Against US Intervention in Central America, or even Artists for [Jesse] Jackson, and Artists for Mondale, to the enigmatic—Brooklyn Art Dump, Free Association, Foolish Productions, Temporary Insanity, to the preposterous—Barbarians for Socialism, Up Against the Wall Motherfuckers (Black Mask), and a weekend conference of Left-academic self-ridicule advertised as the Radical Humor Festival which was sponsored by the journal *Cultural Correspondence* at New York University in the Spring of 1984. To this third category we must add a single document about the Institute for Unknown Political Affaires (IUPA), two European artists—Karel Dudesek of Czechoslovakia and Bernhard Müller of Germany—who, disguised as American soldiers, crossed into Communist Poland in 1981 to meet with the free workers' union Solidarność, and also mention a folder on the equally short-lived agit-prop group Union of Concerned Commies (UCC) whose members—mostly malcontent temporary office workers in San Francisco—later went on to publish *Processed World*, a zine dedicated to providing a "creative outlet for people whose talents were blocked by what they were doing for money."[25]

Several vertical files also contain printed materials on late 1960s and 1970s ultra-left political groups including the art-oriented Anti-Imperialist Cultural Union organized by African-American poet Amiri Baraka, but also an extreme militant faction of the Black Panther Party known as BLA or Black Liberation Army which sought to establish a break-away African-American nation in the Southwest United States. But even here a connection to cultural radicalism exists, one born out by the archive. In a separate folder are documents about the

Madame Binh Graphics Collective: an all-white, all-female poster-making cadre that served as the cultural "arm" of the May 19th Communist Movement, one of several militant organizations like the Weather Underground that splintered off from Students for a Democratic Society (SDS). Members of Madame Binh (and members of May 19th) were eventually sent to federal prison on charges that they assisted the BLA in the armed robbery of a Brinks armored car in 1981. The stolen cash was to be used to purchase weapons for the coming anti-imperialist revolution. According to a former member of the graphics collective, Mary Patten, even when the group was faced with the daily grind of prison life they did not stop producing oppositional culture, "we created 'prison art' with permitted materials—collages made from torn-up magazines, toothpaste substituting for glue ... we made portraits of fellow-prisoners [and] mobilized a veritable cottage industry to make drawings, cards, paintings, and paper quilts for our annual 'crafts sale for human rights.'"[26]

One PAD/D folder documents an infamous political rogue, for lack of a better term; the cryptic street-artist William Depperman, whose minutely typed broadsheets once plastered city walls indicting the CIA with assassinating kung-fu actor Bruce Lee and the US government with bioengineering the AIDS virus. There are also materials in the archive with no specific relationship to art and politics per se, such as binders for the 1980s music venues Club 57 and the Mudd Club, or one for the NGO the World Wildlife Fund. Some material documents public art projects of experimental urbanism similar to *Archigram*. One pamphlet sports a grainy black and white image of a crowded Amsterdam square from 1970 dominated by a massive tubular inflatable artwork by Eventstructure Research Group. Only one other uncataloged folder contains information about this group in a different corner of the MoMA Library, however a quick Internet search reveals ERG was a late '60s Dutch collective interested in "notions of perception related to space, time and media." Nevertheless, a substantial portion of the archive's content is not so easily traceable even using current information technology databases. Hundreds of binders are filled with documents sent to PAD/D by individual artists. Most reveal work directly engaged with issues of aesthetics, politics, and society, but here and there are folders for artists who produced abstract or formalist painting and sculpture. In general, few of these individuals (or groups) ever achieved serious visibility like those names mentioned at the beginning of the chapter.[27]

A good portion of the PAD/D Archive contains an assortment of collectively self-published journals, pamphlets, and catalogs, including anti-catalogs. "Smashing the Myths of the Information Industry" is a modest sized orange-colored "cat-a-log" printed by the then emerging alternative media collective Paper Tiger Television in the mid 1980s. Founded by Dee Dee Halleck and rooted in the media criticism of Herbert Schiller, Paper Tiger remains one of the few groups still operating today.[28] Another "uncataloged" file folder contains a stout, palm-sized directory of anti-authoritarian organizations by an anarchist study group in Berkeley called International Blacklist, still another binder contains a single bound issue of poetry and sketches by residents of the Augusta Mental Health Institute Psychiatric Center in Maine. Several now obscure Left cultural journals from the 1970s and 1980s are archived—*Incite* (Canada), *Black Phoenix* (UK), *Cultural Correspondence*, *The Fox*, and *Red Herring* (New York)—most of which have since folded, with the exception of *Left Curve* out of Oakland. But there are also a host of politically playful publications including zines by *Artpolice* from Minneapolis, *CONTROL* out of London, and an early 1980s Situationist-inspired newsprint publication from Long Island New York called *FREEZE & SCREAM*, its yellowing back cover featuring a *détourned* Steve Canyon comic-book panel by Herbert Sigüenzo in which a woman shouts at a befuddled, square-jawed man: "It's simple Steve: why don't you and your boys just get the fuck out of El Salvador!"

Among other scarce publications in the PAD/D Archive is *Presencia de México en la X Bienal de París 1977*, a mutinous "counter-catalog" produced by four radical Mexican collectives: grupo Suma, Tetraedro, Taller de Arte e Ideología, and Proceso Pentágono. After members of Proceso Pentágono came to believe the Paris Biennale organizers were planning to undermine the Leftist intent of their artwork with critical essays by anti-Cuban expats, all four groups organized their own exhibition catalog. Proceso Pentágono was known for staging mock kidnappings and automobile accidents on the streets of Mexico City as a public protest against the rise of a generic and bureaucratic urban modernism: highways and housing projects cutting residents off from neighborhoods, public spaces, and potential sites for gathering and demonstrating. Now brittle and yellowed at the edges, the archived copy of the Biennale Countercatalog testifies to a collision, one of many, in which artists registered their antagonism towards institutional power in print form.[29] A comparable story sits inside another folder marked *an anti-catalog*. Published the same year as the Mexican counter-catalog, *an anti-catalog* was collectively produced by a group of politicized artists and art historians associated with Artists Meeting for Cultural Change (AMCC) in New York. The cover designed by artist Joseph Kosuth offers a text-only manifesto that explicitly calls into question the neutrality of art scholarship and its cultural institutions.[30] Directly inspired by the ground-breaking cultural analysis of John Berger's *Ways of Seeing* book and television program, *an anti-catalog* stridently offered its own critical rejoinder to the Whitney Museum of American Art's Bicentennial exhibition of 1976 in which the organizers planned to represent 200 years of American visual culture using John D. Rockefeller's collection of white male artists (plus one woman and one black painter). The dissident publication also applied social art history scholarship, typically associated with T. J. Clark's work on nineteenth-century France, to an American context, and perhaps for the first time. In an implicitly linked archival folder sits a letter signed by some 75 artists including Vito Acconci, Harmony Hammond, Howardena Pindell, Alan Sekula, and Linda Nochlin protesting the "removal" of editors Max Kozloff and John Coplans by the owners of *Artforum*, presumably for publishing Marxist-inspired art criticism by writers such as Carol Duncan and Alan Wallach, two of the scholars involved in *an anti-catalog*. The Mexican counter-catalog, the AMCC counter-catalog, and the firing of the *Artforum* editors all took place in 1977.

Much of the material in the PAD/D Archive amounts to a call for action and participation, including an open invitation to participate in the re-creation of a Chilean People's Mural on West Broadway in SoHo that was eventually carried out October 20, 1973, one month and eight days after democratically elected Chilean President Salvador Allende was toppled on September 11 by General Augusto Pinochet in a CIA-backed coup. Likewise, several documents by Iranian Students Association ask for "Solidarity with 100,000 Political Prisoners against the fascist regime of the shah." There are also attempts to link art and labor either by treating artists as cultural workers who can refuse to produce, or by linking artists with labor unions. "Would you like to take part in a strike of artists?" begins one brief communiqué tucked inside a folder binder marked *Art Strike*. Dated May 15, 1979, the one-page, typewritten proposal originated nine years after the short-lived *New York Art Strike Against Racism, War, and Repression*, and three years after a call out of London by Gustav Metzger for a three-year artists' work stoppage (between 1977 and 1980) to bring down the art world because a "refusal to labor is the chief weapon of workers fighting the system."[31] But this later call for artistic inaction was intended as a more subjectively based protest against "the art system's unbroken repression of the artist and the alienation from the results of his practice." The petition goes on to instruct its recipient: "For Artists Only!" "No Publishing," and is signed by the enigmatic Goran Đorđević of what was then known as Yugoslavia.[32] Linking artists with other workers was also the aim of "Revolting Music," a dance party held at the Machinists Union Hall in downtown New York City by the collective Group Material featuring 100 guaranteed "danceable hits" by The Clash, James Brown, Aretha Franklin, and Poly Styrene that "demonstrate sexual, class and racial consciousness and the furious desire for social change."[33] Similarly, in 1982, critic Lucy Lippard and artist Candice Hill-Montgomery organized an exhibition entitled *Working Women, Working Artists, Working Together* for the Bread and Roses art gallery, a cultural center founded by activist Moe Foner for the District 1199 Health and Hospital Workers Union. Among the artists featured in the exhibition were Ntozake Shange, Cecilia Vicuña, Vanalyne Greene, Jerri Allyn, and Mierle Laderman Ukeles, who was herself a frequent collaborator with the New York Department of Sanitation workers. But Ukeles is also the author of a remarkable 1969 manifesto entitled *Maintenance Art—Proposal for an Exhibition*, which reads in part:

C. Maintenance is a drag; it takes all the fucking time (lit.)
The mind boggles and chafes at the boredom.
The culture confers lousy status on maintenance jobs = minimum wages, housewives = no pay

Ukeles' declaration about feminism, labor, and cultural criticism forms part of a pink thread that runs throughout the PAD/D Archive right alongside resistance to gentrification and military intervention in Latin America. No More Nice Girls, Dykes Opposed to Nuclear Technology, Women's Art Registry of Minnesota (WARM), Women's Caravan "S.A.C," and Spinsters Ink (one of the first lesbian literary publications in the United States), Seneca Depot October Action Coalition, Everywomen Press—folder after folder testifies to a feminist cultural militancy that not only opposed patriarchal authority, but also broader issues of value accumulation and production. As Julia Kristeva insists, what was at stake in the revolt of May '68 wasn't replacing bourgeois society's values by other ones, but instead "contesting the very principle of Value, i.e. power, lack, life as process of production and work itself."[34]

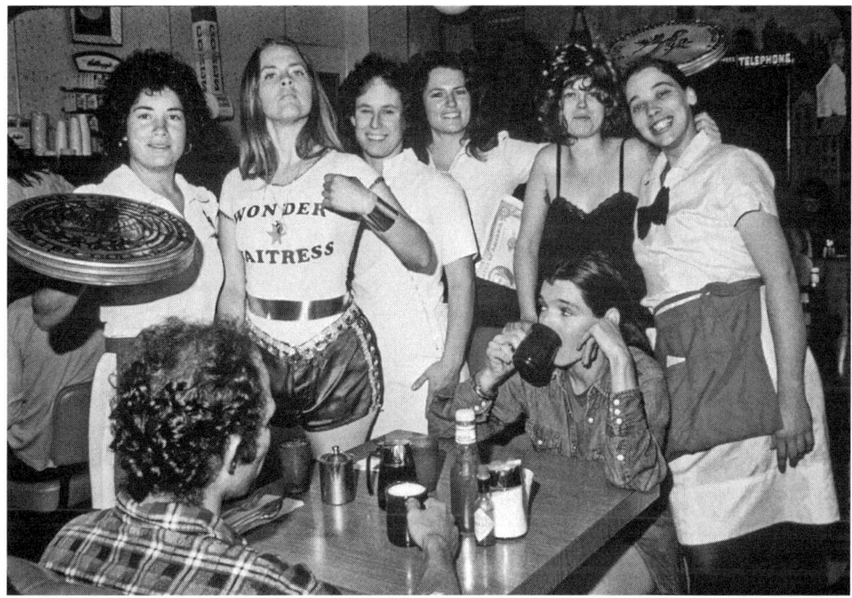

Ready to Order? by The Waitresses was a 1970s site-oriented conceptual art work that took place in several restaurants around Los Angeles, CA, over a seven-day period. The performance project presented vignettes at lunchtime followed by evening panels focused on issues of women's work, female stereotypes, sexual harassment, and the relationship between food and money. Pictured from left to right: Denise Yarfitz, Jamie Wildman, Jerri Allyn, Anne Gauldin, Patti Nicklaus, Leslie Belt in Lafayette's Café, Venice, CA, 1978. Image courtesy Maria Karras.

Material in the PAD/D Archive documents several feminist art groups who explicitly questioned the invisibility of women's "naturalized" service labor within the art world. "See Red Women's Workshop" produced dozens of agitational and educational silk-screen prints and political cartoons in London throughout the mid 1970s into the 1990s. Some of these graphics attacked Prime Minister Margaret Thatcher's cuts in social welfare, or called for support of "our Irish Sisters in Armagh Jail," but many posters dealt directly with women's suffrage such as one that demanded equal pay with men by proposing women should refuse to feed, sleep with, or do housework for them until economic justice was achieved. A similar feminist economic critique fueled the photographic collective Hackney Flashers, an East London-based group whose projects "Work and Wages," and "Who's Holding the Baby?" questioned the social construction of femininity and motherhood through a semiotic critique of gender representation.[35] Similarly deconstructivist, the Berwick Street Film Collective (BSFC) worked with artist Mary Kelly in 1975 to produce *Nightcleaners*, a 90 minute 16 mm film inspired by Brecht's theory of alienation that sought to take critical exposition to another level by serving in a media campaign to unionize women office cleaners in London.[36] Performance art using surreal props was the preferred tactic used in Los Angeles by a group of women who had collectively waitressed for "a total of fourteen years."[37] In order to address abusive treatment of service workers the group's inaugural press announcement states that starting April 25 until May 1, 1978, "we will waitress again," as a group of artists, The Waitresses. Inspired by feminist educational programming at the Woman's Building—an autonomous non-profit started in 1973 by politicized women artists in Los Angeles—The Waitresses staged guerrilla theater in restaurants and café's that served up stories about their experiences as service workers. The group later co-conceived "The All City Waitress Marching Band," several dozen food servers drolly demanding "equal pay for equal work" in lockstep and aprons, and in 1982 founding members Jerri Allyn and Anne Gauldin went on to establish Sisters of Survival (S.O.S.), a quartet of rainbow-colored "nuns" who performed skits and teach-ins about the dangers of nuclear power and military technology, and whose work appeared in the artists' book section of *Committed to Print*. Except for Allyn members of The Waitresses later abandoned the fine arts to pursue theater, graphic design, yoga instruction, and in the case of one former Waitress, the life of a Buddhist nun.

The PAD/D Archive also contains materials documenting the better-known feminist art collective the Guerrilla Girls. In the spring of 1985 the pseudonymous "girls" organized a sustained street-poster campaign mixing dry humor and cold statistics to publicly condemn the world's "retrograde attitudes towards women artists." Strategically placed in the SoHo art district one graphic blatantly listed 20 commercial galleries that showed "no more than 10% women artists or none at all."[38] Almost immediately the group was sought after to give public talks, especially in university settings or alternative, non-commercial art spaces. In order to protect themselves from recrimination within the small quarters of the art industry, members of Guerrilla Girls disguised for these public appearances by wearing plastic Gorilla masks. In the months and years that followed the posters name more names, steadily pressuring an art industry that nom de guerrilla Frida Kahlo described as "one of the last unregulated industries." Which is why the group, who often describe themselves as "the conscience of the art world," can be described as an economic art lobby made up of small cultural manufacturers seeking a greater share of a given market. From a slightly different perspective, however, their guerilla campaign amounts to a seemingly fantastic demand that their labor—mostly unwaged and unrecognized—along with that of other women artists and people of color, should be properly remunerated within the symbolic and material economy of high art. Resistance to the secondary status of "women's work" did not begin in the 1980s. Nor was it always aimed at the commercial art world. Issues of gender and labor arose even within Left-leaning cultural groups such as AWC. As Julia Bryan-Wilson points out, some of the more active women members of AWC wandered away from the group around 1971 in order to form their own feminist organizations including Women Artist's in Revolution (WAR), or the Ad Hoc Women Artists' Committee, or Women Art Students and Artists for Black Artists' Liberation. But since it was mostly women members who had "naturally" been doing much of the administrative and secretarial work, this defection crippled AWC's organizational structure.[39]

What would an equitable distribution of labor mean within a cultural economy like that of the art world? If realized, it would completely upend the existing structure of art market valorization. Economics becomes politics. As Federici explains, the 1970s wages-for-housework campaign in Italy and elsewhere sought to raise consciousness about the unrecognized role of women under capitalism, but it was also a critical strategy aimed at many Leftist and Marxist theorists who similarly ignored women's essential reproductive economic function.[40] Perhaps these gender-based criticisms are best illustrated by the provocative and playful work of Carnival Knowledge, a little-known feminist art collective who, a few years before the Guerrilla Girls, audaciously explored the imagery and politics of female sexuality without regard to reproductive demands using elaborate installations inspired by the vernacular of the side-show and the circus. Posters, correspondence, and several sketches of unrealized projects by Carnival Knowledge reside in the PAD/D Archive, including documents about their collaboration with Times Square porn-workers Annie Sprinkle and "Sexaphonist" Dianne "Moonmade." One exhibition of female erotic art entitled "Second Coming" provoked a censorious attack by Jerry Falwell's fundamentalist Christian group Moral Majority. The show featured a mocked-up image of the conservative televangelist Falwell installed in a kissing booth, as well as an interactive artwork modeled on the popular Mr. Potato Head toy entitled "Build your own Dildo Erection Set." In response, the National Endowment for the Arts (NEA), now led by Reagan appointee Frank Hodsoll, punished alternative space Franklin Furnace for daring to host such a sex-positive display. Nevertheless, insofar as a group of women artists were vilified for openly and playfully displayed interest in their own sexual pleasure without regard to child-bearing or motherhood, this early and overlooked skirmish in the coming culture wars signaled a fateful paradigm shift few feminists or Leftists could have predicted at the time. In hindsight, this relatively obscure moral condemnation can be seen as part of a sweeping rightward strategy to "re-encircle" and delimit the social gains made by feminists and others during the uprisings of the 1960s and 1970s. Key elements of this reactionary program included a call for a return to "family values," the political defeat of the Equal Rights Amendment (ERA), and the fostering of an increasingly well-organized and violent campaign against abortion clinics.

Much of what the Right feared is now sheltered within the PAD/D Archive, and much of what is in the archive documents an unprecedented rebellion by the offspring of well-fed, well-educated workers who angrily rejected the patriotic expectations and stultifying working conditions associated with their parents' world. Carnival Knowledge, Hackney Flashers, Heresies Magazine Collective, Guerrilla Art Action Group, Black Emergency Coalition, Alliance for Cultural Democracy—the artists and groups represented by the PAD/D Archive chronicle a complex artistic response to this radical shift that involves not only explicit expressions of political dissent, but also a desire to liberate the communal, creative, and sexual dimensions of social being. According to Virno, this rebellion represented the "first revolution aimed not against poverty and backwardness, but specifically against the means of capitalistic production, thus, against wage labor."[41] Nor were these rising democratic expectations confined to the privileged classes or elite universities. By the end of the 1960s, lower-middle and working-class college students at Kent State in Ohio and Jackson State in Mississippi staged militant anti-war protests. In May of 1970 both campuses became the site of military repression against activists leading to six deaths and dozens of injuries. Street fighting between students and police outside the Democratic Convention in Chicago in 1968 signaled a level of near-revolutionary intensity that soon developed counterparts in Germany, Mexico, Italy, and most especially France. Meanwhile, industrial leaders and traditional labor unions were beset by a new generation of rank-and-file workers who insisted on being more than a pair of hands on an assembly line. They wanted the democratic and cultural changes taking place around them reflected on the shop floor. This was particularly strong amongst public employees in the US who launched a series of strikes in the late 1960s and early 1970s unlike anything witnessed since the 1930s.[42] But rebellion was also taking shape in industrial cities such as Detroit, where the Ford manufacturing plant and other automobile factories are located in a predominantly African-American city. There black workers organized militant trade unions including the Dodge Revolutionary Union Movement (DRUM) and ELRUM (the Eldon plant version of DRUM). Both groups were connected to the League of Revolutionary Black Workers, which has been compared to the *Comitato Unito de Base* ("United Rank-and-File Committee") organizations in Italy in 1968.[43] Radical unionists repeatedly shut down plant production throughout the mid to late 1960s in a series of coordinated wildcat strikes. They also made contact with their radical union counterparts in Turin, Italy.[44] However, the seriousness of this insurrectionary threat is perhaps most clearly measured by the coordinated level of repression against these activists by the US government through organizations such as COINTELPRO, one of the domestic counter-intelligence programs set up by the FBI and charged to "expose, disrupt, and otherwise neutralize" such groups as the Black Panthers, but also other factions of the New Left, the peace movement, and anyone the government perceived to be an enemy social order.[45] These covert government operations took place against a background that included the murder of Malcom X in 1965, the killing by police and FBI agents of at least ten members of the Black Panther Party between 1965 and 1966, and the assassination of Martin Luther King Jr. in the spring of 1968, days before he was to lead a multiracial "Poor People's March" on Washington aimed at creating an alliance between the civil rights movement, militant unions, and Leftists seeking greater economic and political justice. Despite these setbacks, capitalism and US imperialism appeared to be at a disastrous crossroads. The American military had been defeated by a peasant army in Southeast Asia, the Nixon Whitehouse toppled by the Watergate conspiracy, and the US and much of the industrial world was enduring a prolonged financial crisis brought about by the over-accumulation of capital and a crippling oil embargo organized by third-world Arab nations. The catastrophe continued to unfold. As late as 1979 two US-backed regimes, one in Nicaragua and one in Iran, were defeated by popular insurrections, as a major insurgency emerged in the US client state of El Salvador. This was the same year a near-meltdown at the Three Mile Island nuclear power plant demonstrated to many that an environmentally destructive world order was in rapid and dangerous decline. But while expectations for radical political change rose, even spreading to the center of the liberal Democratic and Labor parties in the US, UK, and elsewhere in the industrial West, the grass-roots liberation struggles of militant labor unions, blacks, feminists, gay liberation activists, Chicanos, Asians, Native and African-Americans were entering a phase of factionalization and organizational decline. Aside from the sizable protests associated with the international anti-nuclear movement, and a smaller, though still tightly organized level of resistance to US military activity in Central America, the era in which the Left could boldly mobilize mass demonstrations was over. By the early to mid 1980s it was not capitalism but the New Left which had imploded as a powerful new conservatism spectacularly demonstrated its authority with Ronald Reagan's decertification of the striking Air Traffic Controllers Union in 1981, and Margaret Thatcher's breaking of the National Union of Mineworkers strike a few years later.

For Italian Autonomist Marxists like Virno and Antonio Negri, as much as for radical feminists, council communists, and similar anti-centralist Leftists including many of the artists represented in the PAD/D Archive, the failed revolution of the 1960s and 1970s was but another articulation of a longstanding desire to break with both the disciplinary routines of capitalism, and the socializing regimes of patriarchal authority. Neither the first, nor the last, this rebellious wave of rising expectations would reassert itself in the late 1990s, however, not before a new socio-economic regime emerged whose salient features, as we have seen, include the amplification of global "surplus" populations, labor redundancies, and individual risk, the implementation of novel workplace disciplines based on flexibility, "creativity," and individual entrepreneurship, and the enclosure of public spaces, histories, and even affects by private, corporate interests. Julian Stallabrass and Chin-tao Wu have written persuasively about the corrosive effects such "risk society" has had on artists and art institutions; Benjamin Buchloh branded the return of figuration in the 1980s a politically regressive backwards slide; and British critic John Walker went so far as to implicate arts administrators in the rightward shift, writing that "some curators who had supported political art in the 1970s welcomed a resurgence of traditional art forms," adding that the 1981 Royal Academy's exhibition *New Spirit of Painting* was an all-male affair that treated the feminist art movement as if it had never happened.[46] And yet as much as the 1980s epitomizes the defeat of Left politics and the rise of enterprise culture, it also bore witness to a new regime of socially oriented artistic interpretation. Henceforth, the aesthetic formalisms long associated with dominant post-war critics such as Clement Greenberg and Michael Fried were unconditionally replaced not only by so-called neo-expressionist painting, but also in general by an interpretive artistic vocabulary based on social history, cultural identity, even value to a specific community. So total was this transformation that today it is virtually *de rigueur* to attach some external meaning or narrative—national, biographical, communal, and on occasion political—to even the most abstract and autonomous of artworks. This "new," post-modern, post-'80s artistic paradigm was in fact long in the works, a culmination of what Grant Kester calls the "post-Greenbergian diaspora" of the 1960s and 1970s most visibly reflected by the political art of Hans Haacke, Leon Golub, and Martha Rosler, as well as the frequently performative work associated with Allan Kaprow, Suzanne Lacey, and Adrian Piper in the US, or with Joseph Beuys, Gilbert and George, and Viennese Actionism in Europe.[47] Nevertheless, it fell to the decade of the 1980s to demarcate this passage that, as one standard art historical reference book bemoans, infected the art world with a "deep unease," producing a feeling that "the old system which had governed the development of modernism almost from its beginning was starting to disintegrate."[48]

No doubt this process of disintegration was hastened along not by the specific radical art practices documented in the PAD/D Archive but by the very presence of its potentially unlimited scope and heterogeneous content. The haunting of the institution begins with what it shelters, often in spite of itself. Still, whether or not the deep unease signaled by the 1980s represents an oblique triumph of post-'68 cultural activism is a question that cannot be separated from the rise of the decade's unabashedly entrepreneurial art world, variously described by even its advocates as glitzy, careerist, and cynical.[49] "At the beginning of the 1980s, a dozen years after the cultural revolution of the 1960s, there was a boom in neo-expressionist painting that signaled "the end of the rich period of experimentation, analysis, and social engagement," writes Hans Haacke, who goes on to point out that with the election of Ronald Reagan and Margaret Thatcher and the dismantling of the welfare state many of these neo-expressionists also flourished in a climate of "mutually profitable collaboration." [50]And yet this was also the moment that content in one form or another, and often of a political or critically social nature, was allowed back into the corridors of the art world. Therefore, perhaps, it is O. K. Werckmeister's term "Citadel Culture" that most unambiguously summarizes the aesthetic imagination of an era typified by the recondite policies of Ronald Reagan and Margaret Thatcher, but also Brian Mulroney in Canada, and Roger Douglas in New Zealand among others.[51] "At the moment of their greatest 'economic success'," Werckmeister comments, democratic, industrial societies produced "a culture contrived to exhibit the conflicts of those societies in a form that keeps any judgment in abeyance."[52] Perhaps even more than the memory-haunted streets of West Berlin, it was the ersatz Bohemia of art, commerce, and gentrification that took root in New York City, which most clearly exemplifies the rise of this 1980s citadel aesthetic.

Cultural Enclosures and Trickle-Down Bohemia

Long known for its militant trade unions, Left-leaning politics, and non-conformist populace, New York City's fiscal crisis provided the new conservative movement with an opportunity to reign-in organized social dissent. This was accomplished primarily through a radical structural adjustment of the city's liberal welfare economy. According to David Harvey, New York in the late 1970s represents the first application of University of Chicago economist Milton Friedman's ultra-free-market or "neo-liberal" policies.[53] While the city's famed 1975 bailout was meant to foster a good business and tourist climate, its long-term agenda redirected public resources away from social services and into the private business sector while effectively draining support from housing activists and other community-based groups. In this sense, the neoliberalization of New York City was like a "velvet" version of Chile's brutal political and economic "normalization" in 1973. Just as Nixon's cut-off of financial aid to Allende's Leftist government set the stage for Pinochet's right-wing coup, so too were New York City's poorest neighborhoods systematically encircled, quarantined, and defunded by banks and other lending agencies. In many places this financial withholding or "redlining" literally reduced entire blocks to rubble. Essential services including schools, transportation, and hospitals were cut to a minimum. This sustained process of dispossession and demolition was followed by the restructuring of city life around notions of risk-taking and entrepreneurship, including real estate and financial speculation, but also cultural ventures that sent prices for contemporary art to new heights. The *I Love New York* campaign was launched to make the crime-plagued streets attractive to tourists, and by the mid 1980s businesses were also returning to the city, not, however, in the traditional blue-collar manufacturing area, but instead in the so-called F.I.R.E. sector: Finance, Insurance, and Real Estate. An incoming wave of young, white professionals, many of whose parents had fled the inner city for suburbia years earlier, moved to low-rent neighborhoods within close commuting distance from Wall Street. Like the shock troops of a new, "creative" working class, these incoming "gentry" absorbed and regurgitated the dissident culture they found in the city—including rap, hip-hop, graffiti, street art and break dancing—while simultaneously, though largely inadvertently, driving up rents, and pushing out poor and working-class residents. The PAD/D Archive is replete with references to the city's housing crisis in places like Spanish Harlem, the South Bronx, Hell's Kitchen, and the Lower East Side.

"Because of the mayor's lack of interest, we are abandoning parts of the city. We are the only city in the world that has ruins that are only 50 years old," intones one of several surrealist influenced photomontage flyers in a dossier labeled "Food Stamp Gallery," then managed by a now obscure artist named Vinny Salas. The artist's advertisements for his "gallery" consisted of impenetrably dense collages deriding the decline of city services, gentrification, and Mayor Ed Koch. One of these Max Ernst-like visual satires shows the smiling head of the Mayor grafted onto a hormone-pumped male torso touting an illegal handgun. Salas' caricature of Koch, who oversaw the first phase of New York's neoliberal structural adjustment, is also an allusion to Bernhard Goetz, the so-called "Subway Vigilante" who wounded several young men, crippling one, after they allegedly tried to rob him on the number 2 train. Goetz was carrying an unlicensed weapon and briefly served prison time. In a city beset by crime Goetz became an instant folk hero to conservative members of the National Rifle Association (NRA). Meanwhile, foreshadowing successor Rudy Giuliani's infamous praise for the motorist and off-duty officer who shot and wounded a homeless "squeegee-man," Koch sided with Goetz's acquittal on murder charges (though he denounced his vigilantism), even as the Mayor simultaneously condemned the indictment of a police officer who shot to death an unarmed African-American woman, Eleanor Bumpers, as she was being evicted for falling four months behind in her rent. Passionately manic, the forgotten collagist's humorous juxtapositions of high and low cultural references also carries over to the amalgamated title "Food Stamp Gallery," insofar as it fuses the opulence of high culture to a government relief program. In fact, the actual "gallery" was a street-level window display case located in "Spanish" Harlem on Manhattan's Upper East Side. No doubt Salas' fanciful conceit was also a parody directed twelve subway stops south at the pseudo-Bohemian fanfare known as the "East Village Art Scene."

Real estate speculators began promoting a portion of the crime-ridden Lower East Side—which was known to its large Latino population as Loisaida—under the moniker East Village.[54] Not an entirely new invention, but one aimed at attracting more affluent renters through an association with the safer Greenwich Village. Hard hit by decades of financial disinvestment the streets of the Lower East Side resembled a semiotic war zone. Tattered wall posters covered landlord-abandoned buildings. Made brittle from daily exposure to weather and layered applications of wet announcements, this "image brawl," as PAD/D members Miriam Brofsky and Eva Cockroft once described it, formed a nearly illegible pelt of faded type and bleached colors publicizing Punk bands such as the Meat Puppets, Big Noise, and the Slits, or calling for protests against the CIA, or simply staging notices from people offering services, selling off possessions, or looking for rideshares to other cities.[55] Here and there a local schizophrenic ranted in fine point type not far from an equally feverish-looking flyer by Jenny Holzer, one of countless young artists drawn to the cultural and visual bedlam of the area. By the mid 1980s the East Village had not only became a favored destination for the new F.I.R.E workforce, but enterprising commercial art galleries garrisoned themselves within this ethnically diverse, though financially impoverished neighborhood, all of which added inflationary pressure on residential and commercial rents. At its height in the mid 1980s, the so-called East Village Art Scene consisted of over 100 art dealers primarily fixated on paintings featuring an assortment of cartoon characters, graffiti, and pornographic imagery. "The American dream's dark underside, its evil twin, its inner child run amok," is how one contemporary curator later described the alleged youthful subversiveness of East Village Art.[56] Outwardly, this campy Bohemianism seemed exactly the opposite to neoconservative pieties concerning private property, sexual abstinence, and family values.

On the one hand, this new art scene was like a seductively lurid counterpart to the glitzy *I Love New York* campaign. It attracted its own congregation of niche businesses especially in the fashion, food service, and leisure industries. With

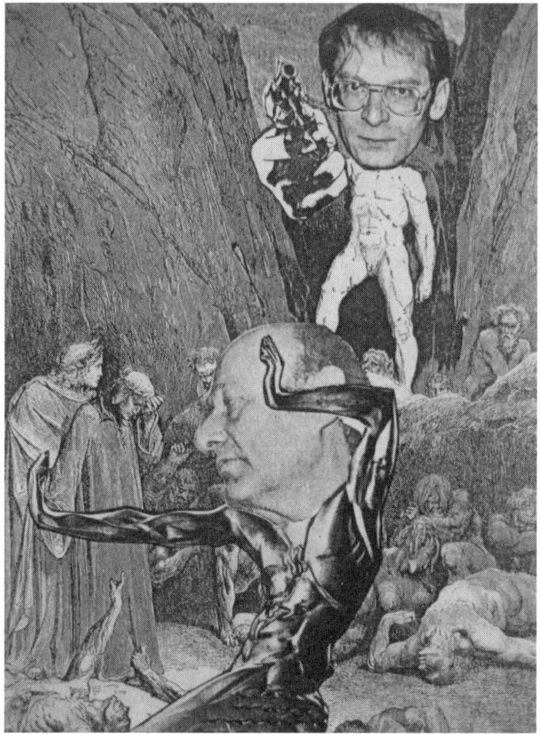

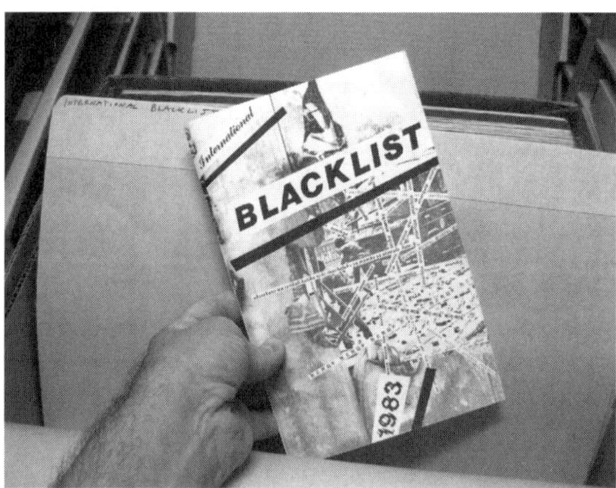

A photocopied collage (top) by Vincent Salas, founder of the Food Stamp Gallery, shows New York City Mayor Ed Koch as a dancing Anubis strutting before subway vigilante gunman Bernhard Goetz; and International Blacklist (bottom), a directory of anarchist organizations published by the Anti-Authoritarian Studies & Blacklist Group from Berkeley, CA, both from the early 1980s and just two of the thousands of items stored in miscellaneous uncataloged materials that make up part of the PAD/D Archive at the MoMA in NYC. http://arcade.nyarc.org/search~S8. Images courtesy Vincent Salas and Gregory Sholette.

capital flowing from Japanese and German art collectors and an unprecedented expansion of art museums underway in the United States, the demand for fresh artistic products had never been greater. On the other hand, it was a new cultural paradigm turned profoundly inward on itself in which the performance of "deviancy" appeared radical, and the avant-garde's long relationship with Left politics virtually abandoned. But this citadel culture had its detractors, including the late Craig Owens, as well as critics Rosalyn Deutsche and Cara Gendel Ryan who wrote prophetically in 1984 that the East Village Art Scene was financed by big capital as a "war of position against an impoverished and increasingly isolated local population."[57] The rise of the "revanchist city" in the aftermath of this battle is taken up in the next chapter. Meanwhile, a few artists, like Salas, identified enough with those being displaced to critically engage with this new cultural franchise and the politics it represented.

A binder in the PAD/D Archive documents one group of artists who lodged their protest against the Koch administration in the early hours of January 1, 1980, by squatting a "warehoused," city-owned building on Delancy Street and installing an exhibition denouncing landlords and local gentrification just hours before police shut their intervention down later that same day. The Real Estate Show would eventually became a local cultural center known as ABC No Rio, but not until after a well-publicized visit by German art superstar Joseph Beuys shamed the Mayor into providing the artists with a venue for their critique.[58] Other artist-run associations including Collaborative Projects (COLAB), Group Material, and Fashion Moda (located in the South Bronx) exhibited work critical of urban policies favoring the wealthy and so-called "reverse white flight," although more often than not this protest was expressed indirectly, through thematic art exhibitions focused on hip-hop culture, suburban sensibilities, or the fate of "homeless" animals living on city streets. Gentrification and urban dissolution were also recurring themes in the paintings and collages of Anton Van Dalen, Jane Dickson, David Wojnarowicz, and John Feckner, whose South Bronx street stencils "DECAY" and "BROKEN PROMISES" spray-painted on an abandoned tenement building were later appropriated in an act of *counter-détournement* by Ronald Reagan's presidential campaign—standing in front of Feckner's accusatory graffiti, the soon to be elected governor of California railed against the failed urban policies of "tax and spend" liberals. Published on the cover of the *New York Times* this photo-op revealed a signature trait of citadel culture, the enclosing and annexing of indigenous, sometimes illegal forms of resistance such as stencils, graffiti, and street art for commercial or politically reactionary interests.

PAD/D launched its own critical détournement of the East Village Art Scene, *Not For Sale* (NFS), in April of 1984, "throwing up" four illegal street art galleries: The Discount Salon, Another Gallery, The Leona Helmsley Gallery and, somewhat prophetically, the Guggenheim Downtown. Christened with cans of Banner-Red and Krylon spray paint this quartet of fictive exhibition venues were in reality the disheveled walls of several derelict buildings, temporarily commandeered by a group of interventionist artists who sought to draw local residents, including artists and art dealers, into a public debate about their role in the gentrification of the neighborhood. The "exhibitions" consisted of illegally posted hand-painted posters, photocopies, and silk-screen prints decrying the displacement of low-income residents while calling on artists to become involved in local efforts to prevent real estate speculation. New York's Mayor Ed Koch is pictured by PAD/D member Jerry Kearns dancing as the city burns behind him; a two-meter tall, hand-cut poster by an unknown artist shows a hydra-headed speculator who appeared to be stalking local real estate options; and a colorful screen graphic by Michael Corris and Mary Garvin extolled squatting or communally refurbishing buildings deserted by landlords (the majority of properties on the Lower East Side in the early 1980s had been commandeered by the city because of non-payment of taxes by building owners). One smaller street flyer by Ed Eisenberg was entitled "Reaganomic Galleries." Its message sought to link the President's infamous trickle-down economics—that first, failed attempt to positively brand American neoliberalism—with the ersatz Bohemianism already emerging around the alphabet streets South of 14th Street and East of the Bowery. The NFS Project—which takes up several document binders in the PAD/D Archive—was inspired in part by Loraine Leeson and Peter Dunn's Docklands Community Poster Project in London, another anti-gentrification public work with records in the collection. Officially, the NFS Project opened at the "Guggenheim Downtown," the windowless façade of a vacant tenement on the corner of 10th Street at Tompkins Square Park, itself the site for numerous clashes with authorities since the mid 1800s. On hand were local housing activists to register voters and encourage neighborhood resistance to gentrification. Four years later, Tompkins Square's homeless, gathering in ever greater numbers as rents rose in the city, became both audience and participants when Polish artist Krzysztof Wodiczko rolled out his homeless vehicle into the park: a mobile unit for sleeping, storage, and cooking. Months later the park would become the site of what the *New York Times* described as a "police riot." By 1988 the city's homeless population had reached over 30,000, and Tompkins Square Park had become a tent-city filled with hundreds of literally *dispossessed* New Yorkers.[59] One August evening this encampment, along with groups of anarchist protesters, punks, and skinheads also "squatting" in the park, was forcibly evicted by police in a mêlée that spilled violently into nearby streets and businesses.[60] Police were videotaped attacking not only their initial targets from the park, but people eating and shopping in the posh restaurants and shops of the gentrified East Village. After the riots the park was closed for a complete renovation that brought it more into line with the ever more prosperous neighborhood surrounding it. For both activists as well as the new "gentry," the Tompkins Square event came to represent a pivotal turning point in New York's future.[61] During this four-year interval between the homeless evictions and the reopening of the refurbished park, East Village artist David Wojnarowicz had died of AIDS, graffiti writer SAMO turned art world mega-star Jean-Michel Basquiat had died of a drug overdose, and most of the art galleries had vanished, largely victims of escalating commercial rents they had helped inflate. At the same time neither PAD/D nor its archive of political art, any more than the exhibition *Committed to Print*, had done anything to slow down the rise of an increasingly global citadel culture that, true to its paradoxical nature, even created a modest opening for a representational handful of "political artists" within its new, entrepreneurial Bohemianism.

The Crypt

The documents within the archive effectively "speak the law" as Derrida implores, establishing an economy of interpretation that falls under the regulation of the household (*oikos*), and "its laws of domesticity."[62] Likewise, the very *archivalization* of post-'68 radical art by the various museum households of the art establishment could have only been made possible once any actual threat to institutional authority had fully passed, that is to say, once the spirit of a militant, confrontational Left culture with its promises of autonomy, democratic transparency, and collective solidarity, had fallen into irreparable ruin. And yet this familiar space of the household, be it an archive, museum, library, or the entire cultural economy, is not just the site of domestic disputes and struggles—internecine battles over art world turf or resistance to patriarchal and racial privilege—it is also where ghosts inevitably return, unannounced and unwanted. A significant question therefore asserts itself: What role does such a rebel archive play within an institution such as the MoMA, especially given the fact that PAD/D's repository of social and political art was premised on animosity towards institutional authority itself? For if on the one hand the museum's loving interment testifies to the generosity of the institution, it also reveals on the other hand a capacity to exert power "all the way down," into the finest of details and historical shadows. At the same time, the very presence of such an archive, with its prodigious index of forgotten but self-selected names, projects, groups, actions, and so forth, attests to the fact that opposition to established cultural hierarchies is not in the least uncommon. Still other factors come into play, including the familial nature of this particular entombment by the MoMA Library. Whatever internal disputes or expectations the acquisition of the PAD/D Archive may have generated within the museum remains unknown; however, we might read this minor, generally unnoticed supplement to the proper historical canon as an internal mark or bruise alluding to a far larger corpus of excluded cultural production. As curator and critic Simon Sheikh has perceptively observed, institutional memory requires the omission of certain subjects, not because of willful acts of exodus or rebellion, as many artists would like to think, but because "expulsions at the very center of institutions ... allow them to institutionalize?"[63] Which is to say the supplemental, even redundant archive of radical art does not belong to some fantastic world apart, but is instead fully inscribed within the institution's ideological architecture as a necessary if mute presence filled with micro-histories, resistant practices, and partially submerged "outlaw" memories. One thing is clear, in the intervening years since, no exhibition as politically charged as *Committed to Print* was ever again attempted by the museum.

The Grin

In the weeks leading up to the May 1968 events in Paris, filmmaker Chris Marker recalls a meeting with Louis Althusser. "For him, as for others, Revolution was in the air, and had to be, like the grin of the Cheshire Cat." Marker adds that while the brilliant Marxist theorist would always see that grin, "He wouldn't (nor would anyone) ever see the Cat."[64] Of the scores of materials and documents delivered to PAD/D between 1980 and 1988, the only submission rejected by the Archive Committee was a folder containing several woodcut prints of house cats. Sometimes however, a grin is all one has to work with.

3

HISTORY THAT DISTURBS THE PRESENT

There is no such thing as society.
Margaret Thatcher

Queer Signs

The Meatpacking District in Manhattan stretches just a few blocks south and wide along the Hudson River near 14th Street. In the late nineteenth century the area was home to several hundred slaughterhouses and meat processing plants. About 100 years later the area was largely abandoned to black market activities including illegal drugs and transsexual prostitution. Throughout the 1970s fiscal crisis these shadow economies generated their own set of rules and cultural meanings, as well as an alternative historical narrative transmitted largely by word of mouth. One of these counter-histories involved Marsha P. Johnson, an African-American drag-queen and transgendered social activist. According to available records, Johnson had taken part in the legendary Stonewall Inn Uprising of 1969, in which gay people rebelled against constant police intimidation during several days of street riots in Greenwich Village. In the 1970s she co-founded along with Sylvia Rivera an informal organization known as Street Transvestite Action Revolutionaries, or STAR, which aimed to assist young and frequently homeless transgendered runaways, many of whom turned to prostitution for a living. Along with providing runaways with shelter and food, STAR also put pressure on mainstream gay and lesbian groups to recognize the civic rights of transgendered people.[1] Johnson remained socially active until 1992 when, on the morning after that year's annual Gay Pride Parade, her dead body was discovered floating in the Hudson River. Officially, the New York Police Department listed her death as suicide. Unofficially, according to members of the transgendered prostitute community in New York City, Johnson's death was the result of gay bashing, a physical assault by several men that reportedly took place the night before the parade.

Two years later a group of cultural activists brandishing a temporary city permit mounted a pink triangular marker on the pier near to where Johnson's body had been found. Printed on this sign was a tersely worded eulogy to the drag

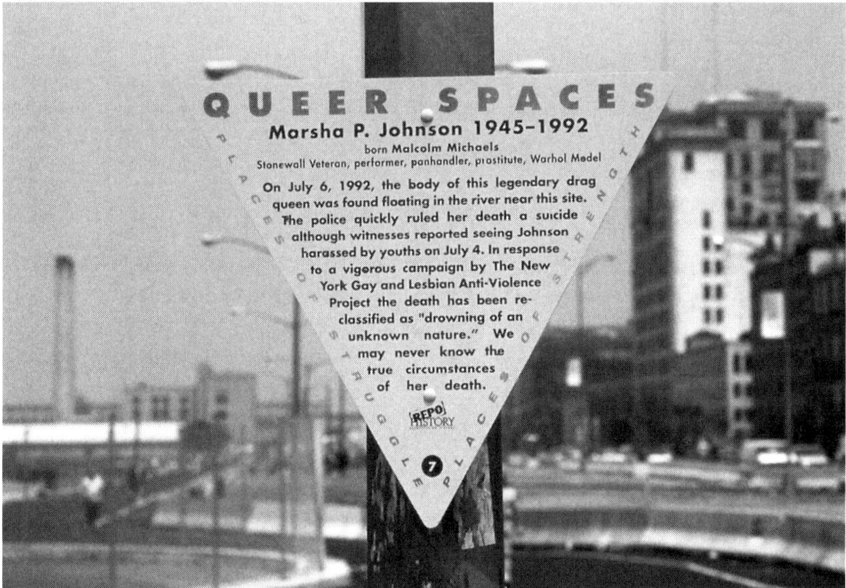

1994 REPOhistory street sign memorial for transgendered political activist Marsha P. Johnson (1945–92), located in the Meat Market area of Manhattan, one of nine placards making up the Queer Spaces project sponsored by the Storefront for Art and Architecture, NYC. Image courtesy Jim Costanzo.

queen, describing her activism amongst the Meatpacking District's transgendered subculture as well as her untimely death. The rose-colored testimonial's presence was unusual, though unspectacular. It was a relatively small, text-covered object nestled among New York's dense network of signs regulating parking, traffic, city utilities, and the movement of pedestrians. At the same time, it's function was not regulatory. The "solemn" tone and serious-looking typography suggested an official historical marker. However, its shape and color undermined this reading because most official historic preservation takes the form of substantial bronze plaques or figurative statuary commemorating civic, military, or political leaders. It was a "queer sign" that commemorated an individual few had ever heard of and a city that was no longer visible. As though from the grave it summoned to light something missing, forgotten, and, in Johnson's case, literally discarded. Its phantom jurisdiction briefly haunted one small corner of a gentrifying Meatpacking District, calling forth an *other* city, a spectral city, with its own, unremembered rules and regulations, myths and memories.

Johnson's temporary memorial was one of nine similar historical markers—all triangular, all pink—attached to lamp-posts and traffic posts around Manhattan's Greenwich Village between June 18 and August 31, 1994. The project was entitled

Queer Spaces. It coincided with the 25th anniversary of the Stonewall Uprising and was the second in a series of historical public sign projects organized by REPOhistory, a varied group of artists and activists whose primary conceit was to act as the self-appointed amateur historians of those who lacked visibility within public spaces where official commemorative statues and bronze plaques held sway.[2] One pink sign was mounted near the former offices of the Daughters of Bilitis, a lesbian political advocacy group founded in the 1950s; another plaque was located at the corner of Wall Street and Broadway where a militant demonstration against pharmaceutical company profiteering took place in 1987 and signaled the formation of ACT UP, or the AIDS Coalition to Unleash Power. Further uptown, at the site of the former Everard building, a triangular placard described the pre-AIDS-era Turkish-style bathhouse as part of "a network of gay bathhouses that were an integral part of the sexual life, folklore, and economy of New York's gay community."[3] Nestled among New York's dense network of signs regulating parking, traffic, city utilities, and the movement of pedestrians REPOhistory's pink triangles appeared to offer their own set of laws, as if an additional set of instructions were necessary for everyday transit to work, home, leisure, shopping or, perhaps more to the point, as if passersby required some kind of supplemental information in order to fully grasp how and why they were in this particular city, at this specific time and place.

REPOhistory was initially informed by multicultural readings of lost, forgotten, or suppressed narratives, writes group member Jim Costanzo, after which it sought to remap this information directly onto "the public sphere with the goal of using history to comment on contemporary social issues from progressive perspectives."[4] Fredric Jameson has proposed that such cognitive mapping helps situate a fragmented sense of identity within a shifting post-modern landscape. In a sense, REPOhistory momentarily did this by writing directly on the skin of a gentrifying New York using *détourned* versions of the city's own semaphores, signs, and rules of conduct as its medium. Between 1989 and 2000 the group produced six historical public marking projects, three in New York City, as well as two in Atlanta, Georgia, and one in Houston, Texas. All were similarly pragmatic: a series of traffic sign sized panels were attached to a signpost or lamp-post. An image was printed on one side, a text on the other. For each sign a different individual or individuals researched the specific site to be marked using guidelines provided by the collective. Initially intended to be an illegal, guerrilla art intervention, REPOhistory eventually obtained nine-month-long installation permits from municipal authorities for most of its projects. Once in place, a printed map plotting the location of each site-specific marker was freely distributed through a variety of institutions: city agencies, art galleries, and the US postal system. In addition, a press agent was commissioned to publicize the installations, thus expanding the informational range for each project. The group's projects were not only site-specific, they simultaneously aimed to re-articulate the flattened temporality of the post-industrial city. REPOhistory's critical theory of site specificity, therefore, was realized at two levels: first as a re-narration of a given place using documents, oral histories, public records, and so forth, and second as an interrogation of standard historical representation. The importance of the latter, de-mystifying approach is summarized by group member Lisa Maya Knauer who points out that "histories didn't just exist or emerge by magic; they are produced, reproduced and contested—in various arenas, including public school curricula, museum displays."[5] However, compared with other public artworks of the 1990s, REPOhistory's projects appear understated and prosaic, as if the group were possessed by an archive, which demanded that its content be permitted to "speak for itself." Furthermore, while the *New York Times*, *Village Voice*, *New York Newsday*, and other mass circulation newspapers did report on REPOhistory's work at the time, and in several instances reprinting the entire project map, few art-related journals or publications even noticed the group's work. [6]

In the year of REPOhistory's founding, sculptor Richard Serra's provocatively austere *Tilted Arc* was de-installed from the Federal Plaza in downtown Manhattan following public controversy.[7] Four years later, in 1992, as the group launched its first sign-project in downtown Manhattan, Jeff Koons' four-story topiary *Puppy* towered over pedestrians in the town of Bad Arolsen, Germany. One year later Rachel Whiteread's *House* stirred up local opposition in East London when the artist transformed a unit of actual public habitation slated for demolition into a ghostly plaster monument. Perhaps most dramatically, in 1995 artists Christo and Jean-Claude wrapped the entire Reichstag in fabric shortly before it resumed functioning as the parliament of a recently reunified Germany. Each of these large-scale projects conspicuously announced their aesthetic disposition through the use of improbable materials or dramatic shifts in scale. By contrast, REPOhistory's first public installation was entitled simply the *Lower Manhattan Sign Project* (LMSP), and took place in Manhattan's Financial District in 1992. It was intended to function as a critical counterpoint to the Christopher Columbus Quincentennial celebration of that same year. Focusing on the city's multiethnic and working-class history, the group's alternative street signs temporarily marked the location of the city's first slave market, the offices of a successful nineteenth-century abortionist named Madame Restell, the contour of the island's pre-Columbian coast line, the site of an alleged slave rebellion in 1741, and the historic visit by Nelson Mandela to the city just two years prior to the LMSP installation. Near City Hall the group marked the site where pacifist demonstrators were arrested in the 1950s for refusing to take part in civil defense drills; nearby a sign commemorated where radical New York Congressman Vito Marantonio had collapsed of a heart attack in 1954; a few hundred feet away another sign marked the location of a public address by abolitionist and feminist Frances "Fanny" Wright, who proposed deliberate miscegenation as a solution to racism.

Much of the visibility for this project can be traced to a little-known figure within the New York City Department of Transportation (NYCDOT) who issued REPOhistory its installation permit. Frank J. Addeo was known "off the record" as a strong supporter of public artworks, including the seriously humorous street signs of Ilona Granet that cautioned men to "curb" their animal instincts, as well as more controversial projects such as Gran Fury's 1990 street-sign project that read, in part, "10,000 people with AIDS are homeless. NYC's cost effective solution: DO NOTHING." But Addeo's relatively informal approach to granting artists access to city streets would soon become a casualty of increased governmental supervision during the administration of Republican Mayor Rudolph Giuliani. In the meantime, it was David Dinkins who governed New York. A staunch Democratic Party loyalist, he ran on the promise of reducing racial tension and described New York as a "gorgeous mosaic" of ethnic diversity. One measure of this illusive goal can be read by REPOhistory's official reception. The day the LMSP opened the group received an honorary scroll from the City pronouncing June 27, 1992, "REPOhistory Day."[8] Dinkins remains the only African-American Mayor of the city to date. All subsequent REPOhistory projects would be carried out under the administration of former prosecutor Rudolph "Rudy" Giuliani, whose anti-crime, anti-taxes platform overwhelmed Dinkins and the liberal Democratic Party in the election of 1994, the year of *Queer Spaces*.[9]

Not long into Giuliani's second term, REPOhistory was ready to launch a new street-sign project, this time in collaboration with the not-for-profit organization New York Lawyers for the Public Interest (NYLPI). Founded in 1976, NYLPI's mission is "to serve the legal needs of underserved, underrepresented New Yorkers and their communities."[10] The resulting REPOhistory/NYLPI collaboration was entitled Civil Disturbances: Battles for Justice in New York City: 20 graphic street signs commemorating specific legal precedents that literally shaped the fabric of life in New York City as much as the "streets on which we walk and the buildings in which we live and work."[11] But in spite of the group's previous record of obtaining temporary installation permits from the NYCDOT this time the agency refused REPOhistory's request for permission to install Civil Disturbances. Giuliani's "Quality of Life" campaign seemed bent on systematically erasing traces of the New York REPOhistory struggled to remember, as if eliminating an invisible legion of ghosts was as essential to neoliberal reforms as was balancing municipal budgets, or providing tax breaks to wealthy landlords and corporations. Meanwhile, holed up inside City Hall, the Giuliani administration appeared increasingly besieged by journalists and advocates of free speech who pursued charges of censorship and political authoritarianism against the Mayor. Indeed, by 1998 six lawsuits had been filed over denial of access to information about municipal budgets, real estate deals, conditions in homeless shelters, freedom of speech violations, and city housing and law enforcement policies.[12] By comparison, REPOhistory's art installation was a relatively modest excavation of the past. A series of street signs—by now the group's signature medium—were to be installed at 25 specific locations in Manhattan, Brooklyn, and the Bronx. Each site marked by REPOhistory related to a different moment in the City's legal history: a corner where street artists were arrested for selling un-permitted merchandise, a downtown courthouse where battered women filed petitions for increased protection, a Greenwich Village co-op sued by AIDS sufferers for trying to close the building's first floor medical clinic, a Federal courtroom where welfare recipients collectively regained benefits lost under the Reagan administration, a street where Chinatown labor activists stopped real estate speculators from further gentrifying the neighborhood, the entrance of the Empire State Building where wheelchair-bound disabled people chained themselves to doors, demanding access to sidewalks, parks, and public buildings, as well as multiple locations in low-income neighborhoods and public housing projects where Latino and African-American victims failed to have murder charges brought against violent police officers. In an atmosphere of eroding civil liberties the corporate law firm Debevoise & Plimpton entered into a series of discussions with City attorneys on behalf of REPOhistory. One year earlier the Giuliani administration lost a class action suit brought against the City by street artists. The precedent set by Lederman/Bery et al. versus City of NY, a case that REPOhistory included in its Civil Disturbances sign project, underscored the First Amendment rights of free speech for artists. The decision was a stunning loss for Giuliani, whose so-called "Quality of Life" campaign hinged on regulating behavior by enclosing and micro-managing urban spaces. Possibly fearing another defeat, the City finally withdrew opposition to Civil Disturbances, and the signs were successfully installed on August 4, 1998, about ten weeks later than anticipated. Nevertheless, this victory over City Hall did not end censorship of the project, which was subsequently carried out by local landlords, politicians, and businesses.

Almost as soon as the project was installed several individual signs "disappeared" from public view. Among these was "REPOhistorian" Janet Koenig's sign that documented the Empire State Building's prolonged non-compliance with the Americans with Disabilities Act (removed by building managers); Marina Gutierrez's work critiquing housing discrimination by the City against Puerto Rican families in her Brooklyn neighborhood (taken down by local politicians); and a REPOhistory street marker designed by former Archigram member William Menking detailing the illegal demolition of several, low-income hotels just blocks away from the "Disneyfied" post-1990s Times Square. Owner and art collector Harry Macklow had the lot cleared one night, later selling the land to a London-based international luxury hotel and resort chain. That corporation built its flagship New York hotel on the site. Today the Millennium Premier offers an

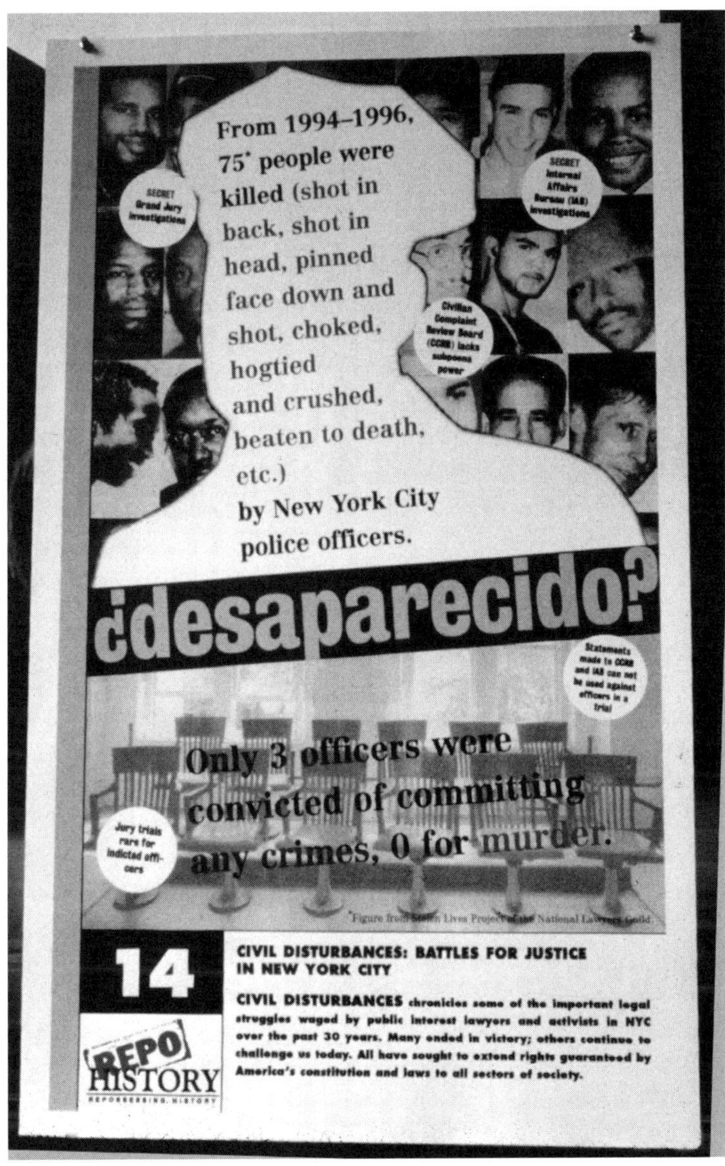

1998 REPOhistory street sign by artists Jenny Polak and David Thorne, describing the inadequate investigation of criminal activity by New York City police officers for committing violent acts against residents. The sign was one of 20 graphic markers making up the project Civil Disturbances: Battles for Justice in New York City (1998–99), which was initially delayed by several months when City officials objected to public works highlighting the use of legal action to expand the rights of homeless people, workers, children, and the disabled among others. Image courtesy Tom Klem.

"Oasis" where high-energy service provides a new level of self-indulgence—or at least this is the message that accompanied a full-page advertisement in the *New York Times* soon after the hotel opened. Rendered in a retro, 1930s drawing style, three chicly dressed individuals, a man and two women, sip cocktails and presumably discuss business. REPOhistory's public invocation of the unknown, nearly indigent men and women forced to flee the wrecking ball that made way for this grand new establishment was not well received. The managers of the Millennium removed the legally permitted sign and then delivered a letter to NYLPI threatening legal action if any attempt was made to re-install the artwork either near the hotel, or anywhere else in the City. REPOhistory was divided over how to respond to this threat. Ultimately the group's temporary NYCDOT permit ended before action was taken. Nevertheless, anxieties raised by the possibility of legal confrontation undermined group cohesion and revealed just how fragile cultural activism had become in New York since the days of, say, the Art Workers' Coalition or the Black Emergency Cultural Coalition. REPOhistory carried out one last project in 2000 using the postal system and Internet to distribute its graphics. Much to the chagrin of local public art organizations the Civil Disturbances debacle led the City to close loopholes used to gain installation permits. Many of the more established public art organizations in the City were displeased with this imposition of rules and irritated with REPOhistory for triggering the changes. Nevertheless, it is apparent that the late 1990s was a moment when democratic access to urban space was being curtailed or eliminated in New York in favor of increased privatization and police management. Needless to say, much of the public art installed since—for example the enormous 2005 Gates project in Central Park by Christo and Jeanne-Claude—has sought to deliver a strictly non-confrontational, non-content oriented "aesthetic" experience.

Queer Spaces

What was distinct about REPOhistory's archival recovery projects is that most of them took place just as those who claimed to stand for law and order—Mayor Giuliani and his administration—let loose upon the city a wave of free market, real estate based anarchy that simultaneously sought to "disappear" any trace of the hustlers, homeless, street artists, activists, radicals, union organizers, and anyone else not sympathetic with the new economic and social order. Maintaining the appearance of control became of uppermost importance to the new regime. According to the Mayor and his police commissioner William J. Bratton, stepping up misdemeanor arrests, banishing the homeless from streets and public spaces, and repairing damaged building façades would inextricably lead to the lowering or elimination of more serious criminal offenses.[13] Initially this so-called "Broken Windows" program was directed towards reducing such violent offences as rape and murder. New York City police were given broad search and seizure powers as petty criminal violations jumped dramatically. But before long this panoptic management of public space expanded even further as thousands of surveillance cameras were installed at street level throughout the city, not only by law enforcement agencies, but also by landlords and private businesses.[14] "Freedom is about authority," insisted Giuliani in one of his first appearances before the press after being elected Mayor. "Freedom is about the willingness of every single human being to cede to lawful authority a great deal of discretion about what you do and how you do it."[15] Hand and glove with increasing top-down jurisdiction over urban behavior went the deconstructive processes of economic privatization and deregulation, because only upon the ash of a ruined social welfare state could the revanchist city come into being.

Giuliani had served under Ronald Reagan as an Associate Attorney General. Once elected Mayor of New York he set in place his own form of neoliberal restructuring that including increased private management of public programs and deep budgets cuts for sanitation, social services, and education. The Mayor also slashed commercial rent taxes on corporations willing to move to Wall Street, sold the city's television and radio station, and sought to reduce the City's unionized workforce by 7 percent as he eliminated affirmative action rules established by Dinkins so that city contracts would assist businesses owned by women and minorities.[16] Many of these policies were an accelerated continuation of the bailout program of the late 1970s carried out under Mayor Ed Koch, but which had been slowed somewhat under Mayor Dinkins. According to David Harvey, who extends an argument first made by urban theorist William Tabb, it was New York City in the mid 1970s that became the test site for a radical economic and political makeover in the United States that "effectively pioneered the construction of a neoliberal answer" to post-war economic problems, including the over-accumulation of capital, falling rates of profit, and competition from emerging markets around the globe. Significantly adding to this reconstruction challenge was how to maintain discipline over labor at a time of political disenfranchisement and even overt rebellion.[17] As we have seen in the previous chapter, key to ending the City's lingering fiscal crisis was transforming New York into an appealing location for corporate headquarters as well as a desirable place of residence for the wealthy and for upper-middle-class professionals employed in F.I.R.E—the finance, insurance, and real estate sector. To help secure this workforce, who were to replace the lost blue-collar manufacturing base of previous decades, New York City adopted a global cities strategy.[18] According to sociologist Alex S. Vitale, this meant attracting international capital by adopting "fiscal strategies consistent with the ideology of structural adjustment, which called for a hollowing out of the welfare state in favor of market mechanisms."[19] Financially depleted neighborhoods on the Lower East Side, Hell's Kitchen, and the Meatpacking District were targeted by waves of real estate development. Public housing was privatized, rents skyrocketed, and unions were pressured to give up hard-won benefits. If outwardly these neighborhoods aimed for a scrubbed-clean but superficially Bohemian aesthetic, in reality they resembled suburban gated communities where the poor and traditional working classes were systematically excluded through a combination of high rents, privatized public space, electronic surveillance, and, when all else failed, aggressive police tactics. By Giuliani's second term, places like the Meatpacking District were no longer social and economic hinterlands. Now four-star restaurants, high-end fashion showrooms, and commercial art galleries moved in, some with franchises in London and Berlin. Effectively, "legitimate" business interests catering to the increasingly well-heeled urban gentry were replacing an illicit street economy of recycled goods, drugs, and transsexual prostitution. Not without sarcasm Saskia Sassen calls these makeovers the "glamour zones" of global cities, while Neil Smith acidly describes them simply as the "revanchist city."[20] Beneath its cosmopolitan shell a vengeful provincialism stands guard against the return of any visible symptoms of the "failed" liberal welfare state of old: homelessness, graffiti, illegal drugs, prostitution, and general signs of disorder. Tellingly, and ironically, the 1990s actually produced more homeless New Yorkers than had the 1980s, although unlike the previous decade these men, women, and children were no longer a palpable presence in parks, streets, or subways. However, by criminalizing such everyday acts as sleeping in public, and by increasing penalties for loitering, the City effectively made its homeless problem "disappear."[21]

Invisibles

After leaving office Giuliani formed a security-consulting firm known as Giuliani Partners, LLC (and police commissioner Bratton formed his own Bratton Group, LLC). Among other clients was Mexico City, where officials were introduced to a series of "Quality of Life" and "Broken Windows" urban crime-prevention tactics similar to those used in New York City, including the elimination of panhandlers and "squeegee men," as well as control of graffiti.[22] The widely publicized failure of Giuliani's program in Mexico City not only suggests that crime reduction in 1990s New York City was not solely attributable to increased policing and control of public space, but also raises doubts about the role of corporations and wealthy individuals in what were previously considered public institutions and democratically controlled policies. After all, Mayor Rudolph Giuliani was merely an overt symptom of a far more sweeping ideological shift towards deregulation and the privatization that, ironically, was never as free market based as its neoliberal proponents claimed. In practice, the economic and social restructuring of post-industrial cities involved a great deal of corporate welfare, including massive subsidies to real estate and financial firms as well as culture producers such as "design houses, advertisers, publishing, and music and television production."[23] Meanwhile, the disappearance of unwelcome *signs* of public disorder and class division within New York and other socio-economically overhauled global cities—from graffiti and broken windows to panhandlers, "squeegee men," and cross-dressing prostitutes—coincided with a marked interest by contemporary artists and their followers in representing those marginalized populations forgotten or suppressed by mainstream institutions and their official histories. A singular case in point was the 1992 installation *Mining The Museum* by artist Fred Wilson at the Maryland Historical Society in Baltimore. Invited by the museum to intervene in their collection, the Afro-American/Caribbean artist juxtaposed slave shackles, Klan hoods, and tribal African weapons with colonial-era pewter mugs, nineteenth-century perambulators, and miniature naval sloops. By literally staging a return of the repressed, the exhibition drew an unprecedented audience including many from the surrounding African-American neighborhood who had previously ignored the museum.[24] The following year, German artist Lothar Baumgarten inscribed the interior spiral of Frank Lloyd Wright's iconic Guggenheim Museum with a string of North American indigenous tribes, and Hans Haacke made an explicit reference to the Venice Biennale's links to 1930s fascism by demolishing the floor of the German pavilion. Several years earlier neo-Nazis had fire-bombed Haacke's ironic memorial to Austrian fascism *And You Were Victorious After All* in Graz. Similar mnemonic interventions took place in public space. Native American artist Alan Michelson arranged a circle of stones in downtown Manhattan to mark the perimeter of a now absent Collect Pond, once a source of fresh water in New Amsterdam, but soon polluted from chemical dumping by nineteenth-century tanneries, slaughterhouses, and breweries. Similar attempts at prodding public memory were carried out by Dennis Adams in New York, with his neo-constructivist bus shelter memorializing the state-sponsored execution of Jewish "atom spies" Julius and Ethel Rosenberg, and in Europe with *The Algerian Folie*, a flatbed truck Adams fitted out with images invoking French colonialism and installed outside the Centre Georges Pompidou in a gentrifying Paris of 1989. Several years later Christian Boltanski produced a melancholic reference to the Holocaust by stacking lost luggage on towers of steel shelving inside New York's Grand Central Station. Meanwhile, Chilean-born artist Alfredo Jaar forced an increasingly global museum-going audience to confront photographic portraits of anonymous gold miners in South America; Polish artist Krzysztof Wodiczko projected images related to historical and political violence on buildings and public memorials; and in one inconspicuous corner of Hamburg, Germany, Jochen Gerz and his wife Esther Shalev-Gerz's *Monument Against Fascism* gradually descended below ground to completely vanish from sight between 1986 and 1993.

Appropriating museum displays, monuments, and train station lobbies were not the only tactics of these archival interventions. Like REPOhistory some artists made use of the authorial power vested in administrative signage in an effort to subvert orthodox history. Beginning in the mid 1980s, indigenous artist Hokeayevi Edgar Heap of Birds began erecting his own metal signs, placards, and billboards that made reference, sometimes enigmatically, to the erasure of Native Peoples from the face of the North American landscape. Between 1984 and 1995 architectural historian Dolores Hayden and collaborators produced *The Power of Place: Urban Landscapes as Public History* about the little-known histories of Black sharecroppers, women laborers, Chicanos, and Mexican Americans in the Los Angeles valley; and on Chicago's South Side, artist Daniel Martinez produced a series of metal signs that, together with a street carnival, publicly memorialized the labor and ethnic history of the city's Maxwell Street market, once teeming with African-American vendors and now packed with upscale condos. The project took place under the umbrella of *Culture in Action*, a city-wide art installation organized by Mary Jane Jacob in 1993 that also included 100 small boulders arranged by Suzanne Lacy on city streets embedded with official-looking metal plaques that commemorated women of diverse backgrounds, both living and dead. Most of these historical marking projects were temporary in nature, however, in June of 1993, a series of 17 official-looking street signs appeared in a Berlin neighborhood ominously declaring that Jews were no longer permitted to use public swimming pools, were banned from wearing expensive jewelry in public, and that it was now illegal to sell them cigarettes, cigars, or pets. Each ruling was dated between 1936 and 1945. The posted warnings appeared in a part of the Schöneberg district once home to many Jews including Albert Einstein. Among the signs was the infamous decree of September 1, 1941: *All Jews over the age of 6 must wear a yellow star with the word "Jew" on it.* Two Berlin-based artists, Renata Stih and Frieder Schnock, designed the provocative markers as part of a memorial to the extermination of Berlin's Jewish population. The project, entitled *Places of Remembrance (Memorial in the Bavarian Quarter, Berlin-Schöneberg)*, aroused shock and anger from many residents, who envisioned the reunited Berlin not as a place haunted by the ghosts of National Socialism, but as Germany and even Europe's new cultural and political center.[25] Remarkably, Stih and Schnock's *Places of Remembrance* was not a guerrilla intervention, but an officially commissioned memorial by Berlin's Schöneberg district to commemorate its disappeared Jews. Official monuments and museums to the Holocaust, to Jewish Heritage, and to other victims of European Fascism exploded throughout the Western world in the post-Cold War years, with examples in Los Angeles and the District of Columbia (1993), Austria (1996), New York City (1997), and, perhaps most anticipated of all, in Berlin, where the *Memorial to the Murdered Jews of Europe*, designed by American architect Peter Eisenman, was completed in 2005 after ten years of competition and controversy. Notably, one of the failing bids for the Berlin memorial was submitted by Stih and Schnock, who proposed a fleet of buses that would travel to sites associated with the persecution of the city's Jews. "A giant monument has no effect and ultimately becomes invisible," Schnock commented; on the other hand, giving people a way to "visit the authentic crime scenes would be far more effective."[26] As much as his comments point to the late capitalist, or some would say, post-modern emptiness of historical meanings and interpretation, Schnock also makes an oblique reference to the politics of the archive, and a certain invisibility that paradoxically appeared less and less willing or capable of remaining invisible. At the same time this eruption of historical and ethnic otherness (the two were frequently represented together) into contemporary artistic subject matter signaled a palpable shift within the trajectory of the avant-garde.

Hal Foster observed at the time that artists were increasingly seeking ways to incorporate anthropological methods and its discourse into their practice.[27] Describing this shift as the "ethnographic turn," Foster cautioned that as much as this tendency sometimes challenged cultural orthodoxies, it could also substitute what amounted to a privileged alterity for the work of critical disinterestedness, the ultimate measure of aesthetic value. Foster begins his critique by returning to the roots of artistic radicalism in the twentieth century by reminding us of Walter Benjamin's influential 1934 essay "The Author as Producer" in which the Jewish-Marxist theorist calls upon class-conscious artists and anti-Fascist intellectuals to politicize the content of their work while simultaneously revolutionizing their methods of cultural production. Benjamin urged active engagement with the new, visual and technical capabilities brought about by the mass reproduction and distribution of news, photography, and cinema, which he believed could melt down and reconstruct all previous cultural forms while redefining or eliminating stagnated disciplinary boundaries. Benjamin, Esther Leslie summarizes, exhorted "critics to become photomontagists, authors to become critics, critics to become authors, practitioners to become theorists and theorists practitioners."[28] A politicized avant-garde must produce a new, radical cultural agency, one that betrays its class of origin (the bourgeoisie) in favor of working-class objectives, while actively developing an apparatus of artistic organization that can be continuously modified and expanded upon far beyond any merely propagandistic function. Foster contrasts this politically engaged artistic program with the quasi-anthropological art of the 1990s, concluding that the latter appears to be a fetishization of Benjamin's project insofar as the radical collapsing of authorship with political functionality (think Brecht or Heartfield) now turns almost entirely upon the subversive shock of ontological displacement. Artists were no longer tasked to re-function artistic form and content; radicalism was now simply, perhaps even matter-of-factly, embodied. Without entirely dismissing the subversive intent of this gesture, or, conversely, uncritically embracing Benjamin's displaced proletarian modernism, Foster warns that this idealization of otherness could lead to "a politics that may *consume* its historical subjects before they become historically effective."[29] And yet, suggested Fredric Jameson, it was the very possibility of historically informed political agency that was threatened with erasure by what he called post-modern pastiche: the schizophrenic play of historical and cultural signifiers uprooted from any connection to memory or to narrative.[30] This "surrealism without the unconscious" did not ignore the past, instead it spectacularized such imagery, approaching history not as a project to be analyzed and worked upon, but as a conceptual stumbling block, perhaps *the* impediment (along with class) standing in the way of some new, de-essentialized social agency. Which is to say, it was not that the avant-garde's romance with the world beyond art had ended, rather, some artists had merely shifted their focus from the diachronic to synchronic plane as an old dream of historically driven class consciousness gave way to the apparently static category of a missing *other*. And yet, the projects of REPOhistory, Haacke, Michelson, or Stih and Schnock, among others, clearly deviated from this post-modern tendency by intentionally challenging a certain historical amnesia, even provoking strong, at times violent public responses to their short-lived appearance. Indeed, such work appears to belong to a wave of historically engaged mid 1980s and 1990s visual culture that sharply contrasted with an increasingly dominant post-modern pastiche that, as elaborated upon by Jameson, Terry Eagleton, and other Marxist intellectuals, treated history as a reservoir of floating images detached from memory or meaning. At the same time, this nameless counter-tendency also appears linked with a broader artistic and scholarly response to those who denied the veracity of certain historical events, including most notably the Holocaust. The films of Claude Lanzmann and Dan Eisenberg and the art installations of Ellen Rothenberg all examine mid-twentieth-century Jewish history through techniques of reportage, montage, and poetic imagination without reducing the historical narrative to a post-modern cascade of disconnected signifiers.[31] Meanwhile, a curiously premature illustration of this anti-post-modern tendency is found in the largely ignored work of former Art + Language group member Terry Atkinson, who as early as the mid 1970s turned away from making conceptual art to produce a series of more or less realistic history paintings depicting the trauma of trench warfare amongst British working-class soldiers during World War I. Atkinson's anomalous career even suggests a very different, antithetical reading of post-war painting when contrasted with the highly celebrated works of German painter Gerhard Richter.

REPOhistory perceived the ranks of invisible *others* as poor immigrants, slaves, abolitionists, radicals, feminists, trade unionists, indentured servants, child-laborers, and the forgotten narratives of transients, native people, and gay, lesbian, and transgendered activists. In reality, these disenfranchised minorities shared nothing so much in common as a mutual superfluousness to the mainstream public sphere: its electoral process, its history, but also its museums, cultural institutions, and official educational curricula. Indeed, the public debate over how to teach American history from a culturally "inclusive" perspective also rose to new heights in the early 1990s.[32] It was at this time that the contemporary art world was confronted with its own geographical and ethno-historical centrism as a rising tide of once-excluded artists outside the US and Western Europe were propelled by the dictates of an unprecedented globalization into the markets of the culture industry. It is impossible therefore to dismiss Foster's trenchant analysis as a response to the loss of critical privilege, a kind of white man's panic. Still, what Foster did not anticipate was the degree to which the process of substitution and reification he so cogently identified would itself become a pivotal, virtually automated function of art under neoliberal enterprise culture. The "ethnographic turn" soon morphed into a series of "turns," and turns within turns, including the "outsider artist" turn, the social-relational turn, the interventionist and the "green" turn, and so on and so forth—each seemingly new rotation of contemporary art's privileged subject seeking to economize on an increasingly prosperous art market (that simultaneously produced an exponential flood of surplus artists and artworks).

Between the mid 1980s and the early 1990s, sales of young, emerging artists, especially painters, grew at a phenomenal rate. Anti-theoretical, a-political, and deeply entrepreneurial, the deregulated neoliberal economy reinforced artistic tendencies markedly different from the austerity of conceptual and minimal art in the 1960s and 1970s. Chin-tao Wu describes this change in art world values as *enterprise culture*. But the art market tumbled badly at the start of the 1990s in a delayed response to the stock-market crash of 1987. And then, once again, keeping pace with the fortunes of the financial sector, contemporary art sales rebounded at an even more accelerated rate, this time spurred on by Clinton's so-called new economy.[33] However, between the rise of the Internet that some described as a new cultural commons commingling high and low culture, professional and amateur, plus the massive export of finance capital to developing nations with their own emerging contemporary art scenes, a formerly invisible sphere of imaginative productivity challenged the seemingly well-anchored offices of Western intellectual authority. Something was spilling out of the archive. And conventional methods of managing this excess did not appear to be holding. Perhaps most evident in this respect was the rapidly fading power of academic critics and cultural theorists who claimed to be the primary interlocutors between artists and institutions. Suddenly a breed of fluid and largely independent curators began to build and shape artistic careers much as the art critic had in previous years. "The era of the curator has begun," wrote *New York Times* art critic Michael Brenson approvingly, while Foster soberly mused that these wandering curators mirrored the rise of the equally nomadic artist ethnographer.[34] But it is unlikely this usurpation would have been possible without the increasing power of a new engine of art world expansion: the international art biennial. Within two decades of 1980 the number of these urban art fairs doubled in number to include Havana, Johannesburg, Vilnius, Istanbul, Berlin, Dakar, Tuzla, Porto Alegre, Liverpool, Fukuoka, and Gwangju province in South Korea, among other, once marginal art world outposts. It is possible, in other words, to see the revolving privileging of art world subjects not as an inversion of entitlements, or as the triumph of some vengeful, historical Id over an orthodox canonical ego, but as an economizing maneuver in which real artistic meaning appears to be displaced "somewhere else," only to return to the art world's stockroom of cultural capital with value added. That this machine-like circuit resembles the deregulated operation of deregulated finance capital—invest in an underdeveloped region of the globe, boast that capital has made infrastructural improvements and increased multiculturalism, actively deplete these same regional economies through "open" borders and so-called free market policies favoring wealthy nations, then remove the primary investment at the first sign of economic contraction— is perhaps secondary to a radical transformation the ethnographic turn produced within the world of arts administrative apparatus.

Increasingly the art world resembled the "transnational" corporate sector and was becoming unfixed in space (or so it appeared). A different, more flexible and enterprising approach to arts management was called for as artist's working conditions, always precarious at best, began to resemble that of other post-Fordist industries dependent upon outsourcing and just-in-time production methods.[35] At the same time, capital's geographic fluidity and dependency on information networks was altering the very image of cultural consumers and the globalized workforce. Images of multiethnic harmony began to appear in print and television advertising, perhaps most dramatically in the series of commercial images shot by Italian photographer Oliviero Toscani for the Benetton corporation.[36] In the white suburbs of America, young people embraced inner-city hip-hop culture once contained within what Jeff Chang calls the necropolis of the 1970s South Bronx.[37] Individuals of divergent gender, sexuality, ethnic and class backgrounds were now graduating in waves from a plethora of art programs in schools and universities. Many came from lower-middle or even working-class families where high culture was a distant, even despised phenomenon. They felt no allegiances to the formalist traditions emerging out of either European modernism or the New York Abstract Expressionist School, but instead relished comic books, pulp fiction, movies and television, children's animation, home-crafts, plastic molded figurines, and, in certain ethnic communities, graffiti writers, low-rider automobiles, even seashell embedded alters to the virgin of Guadalupe (*Nuestra Señora de Guadalupe)*, exactly the sort of *objet d'art* that Greenberg abhorred as kitsch.[38] The art world filters meant to prevent this kind of imagery from entering into serious consideration had begun breaking down as early as the 1980s with the East Village Art Scene's adoration of banality and glitz. By the early 1990s, with the financial success of the Young British Artists (YBA) and former Wall Street commodities broker turned artist Jeff Koons, these aesthetic filters were in virtual collapse. Images of serial killers, rotting melons, spin-paintings, ceramic statuary of animated cartoons sent sales of contemporary art to record heights. It was not only a matter of once-rejected content. The sheer quantity of cultural practices by artists, amateurs, mass media, science, overwhelmed previous systems of reception and interpretation. The art critic was forced to either completely ignore this trend, or somehow address four simultaneous and dramatic changes in their field of knowledge including 1) an explosion of professionally trained young artists, many from subaltern backgrounds, 2) a seismic shift in artistic taste that virtually mocked the classical model of detached aesthetic judgment, 3) the extraordinary global capitalization of the contemporary art market, and 4) the diminishing power of critics, interpreters, and theorists to shape this new enterprise culture. One response within academia was the rise of cultural and visual studies, both of which were far more influenced by media criticism and the social sciences of anthropology and sociology than they were by art history, including its Marxist or social-historical variations.

Both the "ethnographic turn," and its criticism, came at a moment of convergence between the forces of capitalist globalization and an electronic form of communication and memory enhancement that rejected the policing of culture's archives. A vast surplus of artistic producers armed with a powerful means of self-representation seemed to be asking: Who gets to produce culture, for whom, and why? The processes of cultural democratization Benjamin sought to harness for the Left now verged on near total attainability, though sans ideology or class-consciousness. No doubt these seismic changes added to the apprehension of art critics.[39] Nevertheless, in the year before his death, Craig Owens had directly sought to address the implications of this broader cultural shift for visual artists by pointing out in 1989 that globalization was turning the once "displacing gaze of colonial surveillance" back upon the colonizers themselves. Drawing upon a range of theorists somewhat peripheral to the art world, including Edward Said, Michel Foucault, and Gayatri Chakravorty Spivak, Owens' critique focused on the many who fall outside the globalization juggernaut. Citing Spivak he prophetically argued that Western artists and intellectuals must begin to confront the growing visibility of "subsistence farmers, unorganized peasant labor, the tribals, and the communities of zero workers."[40] Five years later a group of indigenous people descended from Mayan Indians in the poor, rural Southern state of Chiapas declared autonomy from the Mexican government. Rather than rely strictly on armed struggle, as in previous anti-colonial insurrections such as those in Cuba, Algeria, Southeast Asia, and Peru, the Zapatista Army of National Liberation broadcast their political platform—a form of participatory, libertarian socialism opposed to corporate globalization—via the Internet. But this interruption from below did not remain strictly virtual. Soon a series of massive, carnivalesque demonstrations took shape in Seattle, Quebec, Genoa, Prague, taking up many of the same demands as the Zapatistas: decentralized collective action, local economic control, and political autonomy from globalized capitalist markets. Sometimes referred to as "*the movement of movements*" these highly decentralized and ideologically diverse protests recalled the scale of marches against the Vietnam War in the 1960s and 1970s, and against nuclear weapons in the 1980s. However, unlike many of these past actions the new spirit of resistance appeared cultural first, and political second. A generation of art school graduates confronted the ruins of the public sphere and its panoptic spaces branded with trade names and ringed with surveillance cameras. With nowhere else to go they decided to misbehave. As Brian Holmes puts it, "the image of pink-feathered dancers expressively disrupting the commerce of a Zara store in Milan sums up this new combat perfectly."[41] Meanwhile, despite differences of education, language, class, or geographical location, the participants in this counter-globalization campaign were able to coordinate their actions using the same, networked information technologies essential to transnational capital. The prosthetically enhanced power of memory and communication so essential to the forces of globalization, entrepreneurship, and just-in-time productivity had come home to roost.

Urban Ghosts

No doubt inspired by the unleashing of this once shadowy archive, and by the capacity of the Zapatistas and other marginal groups to make their presence visible on the world stage, a new generation of artists began to intervene in public spaces, often doing so illegally sans permits. Some of these projects were inspired directly by REPOhistory's *détournement* of urban sign systems; others simply invented a similar approach to marking public spaces. The Pocho Research Society in Southern California bolted an imitation metal plaque to a building on Olerva Street in downtown Los Angeles to mark where David Alfaro Siqueiros' 1932 anti-imperialist mural *Tropical America* had been painted over by local businessmen. The group carried out its action without permission in order to "pay homage to historic erasure."[42] Towards the other end of the state, at 55th and Market Streets in Oakland, California, the Center for Tactical Magic (CTM) collaborated with artist Jeremy Deller and former Black Panther David Hilliard to install, illegally without permission, a yellow and black metal sign graphically commemorating the traffic light post on which the sign was posted.[43] In 1967, after the deaths of several school children by speeding automobiles, the residents of this African-American neighborhood requested a traffic signal be installed.

The Oakland City Council delayed action, whereupon a group of Black Panthers began acting as crossing guards, holding back traffic and allowing children to safely cross to school. Within two months a stoplight was installed.[44] Perhaps most ambitious of all, a group of twenty-something artists and DIY amateur historians illicitly installed a series of signs at ten sites around Pittsburgh Pennsylvania, a post-industrial city that began its own economic restructuring in the late 1970s much like New York. Calling themselves The Howling Mob Society (HMS), this informally organized collective chose to commemorate the tumultuous and largely spontaneous Railroad Strike of 1877 in which an estimated quarter of the city's population—all mostly unemployed—participated. The signs which meticulously mimic official historical markers have titles like "STATE VIOLENCE INCITES RIOTING, SIEGE AT THE 26TH STREET ROUNDHOUSE," and "TWENTY MURDERED AND A CITY RISES UP." Thanks to "Google Maps" software the group's website includes an interactive graphic of each site with a pop-up window

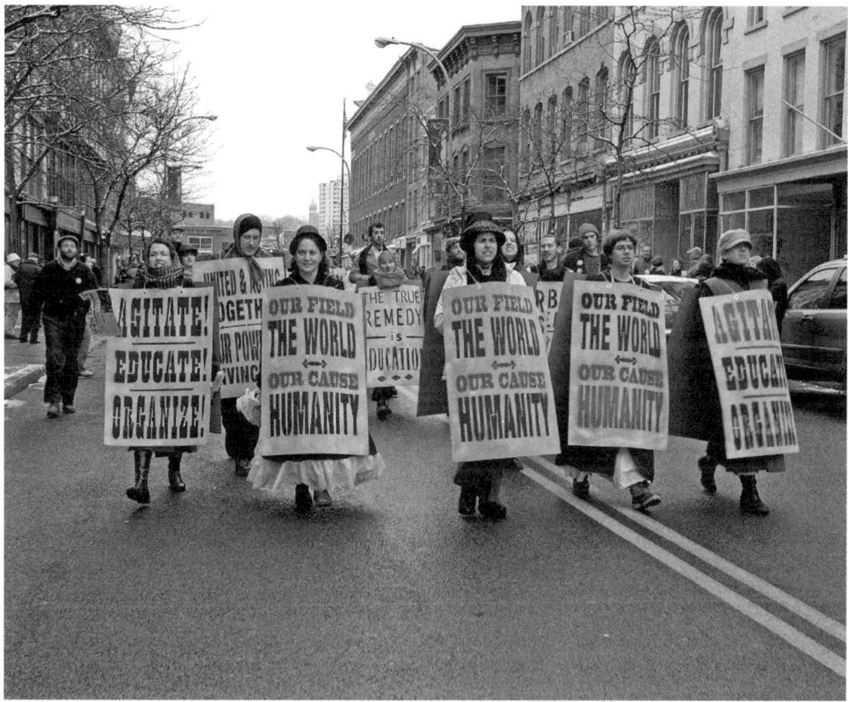

The United Victorian Workers Union was an ad-hoc collective of artists, activists, and academics that came together in the Winter of 2005 to correct the historical misrepresentations of Troy, New York's annual Victorian Stroll. Video documentation can be viewed at www.daragreenwald.com/uvw.html (Organized by Bettina Escauriza, Dara Greenwald, Ryan Jenkins, Josh MacPhee, Amy Scarfone, and Marshall Tramell). Image courtesy Amy Scarfone.

offering the text of every sign.[45] On the same website HMS describes its mission as wanting to give a voice to those marginalized and buried by history, but they go an important step further by seeking to draw "links between historical narratives and current social conditions in order to bring to light the systems of oppression still firmly imbedded in our society."[46]

Meanwhile, in Troy, New York, a group of placard-carrying protestors dressed in nineteenth-century garment workers' clothes inserted themselves into the city's annual Victorian Stroll: a city-boosting event sponsored by the Chamber of Commerce in which the "historic downtown" is transformed into "a magical stage of song, dance, and family enjoyment."[47] Describing themselves as The United Victorian Workers Union the ad-hoc group of local artists and activists carried signs printed in historically appropriate typeface that called for an eight-hour work day as the disarmed business leaders and politicians dressed in Victorian garb looked on in dismay.[48] In a different context, on the streets of Buenos Aires, a groups of artists working with local activists called HIJOS deployed site-specific signs focusing pubic attention on individuals responsible for "disappearing" some 230,000 people during the 1970s Argentinean military junta's anti-Leftist campaign, or "Dirty War." Part of a broader activist campaign known as *escraches*, involving performances, posters, and projections, the street marker projects by the collectives GAC (Arte Callejero, or simply Street Art Group) include graphics that mimic traffic signs such as a yellow, diamond-shaped plaque with an arrow that points towards the home of a former torturer and that even provides the distance to his domicile, or signs that boldly state the name of an individual Junta member with the label GENOCIDA or Juicio y castigo (judgment and punishment); "completely invisible to the art world as 'art actions'; nevertheless they gave the *escraches* identity and visibility."[49]

Outlaws

At a much-publicized 1997 celebrity "roast," in which politicians and press parody each other in a carnival atmosphere, Mayor Rudolph Giuliani came onstage as "Rudia," a blonde women wearing high-heels, a pink satin dress, and an unlit cigar protruding from his lipsticked mouth. "Rudia" or variations thereof, would make several appearances over the years, including immediately after Giuliani's second reelection as Mayor in 2000 when she appeared as a matronly shopper in a department store videotaped flirting with real estate developer Donald Trump who gropes Giuliani's false breasts before the camera.[50] Trump, along with the City's other major real estate developers, received millions in tax breaks during Giuliani's two terms in office. The video became a viral hit on YouTube. But even as the Mayor played at cross-dressing he was successfully blocking passage of an anti-discrimination law aimed at transgendered people's civil liberties.[51]

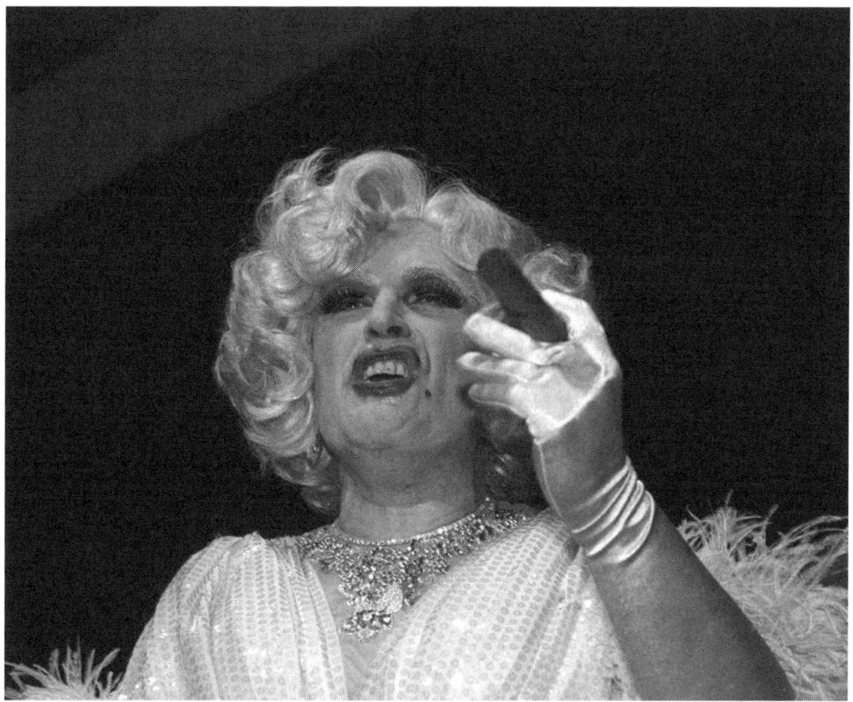

On more than four occasions, as Mayor of New York City and afterwards, Rudolph "Rudi" Giuliani dressed in drag as "Rudia," a female alter ego he once described to reporters as "a Republican pretending to be a Democrat pretending to be a Republican." Image copyright *N.Y. Daily News*.

In a final unprecedented act before leaving office Giuliani moved the mayoral archive accumulated during his eight years in office to a private storage facility in Queens. Journalists and historians were prevented from accessing its several thousand boxes of public papers. Only after hiring a private archivist did he return the municipal archive (presumably intact) to the public. Several years later the former New York City Mayor declared his candidacy for President of the United States. In April of 2003, no longer dressing in drag, Giuliani stood beside fellow neoconservatives and refused to condemn the looting and burning of the Baghdad library and museum as American and other coalition troops stood by without intervening.[52] The archive continues to establish authority over who gets to speak and who has access to visibility. Its juridical power is only eliminated when its contents are confiscated, censored, or reduced to ashes.

Citing the work of Michel Foucault, the art historian Richard Meyer insists that attempts by mainstream society to control the image of the deviant have backfired, producing instead a proliferation of unanticipated counter-images.

Homosexuals, he writes, have frequently adopted and re-staged mainstream society's negative representation of them as a kind of semiotic warfare in which the marginalized embrace society's negative stereotypes as a tactic of rebellion. This act of representational appropriation travels "outside" the law, literally returning an "outlaw representation."[53] Likewise, many of the public signage projects described here also appear ontologically ambiguous, even perverse. They are queer signs. Not surprisingly these urban *hauntings* and acts of *unforgetting* generated resistance from the "Quality of Life" city that had sought to soak up or expunge visible signs of capitalism's social failings—the paperless, marginal workers, the dispossessed, redundant, disappeared, and even the street artist—even as it simulated, in hygienic form, the incubation of a certain manageable artistic creativity. In the case of REPOhistory and similar historical marking projects this confrontation with the counter-archive appeared only briefly, like something frail that was destined to disappear underground once the city of (dis)order was fully ensconced. Indeed, this *other* archive is always elsewhere in time: either in a past that we can never have immediate access to, any more than we will someday stand directly facing Plato's animating fire, or in a promised future that may or may not ever take shape.[54] In which case Marsha P. Johnson comes to us as our mid-day ghost, speaking a counter-discourse in a strangely familiar vernacular that mixes activism and theatrical excess, militancy and camouflage. It is precisely the cunning idiom of a certain "surplus" population whose modest desire simply to cope sometimes erupts into outright disobedience.

"There is no political power without control of the archive, of memory," insists Derrida, adding that "effective democratization can always be measured by this essential criterion: the participation in and access to the archive, its constitution, and its interpretation."[55] Inevitably we are reminded that history, rather than being read as a string of inevitabilities, might be thought of as so many lost opportunities, and that a certain kind of cultural activism may be conceived as a process of recovering these other memories, regardless of whether they are orphaned or suppressed, real or imaginary. And yet the "archive itself" always appears just missed, somewhere prior to or long after the moment we try to ascertain its meaning. That after all is its particular sense of promise. But if we did attempt to redeem the overlooked and the discarded memories that entranced Walter Benjamin, to sniff-out their "social utopian investments," as Esther Leslie suggests, how and on what basis would we go about this rescue?[56] Film scholar Jeffrey Skoller proposes one possible answer by revisiting Benjamin's figure of the brooder (*der Grübler*), the ragpicker as modern allegorist who seeks to construct "some structure of meaning" out of the chaotic jumble of the past by endlessly shifting its random detritus, yet all the while remaining "tormented by his own inability to remember what any of it means."[57] Still, any salvaging operation depends upon some kind of jurisdiction, some interpretive economy linked to the politics of the archive. Generals exposed for war crimes in Argentina, a street sign marking Wall Street's former slave market, the spontaneous "labor uprising" at a holiday fair in upstate New York, or the temporary memorial for a transgendered street-activist in a city selectively forgetting its own past—these varied projects have drawn upon the jurisdiction of an *other*, outlaw archive, briefly reanimating this dark-matter social production within the public consciousness like an accursed gift that nevertheless appeals to an ongoing dream of collective redemption.[58]

Epilogue

The NYCDOT permit required that REPOhistory regularly check on its signs for maintenance and safety reasons. Group member Tom Klem reports that while some of the project signs were damaged or vandalized, the Johnson marker always remained intact. However, it did have a tendency to fade because of its exposure to the sun. On two occasions Klem replaced the Johnson sign. But when he arrived in the Meatpacking District with a ladder and tools he was confronted by transgendered prostitutes. They assumed he was there to remove the memorial. In short, they had adopted the REPOhistory sign, telling him it told their story and what "it was all about." In the end, when the official permit had run its course, Klem simply left the Johnson memorial where it was, and where it remained for several more months before finally disappearing.

4

TEMPORARY SERVICES

Because you can't BUY happiness

Yomango[1]

Prisoners' Inventions

"Every note I have taken" is a collection of classroom memos made by Tiffany Knopow during four years of art education at the University of Wisconsin-Milwaukee.[2] It is a complete archive, Tiffany insists, consisting of hundreds of lined composition pages crammed with penciled equations, jottings, and reminders from courses in Calculus, Geology, American Literature, Physics, and Art History. Each sheet has been scanned, arranged by subject, and turned into a freely downloadable PDF file. There is even a 40-page compilation of notes taken during a course on collections and collecting. "Please feel free to use this information as you need." Since her education was "privately" paid for, she now passes her "property" forward aided by the electronic commons of the Internet. But "Every note I have taken" is less a strict product of cyberculture than it is a variation of the nineteenth-century scrapbook in which the detailed routines and business transactions of life on a Wisconsin farm or prairie were meticulously recorded, along with pressed wild flowers, poems, amateur drawings, or clippings from shopping catalogs. In Tiffany's case, Midwest pioneer culture has been replaced by the regimens of the twenty-first-century "education factory" (her degree was awarded in 2008). However, it is not the obsessively salvaged content of this gift that most impresses, but rather the archive's painstaking devotion to redundancy. For every sheet of paper Tiffany electronically salvaged we know that countless similar documents have been produced, filed away, and eventually disposed of by innumerable other students. What to make of this open-source archive, this digitally enhanced memory? Is it a generous re-distribution of intellectual property, passed forwards to unknown recipients? Or a sly commentary on an educational system that generates too many artists and art historians (among other professions) for the market to absorb? Is it, in other words, both a gift and a critique of the monotonous repetitions of post-Fordism's digital prosthetics?[3]

Tiffany's memo archive is linked to PublicCollectors.org, an online collection of collections dedicated to the "types of cultural artifacts that public libraries and museums do not collect or make available."[4] Artist Marc Fischer manages the site and a modest research center out of his home in Chicago's Logan Square neighborhood. The digital archives of PublicCollectors.org hold inventories of obscure Punk bands, lists of pirated "B" movies, novels read by prisoners, jpgs of found grocery shopping notes on yellow and pink stickies, even snapshots of sidewalk cracks in Mexico City. One set of photographs shows a wall of distressed cardboard boxes packed with thousands of vinyl records awaiting auction on eBay. There is a collection of exploitative pulp comics with gory violent covers from Mexico, photographs of people who are taking photographs of other people in public and at demonstrations, and there is a list of transcribed messages that certain Anarcho-Punk bands included in the dead space of vinyl records. The Dead Kennedys' sardonically scratched into one of their record's metal pressing plates Henry Kissinger's dictum: "POWER IS THE ULTIMATE APHRODISIAC." Another webpage documents a hefty, spiral-bound sketchbook filled with marginally varied drawings of automobiles. Each car chassis is rendered in thick black marker and colored pencil and arranged by manufacturer. The result is like a hand-drawn manual for car dealers as much as it is an inventory of male automotive fantasies. Public Collectors is rife with such archaisms, willful misappropriations, and excesses. It is like a miniaturized sampling of the World Wide Web in which makeshift, amateur, and informal cultural practices are superabundant, and no doubt have always been so. What has changed is that these practices are not confined today to limited groups of aficionados and informal communities. Countless DIY websites for knitting circles, Live Action Role Play gamers (LARPs), zinesters, home crafters, amateur garage-kit sculptors, pirate-radio enthusiasts, crop-circle designers, and the hard-core disciples of Hip-Hop, Goth, Punk, and Do It Yourself (DIY). These now explode into unblinking visibility across the pixilated horizon of a spectacularized society. LARP participants create DIY garments, weapons, social structures, and military campaigns that are performed on weekends and after work in people's backyards. On YouTube one can find some 13,000 homemade videos of these medieval-looking leisure activities that nevertheless take place offline. Untold digital images, videos, blogs, tweets, and so forth evince a widespread antipathy towards "useful" work (much like art), and most of this "other" productivity has an antagonistic or ambivalent relationship to the formal market economy (again, much like art). Therefore, given that art is *the* model of excess productivity *par excellence*, it is no surprise that a growing torrent of professional artists have also taken to representing their work online, while seeking out direct access to buyers. Online art "galleries" such as deviantART, Elfwood, and Gfxartist today host hundreds of thousands of artists, both trained and informal. Social networking sites like

Twitter, Flickr, WordPress, Facebook, and MySpace serve as sales platforms for artists, essentially cutting out dealers and commercial venues in a form of direct marketing. In a very real sense the once-invisible archive has split open. And it has done so with an incomprehensible degree of detail, releasing among other forms of unseen, dark creativity the activist culture that PAD/D once sought to document at the periphery of the art establishment, or the missing data that REPOhistory briefly reinserted into urban space.

Today virtually everything marginalized, overlooked, or made redundant requests our attention. Its call is both like and unlike that heeded by Walter Benjamin who believed the discarded, outmoded, seemingly unrelated materials and technologies found randomly in Paris Arcades were imbued with a radical capacity for signification, perhaps even a deeper potential of historical redemption. Esther Leslie tells us Benjamin "sniffs out the thing-world," his surrealistically inclined archeology picking over society's leftovers as if they were "supercharged with historical meanings." [5] But the postcards, souvenirs, dog-eared ledger books, discarded tickets and snapshots the theorist once used to reconstruct his melancholic image of nineteenth- and early-twentieth-century Western society have been replaced by a different order of detritus, its sheer quantity bespeaking a shift in interpretive approach. Twenty-first-century ruins appear to call upon us more and more from the center, rather than from the margins of enterprise culture. Curiously, what the electronic archive requests is less contemplative than participatory. Its terms are simple, we should "share ourselves," much as Tiffany and Fischer have done, actively erasing the border not only between labor and leisure, but also between the private and public sphere.

Sharing inevitably has a murkier side. A series of digitized snapshots available on PublicCollectors.org is entitled *The Hording Habits of Another Mother*. Offered by a woman— the daughter—identified only as "Beth," the images show suffocating spaces crammed floor to ceiling with rolls of paper, upturned furniture, knitted objects, scattered clothing, unopened packages, knick-knack figurines and souvenirs. In one online image a Sombrero-capped marionette dangles precariously above a tower of carelessly taped shipping boxes. To the left sits a television, its screen blank. A small white blob is reflected there, precisely where Beth's camera-flash left behind proof of her presence as if the daughter were some insurance company adjustor routinely investigating a home break-in. A certain spleenish self-ethnography reveals what most of us knew we would find anyway, another over-consumer's monotonous clutter, though admittedly amplified in the case of Beth's mother. Tedium and a self-surveillance take on a darker pall with "Angelo," an artist and inmate at a maximum-security prison in California whose drawings appear at Public Collectors.

Fischer began corresponding with the prisoner after receiving a letter from him that included "an astonishing ballpoint pen drawing titled *Roman Games*."

Angelo's artwork reveals still another side to semi-visible social productivity, a penchant for displaying the unspoken and unspeakable. In the painstakingly detailed image Angelo renders a group of Roman soldiers "torturing and murdering their Christian captives in the setting of a large arena." Hundreds of additional drawings followed, each elaborate and expressive, and each also permeated by an ambiguously eroticized feeling of constant surveillance "that is central to the prison experience."

> Conflict, fighting, sex, play, games, excursions, adventures, torture, and death always takes place in the company of others. Every event happens within the context of a larger social structure. No one is ever truly alone, except in their thoughts.[6]

Public Collectors concentrates the strange mix of bathos and voyeurism, inventiveness and resentment that dominates the visual and material culture of neoliberal risk society. Still, Fischer admits to his own conflicts about making Angelo's drawings public in publications and online, and not only because of the work's sometimes disturbing content. Issues of exploitation are raised, especially for someone whose privacy is so patently compromised. At the same time, Fischer explains, it is clear that Angelo gets "satisfaction from knowing that people are getting to see some of the things he makes."[7] A kind of counter-panoptic irony is unavoidable. What escapes the prison's surveillance system to ultimately catch our eye is the inner, fantasy life of society's ultimate surplus population: monotonously regimented, intimately scrutinized, but restlessly creative and desirous of communion. And yet the detail and specificity of Angelo's images fascinate for still another reason. In a concrete way his drawings measure the duration of a long confinement (possibly lifelong, though Fischer correctly never asks for details about Angelo's crime or sentence). Human time is literally incarcerated within these sketches, and yet the underlying logic of Public Collectors remains uncannily consistent. Angelo's laboring excesses are like the other side of Tiffany's redundant document scans, or any of the other strange and useless collections, indexes, and obsessions documented on these websites. Instead of selling, or seeking to sell, their labor for a wage this is a type of work without utility, virtually a contradiction in terms. However, by including Angelo in the archive—just one individual among many denied mobility by State, military, criminal, or psychiatric agencies—Public Collectors illustrates the disciplinary system's ultimate retribution: a life filled with endless surplus time in which, ironically, the choice of what one does is insignificant compared to the process of doing work "on oneself." As if to underscore this injunction a top US Appeals court recently ruled that prisoners cannot create or play fantasy games because

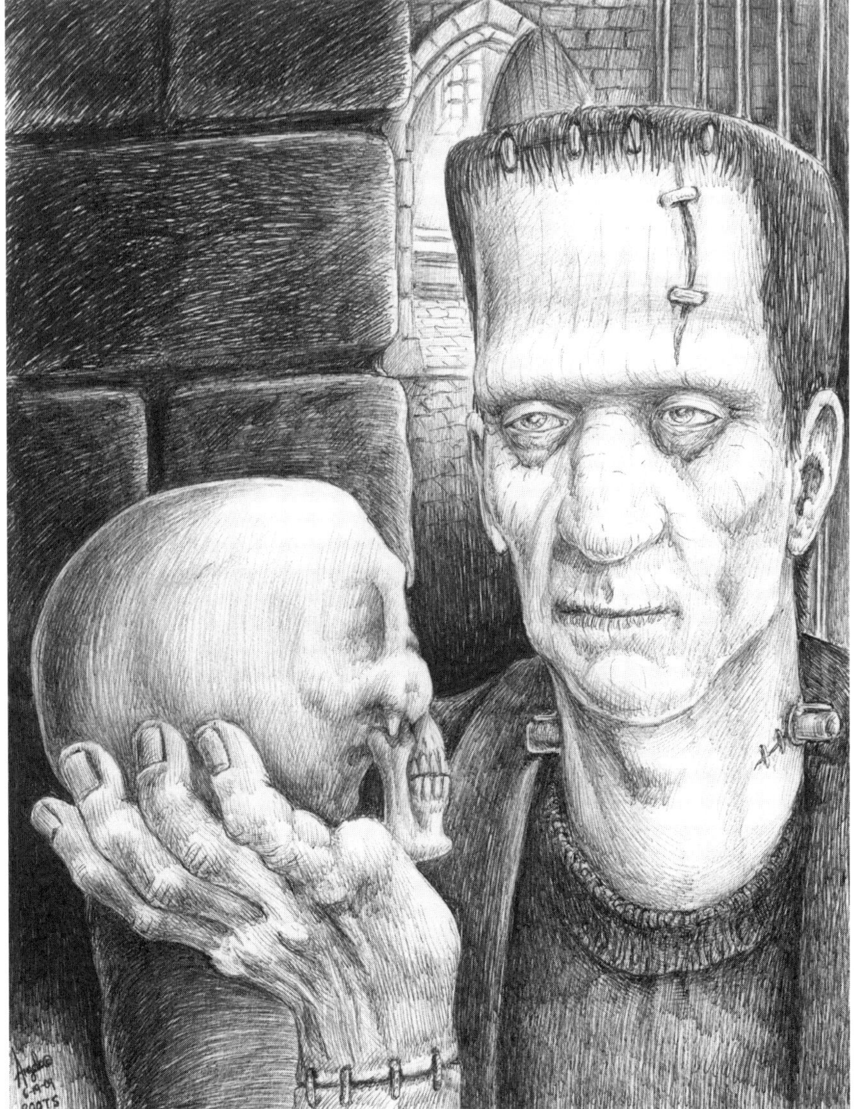

"Roots" is one of hundreds of ballpoint pen drawings made by an inmate in a high-security prison in California named "Angelo" whose work is featured on Marc Fischer's Public Collectors website: www.publiccollectors.org. Angelo's art courtesy Marc Fischer.

they "foster an inmate's obsession with escaping from the real-life correctional environment, fostering hostility, violence and escape behavior."[8]

Angelo's "dirty" pictures are not what penologists had in mind when they devised systems of rehabilitation for the socially unfit. Not surprisingly, Fischer informs us, California prison guards have on occasion illegally confiscated Angelo's artwork charging the inmate with possession of contraband pornography.[9] Angelo is also the author of *Prisoners' Inventions*, a compendium of DIY devices he has gathered from other inmates including chessboards made of toilet paper and small water heaters assembled out of salvaged wire and ballpoint pen parts. The artist-prisoner provides detailed step-by-step illustrations for how to build these inventions, some of which are forbidden by prison authorities. Angelo's book was edited and published by Fischer together with colleagues Brett Bloom and Salem Collo-Julin. The three make up the group Temporary Services (TS), a Midwestern-based artists' group dedicated to erasing the distinction between professional and everyday acts of creativity through archives, exhibitions, publications, and public interventions. Much of what TS is about can be gleaned from another documentary project entitled Public Phenomena. For the past decade the group has recorded the various ways city dwellers, non-criminals in this case, surreptitiously modify their urban environment using improvised materials that reorganize space and communicate warnings and other forms of local knowledge.[10] Peeling gray plywood, wire, and sheet metal are tacked together to form makeshift urban barriers, and along highways assemblages of flowers, ribbon, candles, toys, clothing, and rudimentary crucifixes are affixed to telephone poles, traffic signs, light posts to mark a personal loss to automobile traffic. Derelict materials found on Midwestern streets become improvised contraptions for holding parking spaces, a series of paint buckets serve the same function in Mexico City, and a piece of two-by-four inserted into an upturned packing crate saves a space on a street in Ljubljana. Spot-welded metal boxes protect straggly street plantings on a sidewalk in Mumbai, loops of motorcycle chain covered in thick black rubber spiral about the base of trees, metal poles, and gates in Athens. Those familiar with contemporary art will note the outward similarity of this simple street artistry to the work of Carl Andre, Tony Feher, Thomas Hirschhorn, or perhaps Mike Kelley whose stuffed-animal sculpture consists of forlorn toys and knitted objects that the artist finds in thrift stores and flea markets. No doubt an undercurrent of institutional criticism runs through the archival projects of TS, begging the question of how these informal and anonymous non-art practices differ from what Brandon Taylor refers to as "slack art": the use of ephemeral materials, a marked disinterest in skilled craftsmanship, and an extemporaneous approach to the display of work in which cardboard, reams of masking tape, and used post-it notes suffice as "serious" art?[11] Still, one experiences a distinct visual and sensual exuberance when viewing Temporary Services public phenomena and the accumulated ephemera found in Fischer's Public Collectors archive. This pleasure is derived as much from subtle, rhythmical shifts of scale, location, and improvised materials as it is from voyeurism or some *détourned* expectation about the nature of art. It is the inventiveness of the everyday, the commonplace, and the nondescript multitude. In an age of deregulated aesthetic practice such dark matter inevitably intervenes within the valorization process of official artistic production.[12]

Services

Ninety years ago the Soviet avant-garde artist El Lissitzky prophesied: "There is no reason of any sort for this division into artists and nonartists."[13] Something similarly unguarded, even intentionally naïve, is expressed by Fischer and TS when they intentionally "disrespect" the lines separating artistic labor from that of the researcher, archivist, editor, or arts administrator. The TS mission statement makes this clear. It rejects the typically ambivalent language found in much contemporary art discourse and builds upon a decade of activity in which the group has evolved its own intricate counter-economy of gift giving, publishing, documentation, curating, and public intervention based around a DIY aesthetic of art and life.

> We strive to build an art practice that makes the distinction between art and other forms of creativity irrelevant, [that] champions the work of those who are frequently excluded, under-recognized, marginal, non-commercial, experimental, and/or socially and politically provocative, [that] makes opportunities from large museums and institutions more inclusive by bringing lesser-known artists in through collaborations or advocacy, [and that] puts money and cultural capital back into the work of other artists and self-publishers.[14]

But TS not only attempts to dissolve art back into everyday experience, it seeks to generate a non-market, non-accumulative economy of generosity in the process. In its own peculiar way the group appears to be establishing an autonomous institutional support system from the bottom up, something that would have been the province of the government in the past, or even perhaps the post-revolutionary state in Lissitzky's day. Along with their own archiving and publishing, TS provides modest financing for other artists and helped to establish the multi-purpose exhibition and cultural space Mess Hall on Chicago's North Side, where cooperatively produced free programs range from Heavy Metal festivals and urban mapping projects to slide presentations with roasted corn.[15] "In a gift economy," Ted Purves explains, "transactions are never really over, because each one produces more reciprocal ties."[16] Meanwhile a wave of contemporary artworks, exhibitions, and critical writings have focused attention on art as a form of gift economy including the free biennials organized by artist Sal Randolph, and the 2008 biennial in Iasi, Romania curated by Dora Hegyi entitled "Periferic 8: Art as Gift."[17] The payoff of such gift giving (so to speak) is found in the production of social networks that remain always in motion, or, as Lewis Hyde puts it, the gift must always "move," never aiming to build up an accumulation of capital (either financial or social capital).[18] Nevertheless, even as works of art inspire visions of a non-market gift economy in the minds of various contemporary writers, poets, anthropologists, and even a few neoliberal policy theorists—such as Yochai Benkler who insists, "nonmarket behavior is becoming central to producing our information and cultural environment"—the infatuation with art as a gift cannot ignore the actual global art market valued at its recent peak in trillions of cold hard US dollars.[19]

Contrary to the recent wave of gift art and "relational" art financed by European cultural institutions, major art biennials, and museums, the work of TS takes place in places seldom if ever visited by members of the global art world. In the summer of 2001, TS transformed a fire-escape room adjacent to their small, eleventh-floor office in the Chicago Loop into a free "drop-in" center modeled after the San Francisco Diggers of the 1960s. Clean donated garments were neatly hung within the space, coffee brewed, and copies of the group's signature booklets about urban politics, art, and public interventions neatly stacked for visitors. A sign placed on the sidewalk downstairs encouraged passersby to "come by, drink coffee, look at our booklets, try on clothes in our dressing room and take whatever clothing they want."[20] *One Week Boutique* (OWB) was a conscious experiment in stepping outside the managed parsimony of the mainstream art world. Promoted via emails, photocopy flyers, and word of mouth it took place away from the art gallery scene. Brett Bloom writes that when visitors arrived they "interacted immediately as they would in any clothing store, the questions and strangeness of the situation came only when the economics were discussed."[21] The popularity of the free store led the group to keep OWB going for several months, after which variations of the project were carried out in other parts of Chicago as well as San Juan, Puerto Rico.

The previous year TS had targeted a public institution several blocks away for an intervention aimed at illicitly improving its quality. The Harold Washington Library Center is named after the first and only African-American mayor of Chicago, whose remarkably progressive administration was cut short by his sudden heart attack in 1987. Opened in 1991, its brooding, neo-gothic façade suggests a movie set from Gotham City. But the library is "unquestionably one of the most important, prominent, and valued cultural institutions in Chicago," writes Fischer, who goes on to add that despite its "great size, beautiful architecture, massive holdings, and extensive art collection, Temporary Services feels that this library should offer the public a little more."[22] The little more included some 150 surreptitiously added books and book projects that the group spontaneously inserted onto the library's stacks, each publication complete with stamped due dates and reference stickers identical to those found in legitimate volumes. One aim of the library intervention was to bring "obscure, subversive, self-published, hand-made, or limited edition works by underexposed artists to a wider audience." Among the "books" inserted into the library was a 1973 list of 1,800 "secrets" collected by conceptual artist Douglas Huebler; a *Ghost Book*, containing a motion detector by artist/geographer Trevor Paglen that set off a noise when people walked by it; and *The Somnabulist*, a copy of the short-lived journal loosely connected with the anarchist inspired Chicago Surrealist Group that dates back to the mid-1960s.[23] There were also a number of book-objects or physically altered publications, which had been stitched, wired, buttoned, re-assembled and Velcroed in assorted ways by Emily Forman, Paul Gebbia, Josh MacPhee, Laurie Palmer, Chemi Rosado Seijo, and the late Michael Piazza among other local artists.[24] Although some of these books disappeared from circulation the library staff eventually adopted many others into their official cataloging system.

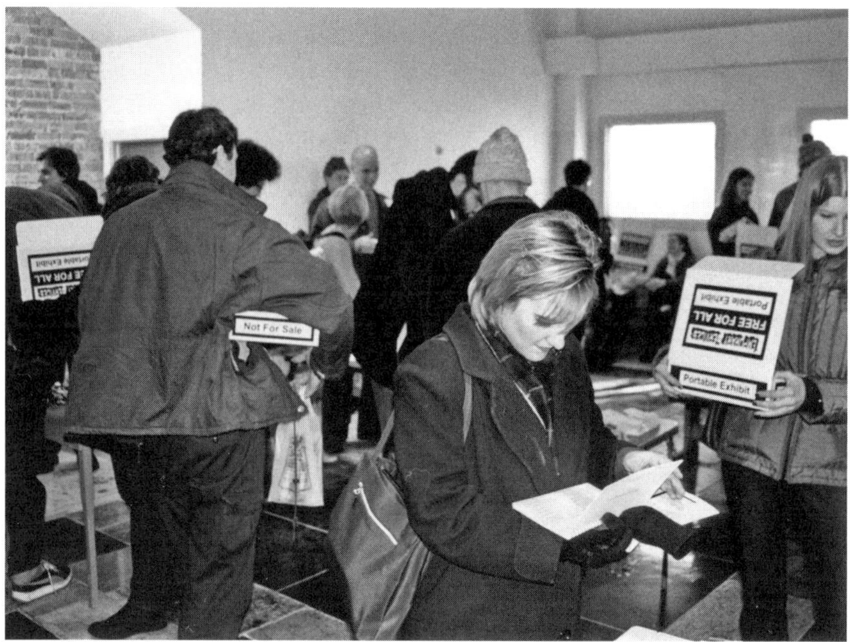

Temporary Services one-day project *Free For All* took place in Chicago. Inside a temporary gallery space the group arranged folding tables upon which numerous small artworks and booklets were stacked. Each visitor was permitted to load up one cardboard box with free materials. When all of the art was disbursed the project ended (2000). Image courtesy Temporary Services.

OWB and the Harold Washington Library intervention were experiments in the borderland between art and the public sphere, or perhaps the failure of the public sphere to live up to expectations. By contrast, the daylong exhibition *Free For All* (FFA) was a critique largely directed towards art world economics. Once again in 2000 TS filled a storefront space located in a primarily residential

Chicago neighborhood with dozens of folding tables. About a hundred small cardboard boxes resembling take-away food containers were arranged on a table near the entrance. Printed on each box was the label "Temporary Services / *Free For All* / Portable Exhibition." Participants picked up one *Free For All* box and then proceeded to walk about the space filling it with an assortment of gifts arranged on the remaining tables. Among the items offered were modified stamped coins, graphic decal stickers, video tapes, cassette recordings, reprints of various found texts, a selection of published religious tracts and even shoe-shine mittens appropriated from a hotel chain. Visitors were permitted to examine and choose one gift box to take away with them. Once all the free gifts were claimed the exhibition came to an end. However, three common elements were found in every box prior to any additional gifts: a booklet listing 1-800 phone numbers useful for obtaining free sample products; an inventory of the contents of all the boxes (essentially the exhibition "catalog"); and a DIY pamphlet outlining strategies for reproducing the project that read, in part, "if you obtained a variety of free materials from this show, you probably have enough things to mount a small exhibit of this work on your own."[25] Included in the booklet were step-by-step instructions challenging visitors to reproduce the group's project, free of copyright or credit. But *Free For All* was not only a critique of the mainstream art economy's dependency on administered scarcity and exclusivity, it also served to illustrate an alternative system of cultural distribution and generosity. It did so, however, by symbolically appropriating institutional authority. Printed on the free project pamphlet was the phrase "You are a collector now," as though a scripted speech act could magically confer on the recipient some kind of official status within the hierarchical structure of the art world. The directness of tone, the disregard for art world decorum—if this is a mode of institutional art critique then it is quite unlike the well-administered forms such self-criticism has recently taken. The cultural politics of TS, and other groups like them, is that of the non-center, which paradoxically exists in many places around the globe, not least in the American Midwest.

City of Big Shoulders

Chicago is a city of small neighborhoods surrounded by monumental canals, warehouses, and railroads that still dominate the urban landscape as remnants of its once massive meatpacking and manufacturing industries. Not that this gritty afterlife has halted the advance of neoliberalization and gentrification. As Richard Lloyd points out in his book *Neo-Bohemia: Art and Commerce in the Postindustrial City*, cultural entrepreneurs in Chicago and other global cities take advantage of a concentrated pool of creative labor that "largely bears its own costs of reproduction." "Today, workers must be competent to the task demands of flexible production—able to demonstrate 'individual creativity' to an unprecedented degree—and they must also be able to acclimate themselves to enormous amounts of uncertainty and risk."[26] The Neo-Bohemian culture industries that have taken root in the "Second City" also reflect the region's deeply engrained working-class sensibility and nostalgia insists Lloyd.[27] While creative young hopefuls in New York City might find supplemental employment servicing the massive legal, financial, and real estate sectors—proof reading, teaching English as a second language to overseas corporate executives, or until recently perhaps even selling condos or working as day-traders on Wall Street—moonlighting in Chicago as an immaterial service worker is much harder to come by. Members of the city's creative class often make a living at lower prestige service labor jobs such as distributing flyers, waiting tables, or bartending, regardless of whether their background is middle or working class.[28] But as Lloyd points out, serving drinks in fashionable bars or clubs in Wicker Park permits artists to mingle with potential "industry scouts," customers who may help them realize their "actual" life's vocation. At the same time these hovering artistic souls provide their employers with a free bonus: the cool hipness of their very presence. Perhaps it is not a coincidence that a group like Temporary Services has emerged out of this mix of surplus talent and prickly, working-class imagination. It may also be why Chicago's DIY aesthetic appears to form a link within a new alternative art scene stretching across the Midwest region and beyond. As if by fiat, many of the region's artists appear to be constructing their own shadow municipality loosely centered within this city described by its native son Nelson Algren as a "lover with a broken nose" (though "never a lovely so real").[29] Together with Experimental Station, Stockyard Institute, inCUBATE, Versionfest, the aforementioned Mess Hall, and such dissident (on and offline) cultural publications as *The Baffler*, *Proximity*, *Lumpen*, and the geopolitical research journal *AREA*, it seems that Chicago's dissident culture uniquely shares certain features with artists and intellectuals in other marginalized global regions, especially those of post-communist Eastern Europe undergoing rapid neoliberalization.[30] This "Second City" effect may explain why Temporary Services has received more attention from curators and art spaces in places like Zagreb, Vilnius, Ljubljana, Copenhagen, Redfern Sydney, or Turku Finland, than the major art centers of New York, London, or Berlin.

In 2007 TS traveled to Zagreb at the invitation of the Croatian-based curatorial collective What, How & for Whom (WHW). There they exhibited several projects including the Public Phenomena archive and a collection of photocopied leaflets that appeared for one year on Chicago streets in 2000 warning residents of a mysterious conspiratorial organization called the Ancient Order that had allegedly inspired Charles Manson's murder spree, brought about the Oklahoma City bombing of 1995, and, in a strange echo of New York's William Depperman

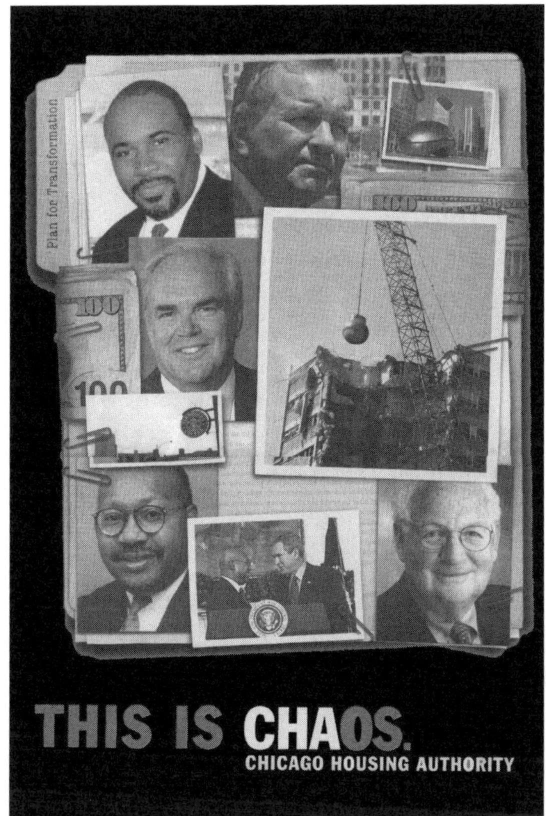

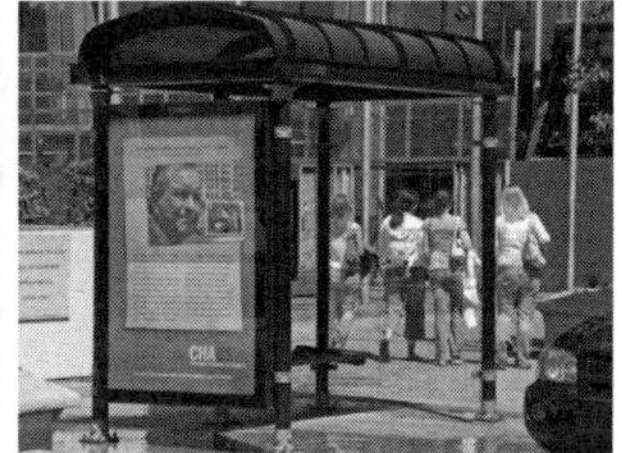

Mayor Daley CHAos Campaign poster asking "Are tourists more important than the poor?" installed in Chicago's Loop business district in 2005. CHAos was a 2005 propaganda campaign aimed at the Chicago Housing Authority (CHA) and its then-freshly branded identity: CHAnge. The CHA intended to illicit a positive interpretation of their large-scale multi-year effort to tear down Chicago's public housing. The CHAos campaign combined research and outreach with a multi-pronged media stunt which illegally installed nearly 100 subway and bus-shelter advertisements which contained a scathing critique of public housing policies. As Micah Maidenberg states in his article in *AREA Chicago*: "The principals behind the CHAos campaign spent three months researching the recent history of the Plan for Transformation, talking to public housing residents, lawyers, and advocates. They drew up a top ten powerbroker list ... including Chicago Mayor Richard Daley, CHA CEO Terry Peterson, two private housing developers, and Alfonso Jackson, the Secretary of the federal Housing and Urban Development agency." Image courtesy CHAos.

a decade earlier, caused the death of kung-fu actor Bruce Lee in 1973.[31] More recently the artists Zanny Begg and Keg de Souza of You Are Here sponsored TS to recreate a public project for a primarily Syrian and Aboriginal neighborhood in Sydney that was first carried out in Chicago in 2000. In both cities the group assumed its signature fictitious role as unofficial "public servant," distributing questionnaires that asked local residents to comment on public "plop-down" sculptures, which they had no input in selecting.[32] In Chicago, TS posted its street survey directly next to a looped steel artwork at the corner of Western and Grand on Chicago's Near West Side. Anonymous responses to the abstract public art ranged from "Eye Sore," "Twisted," "Enchanting," "For white people only," and "Prefer Army tank that was once on this site" (four people signed on to this last comment). In the Redfern "black heart" section of Sydney, Australia, most commentators (who had the option of emailing their opinion) pointed out that the abstract sculpture's upright metal spikes reminded them of the grisly death of local teenager Thomas "TJ" Hickey. The metal sculpture was supposed to invoke the nest of the Bowerbird, but brought back memories of Hickey, a 17-year-old Aboriginal youth who was impaled on a metal fence after being thrown from his bicycle with police cars in pursuit. The incident led to rioting in 2004, as well as claims of a cover-up after white authorities were cleared of all wrongdoing. One annoyed Australian respondent uncannily echoed the Chicago project thousands of miles away by asserting that "only someone who has visited normandy can fully appreciate the need for tank traps and anti personal defences like we have on the corner of regent and redfern."[33] However insightful or simply misinformed, these contrasting references to militarization and segregation in Chicago and Sydney underscore an implicit critique made by Fischer, Bloom, and Collo-Julin: the alienating absence of democratic input regarding what was once thought of as the public commons.

Gifts of Resistance

The new social and cultural practices of generosity that TS is a part of no doubt rekindle an old vanguard desire to dissolve *art into life*, one that seeks to break down divisions between artists and non-artists, producers and spectators. In this sense this new wave of collectivist art invokes not only the post-revolutionary activities of Constructivists and Productivists in the USSR who sought to merge their work with everyday factory labor, but also the post-war practices of Cobra, and later Fluxus, AntFarm, Video Freex, and other conceptual and photographic-media based artists who developed a political practice in consort with a broader critique of capitalism and imperialism waged by students, feminists, minorities, and workers in the 1960s and '70s. This history of course has even older historical precedents dating back more than a hundred years if we allow for William Morris and the Arts and Crafts Movement of the late nineteenth century, or even earlier if we include the populist parades organized by Jacques-Louis David for the revolutionary French government in the late 1700s. Austrian philosopher and activist Gerald Raunig makes excellent use of this history as a backdrop to current interventionist practices in his recent book *Art and Revolution*, but here we should note that still older populist cultural forms such as carnival also involve interruptions of everyday life, and have frequently been cited by socially engaged artists as an influence on their work, even though this low visual culture does not fit easily within the orthodox narrative of Western art history.[34] In 2000 Raunig initiated a collaborative multi-lingual web project called Transversal that is itself a form of digital gift economy in which overlapping theoretical texts on art and politics are translated into several languages and made available free online at www.eipcp.net. Notably the name eipcp, or European Institute for Progressive Cultural Policies, was initially intended as an ironic jab at the proliferation of online and actual policy think tanks, but has since then morphed into a full-blown "project institution" in its own right, not unlike similar mock-institutions that are discussed in Chapter 7.

The list of contemporary interventionist collectives, groups, and cooperatives, some of which were surveyed for this book, is extensive and growing. Along with Temporary Services it includes 6Plus (Tuscon), 16 Beaver Street (NYC); Ala Plastica (Argentina); Baltimore Development Cooperative (Maryland); Basekamp (Philadelphia), Brainstormers (NYC); Broken City Lab (Windsor, Canada); Chainworkers (Italy); The Change You Want To See (Brooklyn); Chto Delat?/What is to be done? (St. Petersburg); Cuckoo (New Zealand); Huit Facettes (Senegal); Critical Art Ensemble (US); Department for Public Appearances (Munich, Germany); Grupo Etcétera (Argentina); Free Soil (Denmark, various locations); Future Farmers (San Francisco); Glowlab (Brooklyn); Grupo de Arte Callejero GAC (Argentina); Haha (Chicago); Icelandic Love Corporation (Reykjavík); Institute for Applied Autonomy IAA (US); La Lleca (Mexico City); Laboratory of Insurrectionary Imagination (London); Los Angeles Urban Rangers (California); Mischief Makers (Nottingham, UK); neuroTransmitter (Brooklyn); Oda Projesi (Istanbul); Office for Urban Transformation OUT (Milan); Otabenga Jones & Associates (Texas); Park Fiction (Hamburg); Platform (London); PVI Collective (Perth, Australia); Rags Media Collective (India); Red76 (Portland); Sari (India); Space Hijackers (UK); Spanic Attack (NYC); subRosa (US); Superflex (Copenhagen); Ultra Red (Los Angeles); Visible Collective (NYC, 2004–6); The Yes Men (US); YNKB (Copenhagen); What, How & for Whom? WHW (Zagreb); WochenKlausur (Vienna); Xurban (NYC, Istanbul).[35]

It was the Situationists who first elaborated a theory of informal, everyday resistance as anti-capitalist cultural practice. Inspired by the writings of Henri Lefebvre (though no doubt indirectly linked to György Lukács' work on reification), the SI imagined a series of subversive tactics including *détournement*, "Unitary Urbanism," and *Derive* or drift that would interrupt the day-to-day world and refocus public attention on actively transforming society, rather than passively watching its spectacle pass by. The first of these disruptive techniques—*détournement*—is perhaps the best known and involves defacing advertisements, popular culture, cinema, and even artworks in an effort to reveal the underlying ideological structures of what Hans Magnus Enzensberger called the consciousness industry.[36] In a roundabout way *détournement* fueled the first wave of art world institutional critique when artists such as Daniel Burren, Hans Haacke, or Michael Asher used their work to reveal the hidden social, political, and economic framework of museums and galleries, often as it was directly manifest in architectural space.[37] The latter two Situationist techniques were more like experiments in deforming and re-experiencing space by psychologically reassembling a fragmented post-industrial landscape. But the Situationists also espoused an alternative to capitalist economics based on the concept of the potlatch ceremony. As observed by French sociologist Marcel Mauss, native people in the Pacific Northwest of Canada redistributed their property downwards, in the form of gifts that traveled from those better off to those less so, thus raising the status of the gift-givers within the entire community.[38] But the generosity of the Situationists was not without certain expectations of reciprocity. The North American potlatch ceremony may have been a way for some to advance their status in tribal society, and the Situationists, as well as their admirers then and since, anticipate some form of political payoff, some shift in consciousness and engagement with the world. Their generosity therefore might be thought of as a gift of resistance. And its circulation would be described in today's terms as a type of viral politics: a gift passed forwards with the hope that it will alter the "ideological DNA" of future recipients. Such pedagogically programmed gifts of insurgency might also explain the intensive labors of the "Freedom Singers" touring gospel groups organized by the Student Non-Violent Coordinating Committee (SNCC) in support of the civil rights movement in the Southern United States of the 1960s, or the free stores and "death to money" parades organized by the San Francisco Diggers in the 1960s whose "invisible street circus" was modeled after the agrarian communist Diggers of seventeenth-century England. Significantly, as researcher Bradford D. Martin has shown, the line between politics and the counter-culture of the post-war era was not always clearly defined.[39] However, even in a socialist country like Czechoslovakia, dissident post-war youth began rejecting the inherited tropes of nineteenth-century "worker's culture" in order to embrace underground art, music, and a *détourned* versions of the "theater of small forms," a form of intimately staged agitational performance and "living newspapers" first developed in post-revolutionary Russia, though given an absurdist, anti-State twist by Czech dissidents in the 1950s and '60s.[40]

Certainly, capital in all its national and corporate modalities was forever shaken in and around May 1968. In cities from New York, Berlin, and Paris, to Mexico City, and even in some socialist nations, a sweeping series of militant protests by students and workers sought to overturn the post-war social, cultural, and economic order. Suddenly "work," as defined within the hierarchical, Fordist assembly-line regimes of both the capitalist liberal welfare states of the West and the State social-capitalism of the East, was being rejected by a generation of well-educated young people who demanded more than free weekends and evenings in exchange for (alleged) cradle to grave security. Predictably, states responded with violence. In the Tlatelolco neighborhood of Mexico City alone several hundred protesting students were executed by the military.[41] Despite effectively subduing dissent and restoring social order anxious corporations began turning to less volatile places for the production of goods and services: places where the local population presumably had lower expectations regarding wages and quality of life than in the wealthier Northern hemisphere. Resistance moved underground. Jobs shifted away from brick and mortar factories as workers became redundant, even in once highly unionized regions of the UK and Northeastern US. Meanwhile, a burgeoning class of entrepreneurial financiers demanded national borders open up to transnational investment. Freed from regulations in place since the depression of the 1930s, capital's new fiscal fluidity further degraded the economic status of industrial towns like Youngstown Ohio (although one could just as easily substitute Detroit, Buffalo, Liverpool, Belfast, or Cardiff). Here was a highly segregated working-class city that once produced a third of the nation's steel.[42] The protracted economic crisis of the 1970s and the evisceration of the welfare state by an emerging neoliberal political regime reduced the once elite economic status of America's white workers like these to that of a surplus population. "The new economic theory made each worker responsible for his or her own job security" writes Louis Uchitelle in his book *The Disposable American*.[43] Yet the wave of manufacturing layoffs beginning in the late 1970s in the United States, Britain, and other industrial nations was not perceived as a top-down, structural adjustment in class relations brought about by the financial needs of capital. Instead it came as proof that one had simply become "an inferior worker."[44] Still, the resulting mix of humiliation and rancor was directed down the economic ladder, like a poisonous gift, towards unskilled workers, immigrants, and inner-city Blacks and Latinos who had always been structurally excluded from full participation in the "normal" socio-economic order. "Hip hop rose-Phoenix like from the ashes of 1970s New York" writes Sohail Daulatzai, "it was an aesthetic vanguard and a chin check to White America."[45] Unlike the underground rap and hip-hop culture of the 1970s Bronx, or the Chicano culture in East Los Angeles, traditional forms of white working-class dissent were blocked from realizing new forms of cultural expression, or in many cases accessing older forms once made possible through the organized labor movement as well as left-wing and socialist parties. A broken, white working class stood alone, confronting a ruined and fragmented political landscape as jobs once thought to be their unique entitlement disappeared over the border or across the ocean. Left behind was a certain imaginary that jumbled together blocked and defeated utopian fantasies with a bitter dose of bad faith.

The new society of risk may have distributed vulnerability in all directions, exposing each level of class stratification to its own superfluousness, but now more than ever capitalist order depends upon the unabashed maintenance of material inequalities. Yet even as this new and expansive form of neoliberal capitalism with its digitized, social factory sets out to mine these once shadowed archives of mind, emotion, and body, it is plagued by a host of prior longings and troubled memories inevitably stirred by these interventions. We do not have to invoke the militant resistance found in some parts of the Middle East and North Africa to locate a simmering discontent that nonetheless makes use of global networking technology to transmit its bad faith.

Ressentiment

Acid green and grainy, the four-minute streamed snuff video *Homeland Security Part 2* is framed in a dark, circular vignette. Allegedly shot through the lens of a night-vision riflescope we see a distant rock outcropping that appears as if underwater. Then a male voice, in English. "He's low crawling ... Guy with a backpack. I bet ya it's probably full of dope." Breaking from the rocky ridge is a shadowy figure moving tentatively across the desert ridge in the dark. "You know what?" a second male voice responds, "I'm going to take a fuckin' shot." A cracking sound, and a bit more conversation: "Get the shovels, get some lime ... and hey, grab me a 12 pack, too." "Roger that. We fuckin' nailed him, dude!"

Purportedly the video shows the murder of an unarmed illegal immigrant somewhere in the desert border between Southern California and Mexico. The snuff movie was made by members of the Mountain Minutemen, one of over a hundred informally organized vigilante groups that emerged after the terrorist attacks of September 11, 2001. This particular video appeared briefly on YouTube in August 2007, and was removed from the Internet after thousands had seen and commented on it, many with a grisly appreciation. After an investigation by the local sheriff the video's authors insisted it was staged, and that no one had been killed. Although some members of the broader Minuteman Project publicly denounced the alleged farce, describing its makers as "renegades," the farce has since taken on a mythic status amongst anti-immigrant extremists and white supremacists.[46]

Minuteman Project co-founder Jim Gilchrist graphically depicts himself superimposed over the United States Constitution on his own website. He sports an arsenal of compact surveillance equipment: a short wave radio, cell phone, and small video camera that he clutches much like a handgun, finger crooked as if ready on the trigger.[47] Another website for the Campo Minutemen shows an image of a

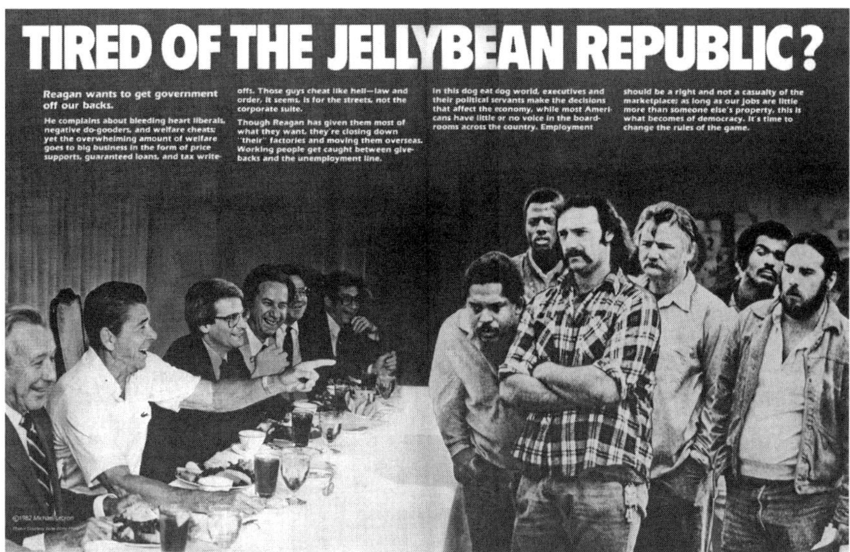

Artist Michael A. Lebron created this photomontage in 1984 and sought to have it installed in the Washington DC subway system using his own funds to purchase advertising space. The local transit authority refused to accept the work, describing the poster as "deceptive." Lebron sued, lost, and finally won on appeal. The piece reads in part "Reagan wants to get government off our backs. He complains about bleeding heart liberals, negative do-gooders, and welfare cheats; yet the overwhelming amount of welfare goes to big business in the form of price supports, guaranteed loans, and tax write-offs. Those guys cheat like hell—law and order, it seems, is for the streets, not the corporate suite." Image courtesy Gregory Sholette Archive and M. Lebron.

man speaking into a walkie-talkie with a rifle slung over his back. He is silhouetted against a spare desert landscape at sunset. The website banner reads: "Doing For Our Country What Our Government Won't."[48] This slogan, much like Gilchrist's montage, or the nocturnal snuff film's ironic reference to homeland security, simultaneously invokes "the law," only to insist that it is either fraudulent or too abstract and therefore insufficient. No written statute it seems can protect the homeland, only flesh and blood guardians who grasp its deepest, most basic truth: vigilance and sacrifice. "At some point," reads one anti-immigrant manifesto, "we must stop this interminable flood of humanity or suffer our demise by its sheer numbers as they impact every aspect of our teetering society."[49] A sense of visceral, existential panic comes across in this nearly Biblical representation of pending disaster. Nevertheless, the representational violence and racism only hinted at on the websites of informal border patrols is granted full expression elsewhere. A visit to the webpages of the far-Right Militia Movements, or the openly fascist Stormfront Media Portal, reveals what the Minutemen dare not say: the rising flood on the nation's borders is not just a tide of unwanted surplus, it is also a *non* white surplus.[50] Sartre might have described this thinking as Bad Faith: a kind of self-deception in which an alleged external threat—in this case the rising tide of dark human surplus—is in fact a response to the wounded fantasy of those whose sense of national integrity and personal identity has been forever ruined by an era of deterritorialized global capitalism.[51] Still, no less than De Certeau's "everyman," this grotesquely retrograde resistance appears inseparably woven into the networks of neoliberal enterprise culture, and the darkest of its "dark matter" reinforces what Eve Sedgwick Kosofsky described as *ignorance effects* that are capable of being "harnessed, licensed, and regulated on a mass scale for striking enforcements."[52] Proponents of the new, networked economy insist that digital technology is fundamentally changing for the better how individuals "interact with their democracy and experience their role as citizens ... and their relationship to the public sphere."[53] The notion of networked *ressentiment* does not seem to have crossed their minds.

Nietzsche's *Genealogy of Morals* pivots on a dialectical flash, an instant when the blocked desires of the subservient class first gain knowledge of their collective advantage over their masters. It is first and foremost an opposition to a world that exists outside the self, a new form of negative creativity the philosopher calls *ressentiment*. The word conjures not only resentfulness, but also active repetition and the folding back upon oneself. Out of the repeated experience of humiliating submission the meek give birth to intelligence and self-knowledge. *Ressentiment* is a reactive project of survival, and with it emerges a previously unrecognized repertoire of skills: the ability to counterfeit and conceal oneself, to be patient in getting what one desires. Against this furtive artistry Nietzsche opposes the fierce appetites of the master class who have no need for self-consciousness or hiding places. Although Nietzsche is openly contemptuous of this new servile morality, he also acknowledges that "a race of such men of ressentiment will inevitably end up cleverer than any noble race."[54] One thing is clear, whether merely bitter or revolutionary, undeveloped or reactive, this survival project inevitably makes use of whatever resources it finds at hand, including the misappropriation of the "master's" own voice, the principal means of expressing political will today. The non-market dark matter that Benkler refers to is shot through with just such stealthy, frequently ambiguous expressions of resentment and rebellion. It is replete with acts of theft, rich with *double entendre* and knowing acts of indirection. Scott describes these "weapons of the weak," and African-American scholar Cornel West lectures that as "Nietzsche noted (with different aims in mind), subversive memory and other-regarding morality are the principal weapons for the wretched of the earth and those who fight to enhance their plight."[55] But this insubordinate dark matter can just as easily take the form of regressive brutality like that associated with racist football hooligans in the UK and elsewhere. Sociologist John Wilson describes the participants in such disconnected collectivism as "unclubbables" who are eager to take advantage of public festivals and fanfare to stage group transgression of disciplinary controls.[56] However, we might also describe this species of angry dark matter as a kind of poisonous gift that circulates as much in "real spaces" as in cyberspace.[57] Fortunately, as West assures us, the forces of subversive memory born of repeated failure also seek to establish a kind of shadow jurisdiction with their own outlaw justice and bottom-up counter-institutionality. Indeed, the archives, public projects, exhibitions, and publications of Temporary Services, PAD/D, AWC, Critical Art Ensemble—and for that matter even the premise of this book—would probably not be conceivable without the creative negativity made possible by a shadowy *ressentiment*.

Angry Gifts

At the height of the financial collapse in Argentina in 2002, a group of self-organized cultural interventionists calling themselves Etcétera carried out "mierdazo," a human shit-tossing festival in downtown Buenos Aires. The cultural activists gathered local participants, many wearing masks and banging on pots and pans, in an action often called *cacerolazo*. They then publicly collected excrement and took turns flinging it at the façades of the Chamber of Deputies, and at the headquarters of HSBC, one of the banks credited with undermining the country's economy.[58] For several years Grupo Etcétera worked loosely with H.I.J.O.S., a movement of political activists seeking social justice for the (now) adult children of the "disappeared," students and leftists murdered during the dirty wars of the 1960s. More recently Etcétera inaugurated what they call the *International Errorist Movement*, insisting that for an errorist, an error is something good. "Errorism isn't the waving of a drowning man. It's obvious that the shipwreck happened and we were on it, we can't deny it." [59]

In the face of seemingly overwhelming odds there is something bittersweet about such resistance. As historian Ana Longoni writes "let us leave it there, then, with a laugh that weighs up and conveys some of the sadness of retreat, a laugh that celebrates, as a small and unexpected triumph, the fact that something from the universe of activist art should be taken on and owned not just by the new social movements, but even by the old Left."[60]

A year after the fecal festival in Buenos Aires, Yomango entered the lobby of the Santander Bank in Barcelona, Spain. The lose-knit performance collective carried bottles of champagne stolen from a nearby supermarket during a public shoplifting performance the previous evening. To the punchy rhythm of Argentinean tango music group members danced and uncorked the agitated beverage, spraying the

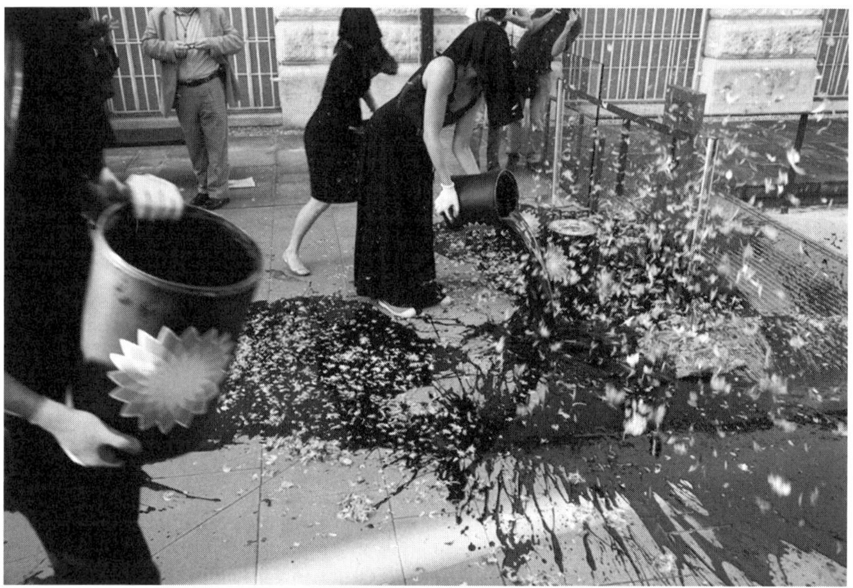

Black molasses is splashed onto the steps of Tate Modern from buckets adorned with the logo of BP. Organized by the group Liberate Tate, the June 28, 2010 protest took place as the museum celebrated 20 years of BP sponsorship, even as the corporation's leaking oil well spewed more than 35,000 barrels of crude oil a day into the Gulf of Mexico. A letter condemning BP by the environmental art group Platform was simultaneously published in the *Guardian* newspaper that read in part: "Every day Tate scrubs clean BP's public image with the detergent of cool progressive culture. But there is nothing innovative or cutting edge about a company that knowingly feeds our addiction to fossil fuels." Image courtesy Immo Klink Studio.

lobby in a frothy protest against the bank's participation in Argentina's economic implosion. Documentation of this "Yomango Tango" in the form of a music video shows bank managers and employees, more puzzled than alarmed, attempt to continue working as the party spins on about them. "Yomango" is Spanish slang for "I take," as well as a word play on the popular Mango chain stores that sell relatively low-priced working women's clothing and accessories. With thousands of stores opening in the Middle East, Asia, and in the United States, the Barcelona-based corporation has become a global lifestyle brand. By contrast, Yomango's branding "from below" gave birth to a series of informal "outlets" or franchises in other parts of Europe, Mexico, and South America. Using the Internet to replicate its counter-brand, Yomango marketed baggy clothes for hiding products, customized accessories with secret pockets for disappearing goods, even training lessons in how to shoplift. Nevertheless, group members insist that the aim of these highly staged "five fingered discounts" was never personal profit. Pilfered goods were not resold, but consumed or freely redistributed during carnivalesque public actions intended to serve as collective "disobedience and direct action against multinational corporations."[61] In one highly publicized action the group removed a 9.50 Euro "sale dress" from a store, and put it on display at the Center for Contemporary Culture in Barcelona, thus producing an instantaneous Duchampian readymade while underscoring the link between art and capital. The dress, along with other stolen clothing, was later returned to the store in an absurdist "fashion show." The group's "magic act" of transmuting dross to gold was gifted forward as an online streamed video contagion. "More than important, the internet has been fundamental for the diffusion of Yomango," insists the group in a text posted on Raunig's eipcp.net. Yomango goes on to explain that the group initially began working within the physical space of the city but later emerged as a "viral brand whose avowed aim was to arrive at losing control of itself."[62] The giddy chaos of the bank lobby intervention in Yomango Tango ends with Liza Minnelli belting out lyrics from her signature performance in "Cabaret": "I used to have a girlfriend known as Elsie, with whom I shared four sordid rooms in Chelsea, the day she died the neighbors came to snicker: 'Well, that's what comes With too much pills and liquor.'" But the song ends with Minnelli sweetly singing, "She was the happiest corpse I'd ever seen."[63]

A lovely corpse, plumes of expensive champagne, a barrage of animated shit—if capital reduces us to one vast interchangeable surplus of expenditure and consumption, so much bio-rubbish poked with pharmaceuticals and lured with over-codes (and no longer even worth programming to respond to an old-fashioned work ethic), then Yomango instructs us to, "Dare to desire ... Because you can't BUY happiness."[64] In Annalee Newitz's book *Pretend We're Dead* the history of capitalism is narrated as a monster movie "from beginning to end."[65] But perhaps the real nightmare is a post-Fordist musical in which a veritable army of stand-in zombies lingers off-stage, waiting to pretend it is alive.[66] *Be happy, insultingly happy. YOMANGO: feel pretty!*

5

GLUT, OVERPRODUCTION, REDUNDANCY!

What is neoliberalism? A programme for destroying collective structures which may impede the pure market logic.

Pierre Bourdieu[1]

Glut

The glut of art and artists is "the normal condition of the art market," Carol Duncan commented in 1983.[2] More than 20 years later a 2005 Rand Corporation study of visual artists in the United States updated her observations, describing an even more unsettling picture of the art world. Its key finding was that although the number of artists had greatly increased in recent decades, the hierarchy among artists, "always evident, appears to have become increasingly stratified, as has their earnings prospects." The report goes on to add that although a few "superstars" at the top of this economic pyramid "sell their work for hundreds of thousands and occasionally millions of dollars, the vast majority of visual artists often struggle to make a living from the sale of their work and typically earn a substantial portion of their income from non-arts employment."[3] Certainly, if post-modernism has taught us anything is it not that individual authorship should be viewed with intellectual suspicion? Why, then, more than 40 years after Barthes' legendary essay "Death of the Author," does the Rand Corporation report reveal increasing art world disparities based on the success of "a few"? Several important questions flow from these observations. First, if the oversupply of artistic labor is an enduring and commonplace feature of artistic production, then the art world must inevitably draw some specific, material benefit from this redundant workforce. Second, the fact that inequality between artist producers has become increasingly evident in recent years suggests that processes of deregulation and privatization within the broader enterprise economy directly affect the working conditions of artists.[4] What possible consequences would result from a mutiny within the global art factory? That is to say, if this inert surfeit of cultural production were to mobilize itself in opposition to the exclusionary mechanisms of the art market? First it would need to awake to the fact that its seemingly natural condition of underdevelopment is contingent, constructed, and that its invisible status renders the efforts of most artists no different from that of the joyful labor of the hobbyist, amateur, or Sunday painter. We appear to be far from witnessing some general art strike today. Still, conditions for unprecedented self-organization are readily available to artists as an increasing number of professional cultural producers turn to social networking sites, online art galleries, and individual webpages as a way of directly distributing images and information about their work. It is a trend that follows the actions of informal artists who have joined such DIY exhibition platforms as deviantART and Elfwood in the millions over the past decade. What would it take to politicize this dark mass of redundant cultural production and what might this politics look like? One thing is clear: thus far, in spite of a burgeoning wave of newly minted talent fresh from art schools and universities with direct access to the means of self-representation, the familiar, pyramidal structure of the high culture industry has not only been unfazed, it appears to have become more entrenched than ever before. Of even greater concern is the degree to which this business as usual appears to be de-politicizing the longstanding role of the artist as a force of independent social criticism.

In her breakthrough study of the visual arts during the rise of neoliberal enterprise culture, art historian Chin-tao Wu concludes that corporate intervention into the world of art has radically altered the way museums, government cultural programs, and other public institutions operate.[5] The shift towards privatization also affects the content of art, as well as the working conditions of artists. Corporations are not known for their support of controversial political work for example, and the exaggerated differences between a few successful artists and all others reported by Rand appears to reflect the ultra-competitive rules of business, as opposed to the collaborative networking of culture. Wu does not dismiss the longstanding involvement artists have always had with capitalist markets; she does however suggest a qualitative shift has occurred in the current neoliberal economy. As complicated and controversial as public arts funding was prior to the 1980s, by enclosing culture within their private business interests global corporations have since "reframed the space and redefined discourse on contemporary art." What then to make of the fact that an increasing number of individuals now identify themselves as "artists" in such an entrepreneurial environment?[6] Is it possible that this enterprise culture has so de-radicalized artists that something approaching an historic compromise or *détente* is taking shape whereby artists gain improved social legitimacy within the neoliberal economy while capital gains a profitable cultural paradigm in which to promote a new work ethic of creativity and personal risk-taking? Far from merely an academic question the possibility of an historic collaboration between art and capital holds out serious consequences for anyone who believes artistic production should retain some degree of autonomy from the market, or that cultural work is more than just instrumental labor, or most urgently of all that it is the historic mission of art to fearlessly engage in social dissent.

Overproduction

That the art world is awash in surplus labor is not a startling insight. Tens of thousands of individuals now have undergraduate or graduate degrees in fine art. Their webpages complete with project descriptions, résumés, contact information, and blogs are spread across the World Wide Web like leaves after a storm. A few commercial entities have begun indexing these sites for a fee, however it is The Saatchi Gallery that has developed the most comprehensive online art platform providing artists with free digital space for their work (jpgs and videos), but also investing in the future of this lucrative industry by appealing directly to art students. According to information on the site some 120,000 artists and art students use their services worldwide. Saatchi takes no commissions for any sales made through its website, and boasts that since launching the platform in 2006 some 130 million dollars in transactions have taken place. The number is difficult to believe. As far as can be ascertained, cyberspace has yet to launch the career of any previously unknown artist into stardom. Most serious Internet sales appear to be backed by the legitimating collateral of a respected art dealer and physical gallery space. One noteworthy alternative model of autonomous online repre-

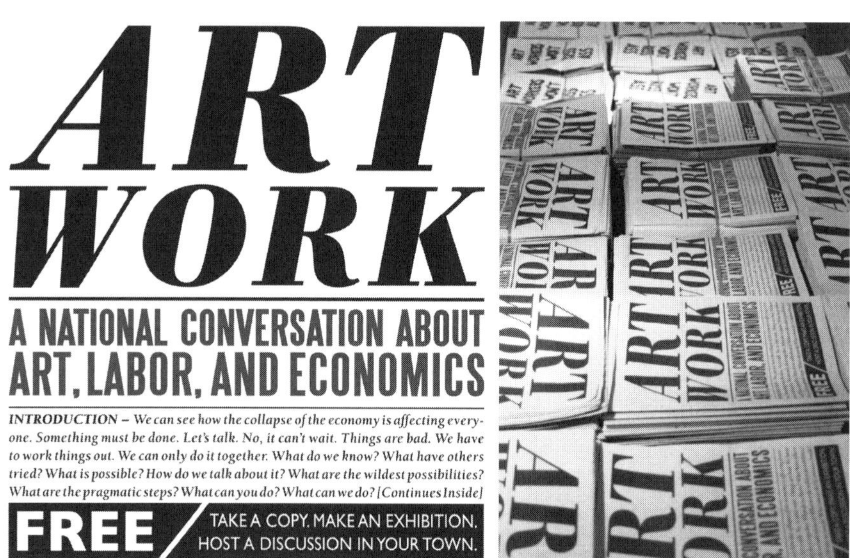

Artists have historically self-organized in response to their own precariousness; a recent example is *Art Work*, a newspaper and accompanying website published by Temporary Services with writings about the effects of the current economic collapse on artists' working conditions. The newspaper is available online and from Half Letter Press in Chicago and has been distributed for free in over a dozen cities around the world since September 2009; see www.artandwork.us/tag/temporary-services. Images courtesy Temporary Services.

sentation is Justseeds.org, a cooperative web platform made up of left-leaning artists from Canada, Mexico, and across the United States (although primarily from the west coast and Midwest). Thematically focused on issues of social justice and anarchist history, Just Seeds artists produce "traditional" graphic works—silk-screen posters, spray-painted stencils, even linoleum block prints. The pieces are displayed as digital images on the website and sell for modest prices, often between 10 and 75 dollars. As if illustrating the long-tail theory of retailing in which numerous specialized interests form a proportionally larger consumer base than that of mainstream buyers, Just Seeds' tiny sales add up to at least enough to sustain both the website and provide a partial income stream for participants.[7] Despite the simplicity of this model, made all the more effortless thanks to the Internet, such cooperation is still rare among contemporary artists. Instead, the growing army of surplus art producers apparently prefer to survive by helping to reproduce the familiar hierarchies of the art world, the same symbolic and fiscal economic system that guarantees most of them will fail.

Some redundant cultural workers are employed by the mega-studios of successful artists. Inside these art factories they might sand and polish resin-cast sculptures or even paint entire canvases, often doing so for little more than the minimum wage.[8] A growing number of these "art extras" operate out of cultural Bantustans surrounding the invisible municipality of the mainstream global art world. In the 1990s New York City's art center shifted away from the downtown scene in SoHo to its present location in "Chelsea" on Manhattan's West Side. But unlike the SoHo that was initially colonized by artists in the 1960s, Chelsea, according to sociologists David Halle and Elisabeth Tiso, represents "the triumph of the commercial gallery system as a mode of showing and distributing art."[9] Practically speaking, few artists can afford to live or work anywhere near this exhibition machinery. Affordable studio space has migrated outwards, away from where the established gatekeeper galleries, museums, curators, and critics are concentrated. The actual production of art has come to resemble a form of outsourced manufacturing or "just-in-time" creativity. The structural partitioning of the culture industry is not limited to New York City. German sociologist Melanie Fasche points out that while 50 percent of the artworks ultimately shown at *Documenta 12* and the 2007 Venice Biennale were produced in Berlin, very little of this work is actually exhibited in Berlin itself. The city has become a "production site" for the manufacture of contemporary art that is shown elsewhere. Along similar lines, French sociologist Alain Quemin's research into France's participation in the global art world came as a shock to that nation's cultural elite when he reported that despite the flow of artists and art institutions between an increasing number of global museums and art biennials around the globe, the majority of artists and the capital (actual and cultural) associated with contemporary art remain concentrated in the US, the UK, and Germany.[10] Which is to say that even as art production appears increasingly distributed in time and space, the processes of cultural valorization remain tied to New York, London, and Berlin. Meanwhile, the majority of professionally trained artists go on reproducing this state of affairs, despite their guaranteed exile from its inner circle.

If the art world still typically represents itself as a top-down process with the cream rising and the dross settling, it effectively functions the other way around, from the bottom up. For what the Rand Corporation does not report, or cannot acknowledge, is that unlike other professions the art industry *must* ghettoize the majority of its qualified participants in order to generate artistic value. But this dark surplus creativity does not function to lower artistic labor costs or the price of artistic goods, as in Marx's classic formula. Rather, the army of under- and semi-employed cultural workers performs a price-enhancing role, though only with regard to a limited number of artworks by a select group of artists whose labor is in turn lavishly rewarded. All the while, as we have seen, these many "invisibles" help reproduce the art world through their purchase of art supplies, journal subscriptions, museum memberships, teaching assignments, but also their informal conversation and gossip, which reasserts the status of leading art brands at openings, on blog sites, at parties, and so forth. Furthermore, as Marcelo Expósito points out, this upwardly distributed art factory system does not extract value on a limited basis as do traditional forms of employment, but does so intensively, continuously, by requiring non-stop forms of "self-educating, training or testing, preparation, production, and so on," all of which are carried out without remuneration.[11] The majority of art world participants are in fact being groomed for failure through a managed system of political (small "p") underdevelopment. Only those who believe that talent (like noble birth) inevitably determines one's individual fortune would describe this as natural. And yet that is typically how the art market is described, as a natural economy in which truly gifted artists are rewarded. What would be necessary to see this the other way around? For one thing it might mean that those who exceptionally succeed become a sort of footnote to a broader social intelligence or collective talent. Furthermore, the closer the art world gets to some sort of full employment, the more it would incorporate a mass larger than its own ideological construction. That would appear to be a logical impossibility, unless a very different art world was imagined, with a very different dispensation of artistic "real estate."

The Grammar of Art Worlds

Sociologist Howard S. Becker famously used the plural term *art worlds* to describe the multiple inputs that make possible the production of any work of art (a painting, sculpture, novel, or concert). In the visual, plastic arts this multiplicity includes canvas and paintbrush manufacturers, as well as critics and museum administrators. Becker insisted that such art worlds have soft and frequently contested boundaries that sometimes allow acts of aesthetic innovation to upset and displace cultural norms and hierarchies. From the vantage point of the early 1980s, when Becker devised his famed formula, he was looking back at a period of substantial public beneficence on the arts in the United States, fueled in large part by an ideological conflict with the Soviet Union and its allies.[12] Federal arts funding peaked in the late 1970s, but not before giving birth to a cluster of artistic institutions that in some cases sought to disengage, or openly contest, the world of art and commerce.[13] Artist Martha Rosler explains that ample government funding in the 1960s and 1970s not only helped spread cultural equality amongst artists, but also expanded cultural support to many smaller American cities wherein prospered "active art scenes that were not oriented toward making (a lot of) money from art."[14] In New York City a series of "alternative" exhibition spaces emerged including 112 Greene Street, Artists Space, and The Kitchen.[15] While these spaces indeed functioned somewhat autonomously from the established art world they did so largely because of steady funding by the National Endowment for the Arts (NEA), as Julie Ault has shown.[16] Once the Cold War ended, so did a great deal of public support for this non-market-oriented experimentation. Which is why the art dealer who bluntly explained to Rosler that your either on or off the artworld's "table" was not exaggerating, but was nonetheless speaking from a decidedly post-1980s perspective.[17]

Today, more than 20 years after the collapse of "actually existing socialism," and some 30 years after the rise of ultra-free-market capitalism, the art world is inundated with participants yet increasingly devoid of Becker's pluralistic "s." Despite a proliferation of international biennials, national museums, gatekeeper galleries, not-for-profit spaces, and commercial art fairs the same acknowledged art luminaries and their proven goods tend to be circulated at all levels of the system. Paradoxically, the contemporary art world is at once more global and yet less varied, more visibly diversified and yet neither porous nor malleable in its aesthetic range. Certainly no single artistic style rules this scene, or, to employ a term popular amongst some younger artists, no single artistic brand holds market supremacy. On the contrary, contemporary art appears indiscriminate in appetite; a maw perpetually opened in uninterrupted consumption as vats of chemicals, butchered animals, dirty mattresses, mass produced commodities, disposable packing tape, cast-off pieces of cardboard, even acts of coitus enter the art world through its specialized showrooms in New York, Los Angeles, London, Berlin, Paris (and, minus the sex, also now in Beijing, Shanghai, Dubai, and Abu Dhabi). Animal, vegetable, mineral: like a steady flock of coarse penitents, the more profane in outer appearance, the greater the artistic yield. For there seems to be one constant leveling everything entering this global cultural matrix: faith in the institutional art world's ability to drag some aesthetic meaning out like a confession from any object, person, or situation.

In this sense, the contemporary art factory deconstructs and reconstructs the world in its own image and for its own ends much as capital has from the start. In both instances—contemporary art and global financial systems—the level of complexity, number of transactions, and volume of participants makes it all but impossible to disentangle physical products and forces of production (labor plus technology) from regulatory, legal, and discursive practices. In addition, the material and symbolic sides of these economies appear to endlessly amplify each other. Think of the way neoliberal "financialization" entangles material goods, from shoes to genes, seeds, or plumbing supplies, with such intangibles as electromagnetic fields, exotic financial instruments, and intellectual property rights. This is perhaps why someone who collects contemporary art, but who also teaches marketing to MBA students, can confidently assert that the art dealer brand "often becomes a substitute for, and certainly is a reinforcement of, aesthetic judgment."[18] From this perspective, an era known for its "toxic business assets" is logically epitomized by Damien Hirst's sculpture *The Physical Impossibility of Death in the Mind of Someone Living* (1991), a chemically embalmed stuffed shark. And, not surprisingly, the same knotting-together of art and commerce leads some to despair.

Art historian Julian Stallabrass skeptically describes the world of contemporary art as *Art Incorporated*; artist Andrea Fraser caustically insists "It's Art When I Say It's Art"; and historian Chin-tao Wu insists that "while contemporary art, especially in its avant-garde manifestations, is generally assumed to be in rebellion against the system, it actually acquires a seductive commercial appeal within it."[19] But what if we could set principles aside for a moment? After all, Stallabrass and Wu seem to be applying what some might describe as outmoded ethical standards more in keeping with nineteenth- and twentieth-century notions of "high" art as something exemplary and noble. What if we could re-imagine the conflict pitting producers against proprietors by lifting this age-old struggle out of its moorings in an outmoded essentialist language and reconfiguring it as a horizontal network of scripts and textual articulations? In other words, if we stop expecting art to be a qualitative measure of a civilization's or an artist's deeper spirit or truth, then such aesthetic and ethical complications should disappear. Unlike Becker's bottom-up interpretation of art-making as a collective process, sociologist Olav Velthuis is concerned with the fluid world of art prices at the other end. But top becomes a bottom of sorts as overlapping "cultural constellations" establish aesthetic values through a web of discursive networks made up of gossip, price-setting games, and the exchange of monetary and informational "gifts" between art dealers, collectors, and artist-producers. Becker's *art world* is reborn as a symbolic economy in which all players—gallery owners, patrons, and artists—now allegedly share "the same business culture."[20] Perhaps it's not a coincidence that this description of artistic enterprise culture resembles the ineffable flow of derivatives, puts and calls, and "dark liquidity" that also make up the financialized neoliberal economy.

Velthuis begins by challenging Pierre Bourdieu's concept of cultural capital. According to Velthuis, Bourdieu understood art as an economy of symbolic goods that nevertheless ultimately serves to enhance the actual, material wealth of a group or individual.[21] Thus, "real" capital is always concealed within (or exchangeable for) what Bourdieu famously called cultural capital. This "economistic" tendency, writes Velthuis, incorrectly emphasizes old notions such as the forces of production, exchange, accumulation, and the sort of antagonisms between producers and owners (artists and dealers) that hint at an art world version of class politics. Perhaps it is also no coincidence that Velthuis' description of the contemporary art world as a messy, interconnected discursive field closely resembles Laclau and Mouffe's radically de-centered field of political antagonism?[22] But the art world is even less antagonistic than this because its many players "visit the same or similar shows, are interested in each other's gossip and rumors and read the same arts magazines."[23] And what begins as an analysis of how art is priced morphs into a comment on artistic value in general. Even more unequivocally than the author of the *$12 Million Stuffed Shark*, Velthuis declares that the sort of detached aesthetic judgment once called for by Immanuel Kant can never be disentangled from the instrumentality of the global art market. Instead, he insists, when it comes to establishing an artwork's worth, "value and price seem to be entangled in an ongoing dialectic," and that artistic quality "is avoided explicitly as a direct determinant of price."[24] Why would anyone seek some mysterious underlying cause and effect for how artistic value comes and goes, rises or falls? We need only look to the language games (expressed in prices) displayed by the market's social players to discover these answers already exist. The sociologist of prices concludes with a twist on a familiar post-structuralist maxim: there is nothing outside the market.

Velthuis is certainly correct to point out that it is impossible to fully, meaningfully disentangle contemporary art practices from art discourse; both involve production that is always already social, plastic, and unfixed. He is also right to imply that this model is universal, or nearly so. Even those artists who claim to care nothing about the "art world" in New York, London, Berlin, and so forth, or those artists who produce "community-based" projects and installations in small cities and towns, or those who operate collectively at the outermost spatial and geographical regions of the market, still inadvertently play a role within this world. No matter how obscure or seemingly radical one's creative activity may be there is an avaricious interest at work within the art world's restricted economy, a hunger not only for the new, but for everything. And this desire is enhanced today by a prosthesis made up of technologies and protocols such as the Internet, html, various graphic interfaces, email, cell phones and cheap, print-on-demand (POD) publications. You can be sure that at any given moment an essay is being written, a paper delivered, a conference planned, an exhibition curated in which all but the darkest corners of this entangled cultural universe are included, however briefly, or superficially. Velthuis most likely gets this, and yet his particular post-modern interpretation prevents him from drawing the obvious *political* conclusion: that what he calls prices are dependent upon an inherent asymmetry of productive forces in which most artists are transformed into a precarious culture proletariat, gleaning and extracting what value can be wrested from the material and symbolic economy of the actually existing art world. By not challenging the processes through which cultural values are produced, circulated, and accumulated, or seeking to ask by whom and for whom these values (or prices or scripts) are established, the sociologist winds up offering little more than a cheerful bromide for coming to terms with neoliberalism and what appears to be a "natural" situation whose new "Social Darwinian" playbook we are all supposed to accept and happily comply with.

This "naturalized" system of asymmetrical risks and benefits is eerily similar to the theory of desired rates of unemployment proposed by ultra-free-market guru Milton Friedman. Post-depression era efforts at creating full-employment, Friedman argued, led to greater bargaining power amongst workers, which in turn inflated wages and ultimately also the price of all commodities, not just labor. As a result, conservative free market policy makers in the late 1970s and 1980s promoted increasing unemployment through industry deregulation, directly opposing the managed approach to capitalism associated with John Maynard Keynes.[25] But this calculated unemployment inevitably led to increased precariousness amongst workers. It is, insists the Midnight Notes Collective, a disciplinary mechanism aimed not just at stopping the economic redistribution of wealth, but at halting the re-appropriation of social capital underway in the 1960s and 1970s by labor, women, people of color and other minorities. If we compare this system of social discipline in the economy at large with the more limited sphere of the art world some curious similarities emerge. Contrary to the oft-cited canard that artists are too individualistic to work together, we find in the United States alone a substantial history of non-governmental guilds, unions, associations, and collectives organized by artists. Efforts to provide greater employment for art workers in the 1930s, through the Work Progress Administration (WPA), or in the 1960s and 1970s, through the NEA, CETA (Comprehensive Employment and Training Act), and Artist in Residency (AIR) programs, led again and again to acts of organized, often militant confrontation in which artists actually demanded even greater autonomy and social security. Their demands included better pay and greater job security from Federally funded programs associated with the WPA, and the Harlem Artists Guild of 1935 also tackled the issue of race-based discrimination in the government's hiring of artists. Some of these artist-led organizations were wholly independent, others initiated by the Communist Party USA. Although difficult to trace, the organizational tactics developed by the political Left during the 1920s and 1930s appear to have had some influence on the thinking of artists groups in the late 1960s and 1970s and perhaps later.

Since then, in the age of neoliberal enterprise culture that has followed the Reagan/Thatcher "revolution," we find a tremendous lowering of expectations amongst artists and a cooling down of efforts at collective action. Significantly, this trend towards passivity appears about to change once again in the wake of the current economic collapse. Nevertheless, precariousness, or simply "precarity," has become the "new normal" for workers in the current "jobless recovery."

The Precarity this Time

Out of necessity, artists are expert at juggling intermittent bouts of barely profitable creative work with more numerous and routine jobs in construction, standardized graphic design, and other service industries. Artists not only incessantly retrain themselves to satisfy novel working conditions, they establish complex social networks made up of other, semi-employed artists, as well as family members, friends, and on occasion, the patron. These networks circulate material support, as well as a great deal of intangible, informational assistance in the form of opportunities for auditions, exhibitions, publications, technical solutions, even gossip. Supplementing this precarious existence is the occasional monetary gift from a parent or a foundation grant or residency. A small percentage of artists also procure additional income from part-time teaching, although in the United States such positions typically exclude benefits such as health insurance or retirement pay. According to an unpublished study, one third of those who graduated from a major US art school in 1963 had given up making art by 1981 and were actually earning more money than those who continued being artists.[26] Visual, plastic artists— painters, sculptors, installation, new media, and performance artists— also benefit from the sporadic sale of artwork, although only a small percentage will ever be able to depend on direct sales in any meaningful way. Instead, for most artists, especially for the majority of visual artists, actual working conditions remain much the same under neoliberalism as they have for centuries. As French Sociologist Pierre-Michel Menger points out, artists as an occupational group tend to be "younger than the general workforce, better educated, and concentrated in a few metropolitan areas." However, artists also reveal:

> higher rates of self-employment, higher rates of unemployment and of several forms of constrained underemployment (non-voluntary part-time work, intermittent work, fewer

> hours of work), and are more often multiple jobholders … artists earn less than workers in their reference occupational category (professional, technical and kindred workers), whose members have comparable human capital characteristics (education, training and age). And they experience larger income variability, and greater wage dispersion.[27]

Menger insists that studying artists' careers is useful insofar as it illuminates "how individuals learn to manage the risks of their trade." In the case of artists this involves the continuous transfer of risk downwards into a "highly flexible and disintegrated organizational setting." All of which leads the sociologist to depict a Lilliputian version of neoliberalism in which artists operate within a continuous state of *oversupply disequilibrium*. And yet despite this inherent precariousness and the built-in "income penalty" the market charges for becoming an artist, the number of people claiming that title is on the rise. In the US the population of artists doubled between 1970 and 1990, roughly the same time frame in which deregulation and privatization delivered us the entrepreneurial risk society.

According to the 2005 US Census, nearly 2 million Americans listed "artist" as their primary employment. Another 300,000 claimed it was their second job. This makes the "job" of being an "artist" one of the largest single professions in the nation, just slightly smaller than those employed in the active-duty military. The actual number of "professionally trained" artists in the United States, or in the world for that matter, is difficult to quantify. Perhaps some idea of this mass can be gleaned from the fact that over 150 specialized "art schools" are dedicated solely to turning out artists in the US, and that most other colleges and universities now offer a bachelor or graduate level degree in fine art.[28] Likewise, although visual artists are only one portion of creative industry workers typically surveyed by the EU, its cultural sector reportedly employed at least 5.8 million such people in 2004, which is more than the total working population of Greece and Ireland put together.[29]

At the same time, although the overall number of artists in England has kept pace with other types of labor, employment in the arts has allegedly increased by some 150,000 jobs between 1993 and 2003. An estimated total revenue of between £23 and £29 billion was reportedly generated by the cultural sector in London alone, making art second only to the city's business sector, according to the Arts Council England in 2004. The growth of artists in Germany is even more astounding. While the majority of the German workforce showed zero growth between 1995 and 2003, the cultural sector grew at a rate of 3.4 percent. As in other post-industrial economies Germany's workforce is increasingly self-employed, but self-employment among cultural workers is four times that of the rest of the labor force.[30] Just as remarkable is the spike in Canada's artistic population. Between 1991 and 2000 the number of artists in all provinces grew

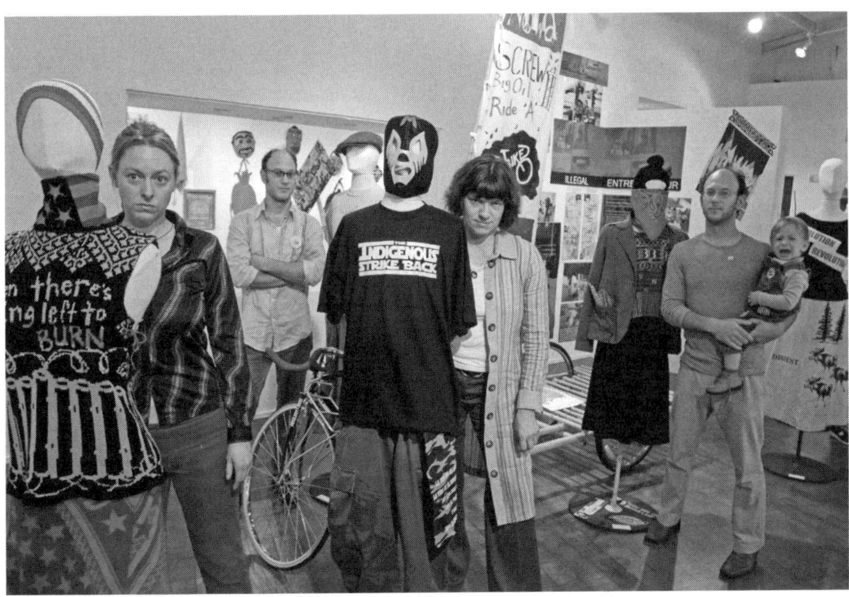

Editors, and a future editor, of the *Journal of Aesthetics & Protest* (JOAAP) pose amidst items displayed in an exhibition they organized entitled "Street Signs and Solar Ovens: Socialcraft in Los Angeles" for LA's Craft and Folk Art Museum in 2006. Much like the editorial outlook of the journal itself, the exhibition highlighted a range of items that fell on the outer margins of formal art practice made by individuals, groups, and artists, including work about foraged foods, seed bombs, radical knitting, pirate radio technology, and sustainable urban culture. Challenging normative ideas of artistic valorization and who is defined as an artist appears to be at the core of JOAAP and many similar, informal collectives. The JOAAP editors are, from left to right: Cara Baldwin, Robby Herbst, Christina Ulke, Marc Herbst, Anselm Herbst. Image courtesy joaap.org

at a rate three times that of the overall Canadian workforce. The authors of the Canadian Council for the Arts report appear genuinely surprised by the fact that some 131,000 Canadians now "spend more time on creating art than on any other occupation." They go on to suggest that this number is probably too low since many "artists" who drive taxis at night or work civil service jobs during the day are simply invisible.[31] Considering the overall reduction in social security since the 1980s, and especially in light of the near-total elimination of direct subsidization to artists in the US at least, one might conclude that the volume of new cultural producers would contract, or remain static. If, as Menger and others maintain, art is the precarious profession *par excellence*, why then does it appear to be thriving in an environment of deregulation, privatization, and risk?[32] Bluntly put, might there be a secret bond between post-Fordist enterprise culture and contemporary art?

AWC v. APT

One example of an allegedly mutually beneficial partnership between artists and free-marketers is the recent invention of Artists Pension Trust (APT). Created in 2004 by Moti Shniberg (a "new" economy technology entrepreneur), Dan Galai (onetime accomplice of the late economist Milton Friedman, father of Reaganomics), and David A. Ross (former SF MoMA and Whitney Museum of Art director), APT now has offices not only in New York, Los Angeles, London, and Berlin but also in the budding art-market centers of Dubai, Mumbai, Beijing, and Mexico City. The fund's goal is to collateralize the chronic insecurity of art professionals by enlisting artists—generally those who have already achieved a certain level of market success—to invest some of their work alongside a "community" of select peers, thereby providing "a uniquely diversified, alternative income stream."[33] In theory, only a few APT artists need become cultural superstars to raise the raft beneath the entire "community," including of course the trust fund's founders, managers, and curators. Officially, legally, APT is located in the British Virgin Islands (BVI), a Caribbean territory of the UK that provides a legal tax haven for the company's assets. The mission of APT is to apply "the discipline of financial services and the concept of risk diversification in creating the first investment program specifically dedicated for artists."[34] APT's model of privately collateralized risk management contrasts sharply with the universalist aspirations of collective security made by several informal artists' groups in the late 1960s and early 1970s.[35] Between 1967 and 1968 the Canadian Artists' Representation/Le Front des CARFAC (later CAR) organized to demand that commercial galleries respect copyright for all Canadian artists and provide royalties from sales and rental-like fees for exhibiting work. (CAR continues to serve artists today.) Several years later two short-lived London-based organizations briefly expressed concerns about social security for artists. One did so with solemnity, the other sardonically (though not without a kind of critical seriousness). In 1971 Mary Kelly, Kay Fido, Margaret Harrison, and Conrad Atkinson founded the Artists Union and immediately sought to establish resale rights for all British artists.[36] But the year before, artists Gustav Metzger, Felipe Ehrenberg, Stuart Brisley, and others led a march on the Tate Gallery under the name of the International Coalition for the Liquidation of Art. Their objective was to debate museum "visitors and staff about the complicity of museums in racism, sexism, war," as well as demand the "equal representation of women, ethnic minorities, and greater decentralization of culture."[37]

Meanwhile, in Buenos Aires, Argentina, the short-lived Syndicate of Unified Plastic Artists (*del Sindicato Único de Artistas Plásticos*, or SAUP) sought to enhance artists' professional status through a highly politicized trade union with ties to the militant *Tucumán Arde* art project of 1968.[38] However, one of the most militant efforts to garner legal rights for cultural workers began with an international group of artists who resided in New York City. In January 1969, Vassilakis Takis from Greece, Hans Haacke from Germany, Wen-Ying Tsai from China, as well as Tom Lloyd, Willoughby Sharp, and John Perreault from the United States met to establish the Art Workers' Coalition (AWC).[39] Several hundred people soon joined its open-door meetings, including Carl Andre, Benny Andrews, Gregory Battcock, Lee Lozano, and Lucy Lippard. In many respects, AWC functioned much like a trade union that viewed museums, their boards, and their top administrators as a *de facto* managerial class, which effectively represented not the public good, but the interests of the commercial art market. It was the artists' job to reveal this conflict and propose ways of amending it. AWC staged protests outside the Museum of Modern Art, the Metropolitan, and Guggenheim museums. Thirteen demands were formally presented to museums (the following year the list was boiled down to nine). Among the reforms called for was a royalties system in which collectors would pay artists a percentage of profits from the resale of their work, and the demand that museums "should be open on two evenings until midnight and admission should be free at all times." The one definite lasting accomplishment of the short-lived AWC is free-admission museum hours at museums in New York City, but the group also helped to set in motion the Professional and Administrative Staff Association (PASTA) union at MoMA, and inspired the formulation of The Artist's Reserved Rights Transfer And Sale Agreement, a legal agreement that provides artists with several post-sale rights including royalty payments if an artwork is resold for a higher price.[40] Before it disbanded in 1971 AWC members marched in support of striking staff at MoMA, called on museums to set aside exhibition space for women, minorities, and artists with no gallery representation, and staged public actions along with sister groups such as Guerrilla Art Action Group (GAAG) to protest US military involvement in Southeast Asia. However, AWC also called for the establishment of an artists' trust fund to provide artists with social security benefits much along the lines proposed by APT some 40 years later. And yet, this is precisely where AWC and APT most clearly diverge.

The language used by 1960s artists' groups such as CARFAC, Artists Union, SAUP, and AWC was built around an essential antagonism between artists and cultural labor that takes place in and for the public sphere on one hand, and the production of art commodities and art careers necessary for the art world on the other. As Lucy R. Lippard put it:

> As a public and therefore potentially accountable institution, the Museums were targeted in order to make points not only about artists' rights but also about opposition to the war in Vietnam, to racism and eventually sexism, and about the institutional entanglement of aesthetic with corporate finance and imperialism.[41]

As just noted, one of AWC's demands was for the establishment of a trust fund that would provide living artists with "stipends, health insurance, help for artists' dependents and other social benefits." But the endowment for this trust was to have been levied by taxing the work of dead artists in the collections of major museums. More like a public trust, the AWC fund would need to be accessible to all working artists. In fact, the ambitious programs proposed by the AWC and the other self-organized groups could only have been realized if the majority of cultural producers were willing to participate in any given region. Notably, only CARFAC still operates today, some 40 years later, boasting affiliated organizations in more than half of Canada's provinces. Perhaps its longevity is possible because solidarity between artists is easier to sustain in a weaker commercial art market where universal social security remains intact?[42] Regardless, the kind of public accountability that makes up Lippard's premise is exactly what neoliberalism has sought to eviscerate from the public's collective memory. By contrast, APT functions much like a private, gated community set apart from the broad population of artists. And this exclusivity is not optional. In order to focus attention on a select group of artists APT has no choice but to ignore the security and fair trade interests of the majority of artists. Any investment strategy based on market speculation must concentrate value disproportionately. The prevailing ideology of APT and much neoliberal enterprise culture is concisely summarized in the title of a recent, best-selling business book: *The Winner-Take-All Society*.[43]

Modern Ruins

Shorn from the social safety net, exposed to unmediated market penetration by every demand set forth by capital, beyond the reach of effective political power, the so-called free market economy offers two asymmetrical options: either sell oneself "creatively" at the high end of the market—as an IT systems designer, hedge-fund manager, graphic interface specialist, etc.—or join the ranks of the burgeoning surplus workforce who compete for non-unionized, low-skilled, part-time jobs. Between these two poles very little gradation exists. Creative jobs typically provide exceptional individual rewards in terms of salary and benefits, but also in the way productivity is organized. Deviating from the routines of the factory, so-called "creative" industries offer flexible schedules and non-hierarchical work environments that encourage employees to indulge in non-linear problem solving. Many of these workers are not salaried but "independent" contractors responsible for their own health care and other benefits. For creative laborers, intermittent, project-based employment, working from home, and opening an individual retirement account are signs reflecting superior education and imagination. As long as contracts are maintained and clients are available, such workplace elasticity allows high-end laborers to experience a unique sense of personal freedom inconceivable within the traditional brick and mortar factory world of yesterday. By contrast, the low-wage service bottom-end of the neoliberal economy is full of unimaginative, repetitive jobs, a world of retail sales cashiers, truck drivers, waiters and waitresses, nursing aides, janitors, and food preparation workers. It was here, as Saskia Sassen and others have shown, where the most robust employment growth in the United States was taking place until the recent economic collapse (and no doubt this is where job growth will first return).[44] But disciplinary mechanisms exist at both extremes. For the majority at the bottom of the labor market flexible employment is not a gift, it is an ever-present and tangible reminder that joblessness is just one paycheck away. For those who lack the capacity, or desire, to produce on demand in an artistic, self-fulfilling manner the penalty is no different from that which befalls the "failed" artist: exile to the precarious abyss of office cubicles, stock rooms, and fixed-wage servitude. Of course there are significant differences in pay grade, social status, and physical mobility between a dishwasher at McDonald's and a web designer, or between a janitor in an office building and an art professor. Nevertheless, all forms of post-Fordist work are continuously exposed to the disciplinary forces of neoliberalism, including anti-union legislation, the lack of secure social benefits, the use of non-contracted part-time labor, and the corporatization of the academy where part-time instructors dominate the learning environment. The effects of this new "precarity" on the imagination of those it administers have yet to be systematically investigated, but it is not surprising to find that many cultural activists are pessimistic regarding organized politics involving anything larger than informal gatherings of small, cellular groups, a point taken up in Chapter 7. For those at the top of the economy on the other hand, what lies in wait should they fail to be creatively self-motivated is evident all around them: a former executive scans groceries at the supermarket, a discharged securities trader empties ashtrays down the street from the office where he once worked.[45]

Globalization, privatization, flexible work schedules, deregulated markets; 30 years of "neoliberal" capitalism has driven most world governments partly or wholly to abandon their previous function as arbitrators between the security of the majority and the profiteering of the corporate sector. The "free market" oriented state that emerged in the late 1970s does not even pretend to offer citizens full, meaningful employment, directly contradicting the promise of security, however illusory, once offered by the post-war Keynesian state. And this has little to do with lack of training or education. "Rather than a skills shortage, millions of American workers have more skills than their jobs require," insists Uchitelle.[46] The result has been a radical redistribution of potential risk from the collective level—the community, state, nation, society—downward, towards each increasingly isolated member of the populace. Today, one's individual sense of "being" seems to exist in a perpetual state of jeopardy. And yet, this impression is

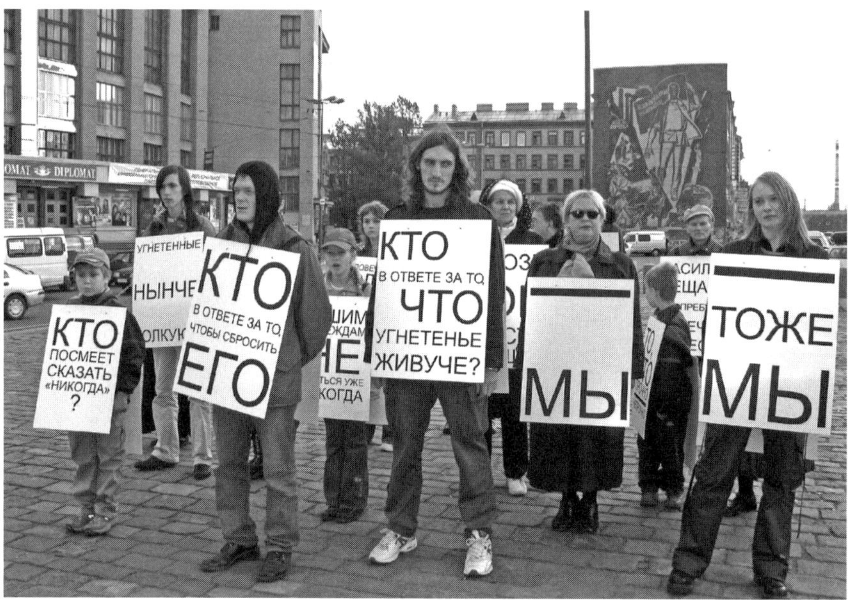

Still from the video project *Angry Sandwich People or in a Praise of Dialectics* (2006), named after a poem by Bertolt Brecht and staged here in collaboration with local political activists by the Russian artists' collective Chto Delat? (What is to be Done?). Participants gathered in a St. Petersburg square where they moved in unison and recited Brecht's poem in a "Soviet mode." "Who dares say 'never'? Who's to blame if oppression remains?" Chto Delat? describes the effect of the reading as resounding "with the depleted pathos of the revolutionary past, a re-collection (*Erinnerung*) of the very language that new forms of protest aspire to negate." Visible behind the performers is a fading 1960s mural displaying the words "Proletariat Unite!" Project realized by Tsapya, Nikolay Oleynikov, and Dmitry Vilensky. Image courtesy Chto Delat?

also unreal, involving an unpredictable set of hazards from multiple sources both real and fictive: the inhalation of invisible toxins, a mutated virus, a government conspiracy, genetically manipulated food, sudden acts of violence, an unforeseen terrorist plot. According to one group of sociologists the essence of this indefinite risk-consciousness is not that it is happening, "but that it might be happening."[47] Compounding these fears is the sublime spectacle of the modern ruin: a blasted skyscraper, a bomb-flattened metropolis, an exploded hospital, devastated marketplace, or pillaged museum, school, library. Perhaps most devastating of all, a geometrically precise pile of naked men forced to display their utter vulnerability in front of some down-market digital camera. Theorist Allen Feldman describes the sadistic snapshots of prisoners at the Abu Ghraib prison in Iraq as pixilated presentations of a "subjugated and damaged interiority." Nicholas Mirzoeff insists these widely circulated obscenities provide Western viewers with a "full spectrum dominance" that ranges from demolished bodies to devastated nations.[48] The result is a vivid display of what philosopher Giorgio Agamben calls "bare life," human existence that has passed beyond the outermost limits of law, language, and society to become a kind of living, biological ruin, a no-longer-human human.[49] For the spectator in developed nations, these bodily and metropolitan degradations always appear to be occurring elsewhere, amongst those unfortunates with the least resources who are already only a few steps away from disposability and abjection: so many distant bodies that help mark-off the outermost margins of our world-image; so many dire cities where society and "bare life" incessantly brush up against each other. The essence of this ontological precariousness is summed up not only by the rise of a 7 billion dollar human trafficking industry, but by the expendable form this modern bondage takes on in an age of weakened national governments and individuated risk. "Slaves of the past were worth stealing and worth chasing down if they escaped," writes activist Kevin Bales:

> Before globalization, people were concerned with "fixed" capital investments, like factories, or lifelong slaves, and long-term planning. The globalized world is more concerned with flexibility than fixed capital, and with processes of production rather than permanence. The same is true of slavery. Slaves are so cheap now that they are not seen as long-term investments, just flexible resources to be used or thrown away as needed.[50]

Given the sweeping integration of the world's economy Bales notes that we may even be directly "using or profiting from the work of these slaves."[51] The risk no longer appears entirely *elsewhere*. A local shipping container reveals a cargo of discarded human sexual slaves; a nearby neighborhood is contaminated with sewage, oil, chemicals; a bank repossesses the home of a friend or family member; the dreaded *pink slip* is deposited in our office mailbox demarcating termination of employment. Instability moves closer. It insinuates itself into our everyday world. And simultaneously, on a far vaster scale that is often beyond comprehension, it takes on an epic dimension: the Asian monetary failure of 1997; the Argentinean economic collapse of 1999–2002 (a preamble to the current crisis?); the botched US government response to Hurricane Katrina in 2005; and the global financial implosion of 2007–9 whose full effects remain ongoing and unpredictable at the time of writing, although it is clear that a structural adjustment of historical proportions is taking place within global capitalism. Despite a recently elected reform government in the United States headed by Barack Obama still scrambling to contain this latest capitalist "malfunction," the line has clearly grown too slender between what once separated manageable economic predicaments—workplace redundancy, unemployment, an uninsured illness, student debt, a failed mortgage—and all-out catastrophe—bankruptcy, homelessness, incarceration, or deportation. Suddenly, it is *we* in the developed world brushing up against bare life. The encounter may be brief, or it may be extended—or it may be interminable.

Without losing site of the dramatically different levels of risk faced by shantytown dwellers, prisoners, or slaves, as opposed to an increasingly at-risk workforce in the cities and towns of developed countries, it is not too difficult to see how such unremitting precariousness reinforces the day-to-day disciplinary mechanisms of neoliberal, enterprise culture.

We Are the Surplus

Like the deterritorialized flow of finance capital, all that is solid, and all that is intangibly social, has been reduced to a kind of raw material for market speculation and bio-political asset mining. It is the social order itself, and the very notion of governance, along with a longstanding promise of security and happiness, that has become another kind of modern ruin. Even if the MFA (Master of Fine Arts) is the new MBA (Master of Business Arts), as some neoliberal business theorists intone, mumbling the phrase like some magic formula, what exactly does enterprise culture gain from its seemingly tender embrace of artists and creative labor?[52] Perhaps, rather than an historic compromise between artistic creativity and the neoliberal economy, what has fixated neoliberalism onto the image of the artist as ideal worker is not so much her imaginative out-of-the-box thinking or restless flexibility as the way the art world as an aggregate economy successfully manages its own excessively surplus labor force, extracting value from a redundant majority of "failed" artists who in turn apparently acquiesce to this disciplinary arrangement. There could be no better formula imaginable for capitalism 2.0 as it moves into the new century. Still, what remains to be seen is how those lost bits and pieces of a ruined society and dreams of collective dissonance might be reanimated through some artistic necromancy by those not yet ready to give in to the disciplinary sirens of enterprise culture.

6

THE UNNAMABLE

It was everywhere—a gelatin—a slime—yet it had shapes, a thousand shapes of horror beyond all memory. There were eyes—and a blemish. It was the pit—the maelstrom—the ultimate abomination.

H. P. Lovecraft

Terror Trials

Known for its carefully researched art projects that explicitly criticize the US corporate and military sectors, the Tactical Media group Critical Art Ensemble (CAE) became an ideal target for the neoconservative administration of President George Bush Jr., which actively engaged in the suppression of domestic political dissent following September 11, 2001. Two and a half years after the terror bombings of September 2001, the United States Department of Justice (DOJ) began a criminal investigation of American artist Steve Kurtz and his scientist colleague Robert Ferrell. In June of 2004, several of Kurtz's associates were handed court subpoenas ordering them to appear before an upcoming Grand Jury hearing or face imprisonment. The artist and scientist were being investigated for bioterrorism. Thus began a four-year legal battle in which the two men faced prison terms of up to 20 years. Kurtz and Ferrell's legal defense ultimately cost an estimated quarter of a million dollars, money raised primarily by members of the art and civil rights communities.[1] Several of the court papers were delivered to potential witnesses at an art opening. The subpoenaed individuals either knew Kurtz as a friend, or had collaborated with him through CAE, the politically engaged, multi-disciplinary artists' collective Kurtz had co-founded in 1986.[2]

In Kurtz's case, what began as a personal loss—the unrelated death of his wife, which sparked a police investigation because of biochemical laboratory materials visible in their house—soon became part of a political campaign aimed at promoting self-censorship amongst dissident artists, scientists, journalists, and academics opposed to the Bush administration's policies.[3] To some degree the government's message, which had already been transmitted before the Kurtz debacle when congress passed the USA Patriot Act in October 2001, achieved its objective when a series of exhibition closings and acts of self-censorship took place across the US art world. Following September 11, FBI and Secret Service agents actively questioned artists, curators, and directors of art galleries at Columbia College in Chicago, the Baltimore Museum of Art, and the Art Car Museum Houston, Texas over reports of "anti-American" activity and put direct and indirect pressure on cultural dissidents. Several museum and gallery directors self-censored their own exhibitions by removing socially critical work or adding to shows artworks with a "conservative" point of view in order to appear more "balanced." Exhibitions at Arizona State University, the City Museum of Washington, the Chelsea Market in New York City, and Ohio University removed artwork that was considered critical of the President or his policies. FBI and Secret Service agents also made intimidating phone calls to university administrators whose faculty publicly opposed the President's war in Iraq. One especially poignant case of self-censorship relayed directly to the author involved an art historian employed by the Smithsonian Institute. While browsing the Institute's own intranet service she discovered that certain images of nineteenth-century paintings were not accessible. The paintings were blocked by the Bush Jr. administration because in them people appeared naked. Only by seeking an added level of clearance would the scholar be permitted to see these works. Rather than call attention to herself, the historian chose to do her research elsewhere.[4]

Professor Kurtz was eventually cleared on all criminal charges in June of 2008 just as the Justice Department (*sic*) was embroiled in its own ethics scandal. And yet even this victory for artistic expression represents a partial success for those seeking to curtail civil liberties when the tens of thousands of dollars and countless hours of volunteer work that went into achieving this one individual's exoneration are taken into account. Needless to say, the sums required to legally defend someone from such serious charges would be prohibitive for any group or individual who had less developed social networks than those of Steve Kurtz and CAE. On the other hand, the FBI and Justice Department's four-year obsession with Kurtz, Ferrell, and CAE also reveals a clumsy and confused response provoked by a group of cultural workers whose particular blending of art and politics—often described as "tactical media" by the group and its followers—is itself a direct response to the ambiguous spatial environment and ruined social institutions of neoliberal enterprise culture.

Critical Art Ensemble

The installations, performances, videos, Internet, and book projects of CAE typically require group members to teach themselves and the public about new areas of knowledge. This autodidactic approach is indirectly linked with 1960s conceptual artists who began to question the institutional limits of art itself by undertaking the self-study of such disciplines as semiotics (Victor Burgin), systems theory and environmentalism (Hans Haacke), linguistic theory (Art + Language), and mathematics (Mel Bochner), and conceptual artist Adrian Piper even went on from studying art to write her dissertation in Analytical Philosophy with John Rawls. Significantly, CAE cites a different set of influences that includes the Situationists, the Yippies, Guerrilla Art Action Group (GAAG), Rebel Chicano Art Front/Royal Chicano Air Force, Gran Fury, Augusto Boal, and perhaps most significantly the interrogation of authority developed by the Feminist Art Movement. A key feature of CAE, therefore, is the group's desire to extend its socially engaged art practices into a broader public commons rather than focus their critique solely on cultural institutions. Along with this pedagogical and socially critical function, CAE also researches and develops new techniques of civil disobedience. One of the aims of this Left R&D work is to adapt outmoded forms of protest to contemporary social and political realities using such insurgent tactics as culture jamming, direct public interventions, and most recently the "reverse engineering" of certain scientific technologies, methodologies, and processes. This includes forms of knowledge that the group claims have been appropriated and enclosed by private and governmental agencies, but which should remain within a democratic public sphere.

Since 1997, CAE's Do It Yourself (DIY) approach has focused on biotechnology, beginning with a live interrogation of advanced reproductive technologies in the project *Flesh Machine*. This was the first performance art piece to bring a working molecular biology lab into public space. Subsequent projects addressed the promissory rhetoric and risks surrounding new biotechnologies including *Cult of the New Eve* (1999–2000); *GenTerra* (2001–3); and *Free Range Grain* (2003–4). As Kurtz became entangled in government investigation the group was exploring government weaponization of microbial organisms in the project *Marching Plague* (2005–7). Among other findings publicized by CAE is the fact that biological warfare planning in the United States dates back to the 1940s. Perhaps the clearest demonstration of the group's engaged research approach is a series of projects undertaken in collaboration with Beatriz da Costa and Claire Pentecost that focused on the political economy of global agribusiness entitled *Molecular Invasion*. In this series, CAE introduced the idea of "Contestational Biology," which aims to employ the materials and processes of biological science in the public interest rather than in the interests of corporate and military power.

Molecular Invasion was first carried out in 2002 as an art installation and live participatory science-theater work at the Corcoran Art Gallery in Washington DC. Its aim was to "reverse engineer" samples of Monsanto's Round-Up Ready corn, canola and soy seed products: Genetically Modified Organisms or GMOs that the US-based multinational has commercially developed, patented, and strictly licenses. These popular cash crops have been manipulated so that they will only grow in conjunction with Monsanto's herbicides, thus locking-in a veritable monopoly on future agricultural cycles. CAE's response to Monsanto's highly technical business scheme was to employ FBS, or "Fuzzy Biological Sabotage," as a means of self-defense for traditional and organic farmers.[5] The Ensemble describes FBS as a type of Contestational Biology exploiting the not-yet-legislated gray zones surrounding new technologies. In this David-meets-Goliath confrontation, harmless biological agents—plants, insects, reptiles, and microorganisms—carry out targeted political resistance against monopolistic control of the global food supply and the patenting of life forms for corporate profit. *Molecular Invasion* transformed the white cube of the art gallery into a provisional public sphere, a cultural re-engineering project complete with juridical evidence: rows of Monsanto seedlings sprouting beneath artificial lights. Within this makeshift courtroom, visitors were encouraged to study, debate, and judge the significant social issues raised by genetic science, especially when it is directed by financial gain as opposed to public welfare. But CAE also explored ways of resisting corporate monopolization of the food supply. Round-Up Ready seedlings were exposed to an environmentally friendly, non-toxic biochemical disruptor during the exhibition, with the aim of making the plants vulnerable to the company's own herbicidal agents. That outcome would, if carried out in actual practice, cripple Monsanto's vertical hold over agricultural production (the company sells 90 percent of the world's genetically modified seeds). But within the context of the art gallery *cum* laboratory/theater/courtroom, CAE's FBS intervention was still only an experimental investigation, a socially engaged "what if."[6] As with most of their work the Ensemble published detailed reports on its democratically inclined amateur research projects. Over the years this has included six inexpensive booklets distributed by Autonomedia Press in Brooklyn (also available free online) that provide step-by-step instructions for carrying out one's own autodidactic exploration of art and science.[7] But CAE's theatrical critique of authority contrasts sharply with the overt criminal charges brought by officials against Professor Kurtz and his co-defendant Doctor Ferrell. "Art follows reality," Bertolt Brecht once wrote as he sought to represent new subjectivities defined by the rise of the petrochemical industry.[8] CAE's attempt to visualize the world of bioengineering appears to have generated precisely the reverse effect as a peculiar combination of fundamentalist Christianity, willful scientific ignorance, neoconservative ideology, and militarized neoliberalism converged into a darkly surreal vortex.[9]

The unreality that swallowed Kurtz and Ferrell began with a tragedy. On May 11, 2004, Steve Kurtz woke to find his 45-year-old wife lying unresponsive beside him in their Buffalo home in upstate New York. He phoned 911. Emergency personnel who responded to his call took notice of assorted laboratory equipment in the Kurtz home, including Petri dishes, test tubes and a DNA extraction unit that was being used in several art projects by Critical Art Ensemble, and alerted the FBI. Within a short time the Joint Terrorism Task Force descended on the

Kurtz home wearing white, head-to-toe Haz-Mat suits. The agents cordoned off the house, confiscated the body of Kurtz's wife, and gathered up his scientific equipment for analysis. They also impounded the artist's passport, lesson plans, books, automobile, and computers leaving his cat in the quarantined house to fend for itself. Kurtz was placed under surveillance. After 22 hours New York's Commissioner of Public Health officially reported that nothing hazardous was discovered in the home and it posed no danger to the public. Both the county coroner and the FBI determined that Hope Kurtz had died from heart failure. Her body was returned to Steve Kurtz for burial. The family cat survived. The incident appeared over. Another case of jittery, over-reactive law enforcement officials who, in the aftermath of September 11 and the still unsolved anthrax mail murders of that same year, responded to a premature death and the presence of unexpected lab equipment with indiscriminate haste. Nevertheless, the FBI retained the artist's passport, books, papers, and several computer hard drives and in fact had already implemented a full investigation into Kurtz some ten days after Hope's death.

Federal agents set about interviewing the artist's academic colleagues at the State University of New York, Buffalo, where he is a professor. They questioned his department Chair wanting to know why the CAE's members identified themselves as a collective rather than as individuals. They wanted to know about their publications, and how they funded themselves. In a revealing and humorous interview with artist Ryan Griffis, the group responded to the same question stating: "We don't understand how to finance work either. No granting agency has ever given CAE money ... We just hobble along from project to project, usually working with an extremely limited budget."[10] Within weeks subpoenas were issued to a handful of Kurtz's associates. Cited on the document was US Code Title 18, Part I, Chapter 10, Section 175: Prohibitions with respect to Biological Weapons. The scope of this statute was greatly expanded by the USA Patriot Act of 2001, so much so that non-pathogenic research bacteria used in college and high school classrooms and by science hobbyists could be re-labeled as hazardous "biological agents." The Department of Justice's multi-million dollar case against Kurtz and Ferrell rested on the purchase and possession of two such harmless microbes—*Bacillus subtilis* and *Serratia marcescens*—both of which were present in the home of the artist at the time of his wife's death. So innocuous are *Bacillus subtilis* and *Serratia marcescens* that they are typically used for "soap testing" sanitary conditions in hospitals and health clinics. The invisible agent is intentionally spread on surfaces by inspectors who then use ultraviolet light to see how far the microbe has spread in order to examine how well employees have followed standard sanitation procedures. Kurtz had in his home samples of both bacteria procured by Ferrell from American Type Culture Collection (ATCC), a standard resource for schools, hospitals, and the biotech industry.

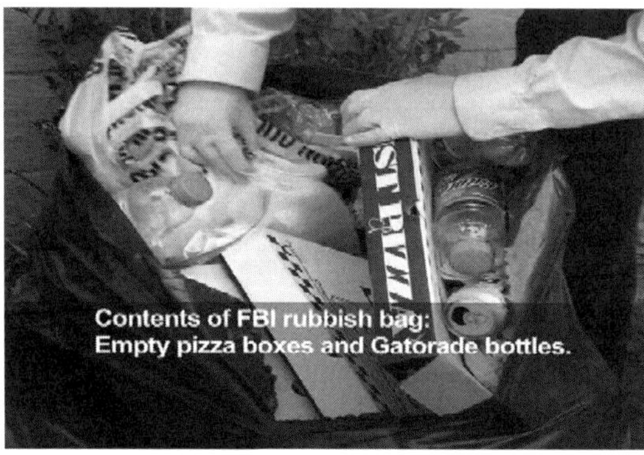

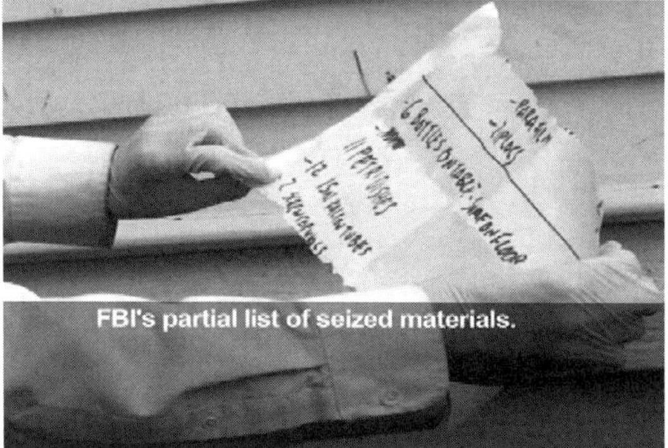

Stills from *Evidence* (2004), a short video work by Critical Art Ensemble, Institute for Applied Autonomy, and Claire Pentecost documenting the trash FBI investigators left behind while occupying the quarantined Buffalo home of CAE group member Steve Kurtz following his wife's death. Image courtesy Critical Art Ensemble.

On June 15, a United States Grand Jury rejected all charges of bioterrorism against Kurtz and his colleague. Twenty-two days later, however, the independent radical press Autonomedia and publisher of CAE's booklets received a subpoena demanding the press submit to the government its list of subscribers. In July, new charges were raised against Kurtz and Ferrell. No longer bioterrorists, the two now found themselves facing up to 20 years in prison on downsized indictments of mail and wire fraud for allegedly purchasing $256 worth of bacterial samples from a scientific supply house under allegedly false pretenses.[11] A committee made up of the artist's friends and supporters was established to raise funds for both men's legal defense. Kurtz hired a high-profile attorney known for his successful defense of First Amendment freedom of speech cases.[12] Autonomedia press was soon dropped from formal investigation; however, it took four years before the charges against Kurtz were finally dismissed as insubstantial.[13] Months before that happened Doctor Ferrell pleaded guilty under government pressure and received a $500 fine with one year's probation. Ferrell was a 27-year survivor of non-Hodgkin's lymphoma, and suffered several strokes after the government charges were brought against him. On April 21, 2008, New York District Court Judge Richard J. Arcara ruled in agreement with Kurtz's attorney that the indictment against the artist "must be dismissed because it fails to allege that the victims [the biological supply company who in fact never leveled charges against Kurtz or Ferrell] were deprived of 'property' within the meaning of the mail and wire fraud statutes, and because it fails to allege that the defendant intended to defraud ATCC and UP of any property."

The court's exoneration of the artist was unquestionably a rebuff to George Bush Jr.'s Justice Department. It took place as other allegations of impropriety were being leveled against the agency and as the President's military involvement in Iraq, already condemned as illegal by the UN, was rapidly eroding his already weak domestic support. Nevertheless, hundreds of hours of volunteer work and tens of thousands of defense fund dollars were required to accomplish one act of justice: defending an artist from being railroaded into prison and made an example of to other would-be critical interventionists. Meanwhile, an unknown number of individuals, though some estimate as many as 1,200, primarily of Muslim Middle Eastern or Northern African background, were detained, investigated, tried, deported, or held on detention based on the new or expanded policing statutes enacted by the post-September 11, homeland security state. Many of these men, women, and children have subsequently been proven innocent of all wrongdoing. Thousands of individuals were detained without trial, others deported, and some sent abroad into "extra-juridical" zones within Pakistan and Syria where human rights do not stand in the way of extreme interrogation methods. The number of people involved in these arrests, disappearances, and renditions and in other forms of detention is difficult to estimate. At the same time, Kurtz and Ferrell's saga discloses several key features unique to collaboratively organized artistic practices, including some that are substantially different from collective formations of the recent past. The first of these characteristics is not especially new. It stems from the nature of collectivism itself. In their publications, exhibitions, and performances CAE members insisted on being recognized not as individuals but as a collective entity, a tendency that motivated the suspicion of government investigators when questioning Kurtz's academic colleagues. Media activist Gregg Bordowitz is explicit: "Though membership is no secret, they prefer anonymity—organized into one entity."[14] The US government has a long history of probing, intimidating, and disrupting collectively organized forms of resistance to its authority or that of big business. One need not look solely at covert action against openly Left factions such as the International Workers of the World (Wobblies), the Communist Party USA, or the Students for a Democratic Society (SDS) to find patterns of government intervention. It is a legacy that includes not only little-known cultural organizations like CAE, but also the active surveillance and suppression of Martin Luther King Jr. and the civil rights movement; of pacifist and religious organizations peacefully opposed to the Vietnam War in the 1960s and '70s; and the intimidation of similar faith-based coalitions opposed to US intervention in Latin America during the Reagan years in the 1980s. As FBI Freedom of Information files show, federal agents not only spied upon these individuals and organizations, they also actively sought to disrupt their activities by submitting false news stories to the media and planting agents provocateurs within their ranks. The framing of actress Jean Seberg for her personal and political affiliation with the Black Panther Party is a well-known case in point.[15]

However, CAE's tactical cultural dissent reflects a very different notion of who or what constitutes political resistance compared with that of most 1960s radicals. One can see this in the way the Ensemble does not seek to establish its own counter-jurisdiction against the mainstream, but instead overtly mimics established symbols and narratives of power in order to reveal the lack of democracy at the heart of the system. Moving within the meshes of enterprise culture this handful of loosely organized, autodidactic artists don lab coats, carry out amateur scientific experiments, publish their experimental findings, and travel about the world under a collective brand offering to share their research with others. They hoist a pirated flag of mainstream credibility. By doing so, they also take advantage of their own lack of a clearly defined image or political position while posing as a far larger and more formidable presence than their modest composition and resources justify. The broader, social significance of this mimicry is scrutinized in the next chapter. For now it is useful to note that such hyperbolic camouflage is an increasingly commonplace feature of contemporary artists' collectives engaged in a decidedly post-1968 form of civil disobedience frequently described as Tactical Media or TM. Along with CAE the practice of TM is most often associated with a cluster of similar, new media-oriented collectives including Electronic Disturbance Theater (EDT), Institute for Applied Autonomy (IAA), Carbon Defense League (CDL), subRosa, The Yes Men, and the Italian television pirates known as Telestreet. A wide range of tactical cultural interventionist groups who make use of electronic networks but manifest themselves in the streets might easily be added to this list: from Code Pink, Billionaires for Bush (defunct), Reclaim the Streets, and the Euro MayDay festivals, to the anti-roads campaigns in Britain and counter-globalization groups such as Tutto Bianco, Chainworkers, and Tendance Floue.[16] While many of the attributes of TM are found amongst socially engaged artists and artists' collectives in general—including a belief that authentic art and culture should align itself with social or political dissent in the form of anti-militarism, increased social justice, the equitable sharing of resources (actual or virtual), and access to participatory democracy—two additional features set TM practitioners apart from other cultural interventionists. The first is their use of inexpensive yet sophisticated media technologies made possible by advances in computer technology and global digital networks. The second is TM's post-communist era "disgust for ideology."[17]

Tactical Media

The viral transmission of TM began in 1997 at a new media festival in Amsterdam known as "the next five minutes." Recapitulating the gestation of all previous avant-garde movements, two cultural activists—Geert Lovink and David Garcia—delivered up a manifesto entitled "The ABCs of Tactical Media." Of course, combining tactics with new imaging technologies was already "in the air" in the early 1990s, and to be entirely accurate, many artists had begun experimenting as early as 1967 with the Sony Portapack portable video recorder to produce a kind of hit-and-run guerilla media through groups like Videofreex, Deep Dish, and Paper Tiger Television.[18] Still, it was not until the mid to late 1980s that the freedom to move between old and new media as well as object making and moving images began to truly become widespread in the art world as an acceptable form of "serious" cultural production, thanks not only to the increasingly diminishing cost of reproductive technology, but also to the collapse of formalist "Greenbergian" art criticism, as discussed in Chapter 2. This shift was so widespread and transformative that even a short-lived art collective in Dublin known as "Blue Funk n. Inf., chiefly Brit. A state of great terror" (1989–94) could ambitiously proclaim in its manifesto, "we are committed to the making and exhibition of media artwork in Ireland. We intend to open a studio with film, video, photography and performance facilities both for ourselves and other artists who wish to work experimentally with these media."[19]

But Lovink and Garcia's manifesto also drew upon a second development in the cultural sphere, involving groups like ACT UP, Gran Fury, and DIVA TV that used increasingly accessible, inexpensive video and print technologies to counteract mass media's homophobic response to the AIDS crisis. Throughout the mid 1980s and early 1990s, organized groups of AIDS activists successfully carried out precise visual campaigns using art, culture, and new media that borrowed advertising tropes from capital's own productive apparatus. Notably, in times of past economic crisis capital often isolated the ill, the disabled, the addicted, or the non-sexually reproducing populations perceived to be superfluous and non-productive. However, a rising economic dependency on creative labor situated at the very core of neoliberal enterprise cultures greatly complicated this ideology of detachment and not-infrequent hostility. It was the tactical sophistication of such groups to play directly off of these frequently contradictory processes of identification and disdain. Both of these precedents—the desacralization of high culture through new technologies and the intervention into shifting social representations—provided Tactical Media with a trove of clever practices rooted in the realm of visual art. But Lovink and Garcia also wedded this evolving concept of aesthetic resistance to the post-Situationist, post-1968 theories of Michel De Certeau and his book *The Practice of Everyday Life*.[20] One could in fact go so far

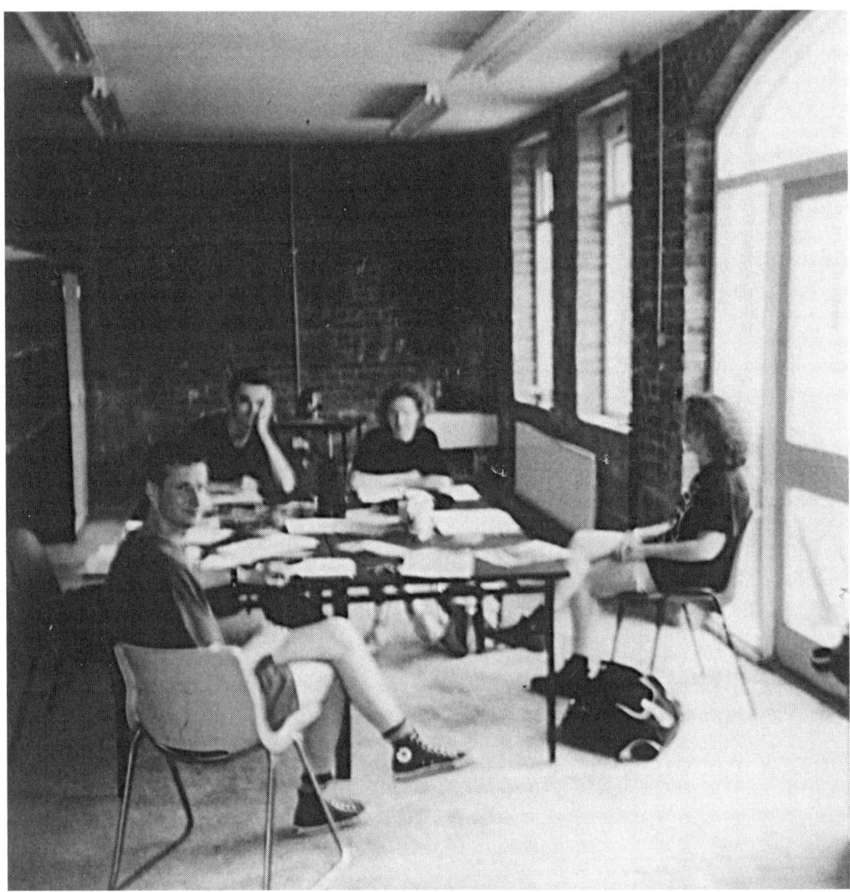

Members of the interdisciplinary Irish collective "Blue Funk n. Inf., chiefly Brit. A state of great terror" (1989–94) seated at the Firestation studios, Dublin, where they will produce a final short film, *C Oblique O*, on the work of a recently deceased member Evelyn Byrne. (From left: Kevin Kelly, Brian Hand, Valerie Connor, and Jaki Irvine). Image courtesy Brian Hand.

as to describe TM as electricity plus De Certeau. Their ABC manifesto called for a new aesthetics of "clever tricks, the hunter's cunning, maneuvers, polymorphic situations, joyful discoveries, poetic as well as warlike."[21] Writing at a moment that some have described as the aftermath of a failed revolution, the French theorist appears to make the best of a bad historical situation by emphasizing day-to-day social resistance over mass action. Rejecting the confrontational and spatially defined politics of leftist parties and unions, De Certeau calls for critical tactics that insinuate themselves "into the other's place, fragmentarily, without taking it over in its entirety, without being able to keep it at a distance."[22] Because it has no space of its own this seemingly fragile, barely political entity depends entirely on opportunities that are seized upon as they arise. These opportunities do not arise in grand confrontations with power such as mass demonstrations or sit-ins, but within everyday situations such as talking, reading, moving about, shopping, or cooking. It holds no political ground because "whatever it wins, it does not keep."[23] It has no laws to apply, no jurisdiction to uphold. Most unsettling of all, De Certeau writes, "it has no image of itself."[24]

With a few exceptions TM completely rejects the organizational practices of the New Left of a quarter century ago. No matter how fragmented and prone to internal dispute, the cultural politics of the New Left showed an unmistakable desire to establish its own separate governance and identity. This counter-cultural ideology is reflected by several of the artist's groups discussed in previous chapters including AWC, AMCC, the Artists Union, and PAD/D among others.[25] By contrast, TM presents itself not as a set of beliefs or a politics, utopian or otherwise, but as a non-identity whose fleeting maneuvers ceaselessly invert normal expectations, including those of traditional socialism or communism. TM is therefore a rejection of most nineteenth- and early twentieth-century leftist movements and of the idea that the working class is a unique and ontologically privileged force of social and historical transformation. The deeply centered "old Left" in the US, Britain, and elsewhere had sought to establish institutions, policies, and ethics separate from those of capital, including those supporting working-class art, music, literature, film, sports, and other forms of cultural development.[26] It represents a full-blown institutional counter-history with its own cultural organizations, including The Artists Union and the John Reed clubs, or the anarchist-based Ferrer School, as well as publications such as *The Masses* and *The New Masses*, and spectacular public events like the Paterson Silk Strike Pageant of 1913 in which leftist artists helped garment workers re-enact their collective walk-out at Madison Square Garden in New York. Left culture even included cigar labels with working-class names and greeting cards imprinted with expressions such as "To My Valentine: I'm a socialist will you be one?"[27] All of this is truly a universe apart from the world in which TM operates, except perhaps in one crucial aspect.

According to Lovink and Garcia, TM takes places place whenever "cheap, 'do it yourself' media, made possible by the revolution in consumer electronics and expanded forms of distribution (from public access cable to the Internet), are exploited by groups and individuals who feel aggrieved by, or excluded from, the wider culture."[28] In other words, the amplification of tactics called for in "The ABCs of TM" was only made possible a decade or more after De Certeau's book appeared, which was itself a timely reflection of a dawning post-Fordist enterprise culture. Nevertheless, there is a kind of political agency at work here after all, but one that appears closer to Walter Benjamin's distracted proletarian film spectator than to a strategically minded working-class radical.[29] Which may explain why, despite protestations, there is also a glimmer of ecclesiastical faith within TM as well, even if it resembles an exotic species of ideological dark matter made visible only as a distributed multitude within neoliberal risk society. TM's most articulate predecessors, the Situationists, sought a total negation of day-to-day fragmentation not through the institutions of art, which they saw as dead, but through a process of turning artistic practices outwards and against monopoly capitalism's spectacularization of day-to-day reality. And yet, as John Roberts notes, the roots of this culturally based opposition are not that different from nineteenth-century *Lebensphilosophie*, a holistic view of human experience in which aesthetic reflection provided a way out, an exit from the continuous subdivision of life into rationalistic categories, or, more appropriately today, from the reduction of life to its biochemical, semiotic, and psychological elements.[30] The broader current of romantic anti-capitalism, to which this philosophy belonged, played an often overlooked role in certain early twentieth-century art movements, suggests Andrew Hemingway, whose study of American Precisionist painters interprets their exacting work as a response to the reification and rationalization of everyday life brought about by industrialization.[31] The Situationists responded differently, but only by degrees. They sought to counter alienation through imaginative situations and poetic actions that interrupted the disciplinary routines of urban space. However, as Scott Cutler Shershow notes, tactical playfulness and artistic generosity ultimately reinvests non-productivity back into positive forms of aesthetic production.[32] And something similar appears to motivate TM's geeky practitioners today, some four decades later. It amounts to an unstated desire to "gift back" a sense of full cultural agency, long since deprived, to those everymen and everywomen who make up what De Certeau calls the "murmuring voice of societies."[33] Ironically, in this roundabout way, this anti-ideology ideology evinces a similar vitalist and aesthetic vision not so different from that of the young Karl Marx, who believed communism would produce a society in which "there are no painters but only people who engage in painting among other activities."[34] For Marx and many Marxists artistic expression appeared to be a mode of self-directed, natural productivity detached from wages and the disciplines of the factory. Artistic labor therefore offers the proletariat a unique pathway back towards the reintegration of everyday lives reified and fragmented by commodity production. However mythical, this commonly held belief remains visible in Hollywood movies, advertising campaigns, and in the swelling ranks of young people studying to become artists. Perhaps it also explains why when artists do occasionally attempt to take control of their working conditions such actions disturb not only the mainstream art establishment, but also the broader, loftier image of cultural production that society holds dear. The public, no less than the specialist scholar, would rather not deal with this other history. On any given Friday night, mostly youthful crowds line up outside the Museum of Modern Art to take advantage of free admission hours. It is a gift that appears to have been made possible by Target Corporation, whose concentric red logo adorns crowd control barriers set up by museum security. What the youthful audience does not know is that it was AWC's rancorous assault on the MoMA some 40 years ago that helped establish their "no-cost" aesthetic experience. Art, in short, appears to be a kind of non-utilitarian play even if in practice that particular dream-image was abandoned long ago by the contemporary art world. Curiously, in spite of its marginal relationship to mainstream art, TM celebrates genuine culture as a liberatory escape from capital. Exodus as a kind of persistent myth, writes Brian Holmes, "points beyond the distorting mediations and structural inequalities of capitalism towards a strange sort of promised land for the profane."[35] Still, as Holmes himself acknowledges, the same intangible creativity that animates TM is also the engine of capitalism's new knowledge factories. Though philosophically at odds with commodified enterprise culture, TM's electronic warriors, hacktivists, and digital ninjas operate as part of capital's own logic, or more precisely, within what military theorist Steven Metz describes as an armed "theater of the mind," even as they search for a way out.[36]

Digital Vitalism

Political agency is no longer found on picket lines, along barricades, or in the visual chaos of urban boulevards as PAD/D once realized it in the streets of Manhattan's Lower East Side. These familiar old spaces of opposition only reinforce existing dichotomies of struggle, polarities that the system allegedly recognized long ago as essential to its very legitimization. Which is why groups like CAE describe the streets as "dead capital" and argue that occupying them is no longer a useful tactic of resistance.[37] Instead, political agency has become ontologically plastic, invisible, even unnamable. As De Certeau explains, the everyday tactician "disappears into its own action, as though lost in what it does," including strolling, conversing, slacking-off, shopping, or perhaps also shoplifting.[38] Small, spontaneous, nearly tactile actions whose aggregate effect on the dominant system is real enough, even if it will never fall like the blow of a hammer, but fester within the system like a low-grade fever. TM counts on the ability of this viral communicability to thicken in connectivity and to seek out other, similar pathogens, nomadic swarms, and ephemeral counter-networks. It is within the evanescent realm of cyberspace that this image of distributed collectivism is most clearly made manifest.

Gliding peripatetically through the digital ether, leisure and work, resistance and play, seem to blur into each other. And yet, there is also something archaic about the polymorphous perversity cyberspace permits us, something akin to De Certeau's adaptive ocean trickster as much as it is to a romantically anti-capitalistic *Lebensphilosophie*, even though this emerging, antagonistic force no longer attaches itself to an ideal of individual wholeness/wellness, but has instead embraced agency as a disbursed, profane, and unnamable *otherness*. The desire for a communal *jouissance* and melting away into the collective imaginary (typically framed in terms of a nationalist imaginary) has frequently been linked to both aesthetics and technological innovation related to the mechanical representation of images (Benjamin), as well as the electronic broadcast of sounds (the voice in particular), and most recently the digital transmission of information.[39] At both extremes, the reified, blocked-up consciousness produced within the spectacle of the global marketplace is rejected. Which is perhaps why the rhetorical tropes of TM are as replete with references not only to pop-cultural imagery, but also to geological, zoological, and cosmic forces and formations. In *The Practice of Everyday Life*, De Certeau compares acts of everyday resistance to the tactics of antediluvian life forms that precede the "frontiers of humanity":

> These practices present in fact a curious analogy, and a sort of immemorial link, to the simulations, tricks, and disguises that certain fishes or plants execute with extraordinary virtuosity ... They maintain formal continuities and the permanence of a memory without language, from the depths of the oceans to the streets of our great cities.[40]

These primordial survival tactics are not only the weapons of the weak; they are linked to a poetic narrative of resistance from below. All the same, one unmistakable impulse loosely binds this ethereal force together: the desire to realize some form of productivity, some vital experience, not strictly determined by economic law. Its collective longing might be utopian, anarchic, technologist, religious, nationalist, aesthetic, or simply nineteenth century, but it manifests itself by *not* producing, or not intentionally producing, for a market that minutely regulates inequalities and hierarchies of winners and losers. Instead, this playful labor is spent killing time, or on itself, or on friends, or friends of friends (what today some call social networks). It is an informal disbursement which is eccentric, even ecstatic, and therefore closer to what George Bataille called a *principle of loss*—expenditure without precise utility—the very abomination of capitalist laws that are based on accumulation, profit, and calculated scarcity.[41] As philosopher Bruno Gulli argues (no doubt with a nod to Melville's cryptic character, Bartleby, the Scrivener), freedom is the "potential not to, the ability to say no, to withdraw."[42] Or, to put this the other way around, man produces not merely when free from physical need but, as Marx wrote, only truly produces "in freedom from such need."[43] Certainly, from a normative, capitalist perspective, economic non-compliance and non-productivity are pathological. For if being *usefully* productive confers membership in the healthy free-market society, then to produce "creatively" but not for capital, or to withdraw one's productivity *from* the market, must signal a deeper social malady. Or does it? For who would deny that something has taken place in the past couple of decades to make this once intolerable sphere of everyday resistance not merely visible, but also, remarkably, somehow of interest to the very marketplace it once spurned and that spurned it? This other [non]productivity with its "missing" cultural mass appears as a gloaming presence on the margins of culture, politics, and business, its fuzzy, distributed mass an object of increasing interest not only to artists and cultural theorists, but also to a faction of twenty-first-century capitalists who, so Tiziana Terranova cautions, would like to control the "unfolding of these virtualities and the processes of valorization."[44] Or, in the jubilant words of neoliberal scholar Yochai Benkler, "the social production of goods and services, both public and private, is ubiquitous, though unnoticed. It is, to be fanciful, the dark matter of our economic production universe."[45] All of which suggests this missing social productive mass is not strictly immaterial or digitized, but rather some hybrid of real and unreal, fantasy and familiar, [wo]man and machine. Furthermore, much of this dark matter partakes of hobbies and techniques that have long been suspect within the world of "serious art," including home and needlecrafts, public murals, street art, air-brushed low-rider automobiles, and countless forms of creative expression often dismissed as kitsch, low culture, or ethnic art. All of these forms and techniques that seem so anachronistic in the digital age now proliferate ceaselessly thanks to the Hypertext Transfer Protocols (HTTP) of cyberspace. The ubiquitous presence of this dark productivity also challenges certain post-war critiques of leisure, including most prominently those of Adorno and Horkheimer who argued that hobbies and amusement under late capitalism are merely a "prolongation of work," or, as Steven M. Gelber put it, DIY projects are "disguised affirmations" of workplace routines. But it is worth noting here Chris Rojek's approving observation that Foucault's interest in the "pathological" activity of prisoners and insane people presents a challenge to traditional Marxist critical interpretation of non-work, play, and leisure activity that is also quite different from the blurring of lines between professional and amateur researchers in, for example, Robert A. Stebbins' notion of "serious leisure," a gray zone celebrated today by advocates of the knowledge economy.[46] For yes, on the one hand, the basement, garage, or "home office" are no longer hiding places from the job and its routines, drills, and enforced timetables. With advances in digital information, micro-technology, and pharmacology the body itself becomes an extension of office discipline made manifest as a seemingly autonomous prosumer or cyberzombie. "Live with your century; but do not be its creature," wrote Friedrich Schiller some 200 years ago. And today a reanimated, highly distributed, though essentially inert mass calls out to capital: fulfill the promise!

Disciplining the Avant-Garde

The once shadowy archive spills open. Blogs, wikis, mashups, fan edits, numberless P2P file-sharing programs and free, collaboratively evolving software evince the revenge of the excluded. But De Certeau's everyday dissident appears on the verge of mutating into something else, something that some neoliberal theorists describe as the networked engine of twenty-first-century capitalism. "Now we have armies of amateurs, happy to work for free," exclaims Chris Anderson, editor of magazine *Wired*, one of the early proponents of the networked "gift" economy:

> Previous industrial ages were built on the backs of individuals, too, but in those days labor was just that: labor. Workers were paid for their time, whether on a factory floor or in a cubicle. Today's peer-production machine runs in a mostly nonmonetary economy. The currency is reputation, expression, karma, "whuffie," or simply whim.[47]

Still, there are filters—ways of pruning, delimiting, and enclosing impurities within this social productivity without completely erasing its fecundity. Shortly before the dot.com crash in 2000 a leading oracle of networked culture prophesized that the initial, giddy, "protocommercial stage" of cyberculture was necessary before profits could be realized. According to *Wired* magazine's founding editor Kevin Kelly:

> The early Internet and the early Web sported amazingly robust gift economies; goods and services were swapped, shared generously, or donated outright—actually, this was the sole way to acquire things online. Idealistic as this attitude was, it was the only sane way to launch a commercial economy in the emerging space. The flaw that science fiction ace William Gibson found in the Web—its capacity to waste tremendous amounts of time—was in fact, as Gibson further noted, its saving grace ... In the Network Economy, follow the free.[48]

There are filters because like all dark matter some of this "amazingly robust" free productivity distributes less commercially desirable offerings. Gifts whose embrace remains suspect including dissident, even poisonous gifts. Right from the start De Certeu's primordial tricksters began to hack the Internet. Open-source programmers developed free software to compete with privately copyrighted commercial programs, The Yes Men produced mirror-images of the World Trade Organization website that "corrected" its institutional identity; and hacktivist culture-jammers built self-detonating "Google bombs" so that someone searching for the phrase "more evil than Satan himself" would find themselves directed to the website of Microsoft Corporation. And yet these tactical games operate in two directions simultaneously. While they provide a means by which the wary and ephemeral fishes of resistance can hide from the panoptic gaze of power, disappearing into some inner fold or temporary autonomous zone from where they can carry out tactical strikes, this same clever mimicry inadvertently projects onto the spectacular screen something that in a moment of panic might be mistaken as an exaggerated menace. Perhaps this is why a deeply compromised government already seduced by the fog of war initially misapprehended the threat presented by Kurtz,

Ferrell, and CAE? Like a mistaken encounter with its own *doppelgänger* the state was first startled, then transfixed. Then its disciplinary apparatus drove forward with one objective: to produce a political show trial in which an unnamable threat would not only be given a name, a fearful name, but ultimately compartmentalized, disciplined, and assigned a numbered prison cell. When CAE transformed various insurgent theories—either avant-garde or radical-corporate—into accessible, DIY procedures, and then directed a diffuse, yet unquestionably resistant force towards select, private and governmental targets, it publicly demonstrated its ability to operate within the same nebulous terrain of power that the state now deems its privileged concession to own, lend out, or direct. When the authorities compare CAE to terrorists, they reveal their inability to categorize what is unnamable. Kurtz and his colleagues sinned yet a second time and really brought down "the man" when they published manuals explicating how to make use of this counter-knowledge, including its tactics and circuitry, and did so not with the ambiguous idioms of art-speak, but rather with the determined hyper-clarity of the techno-geek. This is where something far more grotesque than a simple return to the past begins to be teased out of an otherwise incomprehensible instance of state censorship. It is a warning aimed as much at the "avant-garde" entrepreneurial spirit of many dot-comers, as it is against a group of interdisciplinary TM interventionists who refuse to stay in their assigned role as isolated cultural workers.

Informal spatial manipulations; local politics and forgotten histories mapped onto streets and global digital networks; obsessive acts of hoarding, collecting, and indexing; salacious fantasies, contraband inventions, and the free circulation of private property and personal effects: these non-utilitarian forms of "productivity" parallel or even mock social regulations and proper routines of work. They do so, however, mostly as fragmented, sometimes understated acts of everyday dissent. Internally riven, with contradictory notions of past and future, local and global, the one common feature they share is a memory of repeated failure and banishment from the spheres of social, cultural, and political visibility. How would these isolated forces be politically mobilized in some sustainable way? A return to grand ideas of collective transcendence? A new, revolutionary politics or radical party formation? Or a sweeping aesthetic transformation of society as a whole? Suspicions are immediately raised. And yet something has certainly happened. Some new, or perhaps not so new, collective imagination is materializing, confronting the worlds of art, politics, and business with a seemingly limitless reservoir of surplus activity. This new collectivist fetish inhabits the everywhere and nowhere of social life. Like Lovecraft's unnamable abomination its shapeless shadows issue from the margins, archives, and crypts, somehow operating both inside and outside, nowhere and everywhere, like a maelstrom, a blemish, or a loathsome flood of collective dark matter capable of assuming the very shape of that which once excluded it.

7

MOCKSTITUTIONS

The Cartographers Guilds struck a Map of the Empire whose size was that of the Empire, and which coincided point for point with it.

Jose Luis Borges[1]

Omens

Plato warns us of artistic mimicry. He tells us that Socrates barred imitative poets and painters from his Republic.[2] Artists don't do honest work; they merely represent the work of other laborers. An image of a chair is three times removed from the ideal chair. The first facsimile is that of the carpenter, and yet at least the carpenter's chair can be used for sitting. The artist's feeble, third-order simulation is useless. Worse still, with its fantastic, imitative relationship to the truth an artwork easily misleads citizens (unlike, say, the work of logicians and philosophers). But there is something else in this art of deception, that jeopardizes the very order of the Republic. As philosopher Jacques Rancière elaborates: "The carpenter, baker, shoemaker, blacksmith, all must remain tied to their stations in life. The 'office' of the artist, however, is ambiguous. It is like a phantom profession, one that permits the artist to simultaneously work and not work, to have a 'real' job, and to have a fictional job. And nothing is more subversive than showing other workers the pleasure of not engaging in productive labor."[3] Thanks to this labor of dissimulation artists slide between social barriers; even moving between class distinctions so as to "pass" for what they are not. In Socrates' time artists replicated the works of manual laborers—chairs, bread, shoes, horses' bridles. Today artists imitate a product particular to the post-industrial economy: the administrative, affective, and intellectual power of institutions. For in spite of increased artistic censorship and self-censorship in the wake of the security measures introduced after September 11, and notwithstanding the acute economic uncertainty brought on by the 2008–9 financial collapse, there is one quintessential skill-set that sets artists apart from most other laborers, in the form of a unique aptitude that provides an edge when dealing with the society of risk beyond the longstanding adaptation to structural precariousness and overproduction. In addition to a propensity for flexible work patterns, developing gift-sharing networks, and a capacity for non-linear problem solving, artists possess a sophisticated ability to mimic, exaggerate, or otherwise reshape given reality.[4] We encountered hints of this fictive prowess in the use of hyperbole by PAD/D and REPOhistory, small groups with radical cultural ambitions, or in the demand by AWC that museum boards treat them as a bone-fide labor union, and not an informally structured alliance (and a short-lived one at that), or when Temporary Services imbued everyday people with curatorial status, or sought to give them back lost public authority as a "public service." This is indeed a confidence game. Theorist Gene Ray puts it this way: "as a social stratum of cultural production, artists bring together a dangerous set of capacities. (They're actually human capacities that for most people are structurally blocked.)"[5] However, it involves a representational mimicry not directed towards material objects as in Plato's day, but instead towards the intangible realm of organizational signification and embodiment. Its as though, at a time of derelict institutions and failed states, the imitative artist Socrates warned of has taken up the bits and pieces of a broken world, transforming them into an improved, second-order social reality *extraordinaire*. The map and what is mapped, often critically, ironically, are becoming superimposed upon one another.

The past 30 years have indeed witnessed a curious mimicry at work within the shoals and shallows of enterprise culture.[6] As if responding to the ruined public landscape of enterprise culture, an assortment of ersatz institutes, centers, schools, bureaus, offices, laboratories, leagues, departments, societies, clubs, and bogus corporations have inserted themselves into the deterritoralized space of the spectacular global marketplace. Each of these mock-institutional entities sports its own logo, mission, and website, engaging in a process of self-branding not so much aimed at niche markets or product loyalty, but rather to gain surreptitious entry into visibility itself (although significantly these maneuvers typically provide art world positioning whether intended or not). The most engaging of these phantom establishments do more than just replicate the appearance of lost liberal, institutional structures; they also use their virtual offices to confront and intervene in the real world of actual corporations, businesses, municipalities, and states. The Yes Men, for example, embody stereotypical business executives with such monochromatic precision they gain access to "real" corporate conferences, press events, and mass media coverage; The Center for Tactical Magic mixes together wicca paganism and interventionist maneuvers in an effort to achieve "positive social transformation"; and Chicago-based Temporary Services personify municipal civil servants. Both on and offline, Critical Art Ensemble, Carbon Defense League, and the Institute for Applied Autonomy develop open source "hacks" and reverse engineer technologies for retrofitting computers, public spaces, and genetically modified foods, all in the name of greater self-determination. In Southern California the Los Angeles Urban Rangers are not official park rangers, but rather a group of artists and cultural activists who organize unofficial "safaris" focused on urban policy and environmental justice in a city segmented by highways, onramps, and concrete islands. There is even a counterfeit religious congregation, the Church of Life After Shopping (formerly the Church of Stop-Shopping), presided over by a faux preacher, the performance artist Reverend Billy, a.k.a. Bill Talen. Yet, even if these acts of self-visualization and sham-signification are intended to negate, subvert, or "reverse engineer" the society of the spectacle nevertheless they are conceivable today only because of its deterritorialized networks. But there is also something else. Call it a profound sense of uselessness and redundancy. The phenomenon of mock institutionalism thrives best within a failed society where previous forms of human connectivity have been left in tatters. In a slightly different context, the collective RETORT commented that the counter-globalization "movement of movements is as much a product of 'statelessness' as it is the critique of it."[7] So too does a certain dark matter respond by embracing its own redundancy through overt acts of self-creation and mythification. Indeed, it is impossible to imagine this level of social hacking taking place prior to the collapse of the Keynesian paradigm of an administered society whose intellectual and artistic banalities Adorno resolutely railed against. Prior to the rise of post-Fordist enterprise culture the notion of a broader public good was drilled into the population from birth to old age. Today every individual is in a constant state of warfare with every other individual. Only a radically failed society could give birth to fantasies of triumphant communality such as relational aesthetics or to the hyperbolic pragmatism of self-organized mock-institutions. It might also be giving birth circumstances permitting, to a new conception of the political party, or even the state. Still, the question remains the same as that we started with—whose narrative will ultimately prevail?

At the same time it is inaccurate to imply that artists have only recently adopted tactics of dissimulation including fictional identities, fraudulent artworks, and invented group structures. One need only recall Marcel Duchamp's female alter ego *Rose Sélavy*, or Marcel Broodthaers' *Musée d'Art Moderne*, an imaginary museum that allegedly went bankrupt. Broodthaers even tried to sell his failed institution but was famously unsuccessful. But two distinct factors suggest a recent qualitative shift in these delusive practices. First is the striking art world proliferation of this tendency. Art historian Carrie Lambert-Beatty ingeniously applies the term "parafiction" to this phenomena.[8] She points out that this emerging artistic genre has introduced into the art world a multitude of inventions from parafictional books, archives, television programs, movies, and news stories to make-believe artists, artworks, and scholars. Imagine a small exhibition space in Los Angeles displaying dioramas and artifacts documenting animals, persons, scientific theories, and historical events that may or may not have any basis in fact: a bat that flies through walls and a man who thinks he is a wolf. David Wilson's Museum of Jurassic Technology is a parafiction not because it is a parody of a natural history museum, but because once we are inside its cabinet

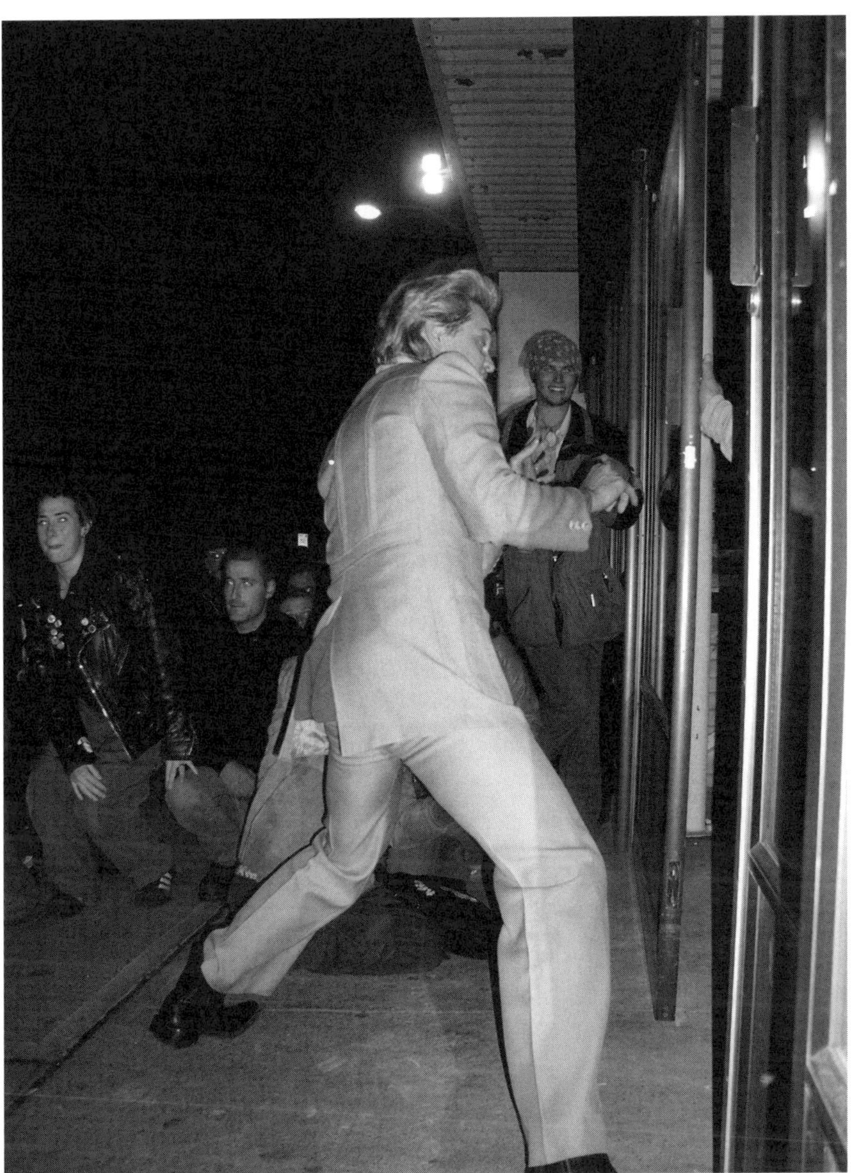

Reverend Billy leads congregants into a store at the Kensington Market in Toronto to hold a town hall prayer meeting about the store's impending sale to a large Canadian super chain. Reverend Billy and The Church of Life After Shopping are a radical performance community based in New York City whose scripture proclaims: "Freedom from shopping is a virulent, contagious threat to the twin forces of consumerism and militarism. The earth is demanding our bravery now. Changeallujah!" Image courtesy Shannon Cochrane.

of wonders veracity itself becomes undecidable. However, it is a different feature of this expanding practice that concerns us here. Fleeting moments of aesthetic parafiction now regularly mutate into full-blown simulations of organizations even as their internal "moving parts" remain administratively deceptive and flexible. For years these artfully crafted counterfeit realities have been migrating out of the art world and into the fabric of the everyday life. Group Material did this, so did General Idea and Videofreex before them, but never to the degree that this leakage of imaginary institutions into the everyday is taking place now, and often with politically tactical intent. This is where the playful, aesthetic stakes of parafiction get complicated, because by the very logic of the counterfeit organization or mockstitution this duplicity can only thrive where the seams of reality and fantasy are worn thin or have completely disintegrated. It may also help explain why some of the most compelling acts of counterfeit reality emerge from geographic places where the public imaginary and public space itself have traumatically collapsed: New York's Lower East Side or South Bronx in the late 1970s and early 1980s; Beirut; or the former Yugoslavia today. It may also explain why as post-Fordist neoliberalism spreads across the globe so too do artist-based dissimulations of authority. Parafiction and mockstitutions are becoming the new norm. Perhaps a clearer way to look at this phenomenon then is to view certain collaborative, collective, and group formations as existing simultaneously as institutions, and as counter-institutional criticism. In other words, they operate in a state of superimposition between the real and the fictional, neither is completely absent or entirely present at any given moment.

Broken City Lab (BCL) is not a laboratory nor is it an official municipal department. It is a six-person "interdisciplinary creative research group" located in Canada's "Detroit," the working-class city of Windsor, Ontario. And like its sister-city Detroit just across the river, Windsor is tethered to a faltering automobile industry. Unstable work conditions and spreading unemployment have led to rising vacancy rates that are among the highest in Canada. Windsor is literally falling apart and broken, but this damaged world is both home to and artistic testing site for BCL, a group of (naturally) precarious art school graduates who are themselves part of the city's ruined physical and social infrastructure. BCL's urban experiments are a response to "the things we see happening in front of us," insists co-founder Justin A. Langlois.[9] This interventionist "research" includes developing informal maps of post-crash urban patterns, hosting open meetings about the hemorrhaging of talent out of Windsor, and creating video interviews focused on the way artists and other residents cope with their broken city. Langlois admits their work is not rigorously methodical or scientific and the reason they even call it a lab is because this terminology "helps us to have some sway of authority, a lab of course sounds different than a club." It seems tangible juridical power flows from even a casual invocation of certain words and phrases, the language of science, technology, and business being an especially potent charm, or perhaps omen?

A laboratory is "a space where small quantities of hazardous materials can have an effect greater than the sum of their parts" insists the London-based collective Labofii, or Laboratory of Insurrectionary Imagination. On its website, Labofii methodically sequences its psycho-geographical experiments in numerical order: "No. 6: Paths Through Utopias," "No. 7: The Great Rebel Raft Regatta," and "No. 8: The People Vs The Banksters" (Bankster being a post-2008 neologism combining bankers with gangsters). Experiment 8 took place on a snowy day outside the Royal Bank of Scotland at Bishopsgate in February 2009.[10]As the effects of the financial collapse accelerated, Labofii members challenged RBS staff to a snowball fight. Few of the bankers (or Banksters) took up the gauntlet. Labofii's Situationist-inspired urban interventions have not gone unnoticed by authorities. According to the group's website Scotland Yard has labeled them: "*not* a normal theatre touring company."

Along with emulating scientific, urban, and corporate research specialists some faux-enterprising artists mimic functions of state. Somewhat like Temporary Services the German group Department for Public Appearances carries out seriously playful appropriations of municipal authority including an eccentric version of a public polling station in Linz, Austria. The project encouraged residents to literally hang their personal thoughts out of doors like oversized post-it notes in the form of colorful banners displayed from the windows and balconies of nearby apartment buildings. In Gdansk, Poland, C.U.K.T. (Central Office of Technical Culture) coolly insists their critical art strategy "could be compared to that of any typical office or institution, insofar as it consists in filling out forms and producing documents."[11] Responding to a question about how they define their artistic practice C.U.K.T. members cite anarcho-theorist Hakim Bey who has called upon artists to engage in "weird dancing throughout the night" and "unauthorized subconscious displays" not made for other artists, but carried out for people who "will not realize that what you have done is art."[12] Meanwhile, in Brooklyn, several artists calling themselves The Aaron Burr Society defiantly re-tool the conservative Tea Party imaginary for left-libertarianism, while distilling illegal, untaxed whiskey as a protest against the economic crash.

Certainly the most comprehensive simulation of a collective national imaginary remains that of NSK or Neue Slowenische Kunst (German for New Slovenian Art), a constellation of Slovenian performers, visual artists, and musicians originally founded in a nation that no longer exists.[13] Since 1984, NSK's jarring artwork has drawn upon the sound and imagery of extreme nationalist movements that, at the time of the group's founding in 1984, remained barely submerged beneath Josip Tito's non-aligned Yugoslavia. But as the socialist republic began to literally fall apart into separate ethno-cultural regions, these ultra-nationalist tendencies became more pronounced, ultimately feeding into an armed regional conflict in the early 1990s. NSK had already become notorious in 1987 for transforming a Nazi era poster of "heroic youth" into a socialist "Youth-Day-Poster." NSK submitted the graphic to the authorities for a national contest and was awarded top prize. Only later did government officials discover the ruse. That scandal, along with the group's other profane mixing of totalitarian communist, Fascist, avant-garde and retro-kitsch imagery, frustrated Yugoslavia's ruling socialist ideologues because, insists Slavoj Žižek, it produced a psychic over-identification with what was officially repressed. NSK forced into the open a disturbing racist reality thinly papered-over by the socialist state.[14] NSK even proclaimed itself a separate state "without territory" opening fictive embassies in several nearby countries and issuing its own NSK passports. Today these parafictional documents turn up for sale online to those desperate enough to believe in their authenticity. Nevertheless, this hacking into the official national imaginary was, and remains, paradoxical and politically risky, though it is no less compelling for this risk, especially in the rapidly privatized post-Communist nations in Eastern and Central Europe.[15] Other regional tacticians have targeted the factory, corporation, and academy. In Russia, the Saint Petersburg's "Factory of Found Clothing" (FNO) is neither a mill nor a sweatshop, but it does manufacture performance and installation art featuring fabrics, garments, and actual sweatshop workers. Founded by Natalia Pershina-Yakimanskaya and Olga Yegorova—two women who never studied art, and who go by the pseudonyms "Gliukla and Tsaplya"—FNO often collaborates with young factory women who design collaborative clothing, engage in social skill-building workshops, and produce consciousness-raising media projects to bolster Russian feminism largely forsaken since the days of liberated radical communists like Alexandra Kollontai.[16] *Three Mothers and Chorus* is a 2008 video opera that musically explores the precarious working conditions of female Russian workers. *Triumph of Fragility* is a 2003 street performance in which a group of sailors were persuaded by FNO to walk St. Petersburg's streets clutching small white dresses to their hearts in order to return the men "their own souls." FNO's faux factory also improbably brandishes its own anti-capitalist manifesto proclaiming "The place of the artist is on the side of the weak!," and "The time has come to return compassion to art!"[17]

For many artists compassion is less a poetic ideal than a practical gift involving the redistribution of state, municipal, and corporate services and property. Far from the cities of the former socialist East one can sometimes obtain a free ride on the Mexico City subway system. The art project known as Mejor Vida Corporation has distributed thousands of counterfeit train tickets gratis to waiting commuters. Among other complimentary "products" that can be downloaded and printed from the ersatz corporation's website are fake student IDs useful for obtaining local discounts and modified barcodes with steeply reduced prices for

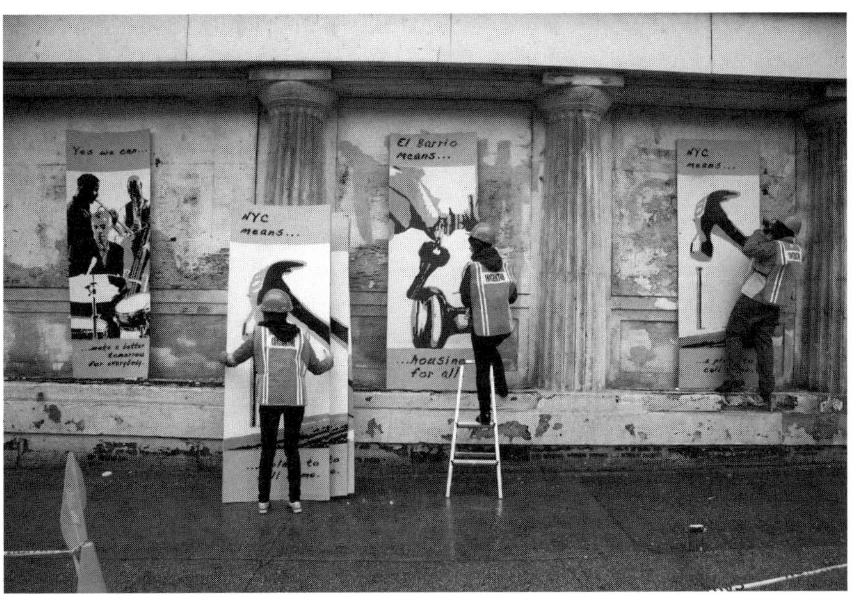

Not An Alternative and allies dressed as street workers in collaboration with Picture The Homeless during a building occupation March 19, 2009, in East Harlem, El Barrio, NYC. The temporary, guerrilla street installation was part of a campaign to bring attention to the contradiction and failure in Mayor Bloomberg's five-year plan to end homelessness by making visible the thousands of City and bank owned properties sitting vacant. Not An Alternative is a non-profit organization based in Brooklyn, NY, whose mission integrates art, activism, theory, and digital technology around core themes of spatial conflict, gentrification, and a critique of the "creative class." Image courtesy Andrew Stern.

staple items such as bread, cheese, and vegetables. So far Mejor Vida provides these adjusted markdowns for San Francisco, Ontario, Canada, and the organization's homebase *la Ciudad De Mexico*.[18] As discussed in Chapter 4, an even more robust version of the "five fingered discount" went global when the Barcelona-based group Yomango's bogus "branding from below" fashion label, producing accessories for everyday shoplifting, inspired a series of informal "franchises" in Mexico, Chile, Argentina, and Germany.[19] In Copenhagen, a less confrontational model of redistributing resources is carried out by YNKB—Ydre Nørrebro Kultur Bureau (Copenhagen) who seek to transform the insignificant into the significant by repairing discarded street furniture and gleaning edible discarded food from local supermarkets. Operating in the crowded, immigrant section of the city known as Ydre Nørrebro the informally organized group has christened itself with the official sounding title of "culture bureau."[20]

In Reykjavik, The Icelandic Love Corporation is not a corporation, it is a three woman performance art collective; the London Police are not constables, but a pair of cheeky, suburban graffiti writers from the East End who honed their art dodging the real London Police; in Winnipeg an informal group of artists much like Paper Rad nominated themselves The Royal Art Lodge, implying perhaps an imaginary link with the British monarchy's Canadian retreat; and, despite its monumental epithet, Atlas Group consists of just one member, the Lebanese artist Walid Raad. Some hyperbolic group nomenclature goes so far as to invoke entire militia. The Infernal Noise Brigade and Pink Bloque—two recently defunct collectives—were dynamic staples of anti-war and anti-globalization protests, and anonymous members of Biotic Baking Brigade spoke "pie to power" by targeting neoliberals and CEOs such as Thomas Friedman and Bill Gates with pastry missiles. Far smaller than the Spanish fleet, The Miss Rockaway Armada is an irregular colony of musicians, performers, and visual artists who ply the Mississippi River on DIY rafts built of recycled trash. But the ultimate hyperbolic expression of militarized play is the Clandestine Insurgent Rebel Clown Army (CIRCA), an informal brigade of protesters with links to Labofii who turn up around the world in oversized shoes and rubber noses to confront arms dealers and G8 leaders. Inspired by the antics of Abbie Hoffman and the YIPPIES, CIRCA describes its colorful slapstick militia as a "fighting force armed with ruthless love and fully trained in the ancient art of clowning and non-violent direct action." A recruitment flyer distributed outside a British Army center in Leeds entreats passers by to "Be rubbish ... join the Clandestine Insurgent Rebel Clown Army." Like a screwball surplus army the future pranksters are required to attend a three-day long "bigshoe camp" in which they learn to uncover their "inner clown and discover the subversive freedom of fooling."[21]

Recycled-rubbish warriors carrying out virtuosic tactics, simulations, disguises, and artful tricks: the legacy of De Certeau but also of Dadaism, Fluxus, and the Situationist International loom large within these plagiarized factories, mock-corporations, and ludic clown armies. Yet, as Brian Holmes argues, activism must also confront "real obstacles: war, poverty class and racial oppression, creeping fascism, venomous neoliberalism."[22] Indeed, some of these jocular artists are little more than youthful pranksters, while others could be described as *psychogeographical* drifters hoping to reinvent the everyday, or at least transform their private experience of monotonous reality into something more tolerable. Some, however, have chosen the tactics of dissimulation in order to make critical interventions in the name of social justice, solidarity, and increased democracy. But one way or another, as hoaxers or intellectuals, lumpen or activists, there is a mutual desire to be *on the side of the weak*, as stipulated by the intrepid Russian art couplet FNO. This unwritten mandate is carried out with a wry, sometimes slapstick frivolity quite unlike the (often) dour leftist political artists of the 1960s, '70s, and early '80s. Even the names of these fantastic groups inspire mirth: Institute for Applied Autonomy, Carbon Defense League, The Yes Men. This is not irony, or parody for its own sake, as it is for example with a comedian like Sacha Baron Cohen (a.k.a. Ali G, Borat, and Bruno), whose giddy spectacles of public humiliation and "id-like" characters substitute for any sustained critique or analysis. But if we again compare the way a certain dark matter surplus self-organizes during an age of enterprise culture and failed nations, as opposed to the post-war era of administered society, these cellular mockstitutions are often so indifferent to proper organizational structure that they adopt any convenient form of governance. And while their masquerade of authority is intended to fail, as Žižek observes, in reality it often works all too well. Paradoxically, the deep suspicion of institutional power has given artists a license to recreate facsimiles of institutions that are superior to what they copy, both symbolically speaking, and often in terms of functionality. The superimposition of reality and fiction, play and power, is only fixed in one state or the other temporally, as expedient, or when a granting authority or the state decides to examine the entity close up. Steve Kurtz and Critical Art Ensemble share something, in other words, with Schrödinger's famous dead/alive cat illustrating the uncertainty principle of quantum physics, a paradox that may also soon prove its existence at least in the laboratory.[23]

One reason these informal forgeries and superimpositions operate like enhanced copies of actual institutions is the unscripted, even opportunistic way artists approach organizational structure. Despite the external impression of logic and order that a graphic web presence and "official" logo provides a mockstitution, it is essentially a plastic framework in which administrative functions are implemented on an as-needed basis depending on circumstances. Rather than building institutional governance hierarchically, in the familiar way, with clearly demarcated rules and offices as so many not-for-profit organizations have in the past, recently established artists' groups and collectives appear to treat organizational structure as just another artistic challenge, as if it were a material or medium to be manipulated. Techniques of management are improvised and organizational forms juxtaposed, as if cutting and pasting together a montage or pastiche out of whatever is available simply to "get the job done." At the same time, one could say that a certain deregulated aesthetic is the "new normal" in an age of enterprise culture. Indeed, from the point of view of many neoliberal thinkers institutional stability is itself obsolete. This may explain why a sampling of artists' groups and collectives queried for this book reveals that a majority have opted out of legal, official visibility altogether (though not out of a forged visibility as discussed above). Most simply never bother to enroll as an NGO, legal charity, or 501c3 not-for-profit (NFP) corporation. A number have even registered as *for-profit* business entities, acknowledging this is mostly a tactic since they have no commercial aptitude or intentions of actually turning a profit.

What follows are several observations extrapolated from an informal survey conducted by Lucia Sommer for the author in 2008–9. The questionnaire, which appears in the index of the book, was sent to a total of 211 geographically dispersed organizations. Most, though not all of the organizations selected for the survey were founded in the past 30 years and still remain active as cultural producers. Ultimately 67 groups responded. The survey, however, is not intended to serve as definitive scientific data, but rather it suggests a likely trend or tendency visible amongst a fair number of contemporary artists' collectives and how they organize themselves in relationship to society and in some cases in relation to the art world.

Organizing Amidst the Ruins

One or more group spokespersons responded to questions about whether or not their organization was legally registered as a not-for-profit, association, or charity; if it has formal rules for membership and decision making; and has the group any relationship to either the commercial or "non-commercial" sector of the art world. The informal survey also inquired about their reasons for working as a group rather than as individual artistic producers. The two most salient results revolve around the changing nature of collectivism after modernism. First, as the art world stigma against belonging to an artists' group or collective has decreased in recent years the visibility of such organizations has increased both within the "non-commercial" sector of museums, biennials, and alternative spaces, as well as amongst a few commercial dealers, though this is still limited. If we invoke the on/off table metaphor here while recognizing the powerful influence wielded by the commercial art market over the so-called non-profit cultural sector today, then it is fair to say that even if a paradigm shift is under way the majority of artists' groups and collectives are marginal players in the culture industry. The second outcome suggested by the survey involves the way these recent groups organize themselves. Previously, in the 1960s and 1970s, foundations encouraged artists in the US who chose to work collectively to officially register as a not-for-profit legal entity known as a 501c3 corporation. They were also expected to establish hierarchical offices and rules of conduct and in some cases to develop external trustees or boards of directors. Growth was also promoted. All of this mirrors the internal structure of the institutions that provide financial support for artists. What is distinctly different about the wave of collectivization since the 1980s is that all but a few of the groups surveyed reveal a willful lack of interest regarding what their legally registered status is if it exists at all. The phenomenon also appears to be evident beyond the US and the UK. Curiously, this does not mean that such groups always reject becoming officially registered. Some even decide to enroll as commercial operations. But the choice of organizational form appears strictly tactical, neither holding any clear ideological or long-term significance to group members, nor taken seriously. There are precedents for this artful deception. As

Julie Ault explains with regard to Group Material in the 1980s, the four-person collective was resistant to the kind of institutionalization demanded by the NEA and other grant foundations. When they did finally receive official tax-exemption the group concocted a "semblance of professionalization and hierarchical salaried staff structure (on paper) in order to be eligible for grants." Privately the group decided to "keep minimal overheads, operate on an adhoc basis, and never have salaried positions in order to avoid any conflict of interest."[24] Perfunctory compliance with official cultural regulators may have been a sporadic though unspoken practice by artists' groups in the past, but today, in an age of overt deregulation and semiotic warfare, such tactics are becoming pervasive, even among groups who, at least on paper, appear to be commercial enterprises.

Ten respondents reported that they work collectively and ideologically against the marketplace, despite the fact they are registered as "for-profit" organizations. Among these are Democratic Innovation (Copenhagen), Gob Squad (Nottingham and Berlin), LIGNA (Berlin and Hamburg), General Idea (Toronto and New York), Com&Com (Switzerland and Germany), and the artists' cooperative Just Seeds representing multiple locations in North America.[25] According to their survey responses, most fail to produce profits and chose to become a commercial entity because it was easier than forming an official NFP or NGO, which typically requires establishing a board of directors, selecting a president or director, and filing annual activity reports, and all of the official trappings Group Material felt compelled to feign. Futurefarmers (San Francisco), an artists' group that is not an agricultural research institute (and yet *is* essentially an agricultural research institute), debated for some time whether or not to become a legal NFP. They finally resolved to remain a sole proprietorship, a business entity in which the owner-operator remains fully liable for taxes, debts, and so forth as opposed to a corporation. Futurefarmers did however, produce an artwork commenting on the entire process in the form of limited-edition bingo playing cards. The game imagery sardonically refers to the elaborate NFP incorporation instructions published by the Internal Revenue Service (IRS) that are mostly intended to nudge church-sponsored gambling operations into seeking non-taxable legal status.[26]

Meanwhile, Orgacom (Netherlands and Turkey) is registered as an NGO in Holland, but its art practice seeks to intervene into commercial markets, while Acces Local (Paris) is a for-profit "company" under French law that simulates business operations by applying "artistic methods to non-artistic purposes, and non-artistic methods to artistic purposes."[27] However, as artist Maureen Connor argues, this blurring of artistic services and commercial services often dulls the kind of institutional critique developed by Andrea Fraser so that such "project-based" artworks begin to literally overlap in "even more disturbing ways with the contemporary corporate workplace" itself.[28] Connor points out that artists willingly sacrifice their autonomy, or what little is left of it, by performing the

META-COMMERCIAL STRUCTURES (10)

officially registered commercial entities with an expedient, equivocal, or critical-interventionist relationship to commercial business practices

1 **Acces Local** France; 1998–present
2 **Com&Com** Switzerland & Germany 1997–present
3 **Democratic Innovation** Denmark; 1998–present
4 **Futurefarmers** USA; 1995–present
5 **General Idea** Canada & USA, 1969–1994
6 **Gob Squad** Germany & UK; 1994–present
7 **Gruppo A12** Italy; 1993–present (non-profit 2000–2005)
8 **Just Seeds** USA, Canada & Mexico 2007–present
9 **Ligna** Germany; 1995–present
10 **Superflex** Denmark & Brazil; 1993–present

NOT-FOR-PROFITS (NPOs) & NON-GOVERNMENTAL ORGANIZATIONS (NGOs) (15)

sometimes operating as adhoc, meta-legal structures in which their small membership informally 'performs' official organizational roles

11 **Ala Plástica** Argentina; 1991–present
12 **cSPACE** UK; 2002–present
13 **Flux Factory** USA; 1994–present
14 **Freud's Dream Museum** Russia; 1999–present
15 **Group Material** USA; 1979–1996
16 **Half Machine** Denmark; 2002–2009
17 **Harwood, Wright & Yokokoji** UK; 2004–present
18 **Icelandic Love Corporation** Iceland; 1996–present
19 **Intermedia Society** Canada; 1967–1973
20 **PLATFORM** UK; 1984–present
21 **Raketa** Sweden; 1998–present
22 **REPOhistory** USA; 1989–2000
23 **Rum46** Denmark; 1995–present
24 **Spanic Attack multi-arts collective** USA; 2003–present
25 **WochenKlausur** Austria; 1993–present

HYBRID GROUPS (3)

officially registered as, or comprised of, both commercial & non-profit structures

26 **Orgacom** Netherlands & Turkey 1997–present
27 **pvi collective** Australia; 1998-present (informally structured 1998–2008)
28 **Videofreex** USA; 1969–1978

INFORMALLY STRUCTURED GROUPS (38)

cellular, flexible, adaptive, few moving parts

29 **Artists Against the War** USA; 2002–present
30 **Artists Meeting** USA; 2006–present
31 **BEIGE Programming Ensemble** USA; 2000–2004
32 **Brainstormers** USA: 2005–present
33 **Center for Tactical Magic** USA, Canada & Germany 2000–present
34 **Chainworkers** Italy; 2001–present
35 **Critical Art Ensemble** USA; 1987–present
36 **C.U.K.T. (Technical Culture Central Office)** Poland, France & UK; 1995–2005
37 **The Fleas** USA & Australia; 2002–present
38 **Free Soil** USA, Denmark & Germany 2005–present
39 **Godzilla: Asian American Arts Network** USA; 1990–2001
40 **Gran Fury** USA; 1986–1994
41 **The Howling Mob Society** USA; 2006–2009
42 **Hydra Poesis** Australia; 2006–present
43 **Institute for Applied Autonomy** USA & Germany; 1998–present
44 **Interim Sites: An Urban Arts Initiative** USA; 1994–1998
45 **iRational.org** UK, Spain, Mexico & Canada 1997–present
46 **Kleines Postfordistisches Drama (kpD)** Germany, Austria & Switzerland; 2003–present
47 **La Lleca** Mexico; 2004–present
48 **Los Angeles Urban Rangers** USA; 2004–present
49 **Meme-Rider Media Team** USA; 2000–present
50 **My Dad's Strip Club** UK; 2002–present
51 **N55** Denmark; 1996–present
52 **Oda Projesi** Turkey; 1997–present
53 **Oliver Ressler** Austria; 1995–present (individual engaged in various collaborative practices)
54 **Parasite** USA; 1997–1998
55 **The Pink Bloque** USA; 2001–2005
56 **Preemptive Media** USA; 2001–2007
57 **Radical Culture Research Collective** Europe & North America; 2007–2009
58 **REINIGUNGSGESELLSCHAFT (RG)**; Germany & Ukraine; 1996–present
59 **RELAX (chiarenza & hauser & co)** Switzerland; 1983–present
60 **Sisters of Survival (SOS)** USA; 1981–1984
61 **Skart** Serbia; 1990–present
62 **subRosa** USA; 1998–present
63 **Surveillance Camera Players** USA; 1996–present
64 **Urban Rats** USA; 1981–1983
65 **The Waitresses** USA; 1977–1985
66 **What is to be done? /Chto delat?** Russia; 2003–present

---

67 **UKK (Unge Kunstnere og Kunstformidlere/Young Artists & Artworkers)** Denmark; 2002–present

"We don't do artworks, we are a political organization... UKK was established in protest to the cultural politics of the right-wing nationalist Danish government. It influences cultural politics both in parliament, in state administration and in the institutions. UKK's field is cultural politics and institutional practices; however UKK does see those as inseparably connected to the politics at large of the government and as such we feel that UKK's political work has an effect beyond art-politics into general politics."

Selected results from the author's 2008–9 survey of artists' groups and collectives. Graphic visualization realized by Worksight.com.

INFORMAL COLLECTIVES VS FORMAL ORGANIZATIONAL STRUCTURES

TOTAL NUMBER SURVEYED: 211

TOTAL NUMBER OF SURVEY RESPONSES:

67

Nota bene: Some of these collectivities refuse the label "artist collective." Often this is due to a critical or distanced relationship to modernist notions of art and/or collectivity. Members may be just as likely to come from other disciplines as from art; and many groups have temporary and changing configurations of members, rather than fixed memberships as implied by the term *collective*. They have been included in this survey because a majority of their activity is cultural work done collectively.

DATE OF FORMATION

1960S	1970S	1980S	1990S	2000S
5	15	20	1	8
19	65	22	2	12
28		35	3	16
		40	4	17
		59	6	24
		60	7	29
		64	9	30
			10	31
			11	32
			13	33
			14	34
			18	37
			21	38
			23	41
			25	42
			26	46
			27	47
			36	48
			39	49
			43	50
			44	55
			45	56
			51	57
			52	66
			53	67
			54	
			58	
			61	
			62	
			63	

RELATIONSHIP TO THE "TWO SIDES" OF THE ART WORLD: MUSEUMS/PUBLIC SPACES VS COMMERCIAL DEALERS/ART MARKETS

LITTLE OR NO RELATIONSHIP TO ANY FORMAL ART SYSTEM

8 ▸ 16 ▸ 41 ▸ 44 ▸ 57 ▸ 64

SOME ACTIVITY WITH MUSEUMS, ART SPACES, & BIENNIALS

1 ▸ 3 ▸ 9 ▸ 11 ▸ 12 ▸ 13 ▸ 14 ▸ 15 ▸ 17 ▸ 19 ▸ 20 ▸ 21 ▸ 22 ▸ 24 ▸ 25 ▸ 27 ▸ 28 ▸ 29 ▸ 30 ▸ 31 ▸ 32 ▸ 33 ▸ 34 ▸ 35 ▸ 36 ▸ 37 ▸ 38 ▸ 39 ▸ 40 ▸ 42 ▸ 43 ▸ 45 ▸ 46 ▸ 47 ▸ 48 ▸ 49 ▸ 50 ▸ 51 ▸ 52 ▸ 53 ▸ 54 ▸ 55 ▸ 56 ▸ 59 ▸ 60 ▸ 61 ▸ 62 ▸ 63 ▸ 65 ▸ 66

SOME ACTIVITY WITH MUSEUMS/ART SPACES/BIENNIALS & COMMERCIAL DEALERS/ART MARKETS

2 ▸ 4 ▸ 5 ▸ 6 ▸ 7 ▸ 10 ▸ 18 ▸ 23 ▸ 26 ▸ 58

AVERAGE NUMBER OF REGULARLY ACTIVE MEMBERS

many groups have informal or flexible memberships and regularly collaborate with others

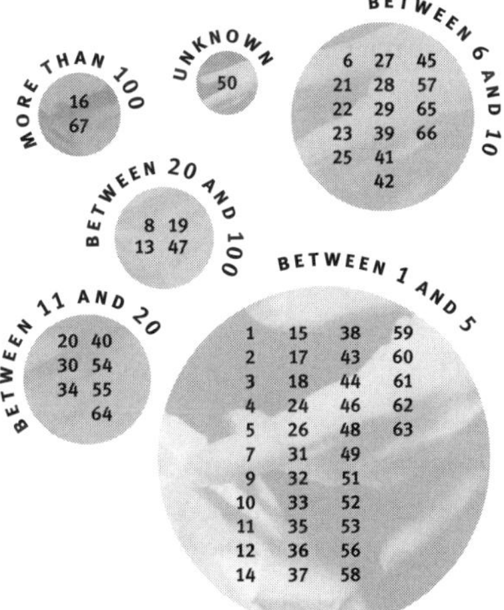

role of service personnel within the precarious neoliberal economy. Businesses, no less than cultural institutions, eagerly lap up this freely offered labor. This includes alterative spaces. Yet what is most engaging about these meta-commercial mock-institutions is less their critical artistic intentions than the peculiar state of difference and similitude they operate within in which antagonism and empathy are superimposed upon one another.

Fifteen of the 67 groups who responded to the survey reported that they are officially recognized not-for-profit organizations under the tax laws of their nation. At the same time most indicated that they operate under non-hierarchical rules of conduct suggesting they are also essentially meta-legal structures who perform proscribed roles as necessary for group survival. Far more commonplace was the complete rejection of any registered legal or taxable status. Thirty-eight, or more than half of all respondents, insisted they are strictly unofficial. This casual, frequently flippant approach to proper institutional formalities is compromised only slightly by the need for one group member to serve as the designated treasurer, and only ten of the total respondents reported not having either a treasurer or a bank account. This concession to organizational structure aside, the majority of these collectives represent their own internal governance as strictly "non-hierarchical," although this idealistic self-image is sometimes qualified by the need for structured decision making, technical expertise, or experienced leadership, such as when the group must manage a complicated project, respond to a mass media inquiry, or, in the case of Steve Kurtz and CAE, confront an external threat. The feminist Tactical Media collective subRosa admits that with sufficient trust the election of a rotating "project manager" or "communications point-person" articulates what is otherwise intended to be a non-hierarchical organizational structure. Icelandic Love Corporation insist they operate under an "artistic structure," presumably meaning they work without top-down authority. Curiously, the lack of hierarchy amongst artist producers is frequently cited not only by artists, but also by the gurus of post-Fordist enterprise culture in books such as the previously cited *Artful Making: What Managers Need to Know About How Artists Work*. And despite their overstated nomenclature intended to project (often ironically) institutional solidity, a substantial number of surveyed collectives are composed of only a few core members, five or six on average, but some consisting of two or only one person.[29] The average age of these participants ranges from the mid 20s to 30s, which is not surprising given that most groups were founded after 1989 and many later still; however, it is exactly this generation that is most likely to have no direct experience of what a non-commercial public realm is, or, aside from the distributed community of social networks, to share any concept of affiliation, solidarity, or collectivity that transcends short-term individual need. The very notion of acting collectively was once considered a political statement in itself, but this is no longer consistently true today. This may be why some contemporary collectives expressed involvement with the commercial side of the art world, a tendency that would have met with mild to serious disapproval in the past. Whereas almost every group surveyed had some involvement with non-commercial art spaces, biennials, or museums, nine groups reported presenting work in commercial galleries, and in several cases, individual members from groups not participating in the commercial art world exhibited their own work in such venues outside the scope of the collective. In fact it is possible that for some younger artists the collective is seen as a safe space within which to experiment at a remove from an increasingly entrepreneurial art world economy. Still, this seems to be a minor feature of collectivism today, and several reasons suggest themselves as to why artists' groups still remain largely, though not entirely, disconnected from what Stallabrass calls Art Inc.[30] In the case of politically engaged artists' collectives of course, the specific imagery or intention of the artwork may be an issue (even the pleasure of being slapped in the face by the avant-garde has some limits after all, though admittedly not many). More often, however, collectors and dealers are simply cautious about investing in multiple-authored artworks. As we discovered with Paper Rad, collectively produced artworks represent a unique challenge within the market for reasons that have little or nothing to do with content. For one thing, artists' groups are often in flux. So much so that a collective can abruptly self-terminate due to an internal dispute or the resignation of a key member, or even a bit of commercial success. Lack of product stability, in other words, is usually not a selling point in the art market. Numerous collectives also encourage participation by non-members; in some instances these are not professional artists. The result is a hybridized aesthetic product that only adds to the non-marketability of group artwork. Finally, projects made by interventionist groups are frequently ephemeral or intangible. Their only permanent existence is as documents or archives, neither of which are valued by collectors to the same degree as painting and sculpture, although that is beginning to change somewhat in an era of privatization and enclosure as the profitable licensing of images, documents, and recordings once thought to belong in the public commons accelerates.

All of this complicates the provenance of a collectively produced artwork as an investment. But there is also substantial reluctance on the part of many informally organized art groups to get near the commercial art market, although this disinclination does not extend to most museums, alternative spaces, or Kunsthalles, judging from the survey results. Many informal artists' groups also seek to elide the specific category of art or artists, even as they operate, or conceivably could only exist in their present form, along the margins of the art world (or in the equivalent "independent media" sphere). In other words, on a practical level, it would be difficult to imagine these masqueraders functioning without some access to the imaginative license granted only to artists. In addition, this vague cultural framing, no matter how ambivalently it may be treated from either side, permits groups to commandeer art world resources, discourse, and networks for political critique, even as it provides essential social capital for group members seeking employment as teachers, cultural consultants, or administrators. This is a paradox that theorist Grant Kester has sought to address through his concept of dialogical aesthetics by applying Jürgen Habermas' notion of communicative action within a public sphere to the activities of socially active artists and artists' groups. For Habermas, beneficial action within a community must be based on mutual trust in which actual social differences of class, ethnicity, gender, or social power are bracketed off from an ideal communicative, discursive environment. Under these circumstances group decision making is directed by reason and faith: facts and superior argument combined with the belief that fellow community members are speaking honestly and in good faith. Feminist theorists such as Nancy Fraser, and Marxist critics like Negt and Kluge, criticize Habermas precisely for his concept of a liberal public sphere which is inherently exclusive of those who either lack the language skills necessary to participate, or of those whose material conditions simply do not allow them to take the time off from trying to survive to even enter the conversation. And yet, despite the growing reality of precarious risk and social fragmentation, the notion of a public sphere, even a compromised one, remains strongly appealing. Which is why Kester's re-application of these public ideals via certain artistic practices is not only compelling but is also a logical response to 30 years of neoliberal social fragmentation. "Subjectivity is formed *through* discourse and inter-subjective exchange itself," he argues, but for this space of relatively transparent discourse to take place it must be momentarily bracketed out from the reified structures of everyday life. Which is where certain types of artistic practice are useful even as they remain a non-instrumental mode of experience. "Aesthetic experience is uniquely capable of producing knowledge about society."[31] Think of this as an epistemology of collective knowledge.

It is this defamiliarization of expectations that artists have been practicing since the dawn of the modern era, if not earlier. Kester is quick to avoid describing this shift away from the familiar as having been brought about by avant-garde shock, something his theory explicitly aims to challenge. However, he does not clarify whether the kind of defamiliarization required to produce a new conversational context is a small rupture different only by degrees or is something fundamentally different from the intentionally disturbing work of many contemporary artists.[32] Regardless, Kester believes that some artists are uniquely capable of reconstructing dialogical exchange because they selflessly (or nearly selflessly) serve as context providers: parenthetical spaces in which conversational experience and informed social judgment is once again possible, if only provisionally. The work of Californian artist Suzanne Lacey, rural Argentinean collective, Ala Plastica, and the London-based Platform all exemplify this dialogical model in different ways. However, there is a fundamental complication to Kester's thesis, one made explicit in the work of Austrian group WochenKlausur, who translate their German name as "weeks of closure."

Since their founding in 1993, WochenKlausur have developed art projects with non-Austrian guest laborers, designed pedagogical programs, and used Austrian cultural funding to improved health care for migrants and sex workers. By temporarily bracketing off dialogical spaces for communication and negotiation with state authorities the group has created short-term public service interventions with measurable benefits for local, marginalized populations.[33] WochenKlausur's desire to intervene in the gaps and broken parts of what is a still very generous and non-privatized Austrian welfare state derives in large part from the influence of the late German artist Joseph Beuys. Somewhat like TM, except minus the electricity, Beuys' theory of social sculpture sought to mend societal defects through direct aesthetic intervention, offering disciples a contemporary version of *Lebensphilosophie*. Beuys remains a controversial figure however, and substantial critiques of his practice and cult of personality have been developed by historians Benjamin Buchloh, Rosalind Krauss, and fellow German artist Hans Haacke, among others. At the same time, Beuys and his activities are often cited as direct inspiration for a generation of socially engaged, European artists including WochenKlausur, as well as for the emergence of artists' centers in Ireland after he established an extension of his Free International University in Belfast in 1974.[34] Like many of the post-'89 artists' groups discussed in this book, WochenKlausur's collective identity is molded in such a way as to attract resources useful for the collective's interventionist mission. This typically requires cleverly reallocating governmental benefits towards invisible groups and individuals who lack access to power, or who have little or no capacity to speak or represent their interests or identities within the broader public sphere. And yet what makes possible this dialogical and conversational medium in the first place is a confidence game in which a seemingly fixed institutional participant—the state, city, corporation, prison, museum, school, even the European Union—is confronted with what appears to be a miniature replica of institutional cohesion and legitimacy. Because all the correct significations of organizational value are artfully displayed there is no other option except to take them seriously and provide governmental support. Its not that WochenKlausur (or most of the artists under discussion here) are insincere—on the contrary, they often take institutional responsibility even more seriously than do those who actually operate within it (even if carried out as a taunt, challenge, or critique). Indeed, this inevitable blurring of artistic representation with actually provided social services may help to explain the election of WochenKlausur's co-founder, artist Wolfgang Zinggl, to a seat in the Austrian parliament in 2001 as a member of the Green Party. Like a chance encounter between Habermas and Derrida on Dada's operating table, the tactical plagiarism of institutional function swings around to occupy the very center of what is cleverly simulated.

What has been born out of this profane coupling is an all-pervasive neoliberal realism, a precarious theater of action in which Zinggl's officious validation becomes the bright flip-side of Steve Kurtz's criminalization. The consequences of this bracketing and re-bracketing, materialization and dematerialization, may vex the prospects for a well-grounded dialogical aesthetic, but they are no less consequential and serious in their ramifications. Which is why, when viewed as an aggregate phenomenon, the most impressive aspect of these informally organized mockstitutions is the degree to which they breathe vitality back into the corpse of civic society and radical politics, strategically occupying the cast-off remains of a now archaic liberal public sphere through acts of puckish necromancy. This includes re-imagining corporate ventures as actually entrusted to the common good, proposing that public education be both public and edifying, and re-envisioning museums and cultural institutions as spaces where an ideal public sphere still buttresses conversation. Perhaps the good faith space of dialogical art is only possible thanks to the bad faith of artistic dissimulation and parafiction? If there is an aesthetic dimension to such tactical resistance it does not manifest itself at the level of artworks such as particular images, objects, installations, publications, performances, or interventionist, participatory actions (although any of these may be part of a given artistic repertoire). Instead, by embracing their own dark materiality and superfluity within capital, these precariously assembled groups, cells, tribes, and collectivities imaginatively secrete an exquisite system of dodges and feints, ploys and maneuvers. Their finest ruse, therefore, is the manipulation of institutional sobriety insofar as it marginally frees these artists from anticipated forms of behavior and disciplinary visibility within the increasingly hegemonic, entrepreneurial art market. Nevertheless, as Canadian artist and critic Luis Jacob warned many years ago, such skillful mimicry can also reveal an "ambivalent attitude of both fascination and apprehension towards corporate culture."[35] It is a caution taken seriously by one group whose corporate plagiarism has become synonymous with the practice of Tactical Media.

The Flying Wing

The art of mocking enterprise culture has been taken to no higher or more sophisticated level than by The Yes Men, a duo of artist-performers who use Tactical Media dissimulations to "correct" the image of corporate wrongdoers.[36] Nevertheless, their strategic leveraging of institutional power depends entirely upon an ability to project a set of recognizable, legitimating attributes from the point of view of mainstream authority and to then allow this "hack" to be publicly exposed through the same media networks the duo briefly pirated. Two aspects of their practice stand out in this regard. First is the simplicity of means by which The Yes Men snare the gaze of established institutions, especially the mainstream mass media. Everything from a particular style of haircut to the choice of color for a tie or business suit is fine-tuned to provide maximum advantage for those lacking capital or resources on par with their chosen advisories. As surrealist Roger Caillois insisted in his startling essay on insect mimicry—a text that inspired Lacan's concept of the mirror stage—an organism imitates aspects of its environment not in order to deceive predators, but as a response to the demands of space itself.[37] One wonders what new theories The Yes Men's soft, invertebrate SurvivaBall would have inspired in the idiosyncratic French intellectual. Once inside its soft spheroid shell a Banker or CEO survives the coming environmental collapse by sucking essential nutrients out of small animals and rolling across the wasted planetary landscape. Yet, even as The Yes Men's actions are becoming increasingly well known and therefore in danger of cooptation by the marketplace spectacle or by the far Right, one important dimension of their actions remains unmentionable. It is an aspect of their work that underscores the closing theme of this book: the rise of new social practices that simultaneously subvert, and yet reinstate sustainable organizational and social structures.

That The Yes Men align their tactical interventions with environmental and social justice campaigns is well known. Less familiar is the way their tactics are timed and coordinated to compliment the specific objectives of particular NGOs.

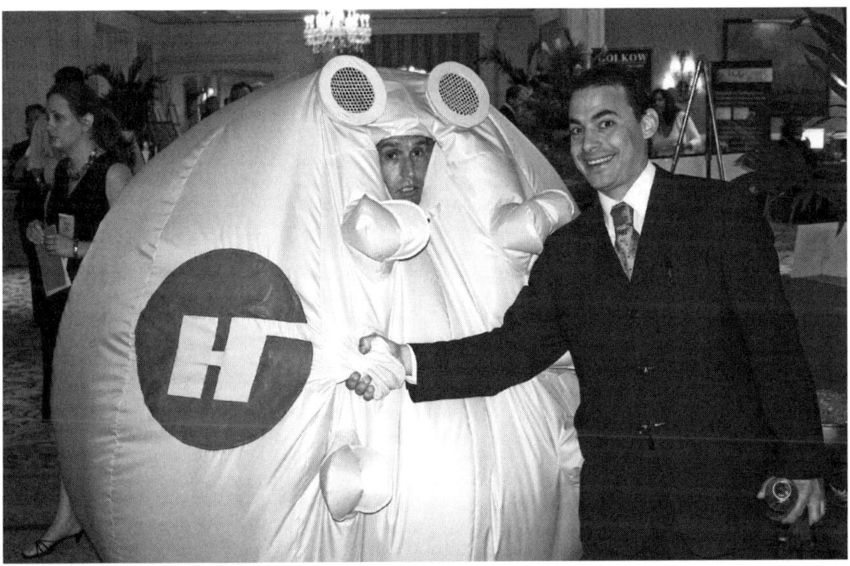

Disguised as corporate representatives of Halliburton, Andy and Mike of The Yes Men display a mock-up of the SurvivaBall Model X7, an autonomous portable environment for surviving environmental catastrophe that the Tactical Media duo insists is "Technological. Profitable. And, dare we say, beautiful." See www.survivaball.com. Image courtesy The Yes Men.

This relationship is not unlike the US military's policy of don't ask, don't tell.[38] As *nom de guerre* Andy Bichlbaum describes the duo's invisible partnership, The Yes Men "shared information and coordinated efforts [with an unnamed NGO] to be sure that whatever we did would be accurate and incisive, and would be of use to the larger campaign if it worked."[39] If the CAE serves as the TM R&D branch for counter-globalization and environmental groups, then The Yes Men are the movement's counter-corporate "flying wing." The term refers to a small group of activists who carry out risky operations in support of an organization's goals, but whose actions are decoupled from that organization for fear of potential legal consequences.

> From our perspective this was an ideal situation: the NGO's extensive knowledge and experience had made our action more resonant and incisive, and we were more comfortable with our action knowing that the "hit and run" aspects our work could contribute to the more sustained effort of a larger organization with a continuing stake in the issues.[40]

One of the most significant of these deniable hit-and-run operations was carried out on December 3, 2004, 20 years after the world's most lethal chemical disaster. In 1984 the city of Bhopal, India lost over 2,000 residents after a Union Carbide pesticide production plant released Methyl Isocyanate (and possibly other toxins) into the atmosphere. The US-based company had already experienced a series of leaks as well as ignored several work actions staged by the local union concerned about the poorly maintained Union Carbide facilities at the factory. After the catastrophe the corporation provided a small compensation to survivors, pulled its operations out of India, and later became a wholly owned subsidiary of Dow Chemical, another US-based corporation. For the twentieth anniversary of the disaster The Yes Men created a mirror image of Dow Chemical's corporate website. When the BBC began researching a piece on the Bhopal disaster it came across the false website, contacted The Yes Men thinking they were Dow Chemical corporation, and invited one of the company's alleged spokespeople to respond to the legacy of the tragedy in which thousands still require medical care as toxic chemicals continue to leach into the ground water some two decades later. The Yes Men complied. They sent Bichlbaum as Dow Chemical's "Jude Finisterra" (Jude, for the patron saint of lost causes, and Finisterra, meaning the ends of the earth). In the televised BBC interview Finisterra proclaims an historic breakthrough for corporate culture. A major transnational business is finally acknowledging its wrongdoing in public, something no other corporation had previously done. The fictive company spokesperson assured viewers that Dow planned to liquidate all of its acquired Union Carbide assets—estimated to be in the billions of dollars—in an effort to compensate the victims of the Bhopal catastrophe. Furthermore, Finisterra promised that Dow would turn over to the Indian authorities Union

Carbide's former CEO Warren Anderson on still-pending charges of mass murder. Immediately following the breaking BBC interview the chemical giant's stock plunged by some two billion dollars, and Dow quickly responded with a press release disclosing Finisterra as an imposter involved in an elaborate deception. Notably, The Yes Men's mission of "correcting" the image of corporate wrongdoers has so far been unhampered by any lawsuits. A definite, tactical lesson of The Yes Men's interventions is that large corporations are unlikely to take legal action against pranksters and culture jammers for fear that a public trial would only amplify the message of their critics. In the theater of semiotic warfare corporations are a priori suspect, and legitimization essential. (Opera companies, artists, and museums know the rules of this passion play all too well.)

The BBC Bhopal prank exposes two truths about enterprise culture. First, the seemingly monumental authority of the media spectacle is vulnerable, quite literally, if only fleetingly, to anyone with some basic graphic art skills, a laptop computer, the willpower to critically apply these resources, and maybe a fresh haircut. This after all is the same message CAE, Lovink, IBM's cyber-strikers, and other practitioners of TM have been insisting upon since the early 1990s: effective civil disobedience pivots today on an ever more accessible sphere of electronically mediated reality, but also upon an awareness of the histrionic nature of this half real–half theater of symbolic action. The second lesson The Yes Men's intervention offers is stark evidence that mimicking institutional power always comes at a price. This is so whether or not the targeted authority is a corporation's public relations officers, scientific experts, city or state authorities, or even the far less formidable jurisdiction of the art world establishment. For The Yes Men, the penalty is an identity adrift within the very same field of corporate culture the artists have declared semiotic war upon for decades. As Nietzsche cautioned—and Caillois reinterpreted some four decades later—be careful as you stare into the abyss for it may begin to stare back at you.

The Yes Men's "flying wing" approach points to an essential problem within Tactical Media and interventionist art—the challenge is to connect radical cultural practices with a broader, more sustainable political critique. This was not always so. Radical artistic innovation has historically been linked, either directly or indirectly, with militant movements focused on social change. John Heartfield's Dada-inspired, anti-fascist graphics were made explicitly for the cover of AIZ, the Workers Pictorial Newspaper (Arbeiter-Illustrierte-Zeitung) published by Willi Münzenberg, a leading force within the German Communist Party (KPD), as well as an elected member of the left-wing Reichstag of the 1920s. Likewise, many of the avant-garde projects and theories generated in the early years of the Soviet Union took place within an approving governmental framework including that of the technical school Vkhutemas. Only later, after the establishment of social realism as the official artistic style in the USSR, did artists such as Tatlin,

Klutsis, and Malevich run afoul of Soviet authorities. Far looser connections between radical artists and political activists appear in the 1960s and 1970s, nevertheless some influential members of AWC including Alex Gross and Jeanne Toche strongly sympathized with the New Left, calling for support of a wildcat postal strike in 1970 that was also endorsed by the militant wing of the Students for a Democratic Society (SDS). In France Jean-Pierre Gorin, who would later join with filmmaker Jean-Luc Godard to form the Dziga-Vertov Collective, was a member of a Maoist splinter group from the French Communist Party. More recently, artist Jerry Kearns, one of the principal founding members of PAD/D, had been active in the Anti-Imperialist Cultural Union, a militant New Left organization founded by African-American poet Amiri Baraka, as well as the National Black United Front chaired by the Reverend Herbert Daughtry in the late 1970s. And today perhaps The Yes Men's hall of mirrors, like the grin of the spectral cat lurking in the PAD/D Archive, are necessary stations, temporary stopping points and trembling superimpositions, waiting for a new generation of antediluvian tacticians to have it both ways, to be nimble interventionists and simultaneously rooted social builders. The Yes Men's latest project called The Yes Lab appears to get this.[41] It is both a pedagogical and an experimental endeavor that calls on social justice, climate change, and anti-capitalist activists to participate in developing the "smartest, most effective" media tactics for accomplishing their political goals. There are definite hints of productivism here, but also a new kind of self-replicating open-source technology known as RepRap that manufactures its own replacement parts.[42] Except unlike a century ago when art aimed to be useful for building a revolutionary society, the aesthetic laboratories and pedagogical experiments of today operate within an ill-defined neoliberal landscape of fractured resistance and temporary anti-enclosures that attempt to remain one step ahead of enterprise culture.

Right to the City

Just outside Washington DC, in Baltimore, Maryland, a group of tactical urban interventionists have produced a series of exhibitions, publications, city tours, pedagogical projects, public interventions, and most recently an organic garden and park that serves to highlight the interconnected role of the local prison system, real estate speculators, and creative industries. Like New York, Chicago, and other urban centers, Baltimore's economically blighted inner-city neighborhoods underwent a process of private urban renewal aimed at attracting members of the "creative class." Meanwhile, the city's large population of low-income, African-American residents has been systematically pushed to the margins or imprisoned.[43] Living communally since their inception in 2005, the three members of the Baltimore Development Cooperative (BDC) were previously known as

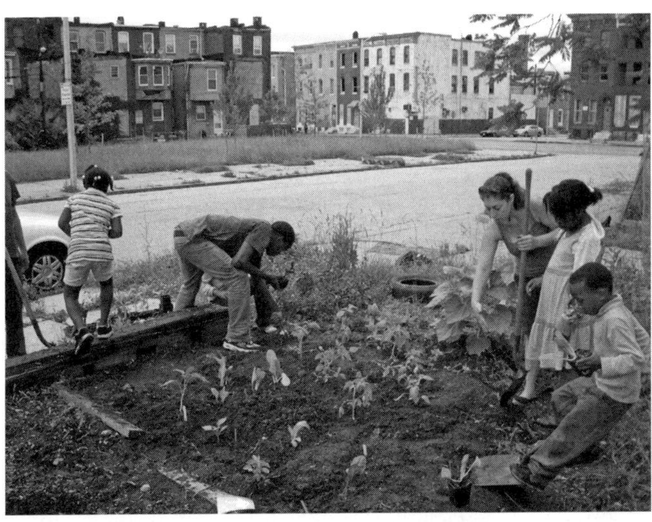

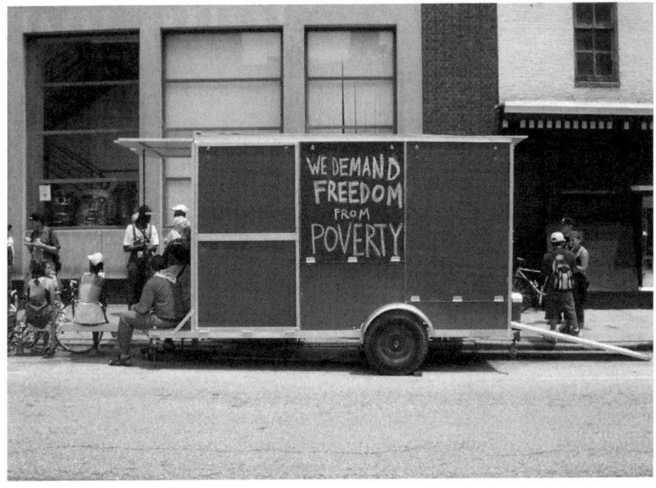

Participation Park is a project of the Baltimore Development Cooperative (BDC): a three-person collective living and working in East Baltimore dedicated to the critical analysis of authoritarian forms of urban planning and the development of more democratic modes of spatial practice. The aim of the park is to not only counter creeping neighborhood gentrification, but also the lack of access to local produce sometimes referred to as the urban food desert phenomenon. In 2007, the group converted a vacant city lot into a "slow food" organic farm and social gathering space. The impromptu park is also used for holding classes on urban agriculture. BDC is made up of former members of Campbaltimore whose 2006 Mobile Trailer project (bottom) offered passersby free classes in sewing and cooking as well as literature about the politics and economics of the city and its "prison-industrial" complex. Images courtesy BDC.

Campbaltimore. Their research focuses on the entwined processes of local incarceration and culturally amplified urban gentrification without sidestepping their own role as white, middle-class art school graduates within this system.[44] After weeks of meetings with local political and social organizers including homeless rights advocates, sex workers groups, tenant unions, and transit activists, the artists transformed their findings into a series of large charts displayed at a downtown art center known as The Contemporary.[45] The group also parked a converted mobile trailer outside of Red Emma's, a worker-owned and managed cooperative bookstore and coffee shop named after the fiery American anarchist and civil rights orator. For about a day the trailer offered free sewing lessons, video screenings, and take-away brochures about urban theory and local social justice organizations before Baltimore police forced it off the street.

Following a subsequent re-composition of its membership the group turned its attention to developing sustainable local projects including an organic garden known as *Participation Park* illegally squatted on a rubble-strewn lot in East Baltimore not far from the city's major correctional center, the same supermax prison facility that played a central role in David Simon's stark television series *The Wire*.[46] *Participation Park* will be expanded to include a band shell for public events and a pizza oven where residents will cook with vegetables from the garden.[47] The group is also teaching seminars on "the right to the city," at Red Emma's, in which retaking the commons is a central theme.[48] Most recently, they organized an ambitious weekend event entitled *The City From Below* in conjunction with Red Emma's and *Baltimore's Indypendent Reader*.[49] With artists from the Just Seeds cooperative designing graphics, the conference organizers invited a range of international cultural and political theorists including David Harvey, George Caffentzis, Brian Holmes, Beka Economopoulos from The Change You Want To See in Brooklyn, Daniel Tucker from AREA Chicago, Christine Ulke from the *Journal of Aesthetics & Protest*, as well as activists such as New York's Picture the Homeless, and Baltimore's United Workers, Kids on the Hill, and Power Inside Baltimore. The three-person art collective produced this event without funding from the city, or any university or foundation, by successfully drawing on their established social networks, charging modest registration fees, and by "leveraging" audio-visual equipment that some participants had access to as local educational instructors.[50]

Several months later BDC was awarded a substantial grant from a city-run foundation that had previously denied the group a similar prize. The money allowed group members to pay themselves a small monthly stipend each for one year.[51] The jury's selection, however, ignited an immediate controversy amongst some members of the local arts community. The tenor of the debate reflects precisely the jagged, often nonexistent line separating the felt absence of social authority and responsibility, and the interventionist culture of groups like

BDC, BCL, CAE, FNO, The Yes Men, or WochenKlausur. One clearly flustered Baltimore art blogger demanded to know why the informal artist's collective had not taken steps to become a legitimate 501c3 non-profit organization? Dwelling on the obvious, the critic points out that the group's name is a "riff on the Baltimore Development Corporation," the city's official bureau of "regeneration" or gentrification depending on which side of the economic fence you are standing on. The blogger acerbically adds that BDC's act of dissimulation is intended to "stir up trouble" by mockingly criticizing the city's urban renewal plans.[52] The group's carefully chosen name provoked awareness of the unspoken class and racial conflict in the city, even as the critic turns a blind eye to the fact that East Baltimore's decline and gentrification, like that of other cities, has been managed from above by municipal, financial, and other neoliberal corporate interests. Nonetheless, with pluck enough to label itself a municipal "development" cooperative, BDC appears to be inventing an art practice precisely suited for the mean streets of Ravenstown, as if filling in a symbolic gap they themselves have carved out of equal parts artistic imaginary and urban wreckage.[53]

The City From Below's conference also laid the foundation for an all-volunteer education program called the Baltimore Free School. Located at Red Emma's Bookstore Coffeehouse the pedagogical project claims inspiration from "a growing network of similar projects in other cities as well as the long tradition of anti-authoritarian education."[54] Courses range from "Patternmaking for Clothing," to "Surrealist Games" and "Breaking Rank: Soldier Resistance Movements, How & Why They Emerge." The BDC artists offer a class appropriately entitled "Right To The City."

This growing network of pedagogical activism is the latest tactical mutation of cultural resistance to the society of risk and its neoliberal enterprise culture. It takes numerous forms, some well grounded, others arriving at a degree of stability as if by accident. Like BDC, New York City's Center For Urban Pedagogy (CUP) consists of a group of cultural workers, artists, and urban theorists involved in issues of city environmental and housing policies, gentrification, and recycling. Also like the Baltimore group, CUP is committed to developing new forms of pedagogy, although their focus is primarily on young people. CUP partners with city schools, developing curricula in which students are encouraged to move out into public space for research projects and class observations. Unlike BDC however, and unlike many of the groups discussed in this book, CUP has lost any interest (if it ever existed) in merely leveraging institutional authority or disguising itself as a municipal agency. For all intents and purposes CUP is an institution founded in 1997, and its educational programs and exhibitions have garnered increasing foundational support and critical attention from the art world; however, the group's founders paint a moderately conflicting picture of the group's initial identity and later development. The evolution of CUP from informal student group to full-blown pedagogical agency is a study in self-organized dark matter inserting itself into the ripped fabric of neoliberal cities *from below*. Damon Rich, CUP's primary founder, insists that even though Situationist theory and institutional critique were strong elements in his architectural education he came to believe it was "most important to build from those insights to create new institutions."[55] Rich also insists that CUP's name "was never meant as a joke or a ruse." Nevertheless, long-time member Rosten Woo recalls that when he joined the group in 1998 "there was certainly something in the name that was intended to be satirical." Woo adds, however, that "we intentionally institutionalized CUP as an experiment in trying to make a different kind of institution than an 'art collective'." In truth this minor difference in CUP's origin story may not really matter given that the operating spaces of neoliberal enterprise culture do not significantly differentiate between the spectacular and the material, except when it comes to how capital is ultimately distributed. Meanwhile, from their statements to their curricula, CUP is shadowed by the lingering influence of Archigram's eccentric city planning projects, Debord's *psychogeographies*, and the unitary urbanism of the Letrists.

Similar pedagogical projects influenced by experimental drifting and *détournement* include tours programmed by the Center For Land Use Interpretation (CLUI) of atomic weapons testing sites in New Mexico and Nevada; a website called Native Resurgence that maps "Native American resistance and ingenuity in the upper Midwest since the 1970s"; the acoustic-activist sound recordings made by Ultra Red out of Los Angeles; and Makrolab, a terrestrial submarine-like structure befitting Captain Nemo built with government and EU funds by Slovenian artist Marko Peljhan in which a group of artists, hackers, radio hams, and the "errant offspring of the military-industrial complex" shared life and research in various semi-isolated locations from Krk Island in Croatia, to Rottnest Island in Australia, to the Campalto in the Venice Lagoon.[56] A series of critical pedagogical initiatives in Chicago explores the use of the city as a learning site for public high school students. Nomadic Studio and the Pedagogical Factory are two programs that emerged out of Jim Duignan's Stockyard Institute, an informal learning center that brings artists together with students in order to develop temporary collaborative projects including: Cafeteria Sessions, in which young people used the school cafeteria to develop digital audio recordings of their school experience that then became a source for an adolescent-specific curriculum; a community radio station in a tent called Urbs in Horto developed in collaboration with the late Chicago artist Michael Piazza; a public message gps sign-board that reads "Don't Mess with My Fro" located atop a taxi cab sponsored by the artist's group Haha; and an imaginary Tourist Bureau co-designed by Davion Mathews that functioned as a traveling oral history of the Austin neighborhood where the Stockyard

Institute is located. Duignan has also forged ties with the University of Hip Hop and AREA Chicago (Art/Research/Education/Activism), the later a publishing and networking platform dedicated to strengthening social justice campaigns and educational innovation throughout the city and Midwest region. On the other side of the Atlantic several members of N55—a Danish collective that partially inspired the work of Chicago's Temporary Services and whose members lived communally together for several years inside a geodesic dome located in Copenhagen Harbor—have recently been working together under the name Learning Site. Like CUP, CLUI, Stockyard Institute, and so forth, Learning Site's projects involve research and pedagogy, however their collective focus is on the exploration of sustainable living. In 2008 they replicated a non-functioning, papier-mâché version of a weathered, 1979 concrete dome that sits atop Palika Bazaar in Connaught Place, New Delhi, and temporarily installed it alongside the original structure.[57] The bazaar itself is a massive underground market built by the Indian state and widely known for its notoriously crowded stalls of cut-rate couture, hand-crafts, electronic goods, and pirated, pornographic DVDs. With the original dome just a few meters away Learning Site's non-functioning, yet full-scale mock-up served as an educational display platform on which to post information about recycling, organic gardening, and day-to-day pro-ecology practices incorporating ideas and methods from environmental theorist Vandana Shiva.

Learning Site's research model is one small part of what is becoming an increasingly widespread phenomenon in which artists and informal cultural collectives combine their desire to re-imagine or literally reinvent organizational structures with an interest in DIY pedagogies and autodidactic forms of instruction. This convergence has recently begun to turn around, implicating its leading protagonists—artists, critics, students, theorists, cultural activists. Some apparently find their own presumably sophisticated education suddenly lacking and seek to create new, self-designed art programs. Others openly reject what in the United Kingdom is referred to by neoliberal policy wonks as enterprise teaching or entrepreneurial learning, or in the United States as the very theft of life itself through a pedagogical system turned graveyard. From the student-occupied campus of the University of California at Berkeley a grim communiqué reads in part:

> Incongruous architecture, the ghosts of vanished ideals, the vista of a dead future: these are the remains of the university ... like the society to which it has played the faithful servant, the university is bankrupt. This bankruptcy is not only financial. It is the index of a more fundamental insolvency, one both political and economic, which has been a long time in the making.[58]

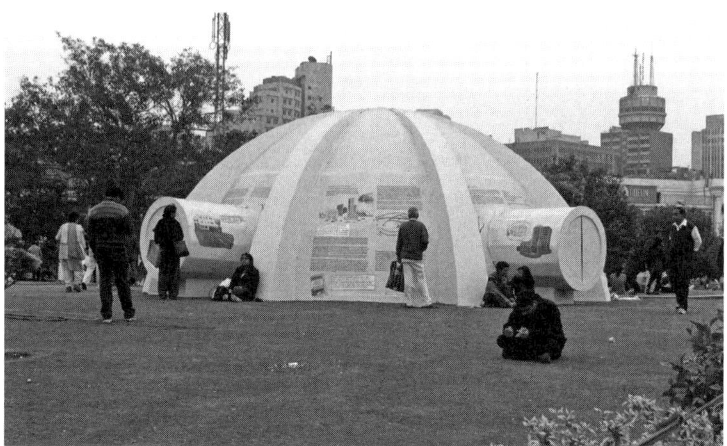

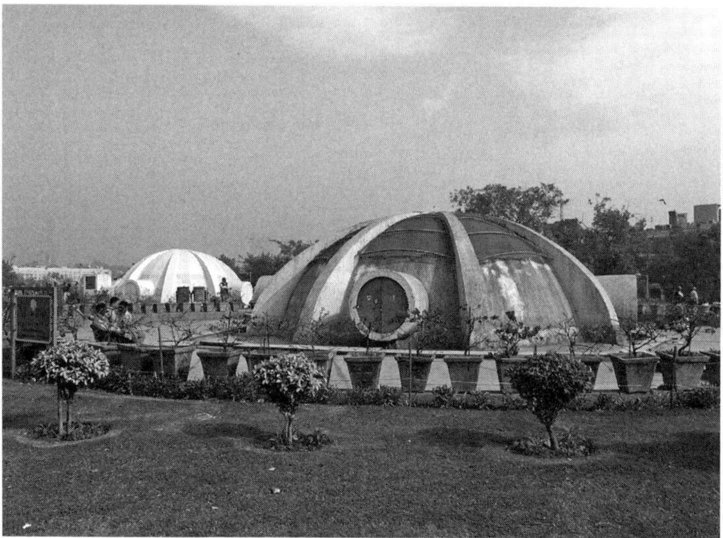

Learning Site's "[Poster Dwelling for Land, Market and Economy]" was a 1:1 scale *papier-mâché* model of the concrete domes that provide light and air to Palika Bazaar, a subterranean marketplace below a public park in New Delhi. The surface of the dome was covered with images and texts that critically explored the tensions between labor, land, and economy, and the role of markets in social and cultural organization. The work was made for the exhibition 48°C Public.Art.Ecology in 2008. The project also included a public lecture and workshop on ecology at the dome led by the Indian NGO Navdanya. A publication containing the texts and images from the dome and other essays is now used by Navdanya in teaching with school children. Images courtesy Rikke Luther and Learning Site.

The Academy from Below?

University students are demanding to be liberated from the "cemetery" of higher education, demanding in fact that they escape the "graveyard" of liberal good intentions in which learned institutions fail to live up even to their own promises of assuring meritocracy, opportunity, equality, democracy in exchange for being processed by the neoliberal edu-factory. The take-over of Middlesex University buildings by students protesting the school's elimination of its renowned philosophy department on financial grounds, or the various manifestos and communiqués from "an absent future" signed by "occupied Berkeley," reflect both the grim state of education at the turn of the century but also its potential rebirth. For two months in late 2009, Austrian students occupied the University of Vienna demanding the abolition of tuition fees, improved working conditions for faculty and staff, and greater democracy throughout the nation's educational system. They were evicted. But in the early hours of December 22 they began organizing new protests in front of the university using digital networks to coordinate flash-mobs: large groups of people who suddenly converge and disperse at a set time in a particular public space, as arranged by an email, Twitter, or cell phone text message—essentially the same technique Iranian demonstrators used to mobilize their opposition to the government of Mahmoud Ahmadinejad. Several months earlier, students at The New School in New York City occupied for a second time in 2009 the privately owned university cafeteria. Barricaded inside they demanded the resignation of New School president Bob Kerry, a strong advocate of the Iraq war and of neoliberal education reform. Violently evicted by police using caustic pepper spray, their actions, along with those of the faculty union and school administrators, appear to have forced Kerry to announce he would not seek a new contract at the end of his term in 2011. Similarly dramatic occupations and protests have swept across the University of California school system following deep budget cuts and other cost-reduction measures in the wake of the recent financial collapse. Other states including New York are no doubt next in line for such upheaval. It appears that many who labor in or who are being "processed" by the neoliberal edu-factory system have begun to mutiny, and the new structural adjustment initiated by the 2008–9 "Great Recession" is beginning to serve as a focusing agent for this rebellion. What's more, theories of tactical urbanism, cultural intervention, and institutional impersonation go hand in hand with this new campus insurgency in which artists, neoliberalism's favorite knowledge proletariat, are playing a key research and development role.

In Los Angeles a group of artists have established their own teaching platform called The Public School. The project developed by several artists consists of an online program that allows participants to design classes they want to take, but can't find elsewhere, from practical, technology related workshops to theoretical seminars. Once enough students register for a particular course an appropriate instructor is hired to teach it, and a modest fee is charged for each seminar. There is no municipal or government support for this educational project, whose name is simultaneously a straightforward reference to the project's open, democratic structure as well as a speech act that "calls the bluff" of the failed California public school system. Since its founding independent clones of The Public School have emerged in New York City, Chicago, Philadelphia, Brussels, Paris, and San Juan.[59] On the East Coast, a new art academy mixes intensifying economic fears brought on by the financial meltdown together with efforts to critically re-imagine art education. The Bruce High Quality Foundation (BHQF) is not a foundation any more than there is anyone named Bruce High Quality. With support from Creative Time (an actual public art foundation) this faux foundation has recently launched the Bruce High Quality Foundation University (BHQFU).[60] The school's online mission statement, in a possible allusion to the French "Invisible Committee" manifesto *The Coming Insurrection*, begins with the stormy words: "Something's got to give. The $200,000-debt-model of art education [in the US] is simply untenable ... [and] mired in irrelevance."[61] That "irrelevant" quagmire is furthermore described as "blind romanticism and a blind professionalism," an academic zeitgeist BHQFU insists has been waging a false battle for the hearts and minds of contemporary art students.[62] The impending insurrection is everywhere these days. On March 9, 2008, Russian authorities closed the European University in St. Petersburg, allegedly on fire-code violations. One month later the first of an ongoing series of impromptu classes was held on a pedestrian street in the center of the city. Organized by then unemployed members of the European University, it included students as well as members of the Russian artists' collective Chto Delat/What is to be Done?[63] The Street University offered classes in student activism, consciousness-raising, and lectures on the Situationists. Other programs featured radical political theories seldom so openly debated in post-Perestroika Russia. After a second, spontaneous street classroom was organized, the European University officially reopened. Nonetheless, Street University (SU) continues to meet, even though its members admit "reorganization during 'peacetime' is difficult."[64] Still, as Chto Delat loudly proclaims "The task of the intellectual and the artist is to engage in a thoroughgoing unmasking of the myth that there are no alternatives to the global capitalist system."[65]

One informally structured program located in Manhattan's financial district for over a decade may represent a rudimentary template for sustaining this new, radical pedagogy from below. 16 Beaver Street (16 B) is both the address and the moniker of a reading group in which participants meet weekly to discuss texts, listen to visiting scholars and artists, and watch videos related to topics of interest generated by group members. There are no restrictions on who is permitted to participate, anyone who shows up and steps off the elevator into the loft is entreated to join in the discussion.[66] Despite its ten-plus years of programming the group has never metamorphosed into a legal entity, commercial, not-for-profit, or other.[67] Funding for events, and for the loft itself, has largely been accomplished by subletting part of the space to a commercial artist, as well as untold hours of in-kind labor provided by members and supporters. But, 16 B's uncluttered, stripped-down organizational model is deceptive. The highly sophisticated intellectual and pedagogical learning made possible by this anomalous [non] organization ranges from topics such as Palestinian culture and resistance to the war in Iraq, to debates about economic neoliberalization, the increasing private concentration of media, art and politics, and the "joys and poetics of resistance to Capitalist alienation."[68] And like the group's stripped-down organizational structure its meeting space is spare and uncluttered, as if it were a tabula rasa awaiting inscription. Other than a few dented track lights, some randomly placed metal eyehooks, and a corridor leading back to a small kitchen, little else occupies the space where several spires of tubular steel and plastic stacking chairs are stored between meetings. On the Southwest wall rippled glass windows look towards Battery Park, except that a nearby industrial building stands in the way, its valves and ductwork glowing milky green both day and night. Against an opposing wall sits a heavy wooden table. Above the table is a mirror with a faux gilt frame. The room's sole purpose on Monday evenings is to accommodate 16 B's ongoing conversations about art and politics, typically accompanied by coffee, fruit, humus, pita bread, and whatever else participants contribute. As with all of the organizations covered in this book, 16 B manages a website that serves as an organizing tool, a bibliography of accessible texts, as well as an archive of past discussions and readings that each week, month, year accumulate like intricate skeins of shared knowledge. Still, these layers remain linked in time and place with actual zones of concentrated art world power.

"The real crisis in art education," artist and cultural entrepreneur Anton Vidokle insists, "appears to be one of distribution: radical, experimental and advanced institutions are clustered in Europe and North America."[69] These regions thus act as magnets for those who wish to participate in advanced art practices, drawing dark matter into the global art machinery. However, since this comment was penned in 2006, an outpouring of new art academies and schools, some large, some small, some barely visible, have sprung up, some at ever-greater distances from the US/EU art world nucleus. In Ramallah the International Academy of Art Palestine brings together local students with practicing artists from the region and abroad. Supported with money from Norway, it awards a Bachelor's degree in contemporary visual art in a region only recently all but exiled in the West as culturally subaltern. Nearby, in Beirut, a new art academy is being organized by Christine Tohme, co-founder of Ashkal Alwan, the Lebanese Association for Plastic Arts and director of the decade-old Home Works program there. Her aim is to use the cultural, political, and spatial complexity of the city itself as both art laboratory and campus. Far from the Middle East, though perhaps also quite near, the artists Judi Werthein, Graciela Hasper, and Roberto Jacoby have established an art school in Buenos Aires, Argentina. El Centro de Investigaciones Artisticas, or simply CIA, is informally structured as well as constantly challenged by a lack of sustainable funding. But the school manages to offer dozens of seminars to aspiring art students each year. And yet Vidokle may have the last word after all. For just like the programs in Palestine and (soon) in Beirut, Argentina's CIA turns out graduates in a location with few resources to sustain professional artists once graduated. Not even the new, networked "knowledge economy" has made serious inroads into these regions, suggesting those who pass through these programs will—barring alternative forms of support and encouragement—eventually be drawn towards the magnetic art mountains of New York, London, and Berlin.

Cramming for the Necrosocial

The Public School, Petersburg Street University, Baltimore Free School, Stockyard Institute, 16 B—add to this list the School of Missing Studies in the Balkans, Red76's Laundry Lecture Series in Portland, Oregon, transit free school in Austria and Eastern Europe, The School of Decreative Methodologies at Basekamp space in Philadelphia, or artist Nils Norman's University of Trash and Exploding School

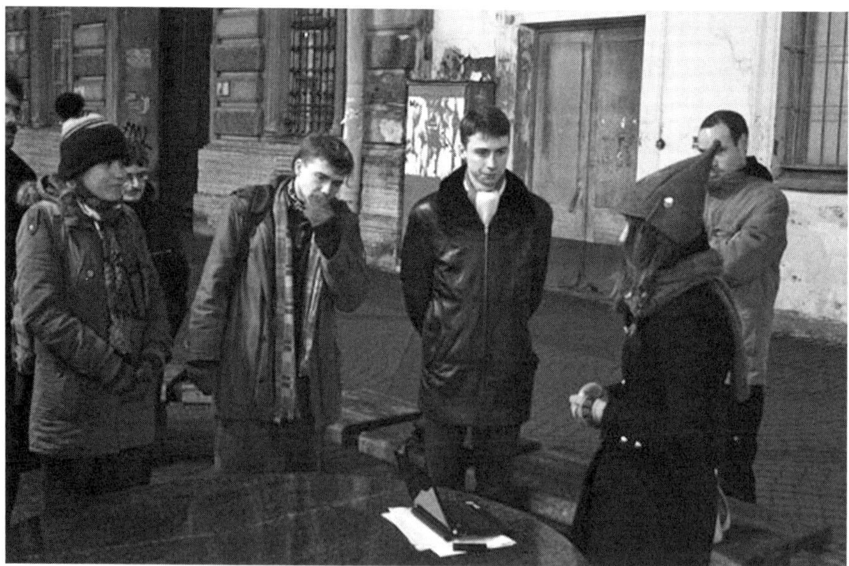

Students gather for a session in the Street University in Saint Petersburg, Russia, Spring 2008, as a spontaneous response to the closing of the European University by authorities. Image courtesy Olga Kopenkina.

projects, and the volume of recent, "bottom-up" pedagogical initiatives begins to become clear. There are even reports that behind the tenth-floor elevator machine room at Saint Martins College of Art in London students gather to clandestinely re-appropriate their education, unbeknownst to program administrators. A provisional simulation of institutional agency appears to be unfolding, step by awkward step. As in Borges' map, the virtual and actual are superimposed on one another. Although Adorno once railed against the intellectual and artistic banalities of administered culture in the post-war era, perhaps it has become necessary now to occupy the ruins of that former society, or more accurately to wear its wreckage like a carapace in the way certain sea creatures camouflage themselves from predators using discarded materials. After all, this accumulated cultural detritus is our shared history, our dark archive of fragmented knowledge and potential liberation. As students occupying Berkeley lament: "This accumulation is our shared history. This accumulation—every once in a while interrupted, violated by a riot, a wild protest, unforgettable fucking, the overwhelming joy of love, life shattering heartbreak—is a muted, but desirous life. A dead but restless and desirous life."[70] Still, what emerges from the grave is always incomplete, impure, time-sensitive, and frequently paradoxical, leaving one outstanding question above all others: how to prevent this bottom-up pedagogical experimentation and Do It Yourself (DIY) academies from becoming part of what the students in occupied UC Berkeley dub the "Necrosocial," a world suited only for the living dead. A materializing dark matter now confronts this so-called future as a grinning archive and antagonistic corpse. Even as the real and digital decay of post-public enterprise culture provides a modicum of protective mediation, a space of temporary action and self-education, these ruins also continue to remind us of what has been lost, for better and for worse, and what promises still wait to be fulfilled.

8

CONCLUSIONS: NIGHTS OF AMATEURS

In the middle of the fight, we learn how we must fight.

Rosa Luxemburg

A Different Durée

It starts like this. The reemergence of activist art, political art, interventionist art, publicly involved social art, collectivized art—though it may be portrayed by some as the birth, or rebirth, of just another artistic genre, it is not. And we know it is not. More than an untapped source of social-historical data, a few new artists useful for sprucing-up the same-old roster canon, this incessant reemergence carries with it a threatening power for the gatekeepers of the artistic canon who eye what they hope is a minor detour with trepidation. But even pure repetition, Derrida insists, "were it to change neither thing nor sign, carries with it an unlimited power of perversion and subversion."[1] If nothing else, the return of a certain real is dangerous, not because its content is necessarily so traumatic, but because it directs our attention towards an ellipsis within the historical record where none is supposed to exist. Furthermore, the types of questioning it provokes, that it has always provoked, provides evidence that from time-to-time those practices and producers within this missing dark matter do sometimes confront their own structural superfluousness, just as we learn to pick over the rags.

From underground economies based on the free exchange of goods and ideas, to the precarious margins of labor where "chainworkers," janitors, clerks, and Starbucks baristas secretly attempt to unionize beneath the downcast eyes of San Precario, patron Saint of precarious labor (or the wide-open pupils of the Wobblies wildcat logo), to the righteous re-occupation of foreclosed homes by the evicted, or the sharing of ingenious contraband inventions for improving life behind bars by prisoners whose only resources are toilet paper, ball point pens, and paper clips, but most of all during the supposedly restful hours of the night when working bodies are meant to rest and reproduce their labor power, yet instead remain alert to read, invent, play, fraternize, and fantasize of another world—in all these cases another productivity, including an eccentric non-productivity, has always found its own time and space apart from the objectifying routines of "work."

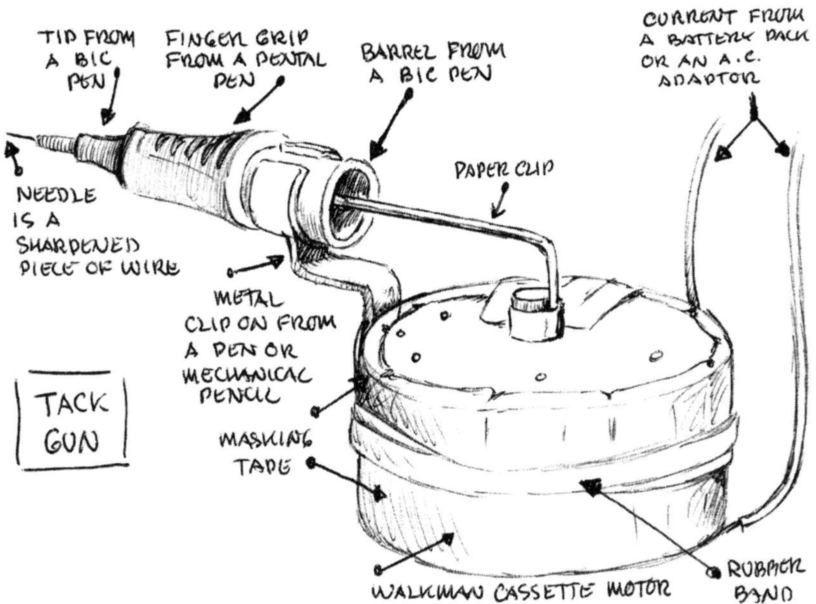

Incarcerated artist Angelo illustrates a book of contraband devices gathered from fellow inmates, in the 2004 booklet *Prisoners' Inventions* published by Temporary Services. Using mostly salvaged materials the designs include: water heaters, cigarette lighters, tattoo guns, and containers made from toilet *papier mâché*. Angelo's art courtesy Temporary Services.

This secretive and adversarial productivity extends well beyond the office or factory. Its trace is visible in New World slave narratives that secretly functioned as manuals for deceiving one's master; quilting circles where women exchanged craft techniques but also informational gossip about men, power, and sexuality; the banned Knights of Labor whose five-pointed star emblem symbolized a labor organization founded on the equality of men and women, whites and blacks; and the articles of agreement forged by pirates, those motley villains of all nations who, as Linebaugh and Rediker note, rejected class discipline in order to give each other a right to vote and a share of stolen wealth, but who also applied their own vindictive justice from below by punishing those maritime commanders who mistreated their crews.[2] If we were to extend our inventory of heroic defiance to include those many minor, sometimes petty acts of everyday disobedience that Michel De Certeau theorized as *tactics* of resistance—the convenience store clerk who silently adjusts his pricing gun to create spontaneous discounts for customers, a painter who inserts images of Nazi storm troopers into a mural commissioned by the Walt Disney Corporation, a low-paid stock exchange broker who creates monetary fluctuations in market shares using his cell phone *just for kicks*, an artist who covertly hangs her work on a museum wall (complete with an official-looking label), or a group of cultural activists performing anti-corporate genetic experiments—then it seems suddenly as if an entire realm of shadowy, non-compliant labor has materialized into gloaming visibility about the margins of mainstream social, political, artistic, and economic discourse.[3]

Nevertheless, isolated flashes of defiance carried out by "cubicle slaves," discontented retail clerks, culture-jamming cyber-geeks, or even minutemen border patrollers, are, at best, disjointed acts of insubordination. They do not necessarily knit together as sustained politics, and they are not inherently progressive or democratic. By and large these are gifts that often "forget themselves" insofar as they are generally not perceived as gifts given or received. Still, insofar as this creative dark activity refuses to be productive for the market, it remains linked, however diffusely and ambiguously, to an archive of resistant practices—past, present, and to come—that Fredric Jameson called a "political unconscious," and that theorists Oskar Negt and Alexander Kluge described in more literal terms as a counter-public sphere made up of dissident affects, re-appropriations, and fantasies.

To realize such a "history from below," or a counter-public sphere, to construct another non-space and non-productivity out of the dense archive of dark-matter social production, means generating filters contrary to those of the market, while simultaneously recognizing that any move towards self-valorized institutionalization is not without the risk of failure or worse, Paris 1871 and 1968 being two cases in point. "What takes courage," writes Alain Badiou, "is to operate in terms of a different durée to that imposed by the law of the world."[4] Militant street theater, counterfeit corporations, interventionist research portals, knitting networks, pie throwers, ninjas, snake charmers, river rafters, amateur scientists—this emerging aesthetics of resistance may be no more than a minor art of attractions and marvels and tactics, a politics of sometimes overt and sometimes tepid acts of delinquency, or even bitter gestures of discontent, and yet their "gifts of resistance" must continue to impart an expectation. We go on picking the rags, but every now and again, this *other* social [non]productivity appears to mobilize its own redundancy, seems to acknowledge that it is indeed just so much surplus—talent, labor, subjectivity, even sheer physical-genetic materiality—and in so doing frees itself from even attempting to be *usefully productive for* capitalism (or *for* Art Inc.), though all the while identifying itself with a far larger ocean of "dark matter," that ungainly surfeit of seemingly useless actors and activity that the market views as waste, or perhaps at best as a raw, interchangeable resource for biometric information and crowdsourcing. The archive has split open. We are its dead capital. It is the dawn of the dead.

NOTES

Exordium

1. Craig Owens, *Beyond Recognition: Representation, Power, and Culture*, eds. Scott Bryson, Barbara Kruger, Lynne Tillman, and Jane Weinstock, University of California Press, 1992.
2. Craig Owens, "The Problem With Puerilism," *Art in America*, vol. 72, no. 6, Summer 1983, 162–3.
3. Owens' article appeared a few months before Rosalyn Deutsche and Cara Gendel Ryan published their landmark essay, "The Fine Art of Gentrification," *October Magazine*, vol. 31, Winter 1984, 91–111; also available on the website of the alternative space ABC No Rio at www.abcnorio.org/about/history/fine_art.html
4. Owens, "The Problem With Puerilism."
5. The term "lumpenography" is borrowed from Nuyorican scholar Luis Aponte-Parés, who describes the very memory of New York City's Puerto-Rican El Barrio during the economically devastating 1970s as a space of arrested development with discontinuous memories and fragmented cultural forms making up its imaginary geography. See Elsa B. Cardalda Sánchez and Amilcar Tirado Avilés, "Ambiguous Identities! The Affirmation of Puertorriqueñidad in the Community Murals of New York City," in Augustín Laó-Montes and Arlene Dávila, eds., *Mambo Montage: The Latinization of New York*, Columbia University Press, 2001, 265.

Introduction

1. Walter Benjamin, *The Arcades Project*, trans. Kevin McLaughlin, eds. Rolf Tiedemann, Howard Eiland, Belknap Press of Harvard University Press, annotated edition, 1999, 546.
2. So suggest the annual statistics gathered by the Craft and Hobby Industry Association: www.hobby.org
3. Walter Benjamin, "The Author as Producer," in *Reflections: Essays, Aphorisms, Autobiographical Writings*, ed. Peter Demetz, Schocken, 1986, 220–39.
4. Professor Kurtz himself did, however, receive Warhol Foundation money during his legal defense on charges of bioterrorism brought by the United States Justice Department in 2004 (see Chapter 6).
5. Carol Duncan, "Who Rules the Art World?," in *The Aesthetics of Power: Essays in Critical Art History*, Cambridge University Press, 1983, 172–80.
6. Martha Rosler, "Money, Power, and the History of Art: A Range of Critical Perspectives," *Art Bulletin*, March 1997, 6–10.
7. Figures about this growth of artistic production are found in Chapter 5.
8. Groys made these comments at The Drawing Center in NYC, during a public lecture for a program "Art and Power," on July 10, 2009.

9. Blake Stimson and Gregory Sholette, "Historicizing Collectivism," introduction to Stimson and Sholette, eds., *Collectivism After Modernism: Art and Social Imagination after 1945*, University of Minnesota Press, 2007, 3.
10. For a recent analysis of this artistic paradigm shift see Gerald Raunig and Gene Ray, eds., *Art and Contemporary Critical Practice: Reinventing Institutional Critique*, MayFly Books, 2009.
11. The PAD/D Archive at MoMA is one of the very few explicitly political art archival collections in the United States, along with the Center for the Study of Political Graphics in Los Angeles, and the All of Us of None Political Poster Archive managed by Lincoln Cushing in Berkeley. Other materials about politicized artists and art groups can be found at the Archives of American Art operated by The Smithsonian Institute in New York and Washington DC, at The Fales Library and Special Collections which houses both REPOhistory and Group Material's documents, and The Tamiment Library and Robert F. Wagner Labor Archives. Both Fales and Tamiment are located in the New York University Library on Washington Square Park in Greenwich Village, NYC.
12. Friedrich Nietzsche, *On the Genealogy of Morality*, trans. Carol Diethe, ed. Keith Ansell-Pearson, Cambridge University Press, 1994; and Eve Kosofsky Sedgwick, *Epistemology of the Closet*, University of California Press, 1990.
13. Olav Velthuis, *Talking Prices: Symbolic Meanings of Prices on the Market for Contemporary Art*, Princeton University Press, 2005.
14. For a compact version of this argument, see Theodor W. Adorno's short treatise "Black as an Ideal," in *Aesthetic Theory*, trans. Robert Hullot-Kentor, University of Minnesota, 1997, 39–40.
15. Alistair Darling, UK Chancellor of the Exchequer, commenting on the aftermath of the financial collapse; see Gavin Cordon (Press Association), "It's Worse Than We Thought, Admits Darling," *Independent*, December 9, 2009.
16. Notably even the label "Great Recession" suggests that media pundits have been forced to acknowledge capital has a history after all.
17. Ernesto Laclau and Chantal Mouffe, *Hegemony and Socialist Strategy: Towards a Radical Democratic Politics*, Verso, 2001 [1985], 98.
18. Ibid.
19. In this same essay Mouffe applies the concept of articulated hegemony to the practice of critical and interventionist art, at which point the weakness of a purely discursive theory premised on antagonistic equivalences dislocated from any specific, historical struggle leads to a vague proposal in support of interventionist art that disrupts "the smooth image that corporate capitalism is trying to spread, bringing to the fore its repressive character" (Chantal Mouffe, "Artistic Activism and Agonistic Spaces," *Art & Research: A Journal of Ideas, Contexts and Methods*, vol. 1, no. 2, Summer 2007, 2; available at www.artandresearch.org.uk). But Mouffe's antagonistic theory is wielded far more sharply by art critic Claire Bishop when she uses it to chastise curator Nicolas Bourriaud's popular notion of Relational Aesthetics by describing his influential theory as little more than a mellifluous fiction of social cooperation (see Claire Bishop, "Antagonism and Relational Aesthetics," *October*, 110, Fall 2004, 51–79).
20. Laclau and Mouffe, *Hegemony and Socialist Strategy*, 88, n. 1.
21. An excellent critique of this post-Marxism is made by literary critic Benjamin Bertram, who writes: "Laclau and Mouffe are, of course, correct in arguing that the fragmentation and proliferation of struggles (for feminists, gays and lesbians, environmentalists, etc.) cannot be dismissed as merely superstructure or the end of ideology.

The politicization of culture and the social is vital to any radical enterprise today. There is no reason, however, why we have to choose between new social movements and totalizing discourses. This opposition has given rise to an essentialist form of separatism that excludes the potential of larger, collective struggles against dominant ideological formations in the United States. The fetishism of dislocation and the related weakness of a theory of ideology limit the possibilities for the development of a sense of what positive liberty might mean in the age of late capitalism" (Benjamin Bertram, "New Reflections on the 'Revolutionary' Politics of Ernesto Laclau and Chantal Mouffe," *Boundary 2*, vol. 22, no. 3, Autumn 1995, 81–110). See also the substantial analysis of Laclau and Mouffe in Grant Kester's forthcoming book *The One and the Many: Agency and Identity in Contemporary Collaborative Art* (Duke University Press).

22. "The steam-engine was from the very first an antagonist of human power [that] enabled the capitalist to tread under foot the growing claims of the workmen, who threatened the newly born factory system with a crisis" (Karl Marx, *Capital, Volume 1*, Section 5, 436, cited in Harry Cleaver, *Reading Capital Politically*, AK Press edition, 2000, 103).
23. See Antonio Negri, *Marx Beyond Marx: Lessons on the Grundrisse*, Autonomedia Press, 1989.
24. W.A.G.E. can be found at www.wageforwork.com/wage.html. Notably, many of the links on the group's website lead to artists' unions in Canada, the UK, and France.
25. This recently founded Teaching Artist Union has no affiliation with the well-established College Art Association dating back to 1912; see http://teachingartistunion.org
26. *ART WORK: A National Conversation About Art, Labor, and Economics* includes texts and graphics by W.A.G.E., Teaching Artist Union, as well as Temporary Services, 16 Beaver Street, Lize Mogel, Nicolas Lampert, Carolina Caycedo, Dan S. Wang, Brian Holmes, Scott Berzofsky and John Duda of Baltimore Development Cooperative (BDC), INCUBATE, Future Farmers Guerrilla Art Action Group (GAAP), Damon Rich of the Center of Urban Pedagogy (CUP), as well as myself. A downloadable pdf of the publication is available at: http://www.artandwork.us/2009
27. With the exception of Helen Molesworth's engaging catalog of her 2003 exhibition "Work Ethic" at the Des Moines Center for the Arts Center, Iowa, and a recent book entitled *Art Works: Money*, by Katy Siegel and Paul Mattick (Thames and Hudson, 2004), there are few in-depth attempts at addressing late twentieth- and twenty-first-century art from the perspective of cultural labor and its market for the English reader. Which is why Andrew Hemingway's *Artists on the Left: American Artists and the Communist Movement, 1926–1956* (Yale University Press, 2002) and Julia Bryan-Wilson's *Art Workers: Radical Practice in the Vietnam War* (University of California Press, 2009) go a long way to help fill this sizable gap in modern and contemporary art scholarship. Another possible marker of the growing interest in artist's working conditions is the selection of Bryan-Wilson's book by the *New York Times*' art critic Holland Cotter as one of his top readings of 2009. Adding to this tendency is Grant Kester's forthcoming book, previously cited, in which the author suggests that certain forms of collaborative artistic labor carried out by groups such as Ala Plastica (Río de la Plata, Argentina), Huit Facettes (Dakar, Senegal), or Park Fiction (Hamburg, Germany) actively maintain a critical tension between specific acts of labor (research and the production of meaning), and the figurative representation of labor as a kind of allegory about present working conditions. Kester believes such "dialogical" friction

is not only capable of transforming consciousness, but can offer new modes of being-together in the world through collective labor.

28. Michael Hardt and Antonio Negri, "The Becoming-Prince of the Multitude," *Artforum*, vol. 48, no. 2, October 2009, 178–9.
29. See "The Internet as Playground and Factory: A Conference on Digital Labor," held at The New School University, November 12–14, 2009: http://digitallabor.org
30. Ironies aside, the conference addressed a number of substantial issues regarding creative work with notable presentations by Scholz, Beka Economopoulos, Lisa Nakamura, and artist Stephanie Rothenberg among others, many now available online at http://digitallabor.org
31. Many of these themes are discussed in Chapters 1 and 3; in addition see the extensive writings by Silvia Federici, George Caffintzis, and the Midnight Notes Collective at www.midnightnotes.org
32. "Who built Thebes of the seven gates?/In the books you will find the names of kings/Did the kings haul up the lumps of rock?" From the poem "Questions from a Worker Who Reads," or "A Worker Reads History," in *Bertolt Brecht: Selected Poems*, trans. H. R. Hays, Grove Press, 1959, 108.
33. See Mike Davis, *Planet of Slums*, Verso, 2007, and David Redmon's "Mardi Gras: Made in China, 2005" in which a string of inexpensive plastic beads purchased in New Orleans is traced back to a sweatshop-like manufacturing plant in Eastern China.
34. Brian Holmes, "A Rising Tide of Contradiction: Museums in the Age of the Expanding Workfare State," in *Unleashing the Collective Phantoms: Essays in Reverse Imagineering*, Autonomedia Books, 2008, 116.
35. See www.kleinespostfordistischesdrama.de; special thanks to artist Kurt Kaulper for the art historical comparison.
36. Bruno Gulli, *Labor of Fire: The Ontology of Labor Between Economy and Culture*, Temple University Press, 2005, 42.
37. Stephen Wright, "Behind Police Lines: Art Visible and Invisible," *Art & Research: A Journal of Ideas, Contexts, and Methods*, vol. 2, no. 1, Summer 2008; available at www.artandresearch.org.uk

Chapter 1

1. Oskar Negt and Alexander Kluge, *Public Sphere and Experience: Toward an Analysis of the Bourgeois and Proletarian Public Sphere*, with a foreword by Miriam Hansen, trans. Peter Labanyi, Jamie Owen Daniel, and Assenka Oksiloff, University of Minnesota Press, London, 1993, 32.
2. Worcester Art Museum website: www.worcesterart.org/Exhibitions/Past/feher.html
3. Miriam Hansen in the foreword to Negt and Kluge, *Public Sphere and Experience*, xxxii.
4. Lippard organized the exhibition "Some British Art from the Left," with works by Rasheed Araeen, Conrad Atkinson, Margaret Harrison, Alexis Hunter, Mary Kelly, Tony Rickaby, and Marie Yates, for New York's Artists Space in 1979. On the back of the invitation card was a note inviting anyone interested to send her documentation on social or political art. The sizable mass of materials she began to receive over the next year led directly to the formation of Political Art Documentation/Distribution. See Chapter 3.

5. PAD/D member and poet Irving Wexler (1918–2001) describes his shift from Stalinist to New Leftist in "New Wine in Old Bottles," *Social Text*, no. 9/10, special issue "The 60's Without Apology," Spring–Summer 1984, 222–6.
6. PAD/D, *1st Issue*, New York City, February 1981. (Note: the title of the PAD/D newsletter was changed to *Upfront* beginning with issue number three.)
7. Scholarship about such alternative, political art practices is, however, growing exponentially: see the bibliography for a select list of some of these new books.
8. PAD/D, *1st Issue*, February 1981.
9. PAD/D, *Upfront*, nos. 14–15, 1987–88.
10. The PAD/D Archive was primarily organized by group members Barbara Moore and Mimi Smith and was donated to the MoMA Library in 1989. It is available for research and its contents can be searched digitally by entering the phrase "Political Art Documentation Distribution" into the Museum's database, accessible at http://library.moma.org
11. The group originally emerged in the Northeast, out of the Fort Thunder scene of the late 1990s in Providence Rhode Island, centered on a warehouse used by numerous noise bands, underground comic producers, and informal trash artists, many of whom were also associated with the nearby Rhode Island School of Design (RISD).
12. Quoted in "Video Mutants: Problem Solving with Jacob Ciocci of *Paper Rad*," *San Francisco Bay Guardian*, posted by Johnny Ray Huston on January 28, 2008; www.sfbg.com/blogs/pixel_vision/2008/01/video_mutants_problem_solving_1.html
13. Related to the author in a September 30, 2005 telephone conversation with the group's dealer at Foxy Production art gallery in Chelsea, NYC.
14. 'What is Paper Rad' at Paper Rad Info: www.paperrad.org/info/info
15. The 2006 "Cease and Desist" letter from attorney Dan Nadel, as well as Paper Rad's own comments about the "controversy," can be viewed at http://paperrad.blogspot.com
16. Allegedly, the popular Austrian art group Gelatin once had open membership, thus its name suggesting an amorphous body, but as success in the global art world dawned the group consolidated its membership and renamed itself: Gelitin, with an "i."
17. Slavoj Žižek, "It's the Political Economy Stupid!," University of Chicago Press, 2009; http://kasamaproject.org/2009/04/14/slavoj-zizek-it%E2%80%99s-the-political-economy-stupid
18. *Craftivists* include anti-war knitting circles and public interventions of crochet and knit graffiti described as *Yarn Bombing* that aims to improve the urban landscape "one stitch at a time"; see http://yarnbombing.com; as well as http://craftivism.com/about.html. Information about microRevolt is available at www.microrevolt.org/web
19. Ulrich Beck, "Risk Society Revisited: Theory, Politics and Research Programs," in Barbara Adam, Ulrich Beck, and Joost Van Loon, eds., *The Risk Society and Beyond: Critical Issues for Social Theory*, Sage Publications, 2000, 213.
20. See *Mute*, vol. 2, no. 0, Precarious Reader 2005: www.metamute.org/node/416/clustercontent
21. Perhaps the clearest outline of this shift is David Harvey's study *A Brief History of Neoliberalism* (Oxford University Press, 2005), but similar accounts have been made by writers such as Naomi Klein, Noam Chomksy, Henry A. Giroux, Alfredo Saad-Filho, and Deborah Johnston.
22. American Social History Project, *Who Built America? Working People and The Nation's Economy, Politics, Culture and Society, Volume 2: From the Gilded Age to the Present*, CUNY: City University of New York, 1992, 597.

23. Silvia Federici, "Precarious Labor: A Feminist Viewpoint"; http://inthemiddleofthewhirlwind.wordpress.com/precarious-labor-a-feminist-viewpoint
24. Doug Henwood, "How Jobless the Future?," *Left Business Observer*, no. 75, December 1996; www.leftbusinessobserver.com/Jobless_future.html
25. Ibid.
26. Gulli, *Labor of Fire*, 125.
27. Kevin Bales, *New Slavery: A Reference Handbook*, ABC-CLIO, Inc., 2000; see also Peter Landesman, "The Girls Next Door," *New York Times*, January 25, 2004.
28. Michel De Certeau, *The Practice of Everyday Life*, trans. Steen Rendall, University of California Press, 1984, xix and xx.
29. Ibid., 37.
30. "Reloading Tactical Media," The GHI of Tactical Media, an interview with Geert Lovink by Andreas Broeckmann, Transmediale.01 Festival, Berlin, July 2001: www.artnodes.com/espai/eng/art/broeckmann0902/broeckmann0902.html
31. Rita Raley, *Tactical Media*, University of Minnesota Press, 2009, 1.
32. Stimson and Sholette, eds., *Collectivism After Modernism*, 2.
33. Chin-tao Wu, *Privatising Culture: Corporate Art Intervention Since the 1980s*, Verso, 2003, 2.
34. Julian Stallabrass, *Art Incorporated: The Story of Contemporary Art*, Oxford University Press, 2004; Theodor W. Adorno and Max Horkeimer, *Dialectic of Enlightenment*, Verso, 1977, 242.
35. Robert Jensen, *Marketing Modernism in Fin-de-siècle Europe*, Princeton University Press, 1994, 10.
36. Ibid.
37. Ibid., 3.
38. Stallabrass, *Art Incorporated*, 183.
39. Tom Peters, quoted by Stefan Stern in "A Guru Aims High on Prozac," *New Statesman*, December 18, 2000; Thomas Hoving quoted in Wu, *Privatising Culture*, 127; and the Amazon.com product description for a book by John Howkins, *The Creative Economy: How People Make Money from Ideas*, Penguin Business Press, 2002; www.amazon.com/Creative-Economy-People-Money-Ideas/dp/0140287949
40. Luc Boltanski and Eve Chiapello, *The New Spirit of Capitalism*, Verso, 2007.
41. Cited in Luc Boltanski and Eve Chiapello, "The New Spirit of Capitalism," paper presented at the Conference of Europeanists, March 14–16, 2002, Chicago, pdf file, 16; www.sociologiadip.unimib.it/mastersqs/rivi/boltan.pdf
42. See Andrew Ross, *No-Collar: The Humane Workplace and Its Hidden Costs*, Temple University Press, 2004, and Brian Holmes, "The Flexible Personality: For a New Cultural Critique"; www.16beavergroup.org/brian
43. Richard Florida, *Rise of the Creative Class: And How It's Transforming Work, Leisure, Community and Everyday Life*, Basic Books, 2003.
44. Florida and his Creative Class Group (CCG) offer policy advice for mayoral administrations and urban planners interested in improving community competitiveness and "urban regeneration." See Richard Florida's website: Creative Class: the source on how we live, work, and play; www.creativeclass.com
45. Angela McRobbie, online document at Be Creative (Der Kreative Imperativ), dated August 2001; www.k3000.ch/becreative/texts/text_5.html
46. These themes will be addressed again in Chapter 5.
47. Plato, *The Republic*, trans. Benjamin Jowett, World Publishing Co., 1946, 136.

48. Kennedy made these remarks, on October 26, 1963, at Amherst College in Massachusetts; two years later President Lyndon Johnson signed the National Foundation on the Arts and the Humanities Act, thus creating The National Endowment for the Arts.
49. For a critical debate on the neoliberalization of education in Europe see the edu-factory collective's web journal at www.edu-factory.org/edu15. Figures on US Student Debt including art schools (whose average tuition is about $120,000 for an undergraduate, BFA degree) are published annually by The Project on Student Debt, October 2008, http://projectonstudentdebt.org. (Note, that in the aftermath of the fiscal crisis, President Obama did sign into law a degree of student debt relief beginning July 1, 2009.)
50. Alaka Wali, Rebecca Severson, and Mario Tongoni, *Informal Arts: Finding Cohesion, Capacity and Other Cultural Benefits in Unexpected Places*, Chicago Center for Arts Policy at Columbia College, Chicago, Illinois, June 2002.
51. John Roberts, *The Intangibilities of Form: Skill and Deskilling in Art After The Readymade,* Verso, 2007, 159.
52. A very rough stab at estimating this would begin with the sales of hobby supplies estimated to be in the 20 to 30 billion dollar range annually by the industry (Craft & Hobby Association Press release found at www.chamembernetworking.org/cms), as well as those new types of art supplies used by both professional artists as well as amateurs. For example, Lyra Research, Inc. estimates that sales of an ink-jet printable canvas paper were estimated to double between 2005 and 2010 (see their "Fine-Art Ink Jet Media Market Assessment, report, August 1, 2006 at http://lyra.ecnext.com/coms2/summary_0290-441_ITM)
53. The AWC's demands to museums and the art establishment are enumerated in Lucy R. Lippard, "Biting the Hand: Artists and Museums in New York Since 1969," in Julie Ault, ed., *Alternative Art New York: 1965–1985*, University of Minnesota Press, 2002, 79–120.
54. Letter from *Group Material* to local residents, dated December 22, 1980, quoted in Jan Avgikos, "*Group Material* Timeline: Activism as a Work of Art," in Nina Felshin, ed., *But is it Art?*, Bay Press, 1995, 85–116. The exhibition's name "Aroz con Mango" is a Cuban expression for "What a mess."
55. Charles Leadbeater and Paul Miller, "The Pro–Am Revolution," November 11, 2004, pdf file, 67; www.demos.co.uk/publications/proameconomy
56. See Charles Leadbeater, "Privatise the Universities!," *New Statesman*, November 22, 1996.
57. Yochai Benkler, *Wealth of Nations: How Social Production Transforms Markets and Freedom*, Yale University Press, 2006, 53.
58. Kristen Fischer, *Creatively Self-Employed: How Writers and Artists Deal with Career Ups and Downs*, iUniverse, Inc., POD publishing site, 2007; Rob Austin and Lee Devin, *Artful Making: What Managers Need to Know About How Artists Work*, foreword by Dr. Eric Schmidt, Prentice Hall Publishers, 2003.
59. Alan W. Moore, "Political Economy as Subject and Form in Contemporary Art," *Review of Radical Political Economics*, vol. 36, no. 4, 2004, 472.
60. Michael Denning, *Culture in the Age of Three Worlds*, Verso, 2004, 40.
61. Walter Benjamin, "Theses on History," in *Illuminations: Essays and Reflections*, Schocken Books, 1969. See also Esther Leslie, who compares Benjamin's sense of time and possibility for historical redemption to cinematic montage and its sudden, remarkable juxtapositions (Esther Leslie, *Walter Benjamin: Overpowering Conformism*, Pluto Press, 2000).

Chapter 2

1. Jacques Derrida, *Archive Fever: A Freudian Impression*, trans. Eric Prenowitz, University of Chicago Press, 1995, 86.
2. *Committed to Print: Social and Political Themes in Recent American Printed Art* was on view at MoMA from January 13 to April 19, 1988, and included a catalog published by the Museum.
3. *New York Observer*, February 22, 1988.
4. For criticism of the exhibition's exclusion of AIDS-related graphic imagery see Douglas Crimp and Adam Rolston, "AIDS Activist Graphics," in Ken Gelder, ed., *The Subcultures Reader*, Routledge, 1997, 439–42.
5. See Francis Frascina, *Art, Politics, and Dissent*, Manchester University Press, 2000, 182–3.
6. The action took place on January 3, 1970. *Guernica* was then still on loan to the MoMA on condition that it not be returned to Spain until democracy was reinstated in the country. Franco died four years later, but the painting only left the Museum for Madrid in 1981. An excellent and detailed history of events surrounding the AWC poster can be found in Amy Shlegel's essay, "My lai: 'We lie, they die'," *Third Text*, vol. 9, no. 31, 1995, 47–66.
7. Sharon Zukin, *Loft Living: Culture and Capital in Urban Change*, Johns Hopkins University Press, 1982; Rosalyn Deutsche and Cara Gendel Ryan, "The Fine Art Of Gentrification," *October*, 31; Winter 1984, 91–111; Neil Smith, *The New Urban Frontier: Gentrification and the Revanchist City*, Routledge, 1996.
8. Midnight Notes Collective, "The New Enclosures," in *Midnight Oil: Work, Energy, War, 1973–1992,* Autonomedia, 1992; www.midnightnotes.org/newenclos.html. See also Harvey's *A Brief History of Neoliberalism*, and Naomi Klein, *The Shock Doctrine: The Rise of Disaster Capitalism*, Picador Press, 2008.
9. See Chapter 3.
10. Derrida, *Archive Fever*, 36.
11. More about these ambitions can be found in a series of interviews with former group members Jerry Kearns, Barbara Moore, Janet Koenig, and Gregory Sholette published in Temporary Services, *Group Work*, New York, Printed Matter, 2007; see also my "A Collectography of PAD/D: Political Art Documentation and Distribution: A 1980's Activist Art and Networking Collective" (2001), available at www.gregorysholette.com/writings/writing_index.html
12. Temporary Services, *Group Work*, 88.
13. Located on Avenue B, between 8th and 9th Streets on the Lower East Side of Manhattan, CHARAS/El Bohio took over the abandoned public school building when real estate values were nonexistent in this part of the city. Together with the Nuyorican Poets Café, the center served as a key part of New York's Puerto Rican cultural Diaspora, thus the amalgam Nuyorican: New York City, plus Puerto Rican. In 1998 Mayor Rudolph Giuliani's administration evicted the center's tenants and sold the building to a private developer who has subsequently allowed the empty structure to deteriorate. In the wake of the latest fiscal crisis new efforts are under way to reclaim El Bohio as a local public institution.
14. See Chapter 1, note 4.

15. A yellow legal pad in the PAD/D Archive lists 70 items loaned to Wye from the collection between August and November of 1986, about three years before it was donated to MoMA.
16. Temporary Services, *Group Work*, 86.
17. PAD/D, *1st Issue*, February 1981.
18. Moore and Smith worked on the collection for 14 years with occasional assistance from Kate Linker, Carol Waag, and Michael Anderson. The PAD/D Archive was officially donated to the Museum on May 26, 1989. The MoMA Archive in which it is housed was established the same year. Soon after, the Franklin Furnace/Artist Book Collection was added, which focuses on a similar time-period of New York City's cultural activity though without the explicitly political framing.
19. "Like so many other institutions entrusted with preserving and transmitting culture, the Whitney has responded to the tide of cultural radicalism by total surrender." (Roger Kimball, "Of Chocolate, Lard, and Politics—1993 Biennial exhibit, Whitney Museum of American Art, New York, New York," *National Review*, April 26, 1993.)
20. For an excellent investigation of these programs see (Under)Privileged Spaces: On Martha Rosler's "If You Lived Here..." Nina Möntmann, in the *e-flux* online art journal at http://www.e-flux.com/journal/view/89#_ftn11
21. Lucy R. Lippard, "Archival Activism," *The Museum of Modern Art Library Bulletin*, no. 86, Winter 1993/94, 4.
22. Ibid.
23. Immanuel Wallerstein, *The Essential Wallerstein*, New York Press, 2000, 363; Paulo Virno, *Grammar of the Multitude*, trans. Isabella Bertoletti and James Cascaito, Semiotext(e), 2004, 110–11.
24. An index to the PAD/D Archive is viewable at http://arcade.nyarc.org/search~S8 and appointments to visit it, or other collections within the MoMA Archives, can be made online at http://moma.org/learn/resources/archives/index
25. See "Some History of Processed World" at www.processedworld.com/History/history.html, as well as *Processed World Bad Attitude: The Processed World Anthology*, Verso, 1990.
26. See, by former group member Mary Patten, *Revolution as an Eternal Dream: The Exemplary Failure of the Madame Binh Graphics Collective*, Half Letter Press (booklet forthcoming 2010).
27. This conclusion is based on a partial alphabetical sampling of the individual artist files found in the PAD/D Archive followed by an online search of any recent career activity. In no way definitive, this research does suggest, however, that at least two thirds of the Archive's named entries—individuals and groups—are like dead letters with no substantial presence in today's highly networked art world.
28. For more about Paper Tiger Television see Jesse Drew, "The Collective Camcorder in Art and Activism: 1968–2000," in Stimpson and Sholette, eds., *Collectivism After Modernism*, 94–133; and Ernest Larsen, "When the Crowd Rustles the Tiger Roars," *Art Journal*, vol. 54, no. 4, Video Art, Winter, 1995, 73–6.
29. See Rubén Gallo, "The Mexican Pentagon: Adventures in Collectivism During the 1970s," in Stimson and Sholette, eds., *Collectivism After Modernism*, 163–90.
30. From the cover of *an anti-catalog, The Catalog Committee of Artists Meeting for Cultural Change*, New York (self-published), 1977.

31. Metzger's entire ART STRIKE 1977–1980 manifesto is reproduced online at www.thing.de/projekte/7:9%23/y_Metzger%2Bs_Art_Strike.html
32. There are no precise records of who produced or managed this simulation, although Mr. Đorđević's name is clearly linked with the project. Đorđević later served as the doorman and docent for *Salon de Fleurus*: a Borgesian fantasy-space concocted in downtown Manhattan in which replicated modern artworks collected by Gertrude and Leo Stein in the early twentieth century for their Paris apartment at 27 rue de Fleurus filled several rooms of a rented townhouse in the 1990s. A more detailed description of *Salon de Fleurus* can be found in Michael Fehr, "A Museum and Its Memory: The Art of Recovering History," in Susan A. Crane, ed., *Museums and Memory: Cultural Sittings*, Stanford University Press, 2000, 57.
33. The complete play list is found in Julie Ault, ed., *Show and Tell: A Chronicle of Group Material*, Four Corners Books, 2010, 38–41.
34. Julia Kristeva, *Revolt She Said*, Semiotext(e) Foreign Agents series, 2002, 26.
35. "Hackney Flashers Collective: Who's Still Holding the Camera?," in T. Dennett, D. Evans, S. Gohl, and J. Spence, eds., *Photography/Politics: One, London, Photography Workshop*, 1979.
36. At the time *Nightcleaners* was produced, the BSFC included Mary Kelly, Marc Karlin, James Scott, and Humphry Trevelyan.
37. The Waitresses (1977–85) founding members included Jerri Allyn, Leslie Belt, Anne Gauldin, Patti Nicklaus, Jamie Wildman, Denise Yarfitz, and Elizabeth Canelake; later Anne Mavor, Anita Green, and Chutney Gunderson Berry joined the group. The All City Waitress Marching Band premiered in Pasadena, California in 1979, and was re-staged in Los Angeles and Bronx, New York as part of a series of exhibitions focused on feminist art history. Besides Allyn and Gauldin, Sisters of Survival (S.O.S.) consisted of artists Cheri Gaulke and Sue Maberry.
38. Kahlo is quoted in Meredith Tromble, "The Guerrilla Girls Make Art Herstory (Again)," *The Gate*, February 26, 1998; www.sfgate.com/eguide/profile/arc98/0226guerilla.shtml. The group's first, pseudonymous, press release explicitly naming 20 commercial art dealers who "show no more than 10% women artists" is reproduced in Ault, *Alternative Art New York*, 73.
39. Bryan-Wilson points out that it is thanks to the routine administrative activities of AWC members like Lucy R. Lippard and Virginia Admiral that the AWC's extensive archives even exist at all, see Julia Bryan-Wilson, *Art Workers*, 160.
40. See Federici, "Precarious Labor."
41. Virno, *Grammar of the Multitude*, 110–11.
42. American Social History Project, *Who Built America? Volume Two*, 597.
43. Chris Aronson Beck, Reggie Emilia, Lee Morris, and Ollie Patterson, "Strike One to Educate One Hundred," Chapter 2, first published in 1986 by Seeds Beneath the Snow; available at www.kersplebedeb.com/mystuff/italy/strike_one_2.html
44. See Dan Georgakas, "Revolutionary Struggles of Black Workers in the 1960s," *International Socialist Review*, no. 22, March–April 2002; www.isreview.org/issues/22/black_workers.shtml
45. See "Supplementary Reports on Intelligence Activities (Book IV); Final Report of the Select Committee To Study Governmental Operations with Respect to Intelligence Activities, United States Senate, Government Printing Office" (1976), 87. Related transcripts of FBI COENTELPRO memos can be viewed at http://whatreallyhappened.com/RANCHO/POLITICS/COINTELPRO/COINTELPRO-FBI.docs.html

46. John A. Walker, *Left Shift: Radical Art in 1970s Britain*, I. B. Tauris, 2002, 255.
47. Grant Kester, *Conversation Pieces: Community and Communication in Modern Art*, University of California Press, 2004, 9.
48. Edward Lucie-Smith, *Movements in Art Since 1945: Issues and Concepts*, Thames and Hudson, revised and expanded edition, 1995, 218.
49. One *New York Times* Arts and Leisure section writer acidly described the 1980s art world as a "show biz–stock market mentality ... whose products share the volatility of, say, pork belly futures" (Grace Glueck, "What One Artist's Career Tells Us of Today's World," *New York Times*, December 2, 1984, 1).
50. Pierre Bourdieu and Hans Haacke, *Free Exchange*, Stanford University Press, 1995, 99–100.
51. O. K. Werckmeister, *Citadel Culture*, University of Chicago Press, 1991.
52. Ibid., 4.
53. See Harvey, *A Brief History of Neoliberalism.*
54. Often accredited to Nuyorican poet Bittman "Bimbo" Rivas, the term Loisaida entered into the cultural wars over who would control the Lower East Side in the 1980s: the city and real estate speculators, or the area's various housing and community activists. The complexity of this ethno-cultural landscape, or "lumpenography" as Luis Aponte-Parés described the Puerto Rican experience in New York, is taken up in relation to other forms of Latino expression by Yasmin Ramirez in *Pressing the Point: Parallel Expressions in the Graphic Arts of the Chicano and Puerto Rican Movement*, an exhibition catalog from el Museo del barrio, 1999.
55. Miriam Brofsky and Eva Cockroft, "The Politics of Street Painting," *Upfront*, nos. 6–7, Summer 1983, 7.
56. Dan Cameron's introduction to his 2004 exhibition *East Village: USA* is available at www.newmuseum.org/exhibitions/387. A more complex rendering of East Village Art set within a broader cultural framework was included in *The Downtown Show* organized by Marvin Taylor and Carlo McCormick at New York University's Grey Art Gallery and Fales Library in 2006. Meanwhile, the East Village scene was swiftly absorbed into the mainstream media spectacle that had begun in the 1980s to link high fashion with contemporary art, amalgamating these into the new "Bohemian" global cities lifestyle still thriving today (though less vibrantly following the 2008 crash); see "LIZA KIRWIN ON EV in the press," *Artforum*, October 1999; http://findarticles.com/p/articles/mi_m0268/is_2_38/ai_57475777
57. Deutsche and Ryan, "The Fine Art Of Gentrification."
58. Alan Moore and Marc H. Miller, *ABC No Rio Dinero: The Story of a Lower East Side Art Gallery*, ABC No Rio with Collaborative Projects, 1985.
59. Robert Fitch, *The Assassination of New York*, Verso, 1993, 17.
60. Michael Wines, "Class Struggle Erupts Along Avenue B," *New York Times*, August 1, 1988; http://select.nytimes.com/gst/abstract.html?res=FB0714FD3D550C738DDDA10894D0484D81. Ultimately over a hundred complaints were officially lodged against the NYPD and a civilian review board concluded a year later that police had used force "indiscriminately." See David E. Pitt, "P.B.A. Leader Assails Report On Tompkins Square Melee," *New York Times*, April 21, 1989; www.nytimes.com/1989/04/21/nyregion/pba-leader-assails-report-on-tompkins-square-melee.html?scp=22&sq=police%20charged%20tompkins%20square&st=cse
61. See Clayton Patterson, ed., *Resistance: A Radical Social and Political History of the Lower East Side*, Seven Stories Press, 2007.

62. Derrida, *Archive Fever*, 2, 87.
63. Simon Sheikh, "Notes on Institutional Critique," in Raunig and Ray, eds., *Art and Contemporary Critical Practice*, 31, also free online at www.mayflybooks.org
64. Chris Marker, *Sixties*, May 2008, booklet published with *A Grin Without A Cat*, DVD, ICARUS Films, 2008, 5.

Chapter 3

1. In 1994 an alternate transgendered people's parade was led by Sylvia Rivera to protest their exclusion from the Gay Pride events; see "Pride Marches and Parades," in Marc Stein, ed., *Encyclopedia of Lesbian, Gay, Bisexual, and Transgender History in America*, Charles Scribner's Sons, 2004.
2. REPOhistory's *Queer Spaces* street project was part of an exhibition sponsored by the Storefront for Art and Architecture, an alternative exhibition and project space located in downtown Manhattan. *Queer Spaces* was conceived and produced by REPOhistory members Megan Pugh, Lisa Maya Knauer, Betti-Sue Hertz, Todd Ayoung, Ed Eisenberg, and Tom Klem. For an insightful look into the process, including internal differences between group members' conceptions of the project, see Betti-Sue Hertz, Ed Eisenberg, and Lisa Maya Knauer, "Queer Spaces in New York City: Places of Struggle/Places of Strength," in Gordon Brent, Anne-Marie Bouthillette, and Yolanda Retter, eds., *Queers in Space: Communities, Public Places, Sites of Resistance*, Bay Press, 1997, 357–70.
3. Text from the REPOhistory Queer Spaces sign number Nine of Nine, 1984 (texts for the entire project are available at www.repohistory.org/queer_spaces/index.php3)
4. Jim Costanzo, "REPOhistory's Circulation: The Migration of Public Art to the Internet," *Art Journal*, vol. 59, no. 4, Winter 2000, 32–7.
5. From an unpublished 1999 essay by Professor Knauer.
6. Notable exceptions include *Artweek* of San Francisco, which singularly covered the first REPOhistory project in some depth, followed by *New Art Examiner*, *Afterimage*, *Index* from Sweden, and *Circa* in Ireland, however, two of these texts were authored by one group member.
7. Coincidentally, 1989 was also the year the People's Liberation Army demolished a plaster model of the Statue of Liberty built by pro-democracy art students in Beijing's Tiananmen Square.
8. Manhattan Borough President Ruth W. Messinger presented the hand-written calligraphic document to the group in 1992.
9. REPOhistory's final project was called *CIRCULATION* and did not involve public signs, but rather small graphics distributed through the postal system along with an elaborate website organized by Jim Costanzo. This final REPOhistory project was realized in 2000, one year before Giuliani left office.
10. Mission statement from the New York Lawyers for the Public Interest website at http://nylpi.org
11. REPOhistory member and project coordinator Mark O'Brien from his essay "Civil Disturbances: Battles for Justice in New York City," in the folded map and brochure for the same project, self-published, 1998.
12. According to the Associated Press a total of two dozen lawsuits were ultimately filed during Giuliani's mayoralty accusing his administration of "stifling free speech or blocking access to public records"; see "Giuliani Accused of Running a Closed City Hall," Associated Press, December 20, 2007; www.msnbc.msn.com/id/22345820.

In his article "Rudy's Rules Of Order" (*New York Magazine*, June 12, 1998, 34), Michael Tomasky describes REPOhistory's legal battle with the City as that of "political dissidents" suppressed by the Giuliani administration.

13. Bernard E. Harcourt, *Illusion of Order: The False Promise of Broken Windows Policing,* Harvard University Press, 2001, 101.
14. According to a special report published online by the New York Civil Liberties Union (NYCLU), entitled "'Who's Watching': Video Camera Surveillance in New York City and the Need for Public Oversight," there were 2,397 public surveillance cameras in Manhattan by 1998, the end of Giuliani's first term as Mayor. Significantly, the report also points out that only seven years later the same number of cameras were recorded in just two Lower Manhattan neighborhoods: Greenwich Village and SoHo (a pdf file of the report is available at www.nyclu.org/pdfs/surveillance_cams_report_121306.pdf)
15. See "'Freedom is About Authority': Excerpts From Giuliani Speech on Crime," *New York Times*, March 20, 1994, regional section.
16. Cassandra Hayes, "Bad Economics in the Big Apple: New York Mayor Rudolph Giuliani kills a program designed to...," *Black Enterprise*, April 1, 1994; www.allbusiness.com/specialty-businesses/women-owned-businesses/422973-1.html
17. David Harvey, "The Right to The City," *New Left Review*, 53, September–October, 2008.
18. Vitale reports that between 1969 and 1980, the city lost more than 330,000 of its 825,000 manufacturing jobs. See Alex S. Vitale, *City of Disorder: How the Quality of Life Campaign Transformed New York Politics*, New York University Press, 2008, 106.
19. Ibid., 101.
20. Sassen, *The Global City*, 335–7; Smith, *The New Urban Frontier.*
21. Vitale, *City of Disorder*, 32.
22. See Katharyne Mitchell and Katherine Beckett, "Securing the Global City: Crime, Consulting, Risk, and Ratings in the Production of Urban Space," *Indiana Journal of Global Legal Studies*, January 15, 2008, 75–99.
23. Vitale, *City of Disorder*, 187.
24. Attendance for Fred Wilson's exhibition was the highest for the Baltimore Historical Society in its 150-year history, according to Judith E. Stein; see her "Signs of Omission: Fred Wilson's Mining the Museum," originally published in *Art in America*, October 1993.
25. For an account of this project see "Remembrance in Schöneberg," available on the website of artists Stih and Schnock at www.stih-schnock.de/remembrance.html (excerpted from a longer piece published in *Alphabet City* 4/5, Toronto, 1995, 6–12).
26. The artists are cited in Juliet Koss, "Coming to Terms with the Present," *Grey Room*, no. 16, Summer 2004, 116–31.
27. Hal Foster, "The Artist As Ethnographer," in *Return of the Real: The Avant-Garde at the Turn of the Century*, MIT, 1996, 171–204. Notably the book was preceded by a wave of new scholarship on art and post-colonialism, ethnocentrism, and cultural production, including: Paul Gilroy, *The Black Atlantic: Modernity and Double-Consciousness*, Harvard University Press, 1993; Edward Said, *Culture and Imperialism*, Vintage, 1994; and Coco Fusco, ed., *English is Broken Here: Notes on Cultural Fusion in the Americas*, New Press, 1995.
28. Leslie, *Walter Benjamin*, 94.
29. Foster, *Return of the Real*, 179.

30. Fredric Jameson, *Postmodernism, or, The Cultural Logic of Late Capitalism*, Duke University Press, 1992.
31. Rothenberg's elaborate Anne Frank Project was itself based on efforts by The Netherlands Institute for War Documentation to definitively authenticate the fated teenager's diary in direct opposition to doubters.
32. See Debra Viadero, "Battle over Multicultural Education Rises in Intensity," *Education Week*, November 28, 1990, 1, 11–13; Henry Louis Gates, Jr., "Whose Culture is it, Anyway," *New York Times*, May 4, 1991; and Julie Ault, Brian Wallis, Marianne Weems, and Philip Yenawine, eds., *Art Matters: How the Culture Wars Changed America*, NYU Press, 1999.
33. "The London-based Daily Telegraph Art 100 Index, which traces prices of works by 100 top artists, rose 26% through November, double the rise for all of 1997," wrote Thane Peterson in "These Prices Are Surreal," *Business Week*, no. 3610, December 28, 1998–January 4, 1999, 170–3.
34. Michael Brenson, "The Curator's Moment," *Art Journal*, Winter 1998; and Foster, *Return of the Real*, 282, n. 44.
35. Just In Time (JIT) refers to the reduction of fixed capital such as prefabricated parts for automobiles or appliances in order to reduce the stockpiling of unsold commodities. Under post-Fordism production takes place more or less when demand rises. This manufacturing flexibility is dependent on global information networks, borderless import and export regulations, and unfettered access to cheap labor markets anywhere in the world.
36. Benetton's "multicultural" ads began in 1986, but did not proceed without controversy. In 1989 the company pulled Toscani's image of a black woman breast-feeding a white baby after public complaints.
37. Jeff Chang, *Can't Stop Won't Stop: A History of the Hip-Hop Generation*, St. Martin's Press, 2005.
38. See Kester, "The Eyes of the Vulgar," in *Conversation Pieces*, 17–49.
39. One of the few well-established art critics who openly embraced the rising visibility of artists of color was Lucy R. Lippard, see her book *Mixed Blessings: New Art in a Multicultural America*, New Press, 2000.
40. Owens, *Beyond Recognition*, 324, 325.
41. Holmes, *Unleashing the Collective Phantoms*, 117.
42. Operation Invisible Monument website: www.hijadela.com/projects/prs/invmon.html
43. "Jeremy [Deller] and I [Aaron Gatch] pulled up in the middle of the day, threw some orange cones out the back of a white cargo van, and went to work. I haven't spoken to David [Hilliard] in a while but last time we did, he mentioned that he still hears people tell stories underneath that sign. We tried to get street signs funded for the whole BP [Black Panther] tour, but nothing ever pulled through" (CTM founder Aaron Gatch, in an email to the author dated January 2, 2010).
44. See the CTM website "Black Panther History Marker": www.tacticalmagic.org/CTM/project%20pages/BPP.htm
45. Google Maps: http://en.wikipedia.org/wiki/Google_Map
46. See the Howling Mob Society website at www.howlingmobsociety.org
47. See the official website of the "Annual Troy Victorian Stroll," sponsored by the Rensselaer Chamber of Commerce, at www.victorianstroll.com
48. A short video documenting the project is available on participating artist Dara Greenwald's website at www.daragreenwald.com/uvw.html

49. Ana Longoni, "Crossroads for Activist Art in Argentina," trans. Zoë Petersen, in Gene Ray and Gregory Sholette, eds., *Whiter Tactical Media*, special issue of *Third Text*, vol. 5, no. 22, 2008, 576.
50. "Rudy Giuliani in Drag Smooching Donald Trump" can be viewed on YouTube at www.youtube.com/watch?v=4IrE6FMpai8
51. Only after Giuliani left office was the law passed by his successor Michael Bloomberg in 2002.
52. Rudolph W. Giuliani, "Toward a Realistic Peace: Defending Civilization and Defeating Terrorists by Making the International System Work," *Foreign Affairs*, September–October 2007; www.foreignaffairs.com/articles/62824/rudolph-w-giuliani/toward-a-realistic-peace
53. Richard Meyer, *Outlaw Representation: Censorship and Homosexuality in Twentieth-Century American Art*, Beacon Press, 2002, 8–13.
54. For an engaging reading of REPOhistory's public interventions in relationship to Oskar Negt and Alexander Kluge's concept of the proletarian or counter-public sphere see Philip Glahn, "Public Art: Avant-Garde Practice and the Possibilities of Critical Articulation," *Afterimage*, vol. 28, no. 3, November/December 2000, 10–12.
55. Derrida, *Archive Fever*, 4, n. 1.
56. Leslie, *Walter Benjamin*, 75.
57. Jeffrey Skoller, *Shadows, Specters, Shards: Making History in Avant-Garde Film*, University of Minnesota Press, 2005, 5.
58. REPOhistory's archival materials are housed at The Fales Library and Special Collections at New York University, along with the documents of Group Material and dozens of other "downtown" artists and organizations: http://dlib.nyu.edu/findingaids/html/fales/repo.html

Chapter 4

1. Yomango, "10 Style Tips" available at yomango.net at www.yomango.net/node/126
2. "Every note I have taken ... a free collection of notes that I have collected, saved, and cataloged," is located on artist Tiffany Knopow's website at www.tiffanyknopow.com/notes
3. Stimson suggests that monotony is in fact the latest expression of post-human affect brought on by the mechanization of aesthetic experience first identified by Benjamin, see Blake Stimson, *The Pivot of the World: Photography and Its Nation*, MIT Press, 2006, 187.
4. See Public Collectors website at www.publiccollectors.org
5. Leslie, *Walter Benjamin*, 75.
6. Marc Fischer, "Angelo," on the Temporary Services website: http://temporaryservices.org/angelo.html
7. Email correspondence between Marc Fischer and the author, October 21, 2009.
8. John Schwartz, "Dungeons & Dragons Prison Ban Upheld," *New York Times*, January 27, 2010; www.nytimes.com/2010/01/27/us/27dungeons.html?scp=1&sq=Dungeons%20&%20Dragons%20Prison%20Ban%20Upheld&st=cse
9. Fischer, "Angelo."
10. All of Temporary Services public art projects can be found at www.temporaryservices.org/past_services.html; their Public Phenomena Archive is located at www.temporary-

services.org/pub_phenom_archive.html. Some of the Public Phenomena images were collected in Joel Score ed., *Public Phenomena*, White Walls, 2008.

11. Brandon Taylor, *Avant-Garde and After: Rethinking Art Now*, Abrams, 1995, 153.
12. De Certeau's dedication in *The Practice of Everyday Life*.
13. El Lissitzky, "Suprematism in World Reconstruction" (1920), in *El Lissitzky: Life, Letters, Texts*, Thames and Hudson, 1967, 333.
14. From the Temporary Services mission statement available online as a pdf at www.temporaryservices.org/HLP_Poster_Booklet.pdf
15. More about Mess Hall and its programs can be found at www.messhall.org
16. Ted Purves, *What We Want is Free: Generosity and Exchange in Recent Art*, State University of New York Press, 2005, 43, n. 1.
17. See also the Independent Curators International's International exhibit *The Gift: Generous Offerings, Threatening Hospitality*; and P.S.1 Contemporary Art Center's exhibition *Mexico City: An Exhibition about the Exchange Rate of Bodies and Values*, Lone Island City, 2002. Other notable critical and theoretical readings of the gift as art include Bruce Barber and Jeff Dayton-Johnson, "Marking the Limit: Re-Framing a Micro-Economy for the Arts," *Parachute*, no. 106, June 2002, 27, 39; and Yates McKee, "Suspicious Packages," *October*, Summer 2006, 99–121.
18. Lewis Hyde, *The Gift: Imagination and the Erotic Life of Property*, Vintage, 1988.
19. Benkler, *The Wealth of Networks*, 56; and on the art economy see Deepak Gopinath, "Picasso Lures Hedge-Fund-Type Investors to Art Market (Update 1)," January 26, 2006; www.bloomberg.com/apps/news?pid=71000001&refer=&sid=aCTxxmKVlgWI
20. TS member Brett Bloom in an email to the author dated October 16, 2001.
21. Ibid.
22. Marc Fischer, "The Library Project," on the TS website at www.temporaryservices.org/library_project_essay.html
23. For more on the little known Chicago Surrealist movement see Franklin Rosemont, Penelope Rosemont, and Paul Garon, eds., *The Forecast Is Hot! Tracts and Other Collective Declarations of the Surrealist Movement in the United States 1966–1976*, Charles Kerr Publishers, December 1997.
24. A copy of the booklet describing the project and a list of books TS "added" to the Harold Washington Library can be found at www.temporaryservices.org/library_project_essay.html
25. From the *Free For All* booklet, Temporary Services, self-published, 2000.
26. Richard Lloyd, *Neo-Bohemia: Art and Commerce in the Postindustrial City*, Routledge, 2006, 240.
27. Ibid., 157.
28. Ibid., 172.
29. Nelson Algren, *Chicago: City on the Make*, University of Chicago Press, 50th Anniversary edition, 2001 (first published 1951), 23.
30. Detailed information about several of these regional art spaces can be found in Nato Thompson, "Until It's Gone: Taking Stock of Chicago's Multi-Use Centers," *New Art Examiner*, March/April 2002, 47–53. *New Art Examiner* was a not-for-profit, Chicago-based art journal that for almost 30 years focused on the Midwestern cultural scene. Thompson's essay is now found online on the website of Temporary Services: http://74.125.47.132/search?q=cache:BZhEyoMs90YJ:www.temporaryservices.org/until_its_gone.pdf+compost+temporary+services+chicago&cd=1&hl=en&ct=clnk&gl=us. See also Gabriel Peimone, "Burgeoning Blackstone: Checking in on the

Experimental Station 5 Years After their Fire," *AREA*, vol. 1, no. 1, 2001, 10, online at www.areachicago.org/p/issues/issue-1/dear-chicago

31. All of the Ancient Order flyers are also available on UbuWeb at http://ubu.com/outsiders/ao.html
32. According to the TS website the Chicago sculpture is entitled "Episodic," made by artist Josh Garber, and the work in question in Sydney is called "Bower" made by artists Susan Milne and Greg Stonehouse. Documentation of the original TS project in Chicago can be found at www.temporaryservices.org/psop.html and the Sydney version at www.temporaryservices.org/publicpoll
33. The lack of capitalization in this anonymous comment suggests it was sent as an email response to the group.
34. Gerald Raunig, *Art and Revolution: Transversal Activism in the Long Twentieth Century*, Semiotext(e), 2007 (originally published in Austria by Turia + Kant, 2005).
35. The survey carried out for this book is discussed below; in addition, Temporary Services has assembled a substantial inventory of self-organized art associations on their site "Groups and Spaces": www.groupsandspaces.net/groups.html
36. Hans Magnus Enzensberger, *The Consciousness Industry: On Literature, Politics and the Media*, Continuum Books/Seabury Press, 1974.
37. See Alexander Alberro and Blake Stimson, eds., *Institutional Critique: An Anthology of Artists' Writings*, MIT Press, 2009.
38. Marcel Mauss, *The Gift: Forms and Functions of Exchange in Archaic Societies*, Norton, 1967.
39. Bradford D. Martin, *The Theater is in the Street: Politics and Performance in Sixties America*, University of Massachusetts Press, 2004.
40. See Lynn Mally, *Revolutionary Acts: Amateur Theater and the Soviet State, 1917–1938*, Cornell University Press, 2000; and Olga F. Chtiquel, "Without Theater, the Czechoslovak Revolution Could Not Have Been Won," *The Drama Review*, vol. 34, no. 3 (T 12), Fall 1990.
41. Gallo, "The Mexican Pentagon," 168.
42. A striking photographic essay on this once prosperous Midwestern steel city appropriately entitled "Images of a Ghost Town" by Mark M. Pecchia is available online at Youngstown State University's Center for Working-Class Studies: http://cwcs.ysu.edu/resources/cwcs-projects/culture/ghost-town-images
43. Louis Uchitelle, *The Disposable American: Layoffs and Their Consequences*, Vintage, 2007, 7.
44. Ibid.
45. Sohail Daulatzai, from the exhibition catalog *Movement: Hip Hop in L.A.—1980s to Now*, curated by Raymond Condrington for the Department of Cultural Affairs, City of Los Angeles, 2003.
46. See Gilchrist's follow-up commentary to his own Op Ed in the *Los Angeles Times* of July 1, 2008: http://opinion.latimes.com/opinionla/2008/07/jim-gilchrist-r.html—the video was briefly offline, but is now viewable again and has received over 17,000 hits (not necessarily unique) as of December 2009.
47. Jim Gilchrist's Minuteman Project at www.minutemanproject.com
48. Campo Minutemen at www.campominutemen.com
49. This is a citation from Minuteman Midwest from November 2008. The site is no longer available. However, the same phrase can be found at www.rense.com/general81/dept.htm. A similar angry, patriotic resentment aimed at the administration of Barack

Obama is evident amongst middle- and working-class members of the newly formed Dallas Tea Party based in Texas: http://taxdayteaparty.com/teaparty/texas

50. Stormfront was founded in the early 1990s as an electronic bulletin board hosted by the Ku Klux Klan and has since morphed into an online news and merchandising source for white supremacist and ultra-nationalist organizations with built-in translation software for Serbian, Croatian, Gaelic, Dutch, Russian, Hungarian, and Afrikaans. See www.stormfront.org/forum/showthread.php?t=218412
51. For a digitally interactive cultural and political "response" to the border vigilante mobilization and other forms of nationalist xenophobia see the free online video game ICED, in which the player assumes the role of a teenager attempting to avoid capture and deportation by officials: www.icedgame.com
52. Kosofsky, *Epistemology of the Closet*, 5.
53. Benkler, *The Wealth of Networks*, 272.
54. Friedrich Nietzsche, *On the Genealogy of Morality*, trans. Carol Diethe, Cambridge University Press, 2007, 21.
55. James C. Scott, *Domination and the Arts of Resistance: Hidden Transcripts*, Yale University Press, 1990; Cornel West, *The Cornel West Reader*, Basic Civitas Books, 1999, 275.
56. John Wilson, *Politics and Leisure*, Allen and Unwin, 1988, 56–61.
57. Here I offer my own observations of several conversations overheard following a 2007 parade celebrating the winning game of a New York sports team in which young white men, presumably from the suburbs and outer boroughs, gleefully described running atop parked automobiles, leaping over crowd-control barricades, and becoming publicly aroused by groups of inebriated female fans, as police watched on helplessly in Lower Manhattan.
58. http://argentina.indymedia.org/news/2002/02/14113.php
59. www.hurriyetdailynews.com/n.php?n=an-errorist-movement-at-the-biennial-2009-09-14
60. Longoni, "Crossroads," 587.
61. Yomango's entire ten-point, anti-capitalist lifestyle tips are available at: "10 Style Tips for a Yomango Life": www.yomango.net/node/126
62. "Whatever Happened to Yomango: Fifteen Answers to a Questionnaire," on the website of Translate.eipcp.net; http://translate.eipcp.net/transversal/0307/yomango/en#redir
63. www.yomango.net/book/export/html/137
64. Yomango, "10 Style Tips."
65. Annalee Newitz, *Pretend We're Dead: Capitalist Monsters in American Pop Culture*, Duke University Press, 2006, 12.
66. For an engaging elaboration on the revenge of the surplus population see Lars Bang Larson, "Zombies of Immaterial Labor: The Modern Monster and the Death of Death," *e-flux journal* no. 15, April 2010, 38–44; and Nikos Papastergiadis, "The Zombification of the Other," *Cultural Studies Review*, vol. 15, no. 2, 2009, 147–78.

Chapter 5

1. Pierre Bourdieu, "The Essence of Neoliberalism," *Le Monde diplomatique*, December 1998, available in English at http://mondediplo.com/1998/12/08bourdieu
2. Carol Duncan, "Who Rules the Art World?," in *Aesthetics of Power: Essays in Critical Art History*, Cambridge University Press, 1983, 172.

3. Kevin F. McCarthy, et al., *Rand Report: A Portrait of the Visual Arts: Meeting the Challenges of a New Era*, Rand Corp., 2005; www.rand.org/pubs/monographs/2005/RAND_MG290.sum.pdf
4. An excellent example of how to read visual artworks (prior to neoliberalism in this case, not solely in terms of iconographic or metaphoric imagery, but in relation to specific conditions of production) is Paul B. Jaskot, "Gerhard Richter and Adolf Eichmann," *Oxford Art Journal*, vol. 28, no. 3, 2005, 457–78.
5. Wu, *Privatizing Culture*, 303.
6. This includes not only visual, plastic artists, but also filmmakers and other media producers together with painters, sculptors, installation and other fine artists.
7. This is essentially the marketing logic behind Amazon.com, explains editor-in-chief of *Wired* magazine Chris Anderson in *The Long Tail: Why the Future of Business is Selling Less of More*, Hyperion Press, 2006.
8. According to reports by several artist friends of the author the going rate for studio fabricators is about 12 dollars an hour in the studio of Jeff Koons, meanwhile the artist Damien Hirst assigns assistants to paint entire canvases that are later sold under his name; see Don Thompson, *The $12 Million Stuffed Shark: The Curious Economics of Contemporary Art*, Palgrave Macmillan, 2008, 65.
9. David Halle and Elisabeth Tiso, "Lessons from Chelsea," *International Journal of the Humanities*, vol. 3, 2005–6, 6.
10. Melanie Fasche, *The Art Market and Regional Policy—Happy Marriage or Troubled Relation?*, Free University Berlin (unpublished paper), 2009, available from http://nuke.creative-regions.org.uk/OutcomesPapers/ThirdSeminarOutcomes/tabid/476/language/en-US/Default.aspx or from the author at melanie.fasche@gmx.de and Alain Quemin, "Globalization and Mixing in the Visual Arts: An Empirical Survey of 'High Culture' and Globalization," *International Sociology*, vol. 21, no. 4, 2006, 522–50.
11. Marcelo Expósito, "Inside and Outside the Art Institution: Self-Valorization and Montage in Contemporary Art," trans. Nuria Rodríguez and Aileen Derieg, in Raunig and Ray, eds., *Art and Contemporary Critical Practice*, 149.
12. There is no question that the National Endowment for the Arts (NEA) was established to win over the hearts and minds of cultural workers worldwide in favor of the seemingly uninhibited freedom of expression granted in the West, even if the exact role that agencies such as the CIA and US State Department played in supporting, say, Abstract Expressionists remains controversial ever since the appearance of essays by Max Kozloff and Eva Cockroft in the pages of *Artforum* magazine in the 1970s. The prominent discussants in this ongoing debate include Serge Guilbaut, Robert Burstow, Michael Kimmelmen, and Nancy Jachec.
13. In dollars adjusted for a 2007 constant the NEA's 1979 budget would be over 400 million dollars, while its allocation in the year 2007 was only about a quarter of that amount ($124,561,844).
14. Rosler, "Money, Power, and the History of Art."
15. A number of superstars including Cindy Sherman, Mike Kelley, and Richard Prince moved from these government-supported venues into mainstream market success, thus demonstrating the underlying capitalist logic of the Keynesian liberal welfare state.
16. Ault, *Alternative Art New York*.
17. Cited in Rosler, "Money, Power, and the History of Art."
18. Thompson, *The $12 Million Stuffed Shark*, 12.

19. Stallabrass, *Art Incorporated*; Andrea Fraser, *Museum Highlights: The Writings of Andrea Fraser*, ed. Alexander Alberro, MIT Press, 2007, 37–47; and Wu, *Privatizing Culture*, 161.
20. Olav Velthuis, *Talking Prices: Symbolic Meanings of Prices on the Market for Contemporary Art*, Princeton University Press, 2007, 18.
21. Ibid., 27.
22. See critique of Laclau and Mouffe pages 14–15, Chapter 1.
23. Velthuis, *Talking Prices*, 27.
24. Ibid., 178, 126.
25. Milton Friedman, *Capitalism and Freedom*, University of Chicago Press, 1962; Midnight Notes Collective, "The New Enclosures."
26. A study of 300 graduates of the School of the Art Institute of Chicago were tracked between 1963 to 1980 by researchers Mihaly Csikszentmihalyi, Jacob W. Getzels, and Stephen P. Kahn in *Talent and Achievement*, Chicago, 1984 (an unpublished report), 44.
27. Pierre-Michel Menger, "Artistic Labor Markets: Contingent Work, Excess," in Victor A. Ginsburgh and David Throsby, eds., *Handbook of the Economics of Art and Culture, Volume 1*, North Holland, 2006, 28.
28. "If all the professional dancers in the United States stood shoulder to shoulder to form a single chorus line, it would stretch from 42nd Street for nearly the entire length of Manhattan. If every artist in America's workforce banded together, their ranks would be double the size of the United States Army. More Americans identify their primary occupation as artist than as lawyer, doctor, police officer or farm worker"; Sam Roberts, "A 21st-Century Profile: Art for Art's Sake, and for the US Economy, Too," *New York Times*, June 12, 2008; http://www.nytimes.com/2008/06/12/arts/12nea.html?ex=1214193600&en=a8f30b5b62faf0f4&ei=5070&emc=eta1; see also the report *Artists in the Workforce: 1990–2005*, a publication of the National Endowment for the Arts, 2008, available as a pdf file at www.arts.gov/research/ArtistsInWorkforce.pdf
29. "The Economy of Culture in Europe," KEA European Affairs, Belgium, November 2006; www.ifacca.org/publications/2006/11/01/the-economy-of-culture-in-europe
30. "Artists in Figures: A Short Statistical Portrait of Artists, Publicists, Designers, Architects and Related Professions in the German Cultural Labor Market, 1995–2003," Federal Commissioner for Cultural and Media Affairs, Germany, March 2007; www.ifacca.org/publications/2007/03/01/artists-in-figures
31. See "More Artists in Canada, but Still Making Less than Most: Study," CBC.CA, October 22, 2004; www.cbc.ca/story/arts/national/2004/10/21/Arts/artsjobstudy041021.html
32. Statistics on artistic labor can easily become misleading or contradictory. Some data gatherers use the term artist to include Hollywood screenwriters as well as painters and poets, thus skewing significant differences between these types of cultural labor. And while this book is not intended as an empirical study, nor do I make any claims to being a sociologist, much of this information gathered from the US, UK, Canada, and Germany is no doubt applicable to the working conditions of artists in other post-industrial nations.
33. APT website: www.artistpensiontrust.org/homepage.asp
34. APT, Frequently Asked Questions: www.artistpensiontrust.org/faq_page.asp
35. Andrew Hemingway, *Artists on the Left: American Artists and the Communist Movement, 1926–1956*, Yale University Press, 2002.

36. See Walker, *Left Shift*, 83–5; see also Mary Kelly, *Imaging Desire*, MIT Press, 1998, 12.
37. Walker, *Left Shift*, 30.
38. See Ana Longoni and Mariano Mestman, *Listen Here Now! Argentine Art of the 1960s*, Museum of Modern Art, 2004.
39. Several excellent histories of AWC exist, including Lucy R. Lippard, "The Art Workers' Coalition: Not a History," in *Get the Message: A Decade Of Art For Social Change*, E. P. Dutton, 1984, 10–19; Bryan-Wilson, *Art Workers*; and Alan W. Moore, "Artists' Collectives Mostly in New York, 1975–2000," in Stimpson and Sholette, eds., *Collectivism After Modernism*, 193–221.
40. Artist Seth Siegelaub and attorney Robert Projansky penned *The Artist's Reserved Rights Transfer And Sale Agreement* in 1971, it has since been used by Hans Haacke and several other artists associated with AWC. For more on this document and its history see: Maria Eichhorn, *The Artist's Contract*, Verlag der Buchhandlung/Walther König, Germany, 2009. An online copy of the contract is available at http://74.125.47.132/search?q=cache:mZdXErfPzpEJ:www.ctrlp-artjournal.org/pdfs/siegelaub.pdf+The+Artist%E2%80%99s+Reserved+Rights+transfer&cd=1&hl=en&ct=clnk&gl=us
41. Lippard, cited in Ault's *Alternative Art New York*, 79.
42. The organization's website is www.carfac.ca
43. Robert H. Frank and Philip J. Cook, *The Winner-Take-All Society: Why the Few at the Top Get So Much More Than the Rest of Us*, Penguin, 1996.
44. Saskia Sassen, "Informalization in Advanced Market Economies," a discussion paper for the International Labor Office Organization, Geneva, Switzerland, 1997, 10.
45. Michael Luo, "Forced From Executive Pay to Hourly Wage," *New York Times*, February 28, 2009; www.nytimes.com/2009/03/01/us/01survival.html
46. Uchitelle, *The Disposable American*, 66.
47. Barbara Adam and Joost Van Loon, "Introduction: Repositioning Risk; the Challenge for Social Theory," in Barbara Adam, Ulrich Beck, and Joost Van Loon, eds., *The Risk Society and Beyond: Critical Issues for Social Theory*, Sage Publications, 2000, 2, 3. But for a more politically critical reading of "risk society" see Anthony Giddens, "Risk and Responsibility," *Modern Law Review*, vol. 62, no. 1, 1999, 1–10.
48. Allen Feldman, "On the Actuarial Gaze: From 9/11 to Abu Ghraib," *Cultural Studies*, vol. 19, no. 2, March, 220–3; Nicholas Mirzoeff, "Invisible Empire: Visual Culture, Embodied Spectacle, and Abu Ghraib," *Radical History Review*, 2006, 21.
49. Giorgio Agemben, *Homo Sacer: Sovereign Power and Bare Life*, Stanford University Press, 1998.
50. Kevin Bales, *New Slavery: A Reference Handbook*, ABC-CLIO, Inc. 2000, 7.
51. Ibid.
52. Katherine Bell, "The MFA is the New MBA," *Harvard Business Review*, April 14, 2008; http://blogs.harvardbusiness.org/cs/2008/04/the_mfa_is_the_new_mba.html

Chapter 6

1. The total sum of monies raised for the defense of Kurtz and Ferrell was about $350,000, of which approximately $241,070 was actually spent. Had the case gone to court instead of being dismissed after four years by Judge Arcara, however, it would have likely cost an estimated half a million dollars. (Note: the author was himself a member

of the CAE Defense Fund, and the committee's usefully informative website remains online as of this writing at www.caedefensefund.org.)

2. CAE members included or include Steve Kurtz and his late wife Hope Kurtz together with the artists Steve Barnes, Dorian Burr, Beverly Schlee, and most recently Lucia Sommer (beginning in 2005). The group's website is www.critical-art.net
3. There is no evidence of prior interest by the government in CAE with this one hypothetical caveat: several years before the FBI investigation of Kurtz, a lecturer at the University of Illinois at Champaign-Urbana baselessly stated that "Critical Art Ensemble paints a picture of cyber-resistance that looks a lot like the descriptions of bin Laden's alleged network." Whether this paper ("Electronic jihad" by Heidi Brush) was even noticed by Federal agents is anybody's guess. It was, however, reported by Kevin Featherly in *Newsbytes* (now part of the *Washington Post*) in a piece entitled "US On Verge Of 'Electronic Martial Law'," October 16, 2001, and the comparison of CAE to electronic terrorists was circulated over the Internet, among other places at Virus.org, an online IT Security News and Information Portal; http://lists.virus.org/isn-0110/msg00110.html_
4. Details on some of the public cases mentioned above as well as others involving US government censorship or intimidation of citizens, tourists, journalists, academics, and students have been compiled by Matthew Rothschild; see the McCarthyism Watch Updates published by the *Progressive* magazine available at www.progressive.org/list/mccarthy. For information specifically involving state harassment of cultural workers after September 11, see the Temporary Services website, "Resurgence of the Culture Wars" at www.temporaryservices.org/culture_wars.html; and John Tarleton, "Busted Puppets: Philly Police Arrest Puppetistas, Toss Their Art Into the Trash," *On the Road with John Tarleton*, August 3, 2000; www.johntarleton.net/philly_puppets.html
5. CAE are not the only cultural activists attempting to defend plants, seeds, and soil against global agribusiness through artistic interventions. Other practitioners include the Swedish artist Åsa Sonjasdotter, who uses Peruvian potatoes in her art installations: www.potatoperspective.org/content.php?page=about&ank=top; the Danish artist Nis Rømer whose project Free Soil combines art, design, and issues of environmental justice: www.free-soil.org; and American artist Claire Pentecost, a CAE collaborator whose online essay "Fields of Zombies" discusses a range of related topics including seed cooperatives and the Svalbard Global Seed Vault in Norway, and threats to genetic seed diversity from GMOs (Genetically Modified Organisms): www.yougenics.net/agriart/pentecost.html
6. CAE carried our several versions of Molecular Invasion. However, according to Lucia Sommer, additional experiments are still needed to prove the effectiveness of the Ensemble's "reverse engineering" process (from an email to the author dated December 18, 2009).
7. Autonomedia Press: http://bookstore.autonomedia.org
8. Bertolt Brecht, "On Form and Subject-Matter," in *Brecht on Theater: The Development of an Aesthetic*, ed. John Willet, Hill and Wang, 1964, 29.
9. For a more detailed look at the case framed within the context of George Bush Jr.'s presidency see G. Sholette, "Disciplining the Avant-Garde: The United States of America Versus the Critical Art Ensemble," in Noah Horowitz and Brian Sholis, eds., *The Uncertain States of America Reader*, Sternberg Press, 2006; available at http://dialogic.blogspot.com/2008/06/gregory-sholette-disciplining-avant.html

10. "We raise funds in three ways. First, we all have straight jobs. Second, we do a lot of visiting artist and speaking gigs in conjunction with writing, so we get royalties, writer's fees, and speaking fees. This money goes exclusively toward projects. Finally, we try to throw as many expenses as possible at any institution that wants to sponsor a project"—CAE responding to questions in Ryan Griffis, "TANDOM SURFING THE THIRD WAVE: Critical Art Ensemble and Tactical Media Production," *Lumpen* no. 81, February 2001 (unpaginated): www.lumpen.com/magazine/81/critical_art_ensemble.shtml
11. Researchers and teachers can purchase these bacteria over the Internet with few restrictions.
12. Kurtz's attorney Paul Cambria has successfully defended *Hustler* magazine publisher Larry Flynt against obscenity charges, invoking the First Amendment right to freedom of speech.
13. For more about the case and its resolution see http://caedefensefund.org
14. Gregg Bordowitz, "Tactics Inside and Out," *Artforum*, September 2004, 212–19; www.thefreelibrary.com/Tactics+inside+and+out:+Gregg+Bordowitz+on+Critical+Art+Ensemble-a0122265007
15. "The FBI vs. Jean Seberg," *Time Magazine/CNN*, September 24, 1979; www.time.com/time/magazine/article/0,9171,947393,00.html
16. See George McKay, ed., *DIY Culture: Party and Protest in Nineties Britain*, Verso, 1998, as well as the various writings of Brian Holmes cited in this book.
17. David Garcia and Geert Lovink, "The ABCs of Tactical Media," 1997; http://subsol.c3.hu/subsol_2/contributors2/garcia-lovinktext.html
18. See Drew, "The Collective Camcorder in Art and Activism."
19. See The Irish Artist-Led Archive webpage: www.theartistledarchive.com/Blue%20Funk.html
20. Michel De Certeau, *The Practice of Everyday Life*, trans. Steven Rendall, University of California Press, 1984.
21. Lovink and Garcia, "The ABCs."
22. De Certeau, *The Practice of Everyday Life*, xix.
23. Ibid.
24. Ibid., 82.
25. PAD/D promoted the creation of a parallel cultural sphere set apart from that of the dominant art market, see Chapters 1 and 2.
26. See, for example, Andrew Hemingway, *Artists on the Left: American Artists and the Communist Movement, 1926–1956*, Yale University Press, 2002, and Michael Denning, *The Cultural Front: The Laboring of American Culture in the Twentieth Century*, Verso, 1998.
27. These and other examples of Left labor's visual and material culture in the United States can be found in the book *Images of American Radicalism*, organized by Paul Buhle and Edmund B. Sullivan, Christopher Publishing House, 1999. A detailed account of the Patterson Pageant is included in Steve Golin, *The Fragile Bridge: Paterson Silk Strike, 1913*, Temple University Press, 1992.
28. Garcia and Lovink, "The ABCs."
29. Walter Benjamin, "The Work of Art in the Age of Mechanical Production," Section XIV, in *Illuminations: Essays and Reflections*, Schocken Books, 1969, 175; see also Gene Ray and Gregory Sholette, "Whither Tactical Media," introduction to a special issue of *Third Text*, vol. 22, no. 5, September 2008, 519–24.

30. John Roberts, *Philosophizing the Everyday: Revolutionary Practice and the Fate of Cultural Theory*, Pluto Press, 2006, 79.
31. Andrew Hemingway, *The Mysticism of Money: Precisionist Painting and the Machine Age*, Periscope Books, 2010; see also Michael Löwy and Robert Sayre, *Romanticism Against the Tide of Modernity*, Duke University Press, 2001.
32. Scott Cutler Shershow, *The Work and the Gift*, University of Chicago Press, 2005, 184.
33. De Certeau, *The Practice of Everyday Life*, v.
34. Karl Marx and Frederick Engels, *The German Ideology, 1845–46*, International Publishers edition, 1970, 109.
35. Brian Holmes, *Unleashing the Collective Phantoms: Essays in Reverse Imagineering*, Autonomedia Press, 2008, 186.
36. "Insurgency is an 'armed theater' where the antagonists are playing to an audience at the same time they interact with each other ... insurgents attempt to prevent the military battlespace from becoming decisive and concentrate on the political and psychological"; Steven Metz and Raymond Millen, "Insurgency and Counterinsurgency in the 21st Century: Reconceptualizing Threat and Response," *US Army War College Strategic Studies Institute*, pdf available at www.strategicstudiesinstitute.army.mil/pdffiles/pub586.pdf
37. Critical Art Ensemble, *Electronic Civil Disobedience: And Other Unpopular Ideas*, Autonomedia, 1996, also available at www.nettime.org/Lists-Archives/nettime-l-9607/msg00004.html
38. De Certeau, *The Practice of Everyday Life*, 82.
39. Blake Stimson draws parallels between an emerging post-national, even post-human collectivism and the flood of monotonous self-representation made possible by photography in *The Pivot of the World: Photography and Its Nation*, MIT Press, 2006.
40. De Certeau, *The Practice of Everyday Life*, xix and xx.
41. Georges Bataille, "The Notion of Expenditure," in *Visions of Excess: Selected Writings 1927–1939*, University of Minnesota Press, 1985.
42. Bruno Gulli, *Labor of Fire: The Ontology of Labor Between Economy and Culture*, Temple University Press, 2005, 6.
43. Karl Marx, *The Economic and Philosophic Manuscripts of 1844 and the Communist Manifesto*, Prometheus Books, 1988, 59.
44. Tiziana Terranova, "Free Labor: Producing Culture for the Digital Economy," *Social Text*, vol. 18, no. 2, Summer 2005, 33–58.
45. Benkler, *The Wealth of Networks*, 117.
46. See Max Horkheimer and Theodor W. Adorno, *Dialectic of Enlightenment*, Continuum Publishing, 1972, 137; Steven M. Gelber, *Hobbies: Leisure and the Culture of Work in America*, Columbia University Press, 1999, 299; Chris Rojek, *Capitalism and Leisure Theory*, Tavistock Publications, 1985, 150–7; Robert A. Stebbins, *Serious Leisure: A Perspective for Our Time*, Transaction Publishers, 2006.
47. Chris Anderson, "People Power Blogs, User Reviews, Photo-Sharing—the Peer Production Era has Arrived," *Wired*, July 2006; www.wired.com/wired/archive/14.07/people.html
48. Kevin Kelly, "New Rules for the New Economy: Twelve Dependable Principles For Thriving in a Turbulent World," *Wired*, September 1997, 10; www.wired.com/wired/archive/5.09/newrules_pr.html

Chapter 7

1. Jose Luis Borges, "On Exactitude in Science," in *Collected Fictions*, trans. Andrew Hurley, Penguin, 1999, 320.
2. Plato, *The Republic*, trans. Benjamin Jowett, BN Publishing, 291–318.
3. Rancière puts it this way, "Plato states that artisans [as opposed to imitative artists] cannot be put in charge of the shared or common elements of the community because they do *not have the time* to devote themselves to anything other than their work. They cannot be somewhere else because *work will not wait*"; Jacques Rancière, *The Politics of Aesthetics*, Continuum Books, 2004, 12–13.
4. Perhaps the only other group who make essential use of this imitative practice are frauds, counterfeiters, grifters, and confidence men, although some would argue, not without warrant, that politicians and preachers belong on this list.
5. Gene Ray, "Art Schools Burning & Other Songs of Love and War," *Left Curve*, no. 30, 2005; www.leftcurve.org/LC30WebPages/Avantgarde.html
6. The reference is to De Certeau's virtuoso sea creatures, *The Practice of Everyday Life*, xix and xx.
7. RETORT, *Afflicted Powers: Capital and Spectacle in the New Age of War*, Verso, 2005, 193.
8. Carrie Lambert-Beatty, "Make-Believe: Parafiction and Plausibility," *October*, 129, Summer 2009, 51–84.
9. All citations are from email correspondence between Justin A. Langlois and the author on January 7, 2010. For more about Broken City Lab see the website: www.brokencitylab.org/about
10. On an identity-correcting webpage Labofii has renamed The Royal Bank of Scotland *The ~~R~~oyal Bank of Scotland*, see: http://www.oyalbankofscotland.com
11. See the Central Office of Technical Culture website at http://cukt.art.pl/test/frame_cukt.html
12. Hakim Bey (a.k.a. Peter Lamborn Wilson) coined the term Temporary Autonomous Zone to describe a radical, ontological break with market culture, in the book *T.A.Z. the Temporary Autonomous Zone, Ontological Anarchy, Poetic Terrorism*, Autonomedia Books, 1991. Bey is quoted here from "TECHNO TRANSGRESSIONS," Jacek Niegoda and Peter Style of C.U.K.T. interviewed by Joasia Krysa, available at Subsol; http://subsol.c3.hu/subsol_2/contributors/cukttext.html
13. NSK conjoins the Slovenian theatrical group Noordung, the visual artists' collective Irwin, with the Wagnarian classical/industrial-pop band Laibach.
14. A short version of Žižek's thesis makes up the introduction to Alexei Monroe, *Interrogation Machine: Laibach and NSK*, foreword by Slavoj Žižek, MIT Press, 2005.
15. Apparently the last edition of the popular travel book *Rough Guide to Yugoslavia* notes that the NSK's own elaborate organizational structure bore a "striking resemblance" to the diagrams found in the country's school textbooks aimed at explaining the socialist nation's "bafflingly complex" bureaucracy to students; see Monroe, *Interrogation Machine*, 107.
16. A celebrant of liberated sex and redefined gender roles, Kollontai became the world's first female ambassador from the USSR to Norway in 1923, see *Alexandra Kollontai: Selected Writings*, translated with an introduction by Alix Holt, W.W. Norton, 1977.
17. FNO Manifesto: http://factoryoffoundclothes.org/?/idiot
18. See Mejor Vida Corporation at www.irational.org/mvc/english.html

19. Yomango, "Whatever Happened to Yomango?: Fifteen Answers to a Questionnaire," translated into English by Rodrigo Nunes at http://translate.eipcp.net/transversal/0307/yomango/en
20. YNKB at www.ynkb.dk/eng/hvem.shtml
21. CIRCA website: www.clownarmy.org
22. Brian Holmes, *Escape the Overcode: Activist Art in the Control Society*, van Abbenmuseum and WHW, 2009, 14.
23. Amanda Gefter, "Curiosity Doesn't Have to Kill the Quantum Cat," *New Scientist*, no. 2603, May 9, 2007, 32–6.
24. Julie Ault with Doug Ashford and Tim Rollins, eds., *Show and Tell: A Chronicle of Group Material*, Four Corners Books, 2010, 11.
25. Just Seeds is described at page 119.
26. The Futurefarmers artwork, *Field of Thoughts: Limited Edition Bingo Cards*, can be viewed at www.futurefarmers.com/survey/bingo.php
27. Acces Local: definitions from their website: www.acces-local.com/index.php?directory_1=local/&directory_2=acces/intentions/&inclu=acces/intentions/definition.txt
28. Maureen Connor, "(Con)Testing Resources," in Elizabeth Mansfield, ed., *Making Art History*, Routledge, 2007, 252.
29. Some 39 groups reported less than six active members, 13 of these claimed only two or three members, and of those remaining only a few rose above ten participants. Some did report working with larger groups of collaborators on particular projects. Note: The Intermedia Society, a Vancouver-based, all-volunteer organization that predates most of the respondents, reportedly involved an unprecedented number of participants during its short lifespan between 1967 and 1972; and in Copenhagen the contemporary art organization UKK (Unge Kunstnere og Kunstformidlere/Young Artist and Art Workers) is also anomalous because it operates along the lines of a trade union for a large number of cultural workers.
30. All but six of the 67 groups and collectives reported that they had shown art in a museum, alternative space, public art gallery, or similar not-for-profit venue, though when asked about relationships with commercial art galleries nine reported some formal ties with an a commercial art space now or in the past, although five others suggested that group members were individually exhibiting in commercial spaces. Some of the answers to this line of questioning appeared downright testy. In response to a question asking if the group or collective had ever sold work commercially one stunned survey participant replied "heavens no," another exclaimed "NEVER," and a still more vehement rejoinder read: "Never, I would rather boil in hell."
31. Kester, *Conversation Pieces*, 9.
32. See in particular Kester's discussion of Willats' work in *Conversation Pieces*, 91, and on the topic of avant-garde shock see pages 83–4.
33. Kester provides an excellent description of WochenKlausur's work in *Conversation Pieces*, 97–101; the group's website is available in English, Spanish, and German at www.wochenklausur.at
34. See Megs Morley's introduction to *The Artist Led Archive* at www.theartistledarchive.com. For Benjamin Buchloh's searing 1980 critique of Beuys see his "Twilight of the Idol," first published in *Artforum*, June 1980, reprinted in Viola Michely and Claudia Mesch, eds., *Joseph Beuys: The Reader*, I. B. Tauris & Co, 2007, 109–27. For an introduction to Beuys' own ideas see *Energy Plan for the Western Man: Joseph Beuys*

in America: Writings by and Interviews With the Artist, compiled by Carin Kuoni, Thunders Mouth Press, 1990.

35. Luis Jacob, from the exhibition catalog *Golden Streams: Artists' Collaboration and Exchange in the 1970s*, Blackwood Gallery, University of Toronto at Mississauga, 2002, 2.
36. The Yes Men grew out of the online Tactical Media group RTMark, which in turn had roots in the 1994 Barbie Liberation Organization or BLO—a group of gender hackers who switched the voice recordings from talking Barbie dolls to G. I. Joe action dolls and then "shop dropped" these gender-bent toys back into stores for unsuspecting consumers to purchase. These tactics were also an outgrowth of media activists Louis Hock, Elizabeth Sisco, and David Avalos in San Diego, who produced a series of posters mocking the city's treatment of illegal labor with the lines "Welcome to America's Finest Tourist Plantation." The publicly displayed graphics were timed to coincide with the Republican National Convention in 1988. For information on the BLO see http://sniggle.net/barbie.php; and on the San Diego cultural jammers see http://content.cdlib.org/ark:/13030/hb2f59n9z3
37. Roger Caillois, "Mimicry and Legendary Psychasthenia," in *The Edge of Surrealism: A Roger Caillois Reader*, ed. Claudine Frank, Duke University Press, 2003, 89–103.
38. DADT: Don't ask if a fellow soldier is gay, and no soldier should admit to being a homosexual, the policy of the United States military signed into law in 1993.
39. Email exchange between The Yes Men and the author, March 22, 2007.
40. Ibid.
41. The Yes Lab is "a series of brainstorms and trainings to help activist groups carry out Yes-Men-style projects on their own": http://theyesmen.org/lab
42. Plans for building your own self-replicating apparatus are at http://reprap.org/wiki/FuturePlans
43. Incarceration rates for African-American men in US inner cities have climbed in recent years so that by 2004 "21 percent were incarcerated. By their mid-30s, 6 in 10 black men who had dropped out of school had spent time in prison," reports Erik Eckholm in "Plight Deepens for Black Men, Studies Warn," *New York Times*, March 20, 2006; www.nytimes.com/2006/03/20/national/20blackmen.html
44. The current group is made up of members Scott Berzofsky, Dane Nester, and Nicholas Wisniewski, all three 2004 graduates from the Maryland Institute of Contemporary Art.
45. The installation was part of an exhibition entitled Headquarters organized by Cira Pascual Marquina at The Contemporary in 2006. Pascual Marquina briefly served as interim director for the institution using its resources to mount a substantial critique of the city despite resistance from board members of the art center. For more on Campbaltimore/BDC's role in this project see "Participants of Campbaltimore, USA in discussion with Gregory Sholette," in the special "Whither Tactical Media" issue of *Third Text*, vol. 22, no. 5, September 2008, 671–8.
46. David Simon's HBO cable television series *The Wire* graphically portrayed the way Baltimore's severe structural unemployment among African-Americans forces many into the illegal drug business, even as the city's compromised police forces, journalists, educators, unions, and municipal officials opt to manage, rather than eliminate, the contraband narcotics economy, knowing full well it is the only steady city employer.
47. BDC's Participation Park shares a certain resemblance to the German project Park Fiction in which local artists and activists asked residents in Hamburg to imagine

how an undeveloped public space might be transformed into a public commons. The resulting collaboration with the community included plans for a flying carpet and palm trees. Once these and other features were built into the park however, the city sought to demolish it. Both artists and residents successfully defended their "park fiction." An excellent account of the project is found in Grant Kester's forthcoming book *The One and the Many: Agency and Identity in Contemporary Art*, Duke University Press, 2010.

48. The term "Right to the City" is both the title of an essay by David Harvey published in *New Left Review*, 53, September–October 2008, and an urban activist organization located in Brooklyn whose website is www.righttothecity.org
49. See *The City From Below*, March 27–29, 2009 at http://cityfrombelow.org/main
50. An account of how these cooperative networks were developed and used for the event is available in Scott Berzofsky and John Duda, "Report On the City From Below," in *Art Work: A National Conversation About Art, Labor, and Economics*, published by Temporary Services Half Letter Press in Chicago, 2009, 20, 21, also available as a pdf file at www.artandwork.us/tag/temporary-services
51. The Janet & Walter Sondheim Artscape Prize amounts to $25,000, thus providing $600 to each of the three group members for twelve months. Notably, this was the same grant that in 2006 the group, then known as Campbaltimore, were first awarded and then denied. At the time the foundation claimed it did not give money to collectives, only to individuals. The city have subsequently changed this rule, a fact that reflects the shifting cultural landscape towards collective practice, but also, as is so often the case, the crusade of one or two individuals, in this case local artist Gary Kachadourian, who was a member of the grant committee.
52. Elizabeth Evitts Dickinson, "The Sondheim and Social Justice," *Urban Palimpsest: Thoughts on Cities, Culture, and Design*, July 15, 2009; http://urbanpalimpsest.blogspot.com/2009/07/sondheim-and-social-justice.html
53. Along with Charm Town and Mob Town, Ravenstown is one of the city's nicknames. It refers to the city's professional football team, which is in turn named after Edgar Allen Poe's poem *The Raven*. Poe, who is buried in Baltimore, also occasionally lived and worked in the city.
54. About The Baltimore Free School: http://freeschool.redemmas.org/content/about-baltimore-free-school
55. Both CUP members' citations are excerpted from email correspondences with the author, dated respectively January 10, 2010 (Rich), and January 11, 2010 (Woo).
56. See Center for Land Use Interpretation: http://clui.org/; Native Resurgence by Nicholas Brown and Sarah Kanouse: www.nativeresurgence.net; Makrolab: http://makrolab.ljudmila.org/phases; Stockyard Institute: www.stockyardinstitute.org; AREA Chicago: http://areachicago.org; and Learning Site: www.learningsite.info
57. "[Poster Dwelling for Land, Market and Economy]" can be found at www.learningsite.info
58. Communiqué from an Absent Future, critical theory and content from the nascent California student occupation movement, September 24, 2009: http://wewanteverything.wordpress.com/2009/09/24/communique-from-an-absent-future
59. The Public School in Los Angeles is part of the Telic institute alternative art center, but all other "branch" locations are autonomous from it, see http://the-flog.com/2008/03/the-public-school-at-telic

60. See the BHQF "Prolegomena To Any Future Art School" manifesto at http://bhqf.org/Site/about.html
61. Compare the BHQF to the opening lines of the book *The Coming Insurrection*: "Everyone agrees. It's about to explode" (The Invisible Committee, Semiotext(e) Books, 2009).
62. The nineteenth-century origins of the art educational "factory" in the Unites States are neatly mapped out in Howard Singerman's opening chapters of *Art Subjects: Making Artists in the American University*, University of California Press, 1999.
63. Chto Delat/What is to be Done? is a Left-leaning Russian artist's collective, founded in St. Petersburg in 2003, that borrows its name from Lenin's 1901/2 essay of the same title. The group's website and archive of political art and cultural newspapers is located at www.chtodelat.org
64. "Street University in Saint Petersburg: a Brief History": http://streetuniver.narod.ru/index_e.htm
65. Chto Delat, "A Declaration on Politics, Knowledge, and Art": www.chtodelat.org/index.php?option=com_content&view=article&id=494&Itemid=233&lang=en
66. For some events the group asks for a modest entrance fee (adjusted for students and unemployed persons) in order to partially cover program expenses.
67. 16 Beaver Street has avoided seeking not-for-profit (NFP) status or tax exemption even though the group's programming record as an established New York cultural institution would likely make them a "grant magnet."
68. Cited in an email from 16 Beaver Street collective member Pedro Lasch to the author, dated January 10, 2010.
69. Anton Vidokle, "Exhibition as School in a Divided City," *Manifesta* 6, 2006, 4. Vidokle runs the for-profit art platform e-flux.com and in 2008–9 organized a series of educational seminars at the New Museum in New York for a group of select students that were para-fictionally christened "Night School."
70. "The Necrosocial: Civic Life, Social Death, and the UC, a Communiqué by Occupied UC Berkeley Students," November 18, 2009: http://anticapitalprojects.wordpress.com/2009/11/19/the-necrosocial

Chapter 8

1. Jacques Derrida, "Ellipsis," in *Writing and Difference*, trans. Alan Bass, Routledge, second edition, 2001, 373.
2. Peter Linebaugh and Marcus Rediker, *The Many-Headed Hydra: Sailors, Slaves, Commoners, and the Hidden History of the Revolutionary Atlantic*, Beacon Press, 2000, 16.
3. Examples taken from *Sabotage in the American Workplace: Anecdotes of Dissatisfaction, Mischief and Revenge*, edited by Martin Sprouse and illustrated by Tracy Cox, Pressure Drop Press and AK Press, 1992.
4. Alain Badiou, "The Communist Hypothesis," *New Left Review*, 49, January–February 2008, 41.

BIBLIOGRAPHY

A Selection of Books on Art and Politics Since circa 1975

Adams, Don and Arlene Goldbard, *Crossroads: Reflections on the Politics of Culture*, DNA Press, 1990.

Alberro, Alexander and Blake Stimson, *Conceptual Art: A Critical Anthology*, MIT Press, 1999.

—— *Institutional Critique: An Anthology of Artists' Writings*, MIT Press, 2009.

Alewitz, Mike and Paul Buhle, *Insurgent Images: The Agitprop Murals of Mike Alewitz*, Monthly Review Press, 2001.

Antliff, Allan, *Anarchy and Art: From the Paris Commune to the Fall of the Berlin Wall*, Arsenal Pulp Press, 2007.

Ault, Julie, ed., *Alternative Art New York: 1965–1985*, University of Minnesota Press and The Drawing Center, 2002.

Ault, Julie, Doug Ashford, and Sabrina Locks, eds., *Show and Tell: A Chronicle of Group Material*, Four Corners Books, 2010.

Becker, Carol and Ann Wiens, eds, *The Artist in Society: Rights, Roles, and Responsibilities*, Chicago New Art Association and New Art Examiner Press, 1995.

Bird, Jon et al., eds., *The Block Reader in Visual Culture*, Routledge, 1996.

Bishop, Claire, ed., *Participation (Documents of Contemporary Art)*, MIT Press, 2006.

Boal, Augusto, *Theater of the Oppressed*, Pluto Press, 1979.

Bourdieu, Pierre and Hans Haacke, *Free Exchange*, Polity Press and Stanford University Press, 1995.

Buchloh, Benjamin H. D. et al., *Art & Ideology*, The New Museum of Contemporary Art, New York, 1984.

Burnham, Linda Frye and Steven Durland, eds., *The Citizen Artist: 20 Years in the Public Arena: An Anthology from High Performance Magazine 1978–98*, Critical Press, 1998.

Bourriaud, Nicolas, *Relational Aesthetics*, les presses du reel, 1998, 2002.

Bryan-Wilson, Julia, *Art Workers: Radical Practice in the Vietnam War Era*, University of California Press, 2009.

Camnitzer, Luis, Jane Farver, et al., *Global Conceptualism: Points of Origin, 1950s–1980s*, Queens Museum/Distributed Art Publishers, 1999.

Cohen-Cruz, Jan, ed., *Radical Street Performance: An International Anthology*, Routledge, 1998.

Cullen, Deborah, ed., *Arte/Vida: Actions by Artists of the Americas, 1960–2000*, El Museo del Barrio, 2008.

Critical Art Ensemble, *Marching Plague*, Autonomedia Press, Brooklyn, 2006.

—— *Molecular Invasion*, Autonomedia Press, 2002.

—— *Digital Resistance: Explorations in Tactical Media*, Autonomedia Press, 2000.

—— *Flesh Machine: Cyborgs, Designer Babies, and New Eugenic Consciousness*, Autonomedia Press, 1998.

—— *Electronic Civil Disobedience, and Other Unpopular Ideas*, Autonomedia Press, 1996.

—— *Electronic Disturbance*, Autonomedia Press, 1994.

Dan Peterman: 7 Deadly Sins and Other Stories, Kunstverein Hannover, 2001.
Deutsche, Rosalyn, *Eviction: Art and Spatial Politics*, MIT Press, 1998.
Duncan, Carol, *The Aesthetics of Power: Essays in Critical Art History*, Cambridge University Press, 1993.
Duncombe, Stephen, *Notes from Underground: Zines and the Politics of Alternative Culture*, Verso, 1997.
—— *Dream: Re-imagining Progressive Politics in an Age of Fantasy*, New Press, 2007.
Durant, Sam, Danny Glover (preface), Bobby Seale (foreword), *Black Panther: The Revolutionary Art of Emory Douglas*, introduction, Rizzoli, 2007.
Esche, Charles and Will Bradley, eds., *Art And Social Change: A Critical Reader*, Tate Publishing, in association with Afterall, 2007.
Felshin, Nina, ed., *But is it Art?: The Spirit of Art as Activism*, Bay Press, 1995.
Finkelpearl, Tom, *Dialogues in Public Art*, MIT Press, 2000.
Foster, Hal, *The Return of the Real: The Avant-Garde at the End of the Century*, MIT Press, 1996.
—— *Recodings: Art, Spectacle, Cultural Politics*, New Press, 1984.
—— ed., *The Anti-Aesthetic: Essays on Postmodern Culture*, New Press, New York, 1983.
The Guerrilla Girls, *Bedside Companion to the History of Western Art*, Penguin, 1998.
Greenwald, Dara and Josh MacPhee, *Signs of Change: Social Movement Cultures 1960s to Now*, AK Press and Exit Art, 2010.
Group Material, *Democracy: A Project by Group Material*, Bay Press, 1990.
Groys, Boris, *Art Power*, MIT Press, 2008.
Hall, John, Lisa Tamiris Becker, and Blake Stimson, *Visual Worlds*, Routledge, 2006.
Harold, Christine, *OurSpace: Resisting the Corporate Control of Culture*, University of Minnesota Press, 2007.
Holmes, Brian, *Escape the Overcode: Activist Art in the Control Society*, van Abbenmuseum and WHW, 2009.
—— *Unleashing the Collective Phantoms: Essays in Reverse Imagineering*, Autonomedia Press, 2008.
(The) Invisible Committee, *The Coming Insurrection*, Semiotext(e), 2009.
Irish, Sharon, *Suzanne Lacy: Spaces Between*, University of Minnesota Press, 2010.
Jacob, Mary Jane and Michael Brenson, *Culture in Action: A Public Art Program of Sculpture Chicago*, Bay Press, 1995.
Jacob, Wendy, Laurie Palmer, and John Ploof, eds., *With Love From Haha: Essays and Notes on a Collective Practice*, WhiteWalls, 2008.
Kahn, Doug and Diane Neumaier, *Cultures and [in] Contention*, The Real Comet Press, 1985.
Kester, Grant, *The One and the Many: Agency and Identity in Contemporary Art*, Duke University Press, 2010.
—— *Conversation Pieces: Community and Communication in Modern Art*, University of California Press, 2004.
—— ed., *Art, Activism, and Oppositionality: Essays from Afterimage*, Duke University Press, 1998.
Knabb, Ken, *Public Secrets, Collected Skirmishes of Ken Knabb: 1970–1997*, Bureau of Public Secrets, 1997.
—— ed. and trans., *Situationist International Anthology*, Bureau of Public Secrets, 1981.
Kwon, Miwon, *One Place After Another*, MIT Press, 2004.
Lacy, Suzanne, ed., *Mapping the Terrain: New Genre Public Art*, Bay Press, 1995.

Lippard, Lucy, *The Lure of the Local: Senses of Place in a Mulitcentered Society*, New Press, 1997.
—— *The Pink Glass Swan: Selected Essays on Feminist Art*, New Press, 1995.
—— *A Different War: Vietnam in Art*, Real Comet, 1990.
—— *Mixed Blessings*, Pantheon, 1990.
—— *Get the Message? A Decade of Art for Social Change*, Dutton, 1984.
—— *Six Years: The Dematerialization of the Art Object from 1966 to 1972*, Praeger, 1973.
Martin, Bradford D., *The Theater is in the Street: Politics and Public Performance in Sixties America*, University of Massachusetts Press, 2004.
McKay, George, ed., *DIY Culture: Party and Protest in Nineties Britain*, Verso, 1998.
McPhee, Josh and Erik Reuland, eds., *Realizing the Impossible: Art Against Authority*, AK Press, 2007.
—— *Stencil Pirates*, Soft Skull Press, 2004.
Meyer, Richard, *Outlaw Representation: Censorship and Homosexuality in Twentieth-Century American Art*, Beacon Press, 2002.
Miles, Malcolm and Mel Jordan, eds., *Art and Theory After Socialism*, Intellect Ltd., 2008.
Mogel, Liz and Lexis Bhagat, *An Atlas of Radical Cartography*, Journal of Aesthetics & Protest Press, 2008.
Monroe, Alexei, *Interrogation Machine: Laibach and NSK*, foreword by Slavoj Žižek, MIT Press, 2005.
Moore, Alan W., *Art Gangs: Political Esthetics in Postmodern New York* (forthcoming, Autonomedia).
Moore, Alan and Marc H. Miller, *ABC No Rio Dinero: The Story of a Lower East Side Art Gallery*, ABC No Rio with Collaborative Projects, 1985.
Naidus, Beverly, *Arts for Change: Teaching Outside the Frame*, New Village Press, 2009.
O'Brien, Mark and Craig Little, eds., *Reimaging America: The Arts of Social Change*, New Society, 1990.
Owens, Craig, *Beyond Recognition: Representation, Power, and Culture*, University of California Press, 1992.
Pasternak, Anne, *Who Cares*, Creative Time, 2006.
Phelan, Peggy, *Unmarked: The Politics of Performance*, Routledge, 1993.
Purves, Ted, ed., *What We Want is Free: Generosity and Exchange in Recent Art*, State University of New York Press, 2005.
Raunig, Gerald, *Art and Revolution: Transversal Activism in the Long Twentieth Century*, Semiotext(e), 2007 (originally published in Austria by Turia + Kant, 2005).
—— with Gene Ray, eds., *Art and Contemporary Critical Practice: Reinventing Institutional Critique*, MayFly Books, 2009.
Raley, Rita, *Tactical Media*, University of Minnesota Press, 2009.
Raven, Arlene, ed., *Art in the Public Interest*, Da Capo Press, 1989.
Ray, Gene, *Terror and the Sublime in Art and Critical Theory: From Auschwitz to Hiroshima to September 11*, Palgrave Macmillan, 2005.
Roberts, John, *The Intangibilities of Form: Skill and Deskilling in Art After the Readymade*, Verso, 2007.
—— *Philosophizing the Everyday: Revolutionary Praxis and the Fate of Cultural Theory*, Pluto Press, 2006.
—— with John Beech, *The Philistine Controversy*, Verso, 2002.
Rosler, Martha, *Decoys and Disruptions: Selected Writings: 1975–2001*, MIT Press, 2006.

Rosler, Martha and Brian Wallis, eds., *If You Lived Here: The City in Art, Theory, and Social Activism*, Bay Press/New Press, 1991.
Roth, Moira, ed., *The Amazing Decade: Women and Performance Art in America 1970–80*, Astro Artz, 1983.
Schor, Mira, *WET: On Painting, Feminism, and Art*, Duke University Press, 1997.
Senie, Harriet F. and Sally Webster, eds., *Critical Issues in Public Art: Context and Controversy*, Harper, 1992.
Stallabrass, Julian, *High Art Lite: British Art in the 1990s*, Verso, 1999.
Staniszewski, Mary Anne, *Believing is Seeing: Creating the Culture of Art*, Penguin, 1995.
Stimson, Blake and Gregory Sholette, eds., *Collectivism after Modernism: The Art of Social Imagination after 1945*, University of Minnesota Press, 2007.
Taylor, Marvin, *Avant Garde and After, Rethinking Art Now*, Prentice Hall, 2003.
Temporary Services, *Group Work*, Printed Matter, 2007.
—— *Public Phenomena*, Half Letter Press LLC, 2008.
—— *Prisoners' Inventions*, Whitewalls, 2003.
Thompson, Nato, *Seeing Power: Art and Activism in the Age of Cultural Production*, Autonomedia Books, 2010.
—— with Gregory Sholette, *Interventionists: Users' Manual for the Creative Disruption of Everyday Life*, Mass MOCA/MIT Press, 2004, 2005.
Walker, John A., *Left Shift: Radical Art in 1970s Britain*, I. B. Tauris, 2002.
Werckmeister, O. K., *Citadel Culture*, University of Chicago Press, 1991.
What, How & for Whom (WHW), ed., Dejan Kršić (design), *On the Occurrence of the 152 Anniversary of the Communist Manifesto*, Zagreb, 2003.
—— *Collective Creativity*, Revolver Books, 2005.
WochenKlausur, *WochenKlausur: Sociopolitical Activism in Art*, Springer-Verlag Wien, 2001.
Wye, Deborah, *Committed to Print: Social and Political Themes in Recent American Printed Art* (catalog), Museum of Modern Art NY, 1988.
Yenawine, Philip, Marianne Weems, and Brian Wallis, eds., *Art Matters: How the Culture Wars Changed America*, NYU Press, 1999.
Zoble, Beatrix and Ula Schneider, *SOHO IN OTTAKRING: What's up: Was ist hier los?*, Springer, 2008.

A Selection of Contemporary Journals Focused on Art and Politics

Adbusters (Vancouver)
Afterimage (Rochester, NY)
aREA (Chicago)
Baffler (Chicago)
Clamor—New Perspectives on Politics, Culture, Media and Life (Ohio)
Journal of Aesthetics and Protest (Los Angeles)
Left Curve (San Francisco)
M/E/A/N/I/N/G (New York City)
MUTE (UK)
October (Mass.)
Public Art Review (St. Paul, Minn.)
Third Text (UK)

APPENDIX: ARTISTS' GROUPS SURVEY 2008

Artists' Collectives Survey Questions*

Basic Information

- What is the name of your group or collective?
- Where are you located?
- How long have you been working/did you work together (since what date—ending what date if applicable)?
- How many people are members or regularly involved in the group?
- What is the average age of group members?
- Are you answering these questions "collectively" as a group, or as one or a few members of the larger group?
- Is there anything else to share about working as a group of artists that we should know?
- Is it OK to cite your collective in the book or do you prefer to remain anonymous?

Relationship to Art World

- How often, if ever, has your collective been mentioned in major art publications (to the best of your knowledge)?
- How often, if ever, has it been linked to website watch-lists such as Saatchi or http://the-artists.org/artist?
- Have you been represented by any commercial art galleries?
- How often has the collective's work been exhibited in a museum?
- How often has the collective's work come up for sale in auction houses?
- Do you have your own art gallery and does it sell work? How much?
- Does the collective fund a majority of its work through sales of work? And/or through grants, lecture fees, or other means? (Please describe.)
- If you have a collective CV would you share it with us?
- In a sentence or two, how would you describe the group's overall relation to the mainstream art world, if any?

Organizational Structure

Have you developed guidelines about your organization's mission and how it governs itself (such as how to agree on projects, or new members, or where to exhibit?) specifically:

- Are there any fixed administrative positions? Are any of these paid positions?
- Does someone take written minutes of your meetings?

* Select results are displayed on page 164. Full results can be found at http://darkmatterarchives.net

- Do you have a designated treasurer? How about a checking account under the group's name?
- Would you describe the group as hierarchically structured or non-hierarchically structured?
- Are there smaller working groups or committees within the larger organization?
- Are you a 501 c-3 (in the US) or other type (outside the US) of not-for-profit corporation?
- If these guidelines are written down would you share these with us?

Reasons for Working in a Group or Collective

- In general, would you say that working in a group is personally satisfying or is it more pragmatic?
- Do individual group members also make projects separate from the collective and show this work on their own?
- Do you see your work in a group as beneficial to you, your art career, your overall happiness?
- If your group is especially engaged in public activism or political art activism, please describe how you see your political mission as it relates to society in general?
- Does the group keep an archive of the projects you create?

INDEX